Assessing
Children's Language
in Naturalistic
Contexts

Assessing Children's Language in Naturalistic Contexts

NANCY J. LUND / **JUDITH F. DUCHAN**

*State University College
at Buffalo*

*State University of New York/
Buffalo*

PRENTICE-HALL, INC.   Englewood Cliffs, New Jersey 07632

Library of Congress Cataloging in Publication Data

LUND, NANCY J.
  Assessing children's language in naturalistic contexts.

  Includes bibliographies and index.
  1. Language acquisition.   2. Language and languages
—Ability testing.   I. Duchan, Judith F.   II. Title
P118.L86   401'.9   82-3786
ISBN   0-13-049668-5   AACR2

Editorial/production supervision by Linda Benson
Jacket design by Miriam Recio
Manufacturing buyers: Edmund W. Leone/Ron Chapman

Printed in the United States of America

10   9   8   7   6   5   4   3   2

ISBN 0-13-049668-5

PRENTICE-HALL INTERNATIONAL, INC., *London*
PRENTICE-HALL OF AUSTRALIA PTY. LIMITED, *Sydney*
PRENTICE-HALL CANADA INC., *Toronto*
PRENTICE-HALL OF INDIA PRIVATE LIMITED, *New Delhi*
PRENTICE-HALL OF JAPAN, INC., *Tokyo*
PRENTICE-HALL OF SOUTHEAST ASIA PTE. LTD., *Singapore*
WHITEHALL BOOKS LIMITED, *Wellington, New Zealand*

We dedicate this book to our intellectual mothers,
those women scholars whose shoulders we stand on,

and

to our biological mothers,
whose shoulders we lean on

Contents

7 Semantics 164

8 Language Comprehension 223

9 Cognitive Precursors to Language Acquisition 255

Preface

This book is about children—how they think, how they talk, and how they understand language. It is different from other books of its kind in that it focuses on helping you, the reader, figure out what it is that children are doing and why they might be doing it. It is not intended to be used as a diagnostic approach for differentiating normal from abnormal children, although there are sections which could help you do that; nor is it intended as a method for deciding what medical, intellectual, emotional, or social conditions are causing the children's behavior. Rather, it is a means for helping you discover what is consistent about a child's communicative interactions and what kind of structures underlie that consistency.

A basic assumption we make in this book is that children's language is woven into the fabric of the event that is occurring as the language is used. Just as pulling a single thread from a cloth changes our perception of that thread, separating language from the context in which it occurs distorts its nature and obscures its communicative function. Descriptions of an individual child's language can be meaningful only when framed by the events and purposes that engender the language.

In order to describe children's language, we advocate a methodology that has been called *structuralism*. It is a methodology that has prevalent use in many disciplines: anthropology, cognitive psychology, linguistics, and sociology. The recent use of structuralism in language and speech pathology has been the result of the fruitful work in child development and psycholinguistics. The focus on structuralism has led us to more informal testing procedures and to reliance on language sample analysis for determining learning patterns for both normal and language-impaired children.

For us, structuralism is not just a new way of assessing language. Rather, it is a new way of viewing children. It leads those who use it to ask why children do what they do, and once they have asked that question, they become committed to viewing children's behavior as legitimate, even when it does not conform to that of other children their age or to that of adults.

In order to ask why children do what they do, we make a distinction between their surface behavior, or what we observe, and the underlying knowledge or sense of the world used to produce surface behavior. This surface and deep structure distinction was first made by Chomsky in 1965 and is a distinction to which this book owes its orientation. Chomsky made the distinction in a formal way, dealing specifically with the language of adult speakers and the deep or underlying structure which can be derived from it. We are making the distinction in a less formal and more general way. Our distinction is between the behavior we see children exhibit and the knowledge we ascribe to them that we assume they use in producing that behavior. This mentalistic framework is one kind of structuralism.

Another kind of structuralism is more descriptive and antedates Chomsky's mentalistic structural analysis. With the descriptive approach, one looks for patterns or regularities in surface behavior and does not look further to determine how those regularities come from underlying knowledge held by those producing the behaviors.

We believe the mentalistic type of structuralism lends the most insight into children's behavior, but it is difficult to do. The descriptive type of structuralism, while not postulating underlying knowledge of language, can readily lend insights for understanding and predicting children's behavior. We have designed our techniques to discover and describe regularities in behavior, and we hope as we get better at the descriptive structuralism that we can go to a more abstract and insightful level of analysis.

A potential problem with merely describing patterns is overinterpretation of surface forms. This has been referred to as "rich interpretation." Clinicians or researchers can look at children in the same way they might look at a Rorschach inkblot. They can make what they see fit what they expect to see. In our discussions of patterns we might be looking at children as if they were Rorschach pictures and read more than is actually there into what they can do. The result is that we may be developing a neat pigeon-holing category system for describing children's communicative behavior which has nothing to do with the category system that the children are operating on to produce this behavior.

We find that describing children with already worked out category systems often leads to missing the more important aspects of children's communication. We do present such categories, but it is only as a guide and with trepidation. We do it only because we feel a need to give you a sense of structural systems and possibilities for structural analysis.

Our plea throughout the book is to ask you as a clinician or potential clinician to allow yourself to see the uniqueness of each child you are evaluating; and to ask you not to rely solely on your preformed categories to describe a child's cognitive or linguistic performance. This "discovery" focus will lead you away from a heavy emphasis on normative data which can present all sorts of categories to feed rich interpretation tendencies.

Although we have included in each chapter a brief discussion of normal developmental patterns, we refrained from presenting structures with age norms because those norms would tend to be used as a category checklist. Instead, we offer the developmental literature as a methodology or set of guidelines for discovering different types of structures in children's behavior. We have found that the structural approach, even with its deemphasis on age norms, is an effective technique for studying normal language and normal children, and we have used this material in courses on language acquisition where the emphasis is on normal development.

The structural categories described contain a bias toward middle-class educated Americans who speak standard English. The bias exists because we are reflecting a biased research literature. The structural method requires that you examine differences for individual children, whether the differences be dialectical or idiosyncratic. We need not and cannot present you with a complete list of those differences. We assume that if we are successful in helping you formulate a structural approach, you will be able to analyze the structure of the dialects your children and their parents speak.

You can tell by the chapter titles that this book is heavily influenced by linguistics. There are chapters covering each of the linguistic levels of language: phonology, morphology, syntax, and semantics. Also reflected is the awareness growing out of the more recent linguistic and psycholinguistic literature that language involves more than people's knowledge of language structure—it also involves their knowledge of the world. The chapters on pragmatics, on language comprehension, and on cognitive precursors to language, in particular, reflect this awareness.

Each of the chapters on domains of language contains suggested procedures for doing structural analysis of a child's performance in that area. The procedures are listed, including means of elicitation, transcription techniques, and how to do the analysis. For some chapters, the procedures are more tangible and explicit than others. That is because the structural categories are more concrete or because there has been more research that we can base our analytic techniques on. For the other chapters we have tried to give you the information, and encouragement, to find procedures that work for you. The chapters also contain a set of exercises for you to test your ability to understand and work with the knowledge presented and to build up a sense of how to do the analysis which was presented in the chapter.

We have come to this project with a healthy respect for the embryonic stage that we are in. Our approach has a natural heritage in other related disciplines. At this point in our developmental history, we should be able to build from what has been done in other areas, changing theories and methods to fit our special needs. We hope that you will join us in that attitude and work with us in our evolution. We feel that through this endeavor we will not only improve our clinical methods as language pathologists, but will also benefit the children the methods were designed for.

Acknowledgments

We want to thank the eight generations of students who read portions of this book and guided us in directions that made it clearer to us and to them. We give a special thanks to Mark Stengel, who first suggested it; to Ray O'Connell, who got us on our way; to Liz Shapiro, who combed it for its errors and offered so many helpful suggestions; and to Fae Johnson, who typed it so accurately and good naturedly. Thanks to our housemates, Alan, Peter, and Steve for their encouragement, sacrifices, and good humor (that's no joke Peter); and to the luck that brought us together as cothinkers, cowriters, cosufferers, and, underneath it all, as friends.

Assessing
Children's Language
in Naturalistic
Contexts

1

Overview
of
Assessment
Approaches

HISTORICAL REVIEW

Speech pathologists have been involved in the assessment of children's language since the 1950s. The intervening years have seen great diversity in the theory and practice of language assessment as changing views of the nature of language have spawned new procedures for sampling and describing language and for categorizing deviations from normal language.

During the decade of the 1950s, two approaches to language assessment were developing. The first, which we could call *normative*, was the approach taken by Johnson, Darley, and Spriestersbach in the first widely used book on diagnostic methods in "speech correction." Their first edition (1952) had no section on language disorders but rather had a brief discussion of measures such as mean sentence length in words, parts of speech used, sentence structure, and ratings of verbal output. Their emphasis was on how normal children at different ages performed on these measures. Normative research for these indices were referred to (e.g., McCarthy, 1930), but no data were presented. In a later edition of their text (1963), Johnson, Darley, and Spriestersbach included a whole chapter on language development and language disorders, reflecting the growth in the study of these topics. Normative data were included from the extensive study by Templin (1957), among others, thus making available to the diagnostician information on what is "normal" for children at different ages with regard to measures such as median number of one-word responses; percentage of responses classified as simple, compound, and complex sentences; mean percentage of parts of speech used; size of vocabulary; and mean structural complexity score, which was computed according to sentence completeness and complexity. The clinician was given no direction for using this information in assessing an individual child's language.

The contrasting approach to language assessment that emerged in the 1950s we will call a *pathology* approach. Based on a medical model, the goal of assessment was to identify the "disease" or underlying cause of the presenting symptoms. Disordered language was viewed as one of a cluster of symptoms that could lead the clinician to diagnosing the problem—i.e., determining the etiology or cause. The presumption was that the condition thus identified explained the speech or language problem, and treatment efforts would be directed toward alleviating the condition rather than further examining the symptoms. The best example of, and most influential force behind, this approach was Myklebust's *Auditory Disorders in Children* (1954). In this work, Myklebust presented symptom clusters which are manifested in the conditions of deafness, mental retardation, brain damage or "aphasia," and emotional disturbance. Originally intended as a manual for differential diagnosis of nonverbal children for pediatricians, psychologists, and audiologists, this approach was readily adopted by speech pathologists, and along with it Myklebust's model of expressive, inner, and receptive language function. While Myklebust emphasized the importance of understanding complex language functioning in order to diagnose the type of disorder, he gave little direction to the clinician for identifying or understanding receptive, inner, or expressive language disorders.

The decade of the 1960s brought new trends in language assessment for speech pathologists. The impact of an older, behavioristic movement in American psychology became apparent when the emphasis shifted from deviant language behavior as a symptom of an underlying disorder to a view that the disordered language itself was the problem. In this framework, language behavior, like all behavior, was seen as developing out of the interaction between the current behavior of the organism and the environmental antecedents and consequences of that behavior (Sloane and MacAulay, 1968). That is, language response was viewed as under the control of both stimulus and reinforcement. The discriminative stimulus, which is the situational condition under which a response will be followed by reinforcement, and the reinforcement, which can be any event which changes the frequency of the response it follows, thus became the focus of the *behavioral* approach to assessment (Schiefelbusch, 1963). Changing the stimuli or reinforcement in the environment became the means for remediating language disorders. Growing out of B. F. Skinner's orientation, as presented in *Verbal Behavior* (1957), language behaviors, or responses, were often classified according to the conditions that prompted them. Responses which function as demands and requests were called *mands,* those that are controlled by a discriminative stimulus (naming, referring) were called *tacts,* and others were classified as being under the control of verbal stimuli (echoing, verbal associations, answering questions). With this approach, the actual response was generally not described, except insofar as necessary to classify it.

Osgood (1957) elaborated the stimulus-response-reinforcement framework of the radical behaviorists. Osgood's behavioristic model included mental associations which an organism can make to a stimulus. According to Osgood, internal associations or *mediations* are also in the form of stimuli and responses. He called them *response mediators* (r_m) and *stimulus mediators* (s_m). These internal associations sometimes led to overt responses and sometimes not. They accounted for some of the jumps in associations people made in their errors on verbal learning experiments. For example, Osgood's model accounted for subjects who answered "joy" instead of the correct word "glee" in an experiment by saying that the stimulus led to an internal, already-learned association between "joy" and "glee."

Kirk and McCarthy (1961) borrowed heavily from Osgood's conceptualization and used Osgood's model to design parts of their now famous test, the *Illinois Test of Psycholinguistic Abilities* (ITPA). The test reflects a behavioristic orientation by virtue of its focus on the stimulus in some subtests (e.g., visual reception, auditory reception), its mediational subtests (visual association, auditory association), and its response subtests (visual expression, manual expression).

The ITPA had a profound effect on the speech pathologist's view of language disorders. It became available at a time when clinicians were becoming aware of language disorders and were becoming frustrated by the lack of direction and assessment tools provided by the normative and pathology approaches. The test thus became widely used and subsequently became for many speech pathologists an operational definition of language.

In addition to borrowing from Osgood's theory, Kirk and McCarthy have subtests of the ITPA which involve memory and closure. These tests reflect another historical trend, the *auditory processing* framework, which combines behaviorism and information processing theory. Auditory processing models began to emerge in the 1960s and are still prevalent (Lasky and Katz, in progress; Levinson and Sloan, 1980).

The auditory processing framework grew out of the behaviorism of the 1950s. It presents the view that language processing begins with the stimulus and proceeds through various steps until it is stored in memory. While rooted in behavioristic sensibilities, it is more elaborate than the Skinner or Osgood formulations—it involves more than chainlike associations because it takes into account factors such as various memories, perceptual processes, and temporal ordering. The tendency toward more mentalistic, psychological constructs of auditory processing shows the influence of computer models of information processing over the last two decades (Fodor, Bever, and Garrett, 1974).

The general format for auditory processing conceptualizations is that information contained in the auditory stimulus proceeds through several encoding steps—it is first received, then perceived, then categorized into meanings, and then stored; and later it is retrieved for future processing. Thus, the test batteries or specific tests have been designed to test children's auditory processing abilities, such as speech-sound discrimination, auditory memory, sequencing, figure-ground discrimination, auditory closure, etc. (Goldman, Fristoe, and Woodcock, 1974).

There are at least two varieties of auditory processing models. One leans more toward a behavioristic framework and treats auditory processing as a set of processing skills which are applied similarly to all types of auditory information (Eisenson, 1972). Another has a more mentalistic focus and regards speech perception as something different from other types of processing, something requiring special innate mechanisms (Sanders, 1977). Both frameworks emphasize processing over rule knowledge or content, both see reception of the language as primary and fundamental to language learning, and both emphasize modalities or channels as significant in learning. They are what might be characterized as "getting-information-in-and-out" models and differ from models such as those developed by linguists that focus on information content rather than on the transmission of information from one person to another.

We can trace our history of *linguistic approaches* to assessment as also originating during the early 1960s when several important studies were done by psychologists examining children's language acquisition. Using analytic techniques and terminology of descriptive linguists, researchers in child language began to formulate grammars or rules that both described and attempted to explain child language. From around the country came reports of investigations of normal children, all confirming that child language is not merely an inaccurate or incomplete version of adult language, but a unique system governed by its own rules (Ferguson and Slobin, 1973). The rules are characterized as making up the child's competence in the various levels of language: phonology, morphology, syntax, and semantics.

Late in the 1960s, a new sense of the importance of studying child language was felt because of issues that were being debated in linguistics and philosophy (Steinberg and Jakobovits, 1971). Noam Chomsky, a linguist, had forwarded a theory of language that differentiated a surface from an underlying structure. His theory of syntax (Chomsky, 1957) proposed that the phrase structure that makes up the sentences we hear can be derived from a more abstract underlying structure through a series of changes governed by algebralike rules. These rules, or transformations, convert underlying abstract phrase structures to their surface manifestations.

If Chomsky's theory of syntax worked to account for such linguistic phenomena as ambiguous sentences and paraphrases, maybe it is a process speakers and listeners actually go through when they speak and understand sentences. This debate about whether Chomsky's linguistic theory is psychologically real was one that created much activity and literature during the late 1960s and produced a new branch of psychology—psycholinguistics. Of most apparent concern was the problem of how people come to know the abstract structure of sentences, since it is not obvious in the sentences they hear; and listeners, according to the theory, cannot understand those sentences without already knowing the abstract structure.

Chomsky's resolution to the paradox was a radical one. He proposed that children are born with knowledge of the underlying structure and that they learn how the deep structures apply to particular surface structures in the course of their exposure to language. Chomsky's nativist theory contrasted sharply with the empiricist and behaviorist notions that language is learned only through experience.

Those who subscribed to the nativistic or innate position looked for evidence from children's language development to support their view. They took as evidence children's common stages of language learning found across cultures and the structures children had in common within each of those stages (Lenneberg, 1967). That is to say, if children in China go through similar stages in learning to speak Chinese as children in England do to speak English, it would follow that they do so from their biologically inherited knowledge of deep structure. If common stages exist in the development of the embryo, why not for the same organism after birth? Empiricists, on the other hand, pointed to differences in children's language learning in different cultures to support the importance of environmental influences and looked for more simple ways to account for Chomsky's abstract structure (Braine, 1976).

The result of the debate and of the linguistic approach for speech and language pathologists has been to look at children's abnormal language in terms of its linguistic structure. Typically, we confine our explorations to surface structure patterns, not following Chomsky's emphasis on searching for more abstract origins of surface patterns (Duchan, in press). Linguistic analyses of children's phonology, morphology, and syntax have led us away from the behavioristic way of thinking about children's language to a more mentalistic approach. That is, we are no longer talking about language as made up of responses pulled from a response repertoire. We now talk about linguistic rules which children and adults use to understand and produce language.

This brings us to the next period in the emergence of language assessment procedures which has come to be called the *semantic emphasis* and which emerged in the mid 1970s. It resulted again from a shift in emphasis in linguistics, but this time generative semanticists formed a renegade group within Chomsky's generative theory camp and argued that Chomsky's emphasis was too much on syntax and not enough on semantics (Lakoff, 1971; McCawley, 1971). The semantic emphasis had its predecessors (Fillmore, 1968), but the focus did not develop a following or have an influence in psychology until around 1975 (Palermo, 1978).

The generative semanticists tried to derive a model for the meanings of words, phrases, and sentences and understandably became heavily involved in philosophical issues and in the differences between language meaning and meanings for things in the world in general. For those studying child language, the emphasis on meaning led to questions about the conceptual bases of first words and two-word combinations (Clark, 1977; Nelson, 1974; Rosch, 1973). Whereas Chomsky's syntactic emphasis led to postulation that words and word phrases derived from deep structure phrases (Bloom, 1970), the semantic emphasis allowed a deep structure that was meaning based, such as having semantic cases (Antinucci and Parisi, 1973), semantic relations (Brown, 1973), semantic features (Clark, 1977), or conceptual prototypes (Rosch, 1973). Thus we find new assessment approaches in language pathology emerging from the cognitive approaches in linguistics which examine children's language for its semantic content and its cognitive base (MacDonald, 1978; McLean and Snyder-McLean, 1978).

In this same time period, in part as a result of the focus on semantics, there was a renewed interest in Piaget's cognitive theory, leading to a *cognitive emphasis* in assessment. Attempts were made to tie the stages which Piaget discovered in cognitive development to those in language development. The sensorimotor period of development, from birth to two years, drew the most attention, and researchers and clinicians attempted to identify which sensorimotor knowledges were precursors to language learning during this early period of life in normal children (e.g., Bates, 1979; Miller et al., 1980). The assessment focus became one which asked whether the language-impaired child had the necessary prerequisite cognitive knowledge for language learning. This type of assessment can be used with nonverbal children who cannot be assessed by procedures built on linguistic structural models. Those models only work if the child is already using language.

In sum, we find new approaches in assessment emerging in the mid 1970s that focus on examining children's language for its semantic content and its cognitive base. Assessment approaches with semantic emphases focus on the meaning expressed as utterances are produced. The cognitive approach to assessment stresses the experiences and concepts that are presumed to be prerequisite to the emergence of language.

This concern in the 1970s about meanings of words, phrases, and sentences led to the realization that sentences derive their meanings from the contexts in which they occur. The same word or sentence means something different on different occasions. This realization then led to a move away from thinking about language knowledge as a fixed set of meanings as listed in a dictionary to an examination of how context influences meaning and how language functions differently for speakers at different times. This contextual influence is the study of language from a *pragmatics perspective* and has come to be the most recent movement in linguistics and psychology. This pragmatics perspective as it applies to language development originated with Bates in 1976 and has rapidly gathered momentum in the last few years. We have begun to see its influence already as we find people looking at children's performance in conversations rather than utterance by utterance (Gallagher, 1977) and as we see them looking for the functions underlying children's utterances (Prizant and Duchan, 1981).

We predict that this pragmatics approach will not be just another addition to our evaluation techniques but that it will shake the very foundations of how we have been approaching children with language problems. Our notion that we can examine children's language by presenting them with controlled stimuli, such as sentences to imitate or formal tests, will come into question. Our idea that language in the clinic is the same as language outside the clinic will be suspect. Our hope that we can measure a child's language ability in one context in a two-hour diagnostic session will be demolished as results from the research in pragmatics become known to us.

But rather than cast our prediction of the pragmatics revolution negatively, we would like to register our enthusiasm and our belief that this approach will allow us to become much more sensitive to our children's sense of language and of the world; and while it will make more work for us, the results will be worth it!

It can be seen from this brief historical account that divergent views of language and language pathology have evolved from a variety of sources. Trying to assimilate all of these orientations into a cohesive model from which to view assessment and intervention is at best difficult for at least two reasons. First, these orientations reflect different theoretical conceptions of language and use categories of observations that are relevant only within a particular theoretical orientation. The second difficulty is that when we attempt to make comparisons about the efficacy of the various theoretical views, we find that they direct us to different diagnostic questions. The normative approach asks questions about normalcy; the pathology approach about etiology; while the behavioral, ITPA, linguistic, semantic, cognitive, and pragmatics approaches direct us toward a description and/or explanation of the problem.

It is important to realize that the clinical observations we make reflect someone's view of language—that is, the categories we use in our observation are deemed relevant because they derive from a theoretical conception of language. Assessment tools and techniques that are available have evolved out of the different approaches we have discussed and thus reflect the diverse views of language. Clinicians should be aware of these differences and realize that using a test or therapy kit also involves adopting the author's view of language.

In sum, we have briefly traced some stages in the history of language pathology. The main point we have been making is that language assessment occurs in a theoretical and practical context, and it is the context that determines our approaches. The periods and dates in our development, like stages and ages in children's development, are somewhat arbitrarily drawn but are roughly as follows:

1950s	The normative approach
	The pathology approach
1960s	The behaviorist approach
	The auditory processing approach
	The ITPA approach
	The linguistic approach
1970s	The semantic approach
	The cognitive approach
	The pragmatics approach
1980s	The pragmatics revolution

ASSESSMENT QUESTIONS

Selection of language assessment instruments should be guided by the assessment questions we are asking. Different questions call for the selection of different tools. All too often this process is reversed—a test is administered because it is available, and then the clinician finds that the test has revealed no new or useful information because it was designed to answer questions other than those of interest. Let us turn to the questions typically asked in language assessment, which we can now recognize as related to our outline of our historical development.

1. Does This Child Have a Language Problem?

This question is generally answered with reference to deviation from average performance of a group and so is best handled with the normative approach. In some cases our initial observation of a child leads us to make the judgment of language disorder because the language displayed is below or different from our impression of what is "normal" for a child of this age. Our knowledge of normal development and our interactions with normally developing children lead us to certain expectations that serve as our standard of normal, against which we compare the particular child.

For more "objective" bases for comparison, there are numerous scales of normal development available, along with data collected byMcCarthy (1930), Templin (1957), and many others on normal children. With these data, it is possible for the clinician to compare a child to others of the same age or to obtain an age-equivalence for a particular child. It remains the clinician's judgment how much deviation from the average is considered allowable. If, for example, the clinician finds that the Mean Length of Response (in words) for three year olds is 4.1 and the three year old in question has a MLR of 3.5, should the child be considered deviant? The answer is largely a matter of clinical judgment, although there are some guidelines which can be followed (see Chapter 10, Tools of Assessment).

There are now many language tests available that have been "standardized" on normal children, so the performance of a particular child can be compared to that of normally developing children taking the same test. Again, the child can be compared to other children of the same chronological age, or an age-equivalency can be determined for his or her language skill. Some tests have "cutoff" scores, or guidelines for the amount of deviation from the average that would indicate a language disorder. Others simply present the data on normal children and leave it to the clinician to decide what constitutes a disorder. Thus, most tests or norm-referenced measures do not lead to a simple yes or no in answer to the question of normalcy but rather lead to descriptions such as the following: below the 10th percentile; 18 months delay; below average; age-equivalent of 4½ years.

2. What Is Causing the Problem?

Attempts to answer this question can take several forms. We may attempt to diagnose an underlying physical or psychological problem through assessment of nonlanguage functions, such as hearing acuity, neurological functions, motor performance, or intelligence. We may rely on the reports of other professionals to give us some of this information. The case history is another tool that is used in identifying possible causes of a language problem. Following the pathology approach, attempts are made to identify clusters of symptoms that are associated with various underlying conditions. For example, a history of a difficult birth, high fevers, and/or convulsions would lead one to suspect the presence of brain damage. Likewise, a history of uniformly delayed motor and social development along with language development would point to mental retardation.

Children often come to the speech-language pathologist with a diagnostic label such as aphasic, autistic, or mentally retarded already assigned them. Occasionally the language evaluation may be part of the assessment procedure designed to arrive at such a label. However, there has been a trend in speech pathology away from engaging in this type of categorical diagnosis, since some of the etiological categories are questionable (e.g., minimal brain damage) and because such diagnostic labels often negatively affect the child. There has also been increased professional specialization since the early publication of Myklebust (1954), and it is often regarded as inappropriate for a speech-language pathologist to make a diagnosis such as autism or emotional disturbance (see Sanders, 1972). This professional territoriality has been a matter with no general agreement, and some authors argue for the speech-language pathologist as diagnostician (e.g., Darley, 1978; Nation and Aram, 1977).

In addition to the classic differential diagnostic labels, there are a variety of comments, such as "forceps delivery," "single-parent family," "tension in the home," and "maternal overprotection," in diagnostic reports which carry the implication that there is, in fact, some sort of causal relationship between these conditions and the child's language. In some cases, terms that were originally used to describe an aspect of the child's behavior or environment have come to be used as diagnostic labels; so we find it has become increasingly common to see a diagnosis of "hyperactivity" or "cultural deprivation" with the implication that these are etiological categories.

Any inference about the cause of a language disorder must be made with caution. If a mentally retarded child has a language problem, we cannot assume that the retardation is causing the problem, since there are retarded children who do not have such problems. We must be even more careful not to imply a causal relationship between the language problem and some behavioral or social description of the child, unless we have supporting evidence that this is appropriate. Most of the time we do not know the cause of a child's language learning problem. Further, knowing the cause is often not very helpful in planning remediation, unless it is a condition that can be changed, since therapy techniques generally do not vary significantly depending on underlying etiology. We must often be prepared to acknowledge that we do not know what is causing the problem and proceed with more productive aspects of assessment.

3. What Are the Areas of Deficit?

This question is directed to a description of the language problem. The behaviorist model, the ITPA model, the auditory processing model, and the linguistic, semantic, cognitive, and pragmatics models can all be used to answer this question, but the description arrived at by each will be different because each defines the areas of language differently. Using a behavioristic model, categories of behaviors, such as mands and tacts or questions, statements, and commands, could be described according to the rate or frequency of occurrence. Deviations from adult language might be explained by constructs such as "stimulus overselectivity" or "response overgeneralization." Generally, with a behaviorist orientation, the primary focus is on changes that occur over time or under different conditions, with behaviors being quantified to make these comparisons.

Using the ITPA model, problems would be categorized in terms of the subtests, such as "visual association problem" or "auditory closure problem." It is not always clear whether some of the deficits identified by the ITPA are meant as descriptions or causes of language problems. For example, the auditory sequential memory subtest consists of strings of unrelated digits. If an individual is found to have a poor memory for digits, do we consider this to be a language problem, or do we instead infer that the poor memory is causing an independently identified language problem? Some of the ITPA subtests seem to be directed more to identifying the cause than to describing the language problem, but this distinction is not made by the test. It is left to the individual clinician to decide how to interpret these areas of deficit once they have been identified.

Auditory processing models would cast areas of deficit into the various processes which the listener is seen as progressing through on the way to decoding information contained in the auditory signal. Separate areas would be evaluated, such as auditory discrimination, auditory memory span, auditory closure, and auditory sequencing.

The linguistic model would lead to the identification of problems within the various linguistic levels, such as "phonological problems" (which might include "articulation disorder") or "morphological problems." As with the ITPA model, distinctions between "receptive" and "expressive" deficits might be identified.

It is more difficult to identify areas of semantic deficit, since there is not a comprehensive framework which covers various areas of semantics. Descriptions of semantic problems within each model do not relate to each other as parts of the same whole as the elements in phonology, morphology, and syntax do. For example, a model built around semantic relations would identify absence of particular relations, such as possession or attribution, drawing from one list of relations (Bloom and Lahey, 1978); while a model which views semantic cases as the deep structure of language would identify deviations within a different or overlapping set of categories, such as agent or experiencer (Miller, 1981).

Language clinicians have used Piaget's rendition of cognitive areas during the sensorimotor period to examine cognitive performance, and thus they test for children's sensorimotor knowledge of object permanence, means-ends distinctions, causality, relation of objects in space, imitation, and development of schemes in relation to objects (e.g., Miller et al., 1980). These cognitive assessments are used to compare children's cognitive performance to normal children and thereby identify cognitive deficits and are also used to see if children have the cognitive competence to learn language.

Finally, the influence of pragmatics on language assessment has just begun to be felt. Pragmatics, like the other areas of assessment, takes its lead from the discoveries in the developmental literature. The areas of pragmatic deficit are even less well defined than those in semantics because the theoretical framework for pragmatics is not cohesive. Thus, deficits are studied and described separately. Children, for example, are said to have problems in areas of turn taking, functions, or use of deictic terms.

After addressing these three assessment questions, clinicians are confronted with a question that is really uppermost in their minds: What should I do in therapy? Knowing that a child is mentally retarded, below the 10th percentile on a standardized test, and has morphology problems is of little use when it is time to begin therapy. We suggest that none of the approaches to assessment discussed thus far will bring the clinician to the point of describing the child's language problem in sufficient detail to plan individual remediation. This planning requires careful observation to determine what the child is attempting and the specific problems the child is having. Such observation leads to recognition of patterns that may appear to be "inconsistencies" until we find that the child performs differently in differing contexts.

This awareness of contextual influences is very important to planning and assessing therapy for a number of reasons. First, we cannot assume that knowledge of any language structure is all or nothing—that is, we cannot assume that if children display the structure in one instance (such as on a test), they "know" it in all contexts; or conversely that if they do not display it appropriately in our sample, they do not know it at all. More typically a child will be correct in some contexts and incorrect in others.

Second, in order to establish meaningful goals for the child, we need to know the discrepancies between what the child is intending to communicate and what is actually being communicated. Also, we need to know the favorable and unfavorable circumstances for expressing intended messages. Recognizing these patterns, we can plan therapy to provide facilitating contexts. Third, in judging the efficacy of our therapy, we must be aware that varying language behaviors are displayed in different contexts. Children's language is often different in the therapy interaction, and we should not unduly emphasize performance only in this narrow framework. Before we can decide on a direction in therapy, we need to answer our fourth assessment question, which addresses the quest for patterns.

4. What Are the Regularities in the Child's Language Performance?

Inasmuch as the previously discussed approaches to language assessment cannot answer this question, we propose an additional approach that requires a more detailed analysis, one that we are calling *structural analysis*. With structural analysis, we arrive at a description of a child's language in terms that go beyond areas of deficit. We describe the specific patterns that the child displays—both what is correct and what is missing or incorrect. Descriptions are in terms of what the child says or does rather than in terms of abstract categories.

e.g., "Has no plural or past tense endings" instead of "Has a grammatic closure problem."

Generalizations are made where possible, with exceptions noted.

e.g., All consonant clusters are reduced to a single consonant except for the /pl/.

Using this approach, the clinician looks to the child's behaviors to determine the relevant areas of language deficit rather than using categories of general deficit areas that reflect the diagnostician's or test maker's conceptual model. We begin our assessment only with the assumption that we do not know beforehand what will be important to look at with this particular child. Also, items on tests are presented in a context which is different from an ordinary communication situation. Since our interest is in how children communicate in their everyday life, we want to see them in more familiar, interactive situations. The clinician or researcher doing structural analysis may intervene by asking the child to do certain tasks, or respond to questions, but the goal of the approach is always to explore the regularities displayed rather than focus on a single instance of behavior as evidence for knowledge or lack of knowledge.

Finally, we can come back to our earlier question about therapy and how to proceed.

5. What Is Recommended for This Child?

Through structural analysis, we identify what is being attempted by the child, what is being accomplished, and the discrepancies that exist between the two. This leads us to our goals for therapy. We can determine an approach to accomplishing various goals by looking to see which behaviors seem to be needed. If, for example, we observe that a child always answers yes-no questions with an affirmative nod in an apparent attempt to be interactive and take turns in dialogue, a goal might be to help the child to understand the consequences of yes versus no so the response can function as an answer and not an empty turn. This goal respects the child's intention—to be interactive—but provides a more utilitarian means to do so. To use another example, if we find that a child can produce /s/ only when it follows /t/, we would recommend working from that phonetic context and gradually modifying it. Recommendations or individual programs thus begin with what we have observed that the child can do and include awareness of how changes in contexts can facilitate behaviors that were previously not possible for the child.

Structural analysis is an ongoing assessment approach. It does not stop when therapy begins because it is a way of observing and thinking that leaves the observer always searching for new patterns and ready to change hypotheses and approaches when the child's performance so indicates. It makes every interaction with a child part of the ongoing assessment of language.

Of the five questions presented, those concerning regularities and recommendations are generally the most relevant to us as clinicians, and they obviously are closely tied together. The body of this book deals with how to find the regularities that help us help children to be better communicators. We begin in Chapter 2 by describing in greater detail the goals and techniques of structural analysis.

EXERCISES

Listed in these exercises are terms or phrases that frequently appear in diagnostic reports about children who have language problems. In light of the preceding discussion, these terms can be understood as attempts to answer one or more of the following four diagnostic questions:
1. Does the child have a language problem?
2. What condition(s) causes the language problem?
3. What are the child's areas of language deficit?
4. What are the regularities in the child's language performance?
5. None of the above

Each of the categories below is an answer to one of the four questions. Fill in the number of the corresponding question, or fill in number 5 if none of the questions applies. Some may correspond to more than one question depending on how they are used by the diagnostician.

1. Severe language problem _____
2. Two standard deviations below the mean _____
3. Hearing loss _____
4. Aphasia _____
5. Auditory processing deficit _____
6. Mentally retarded _____
7. Language age of 4 years _____
8. 89th percentile _____
9. Articulation problem _____
10. Doesn't know colors _____
11. Omits auxiliary verbs _____
12. Two-year language delay _____
13. Autistic _____
14. Problems with conversations _____
15. Shows overextension of meanings _____
16. "Me" for "I" substitution _____
17. Brain damaged _____
18. Plural problem _____
19. Morphology error _____
20. Depressed receptive vocabulary _____
21. Uses pronouns without previous reference _____
22. Slow maturation _____
23. /s/ for all fricatives _____
24. Restricted auditory memory _____
25. Poor grammatic closure _____
26. Uses only action-object combinations _____

REFERENCES

ANTINUCCI, F., AND D. PARISI   Early Language Acquisition: A Model and Some Data, in *Studies of Child Language Development,* eds. D. Ferguson and D. Slobin. New York: Holt, Rinehart & Winston, 1973.

BATES, E.   *Language and Context: The Acquisition of Pragmatics.* New York: Academic Press, 1976.

BATES, E.   *The Emergence of Symbols.* New York: Academic Press, 1979.

BLOOM, L.   *Language Development: Form and Function in Emerging Grammars.* Cambridge, Mass.: The M.I.T. Press, 1970.

BLOOM, L., AND M. LAHEY,   *Language Development and Language Disorders.* New York: John Wiley, 1978.

BRAINE, M. D. S.   Children's First Word Combinations, *Monographs of the Society for Research in Child Development,* 41, 1976 (serial no. 164).

BRAINE, M. D. S.   The Ontogeny of English Phrase Structure: The First Phase, *Language,* 39, 1973, 1–13.

BROWN, R.   *A First Language.* Cambridge, Mass.: Harvard University Press, 1973.

CHOMSKY, N.   *Syntactic Structures.* The Hague: Mouton, 1957.

CLARK, E.   Strategies and the Mapping Problem in First Language Acquisition, in *Language Learning and Thought,* ed. J. Macnamara. New York: Academic Press, 1977, 147–68.

DARLEY, F.   A Philosophy of Appraisal and Diagnosis, in *Diagnostic Methods in Speech Pathology,* 2nd ed., eds. F. Darley and D. C. Spriestersbach. New York: Harper & Row, Pub., 1978.

DUCHAN, J.   Elephants Are Soft and Mushy: Problems in Assessing Children's Language, in *Speech Language and Hearing,* eds. N. Lass, L. McReynolds, J. Northern, and D. Yoder. Philadelphia: Saunders, in press.

EISENSON, J.   *Aphasia in Children.* New York: Harper & Row, Pub., 1972.

FERGUSON, C., AND D. SLOBIN, eds.   *Studies of Child Language Development.* New York: Holt, Rinehart & Winston, 1973.

FILLMORE, C.   The Case for Case, in *Universals in Linguistic Theory,* eds. E. Bach and R. Harms. New York: Holt, Rinehart & Winston, 1968.

FODOR, J., T. BEVER, AND M. GARRETT.   *The Psychology of Language.* New York: McGraw-Hill, 1974.

GALLAGHER, T.   Revision Behaviors in the Speech of Normal Children Developing Language, *Journal of Speech and Hearing Research,* 20, 1977, 303–18.

GOLDMAN, R., M. FRISTOE, AND R. WOODCOCK.   *Goldman, Fristoe, Woodcock Auditory Skills Battery.* Circle Pines, Minn.: American Guidance Service, 1974.

JOHNSON, W., F. DARLEY, AND D. C. SPRIESTERSBACH.   *Diagnostic Manual in Speech Correction.* New York: Harper & Row, Pub., 1952.

JOHNSON, W., F. DARLEY, AND D. C. SPRIESTERSBACH.   *Diagnostic Methods in Speech Pathology.* New York: Harper & Row, Pub., 1963.

KIRK, S., AND J. McCARTHY.   *Illinois Test of Psycholinguistic Abilities.* Urbana, Ill.: University of Illinois Press, 1961.

KIRK, S., J. McCARTHY, AND W. KIRK.   *Illinois Test of Psycholinguistic Abilities.* Urbana, Ill.: University of Illinois Press, 1968.

LAKOFF, G.   On Generative Semantics, in *Semantics: An Interdisciplinary Reader in Philosophy, Linguistics and Psychology,* eds. D. Steinberg and L. Jakobovits. London: Cambridge University Press, 1971.

LASKY, E., AND J. KATZ, eds.   *Central Auditory Disorders: Problems of Speech Language and Learning.* Baltimore, Md.: University Park Press, in preparation.

LENNEBERG, E.   *Biological Foundations of Language.* New York: John Wiley, 1967.

LEVINSON, P., AND C. SLOAN, eds.   *Auditory Processing and Language.* New York: Grune & Stratton, 1980.

McCARTHY, D.   Language Development in Children, in *Carmichael's Manual of Child Psychology,* ed. P. Mussen. New York: John Wiley, 1954.

McCARTHY, D.   *The Language Development of the Pre-School Child.* Minneapolis: University of Minnesota Press, 1930.

McCAWLEY, J.   Where Do Noun Phrases Come From? in *Semantics: An Interdisciplinary Reader in Philosophy, Linguistics and Psychology,* eds. S. Steinberg and L. Jakobovits. London: Cambridge University Press, 1971.

McLEAN, J., AND L. SNYDER-McLEAN.   *A Transactional Approach to Early Language Training.* Columbus, Ohio: Chas. E. Merrill, 1978.

MACDONALD, J.   *Environmental Language Inventory.* Columbus, Ohio: Chas. E. Merrill, 1978.

MILLER, J. *Assessing Language Production in Children*. Baltimore, Md.: University Park Press, 1981.

MILLER, J., R. CHAPMAN, M. BRANSTON, AND J. REICHLE. Language Comprehension in Sensorimotor States V and VI, *Journal of Speech and Hearing Research*, 23, 1980, 284-311.

MILLER, W., AND S. M. ERVIN. The Development of Grammar in Child Language, in *The Acquisition of Language,* eds. U. Bellugi and R. Brown. *Monographs of the Society for Research in Child Development*, No. 29, 1964, 9-33.

MYKLEBUST, H. R. *Auditory Disorders in Children: A Manual for Differential Diagnosis*. New York: Grune & Stratton, 1954.

NATION, J., AND D. ARAM. *Diagnosis of Speech and Language Disorders*. St. Louis, Mo.: C. V. Mosby, 1977.

NELSON, K. Concept, Word and Sentence: Interrelations in Acquisition and Development, *Psychological Review,* 81, 1974, 267-85.

OSGOOD, C. A Behavioristic Analysis of Perception and Language as Cognitive Phenomena, in *Contemporary Approaches to Cognition*. Cambridge, Mass.: Harvard University Press, 1957.

PALERMO, D. *Psychology of Language*. Glenview, Ill.: Scott, Foresman and Co., 1978.

PRIZANT, B., AND J. DUCHAN. The Functions of Immediate Echolalia in Autistic Children, *Journal of Speech and Hearing Disorders,* 46, 1981, 241-49.

ROSCH, E. On the Internal Structure of Perceptual and Semantic Categories, in *Cognitive Development and the Acquisition of Language,* ed. T. Moore. New York: Academic Press, 1973.

SANDERS, D. *Auditory Perception of Speech*. Englewood Cliffs, N. J.: Prentice-Hall, 1977.

SANDERS, L. *Evaluation of Speech and Language Disorders in Children*. Danville, Ill.: Interstate Printers and Publishers, 1972.

SCHIEFELBUSCH, R. Language Studies of Mentally Retarded Children, *Journal of Speech and Hearing Disorders,* Monograph Supplement, 10, 1963, 4.

SHANNON, C., AND W. WEAVER. *The Mathematical Theory of Communication*. Urbana, Ill.: University of Illinois Press, 1949.

SKINNER, B. F. *Verbal Behavior*. Englewood Cliffs, N.J.: Prentice-Hall, 1957.

SLOANE, H. N., AND B. MACAULAY. *Operant Procedures in Remedial Speech and Language Training*. Boston: Houghton Mifflin Co., 1968.

STEINBERG, S., AND L. JAKOBOVITS, eds. *Semantics: An Interdisciplinary Reader in Philosophy, Linguistics and Psychology*. Cambridge, England: Cambridge University Press, 1971.

TEMPLIN, M. C. Certain Language Skills in Children: Their Development and Interrelationships, *Child Welfare Monographs,* no. 26. Minneapolis: University of Minnesota Press, 1957.

2

Structural Analysis

Our form of structural analysis points to finding the patterns in children's performance whether or not those patterns appear on tests or whether or not they have been exhibited by other children. We emphasize language production because it offers a more direct look at ways children use language, though we consider language comprehension just as important. In this chapter we present a general approach for going about structural analysis. We recommend ways to get a sample of naturalistic and elicited language from the child; and we explain how to transcribe it, analyze it for structures, and test for whether its structures are psychologically real for the child. Finally, we suggest ways you might coordinate your results.

We will be assuming in this chapter that these patterns in behavior will be predictable and consistent and that they derive from particular knowledges in the child. Many times these assumptions are not adequate, since the behaviors are likely to vary depending upon the situation and upon the linguistic context. When this inconsistency is structurally analyzed, it often becomes apparent that there is contextual consistency—that is, the patterns are predictable once we understand that they vary systematically under different contextual conditions. For example, the auxiliaries may be dropped in rapid speech; or the language may be telegraphic when the child is being interrogated; or weak syllables may be deleted only in three-syllable words. Studying these contextual influences comes under the domain of pragmatics.

Because context is so important in understanding children's language, most structural analyses will need to involve two aspects: the analysis for units within common contexts and the analysis for variability of those units across contexts. Before we present some steps for doing these two kinds of analyses—

the unit and variability analyses—we will present some general principles and cautions to guide you in carrying out your own structural analysis.

STRUCTURAL ANALYSIS—
THE PRACTICALITIES

Our message is not that you do the impossible—you cannot find patterns for each child in all areas of language performance any more than you can give each child all existing language tests under a normative approach. Rather, our hope is that we can lead you to develop a principled approach for evaluating children's communication abilities, which you can use to select the areas to analyze. Your analysis should lead you directly to formulate clinical goals or design individualized educational plans.

In this section we list some principles and cautions for you as you proceed. First, we ask that you do not use structural analysis unless you are attempting to answer questions about regularities in a child's behaviors. It is only at that point—once you have resolved or taken as secondary the issues of normalcy and etiology—that structural analysis becomes sensible.

Second, we realize you cannot look for patterns in a child's behavior without any ideas about what types of things are characteristic of normal children learning language; so we offer a background of the types of structures that have been studied in the adult and child language literature and suggest it as a way for you to organize your thinking as you proceed. We warn against using these structural categories as a checklist, however, since it may blind you and make it impossible to discover things a child is or is not doing which do not appear on your checklist. Checklists also further the bias toward standard English, which is inappropriate when working within communities that speak different dialects (see Duchan, 1982; Taylor, 1982).

Third, we suggest that you enter into your analysis of a mildly or moderately involved child with the questions: What is it about this child that makes him or her different? What causes the communication breakdowns? Does the problem fall within the phonological, morphological, syntactic, semantic, or pragmatic areas, or does it fall within areas we have not touched on? These questions will lead you to the domains where you can begin your analysis. Perhaps later you will want to look beyond the main problem if you suspect difficulty in other areas, but you cannot and should not try to do everything at once.

Fourth, if the child has problems in all domains, as is often the case for the severely impaired child, you might analyze what it is he or she is doing, rather than focusing on the areas that present difficulty. Thus, the focus for your analysis is not on the source of breakdown, but rather on determining what the child is doing as he or she attempts to communicate, or on how and when the child is responding, and to what.

Fifth, the analyses will vary in difficulty. Sometimes doing an analysis is quick, easy, tangible. This is usually true of structures that are readily observable, such as word endings, and for children whose use of such structures is highly regular and predictable. Other analyses are of less tangible data, such as semantics where the networks of meanings become worked out only after creative use of deep testing and careful study. Analyses are easier once you have done them a few times. For example, once you get used to doing phonological analysis, you will be able to discover patterns such as substituting stops for fricatives much faster. Indeed, you will often not need to go through the transcription but will be able to hear the pattern immediately.

Sixth, regardless of whether the analysis is easy or difficult, we think you will find it is worth the trouble. This is because it leads to the establishment of approaches for helping a child improve. The results of the analysis can be stated in short-term and long-term objectives or educational plans. Thus, for a child whose problem is stops for fricatives, you would work on that, teaching the feature of frication. If your structural analysis is incomplete, you can have as a goal the completion of that evaluation through deep testing.

GETTING A LANGUAGE SAMPLE—SOME PRINCIPLES

There are several principles of language sampling which are found in the literature and in the tradition of those who are doing language sample analysis for how to get a good, easy-to-analyze language sample. These general principles apply to most, but not all, language sampling situations. The amount of pre-planning and control will depend upon the goal of the structural analysis. Obviously if the behaviors being analyzed are rare in natural situations, you will need more controlling methods to elicit them; or if the children are unintelligible, it is important to control the situation so you can know what they are talking about.

Familiar Environment

Better samples are obtained when the child is relaxed and interested and in a familiar environment with a familiar interactant. Labov (1971) pointed this out when he described the difference between informal (vernacular) and formal styles in adult speakers. "Vernacular rules are more consistent than the rules used in formal styles; word classes are more intact, and the vernacular is free of hypercorrection. . . ." (Labov, 1971, p. 460). We have observed that children who have poor intelligibility are considerably less verbal with strangers than with familiar listeners. This implies that the sample of language obtained in the typical clinical situation where the setting, the people, and the activities are all unfamiliar to the child may not reveal the child's true linguistic ability. Observation of the child with family members or school friends will give a better view of the child's typical language performance. This may involve including familiar people in the diagnostic session with the child and clinician or supplementing the clinician's interaction with observation of the child in another situation where the observing clinician is unobtrusive.

Unstructured Activities

Longhurst and Grubb (1974) compared the amount and complexity of language obtained in four situations and concluded that less structured, conversational settings generally elicited language of greater quantity and complexity than the more structured, task-oriented settings. Although asking a child to describe a picture is a frequently used technique for eliciting language, we have found, along with others, that children typically respond by simply labeling objects in the picture, especially if instructed "Tell me what you see" (Bloom and Lahey, 1978; Longhurst and Grubb, 1974). Situations which the adult structures primarily by asking questions likewise yield a restricted sample, since children tend to assume a passive conversational role and merely answer the questions without engaging in more spontaneous interchanges. Children, like adults, are most comfortable talking while they are engaged in some activity of their own choosing which provides a natural topic of conversation.

Length of the Sample

There should be a long enough sample collected to include several occurrences of the behaviors which comprise the domain for the analysis. A minimum of 50 to 100 different utterances is frequently recommended for syntactic analysis (Lee, 1974; Tyack and Gottsleben, 1974), with 50 being accepted as the minimum for computation of MLU. A minimum time period of half an hour has been recommended in one or more situations (Bloom and Lahey, 1978; Crystal, Fletcher, and Garman, 1978). We prefer to observe young children with their caretaker for ten to fifteen minutes before we interact with the child to get an additional sample. With a talkative child, a shorter period of time might suffice, while for a child who says very little, every utterance said in several sessions might be recorded and included in ongoing language sampling and analysis.

Atmosphere Conducive to Talking

Some children talk freely and copiously to any listener in any situation. Most do not, particularly if they have language impairments. It is well to keep in mind that there is no way to *make* children talk; you can only make them want to talk by creating a situation where there is a reason to talk and an atmosphere that conveys the message that you are interested in what they have to say. If you put yourself in the child's place, this is not a difficult principle to understand. Children, like adults, have the right not to talk unless they feel it is to their advantage to do so. Here are some hints for getting the reluctant talker to want to talk.

1. Keep the focus off your attempt to get the child to talk. With children who are very hesitant to say anything, start with activities that demand little verbalization for participation, such as drawing pictures or playing a game. This allows the child to become a participant with you in a nonthreatening way. During this activity you should comment on what you are doing and allow for, but not directly request, the child's verbal participation.

2. Do not talk too much and do not be afraid to allow silent pauses during the conversations. Do not fill up every empty space with a question. This encourages the child to let you take the lead.

3. Select materials appropriate to the child's level of functioning. For example, children operating at a preschool level tend to be more interested in toys than in books or games. Older children tend to like unusual objects or things that can be manipulated.

4. Toys with detachable or moving parts and broken toys generally stimulate verbalization. If possible, you might have the child or caretaker bring in one or two of the child's own favorite toys. Children often have more to say about familiar things than about new ones. When toys become too enrapturing, they tend to inhibit verbal interaction. If that happens, it is best to announce that you will have to put the toy away in a few minutes and do something else or to present an interesting alternative while you quietly remove the distracting toy.

5. Most children are naturally curious. If they know you have something concealed from them, they usually want to find out more about it. Having a big box or bag (or even a pillow case!) from which you withdraw objects may prompt conversation about what else it contains. Likewise, noise sources they cannot see or mechanisms that make toys move stimulate curiosity. It is generally best not to have all of your materials out at once, but you might present alternatives and ask the child which one he or she wants to look at first.

6. If the child will initiate conversation about your materials, let him or her take the lead, and ask questions or comment briefly on what the child is saying. For a more natural and less "testing" atmosphere, insert your own opinions or comments occasionally.

7. If the child does not initiate, make comments yourself about the materials and ask open-ended leading questions, such as "That looks broken. What do you suppose happened to it?" or "Can you figure out what's going on here?" If these prompts do not elicit verbalization, try more specific questions which require minimum output, such as "Do you...?" "Where...?" "What is...?" and then build up to more open-ended questions, such as "Tell me...." or "What about...?"

8. If statements or questions produce no response, demonstrate what you expect of the child. For example, take a toy yourself and play with it, tell about what you are doing, and personalize your account using an imaginary situation. Engage the child in the play as soon as possible and begin to prompt indirectly. For example, make your car crash into the child's car and then ask what happens next.

9. If the child is reluctant to talk about pictures or tell stories, go first and set the stage. A series of sequence pictures provides more story structure than a single picture and therefore is generally easier for a beginning story. You can have the child tell the same story after you or create a new story using different pictures or characters. Unless you are analyzing for storytelling structures, do not ask the child to tell too familiar a story, since it might be memorized and unlike more natural output.

10. Include another person in the elicitation or collection procedure. This might be another clinician or aide who can model the responses you expect from the child or it might be the child's parent, sibling, or friend who can be included in the activities. Having a third party involved tends to take the focus off the child and makes talking more comfortable.

ELICITATION FOR PARTICULAR
STRUCTURES

Language samples are usually taken in natural play interactions. The "natural" part of the interaction must be sacrificed when the data being analyzed do not occur frequently in free play. The situation then needs to be organized to elicit the structures being studied. This can be accomplished either by linguistically structuring the session, with verbal directions or questions to query the child's knowledge directly or by changing the situation from a child-directed free play to a specific activity suggested by the clinician that is likely to elicit particular structures. Children often perform differently in this more structured, elicited context than they do under natural occurring conditions. Thus it is important to evaluate children's knowledge in terms of these contextual constraints and not to make your assumptions about what a child knows about language solely on the basis of these contrived situations.

ELICITED IMITATION   Elicited imitation of utterances is appealing as an elicitation procedure because it is very direct and thereby timesaving. As we indicate in our discussion of sentence imitation tests in Chapter 10, the legitimacy of using this procedure is based on the argument that children often make the same errors on imitated utterances as they would in their spontaneous productions. It must be recognized, however, that elicited imitation is extremely unnatural. While in spontaneous productions children are engaged in an interaction and their utterances have a purpose or intention as well as a meaning, when they are asked to imitate a sentence, the intention is merely to carry out the clinician's instruction. That is, when they imitate "The big green ball is mine" they probably are not intending to inform the listener about the fact that they have a big green ball as they would be if they said the sentence spontaneously.

The most dramatic example of how elicited imitation violates natural pragmatics is observed when clinicians present children with a question (e.g., Are you nice?) and ask them to imitate it. Children often answer the question rather than imitate (e.g., they say yes). Clinicians, because their intent is to get the child to say a question form, consider this an unuseable response and will correct the child, although the response was perfectly appropriate. A second group of structures which do not work well under elicited imitation are pronouns. The meaning of these forms depends on two principles which are violated in a sentence imitation task, namely, *anaphoric* and *deictic referencing*. The anaphoric reference properties of pronouns mean that they refer back to earlier events in the interaction. The meaning of *it* in the sentence "She gave it to her mother" is unclear unless the listener and the speaker know from previous joint referencing what *it* means. Similarly, when you say *I*, the deictic meaning refers to you, the speaker. However, when imitating *I*, the referent changes to the child, and thus the meaning is different. To preserve the meaning, children often change *I* to *you* and vice versa, saying "I am . . ." in response to the model sentence "You are . . ." Clinicians who correct this are penalizing that child for using the language correctly.

The child's attempts to make imitated sentences meaningful might show up in other ways that seem "wrong" from the clinician's point of view. For example, the child knows the event referred to is not happening in the present and so may convert a model sentence given in the present tense to past tense on imitation. It would be inappropriate to analyze this as a semantic or morphological error.

Because of the problems with altered intention and meaning of imitated sentences, we would not use this technique to test for pragmatic knowledge. It is best suited for investigation of phonology, morphology, and syntax and can be used in a limited manner for finding semantic problems. Furthermore, we would not assume that children have particular types of linguistic competence just because they imitate structures correctly. The correct production may come from rote repetition of the model rather than linguistic knowledge. We recommend that you be cautious in your use of this procedure; that is, use only the changes from the adult model rather than correct productions on the imitation task as evidence of a child's linguistic patterns.

Sentences that contain particular structures of interest can be designed for elicited imitation. Table 2.1 shows, as an example, a group of sentences for eliciting auxiliary verbs.

PATTERNING   Patterned practice has long been used in formal instruction in second-language learning. It is a technique which offers a set of similar events, and the learner derives new, analogous responses from the pattern in the presented set. The usual technique is to confine the analysis to simple structures, as in the popular example from children's folklore. The first child introduces the set—"I one it," "I two it," "I three it." The unsuspecting child continues the pattern and is caught saying "I eight (ate) it," when "it" has been described as a singularly unappetizing object.

This elicitation procedure evaluates children's ability to extrapolate patterns from language data as well as shows their knowledge of the structures

Table 2.1   Elicited Imitation for Auxiliaries

(is)	The boy is throwing the ball.
(are)	The kids are riding on the bus.
(am)	The girl said "I am going home."
(were)	The dogs were swimming in the lake.
(was)	The baby was sleeping by the door.
(will)	The men will take away the trash.
(can)	We can sit on the steps.
(should)	The cook should wash his hands.
(has)	The lady has cut the grass.
(have)	We have eaten our breakfast.
(did)	We did like the new cereal.
(don't)	Cats don't like to get wet.
(doesn't)	He doesn't mind if we play here.
(2 aux.)	She will have gone home by now.
(2 aux.)	The men should have been on time.
(3 aux.)	He might have been sleeping when the girl called.

involved. It has the advantage also of being an enjoyable activity. Its disadvantages are that it does not necessarily involve the same psycholinguistic processes used in natural conversation and that children may be benefiting from the routinized nature of the task, thus producing structures that they cannot produce in spontaneous conversation.

A variation on this procedure is to introduce a puppet or doll as a participant in the exercise. This makes it more interesting for young children, and they may be willing to speak to or for the puppet when they are hesitant to talk to strange adults.

Following are examples of patterns which we have devised to elicit particular forms from the child. For additional suggestions, you might look at drill books from foreign language teaching. Also, Slobin (1969) presents some patterned elicitation techniques that have been used with children.

PATTERNED PRACTICE ELICITATIONS

1. Eliciting second person singular

I will say:	This is my book.	
Then you say:	This is your book.	(point to child)
I will say:	This is mine.	
Then you say:		(pause: point to child)
If I say:	This is me.	
What do you say:		(point to child)
If I say:	I hurt myself.	
What do you say:		(point to child)

2. Eliciting auxiliary

I say:	Can he?
You answer:	Yes, he can.
I say:	Will he?
You answer:	Yes, he will.
If I say:	Wouldn't he?

    What do you answer:

    (Continue with Couldn't he? Can't he? Won't he? Could he? Would he? Is he?). This can be repeated with a negative reply (e.g., No, he can't).

3. Eliciting knowledge of functions

    Show the child an object and pattern him or her to answer in the following form:

    You ____ (verb) with a ____ (noun). For example, present a fork and say "You eat with a fork"; then present another object and have the child give the function.

4. Eliciting negatives

    This puppet is bad. He always says no. If his mother says

Come in here	he says	No, I won't.
She is my friend	he says	No, she isn't.
etc.		

5. Eliciting opposites
   This puppet fights all the time. When his friend says

   | It's cold | he says | It's hot. |
   | It's pretty | he says | It's ugly. |

SENTENCE COMPLETION This often-used elicitation procedure works well with forms that occur in the last position in the sentence. The clinician simply says the beginning of the sentence, or constituent, and the child fills in the end—for example, "You eat with a _____." Because this completion technique depends upon the listener's ability to construct what the speaker was going to say, and then to say it, the speaker must provide enough clues so that the possible correct answers are somewhat few in number. Thus, an appropriate completion task would be Berko's (1958) test in which she asked children to extend their knowledge of morphological inflections to nonsense forms: "This is a wug. Now there are two of them. There are two _____."

A sentence completion task can be designed to elicit linguistic knowledge, as in the above example, or conceptual knowledge, as when children are asked to base their completion on an analogy. The Auditory Association Subtest of the ITPA offers some interesting examples of conceptual analogies, such as "Grass is green. Sugar is _____." Interspersed in these examples are test items which do not require that the analogies be based on the conceptual relationship between the words in the first sentence but rather simply require that the second sentence be completed. For example, "Bread is to eat. Milk is to _____." Analogies are more difficult for children than completion where they must simply provide a word that is semantically and syntactically appropriate for the sentence.

Multiple choice items are examples of sentence completion elicitations where children can select an answer from a set of given possibilities. This format is sometimes easier than having to provide the answer spontaneously, because the answer is included. However, you can well remember your own reaction to some multiple choice tests which are harder than regular sentence completion because the foils can confuse the issue.

Following are some examples of sentence completion procedures for eliciting certain kinds of linguistic and conceptual knowledge.

SENTENCE COMPLETION ELICITATION

1. Tag questions
   I'm going to say the first part of a sentence, you say the rest. For example, I'll say "That's mine," and you say "Isn't it?"

   That's yours, _____
   She's my friend, _____
   They don't like her, _____

2. Functions
   We cut with a _____
   I eat with a _____

3. Semantic field knowledge
   Using objects such as utensils, fruits, clothing, ask:
      This is a _____
4. Action analogies
   Birds fly, rabbits _____
   Babies cry, ducks _____
5. Tense
   Today I am shopping. Yesterday I did the same thing. I _____
   Tom can throw a ball. Yesterday he did the same thing. He _____
6. Multiple choice: Tense
   Which sounds better?
      Yesterday I *ate* or
      Yesterday I *eated*
      Yesterday I _____

QUESTIONS   There are several advantages of asking questions to elicit specific structures. First, question asking is probably familiar to the child (Snow and Ferguson, 1977), and second it is a direct and therefore quick and efficient way to elicit certain structures. The disadvantages are that the procedure might seem like an interrogation, inhibiting spontaneous performance or relaxed interaction. Also, responses for some questions may be packaged routines rather than productive structures (see Duchan, 1980; Gleason and Weintraub, 1976; Thomas, 1979).

As with every elicitation procedure, the context influences its success. Children are more likely to answer questions they feel you really want to know the answer to (e.g., "Where do you live?") as opposed to questions you already know the answer to (e.g., "What is this?").

Following is a table of frequently occurring questions and some language forms or meanings which the questions may elicit (Table 2.2, p. 26).

ROLE PLAYING   We have used role playing with children to elicit forms such as commands and directions where the child is the "boss" or the teacher. Having children pretend they are lost and asking directions can elicit question forms. Describing a situation for a "blind" friend or a child from another country elicits descriptive terms. The child might also assume the role of a character in a story who speaks in a characteristic way. For example, playing Goldilocks provides good examples of use of adjectives.

GAMES   Games are speech events which have a prescribed sequence, usually involve taking turns, may have a competitive component, often involve suspense and resolution, and also are regarded by children as fun rather than as work. Any number of gamelike elicitation procedures can be developed. Some familiar games, such as hide and seek, can be redesigned to elicit structures such as prepositions. Objects can be hidden and the child can guess where they are rather than search for them. Other novel games can be designed to elicit particular language performance. The barrier game used by Krauss and Glucksberg

(1969) has children describe unfamiliar designs to elicit nonegocentric role taking. A fruitful game for examining conceptual schemes, descriptive vocabulary, and negative forms is "What is wrong?" where incongruous pictures or statements are presented. Sorting games offer rich opportunities to understand how children classify. Guessing games (Who am I? What am I thinking of? Where does this go?) are usually interesting to children and can be altered to elicit particular structures.

We have successfully used a messenger game for eliciting questions. In this game the child is asked by one person to find out some information from another. The "messenger" aspect of the game may have been experienced be-

Table 2.2   Question and Answer Elicitation

YOUR QUESTION TO THE CHILD	MEANING ELICITED	LINGUISTIC STRUCTURE ELICITED
When	Time	Adverbs, prepositional phrases, tense marker
Where	Space	Adverb, prepositional phrase
Why	Cause-effect	*Because* clause
Who	People	Noun, pronoun, name
Whose	Possessive	Possessive noun or pronoun
Is, are, was, were, am	Identity, quality description	Yes-no
How	Manner-method	Adverb
How many-few	Number	Adjective
much-little	Quantity	Adjective
often-soon	Time	Adverb
far-near	Distance	Adjective, noun, adverb
long	Linear measure or time	
heavy-light	Weight	Adjective, adverb, *as* phrase
big-small	Size	
Would	Probability, *if* condition, cause-effect	*If* clause
Which	Selection, multiple choice	
Do, does		Yes-no
What if	Inference, cause-effect	*If-then* clause
What kind, color, shape, size, day	Classification	Adjective for description, noun for class name
What + be	Identity	Noun
What + do	Action	Verb
What + do + verb + with	Function	Noun
May	Permission	Yes-no
Will you	Request and future	Yes-no
Can	Possibility	Yes-no
Should	Judgment	Yes-no
What happened	Event description	Noun-verb-noun construction, small stories, narrative past tense

Table 2.3   The Messenger Game—A Procedure for Eliciting Questions

This is a suggested procedure for eliciting questions from a child who does not ask them spontaneously. The method works best when three people are involved. The child acts as a messenger, carrying information from one person to another. It is also more realistic if the two people who are exchanging messages through the child are not within view of one another. A problem with the question formulation might be revealed if the child uses the request as a model for forming his or her own questions: e.g., Adult: Ask her how she got to this school. Child: How you got to this school?

MESSAGE CARRIED BY THE CHILD	QUESTION FORM ELICITED
1. Ask her where she lives.	Where + do
2. Ask her when her birthday is.	When
3. Ask her how she got to this school.	How + did
4. Ask her to tell you what this is for.	What + for
5. Ask her who she eats with.	Who + do
6. Ask her what time it is.	What
7. Ask her which one she wants—this one or that one?	Which
8. Ask her how many shoes she has on.	How many
9. Ask her when she is going home.	When
10. Ask her if she will eat out tonight.	Will
11. Ask her what color her hair is.	What
12. Ask her if she wants this.	Do
13. Ask her if she likes what she is doing.	Do (complex)
14. Ask her how she catches a ball.	How + do
15. Ask her when you can go to lunch.	When + can
16. Ask her why she isn't home now.	Why + aren't
17. Ask her is she can jump.	Can
18. Ask her if she will help you snap your fingers.	Will (complex)
19. Ask her why this won't work.	Why + won't
20. Ask her why this is dirty.	Why

fore by the child, thus giving it some realism. Table 2.3 illustrates the types of questions which can be elicited by this procedure.

Some other examples of verbal game elicitation procedures are listed as follows:

1. Eliciting spatial terms. One child is allowed to see an abstract design such as

and must tell another how to draw it, step by step.

2. Listener perspective taking and spatial terms—the map game. One child explains to another how to direct his or her car from one place to another on a map which simulates a geographical space.

3. Categorization—the matrix game. Matrix games are commercially published and ask children what item goes in the empty slot. They must

draw analogies from two dimensions presented in the matrix. For example, what goes in the blank below?

duck	bird	dog
pond	nest	?

4. Strategies to get information and classification—twenty questions. Twenty questions is a game in which children use classification as a means for guessing a targeted object. One player knows an object, the other asks yes-no questions to guess it. The game can be played by younger children if the objects are few and different from one another (Bruner, Olver, and Greenfield, 1966).

INTERVIEWING   Interviewing is a procedure in which you ask children to tell you directly about their use of language or to indicate which structures are allowable in their rule system. Anthropologists use an interview procedure when they ask a member of another culture to explain some aspect of the culture. When this description is applied to language, it is referred to as a metalinguistic task, meaning that it involves language to talk about language. While adults can be asked directly to be introspective about their own language, children generally lack the ability to be metalinguistic until relatively late in development (Gleitman, Gleitman, and Shipley, 1972. For an exception, see Von Raffler Engel, 1965). Roger Brown, for example, tells of asking his famous two-year-old subject Adam "Which is right—two shoe or two shoes?" to which Adam replied "Pop goes the weasel" (Brown and Bellugi, 1964).

For older children, interviewing has the advantage of providing information that might not be uncovered from structural analysis alone. A second advantage of interviewing over other elicitation techniques is that it treats children as responsible coparticipants in the endeavor of figuring out how they use and understand language. It must be recognized, however, that it is difficult even for adults to explain things they do automatically and to reflect on factors that are usually outside of their awareness. The answers you get may not be an accurate description but will still reflect the child's perception. For example, the child with a phonological problem reports that he has trouble with his tongue, possibly because someone explained his problem to him in that way, when actually his problem has to do with his conceptualization of the phonology of the language and not his tongue movement.

We especially recommend the interview procedure for certain areas of structural analysis, such as speech event analysis. Good interviewing is a highly skilled technique and requires considerable sensitivity and insight on the part of the interviewer. The best interviewers pick up on children's leads and go in the direction their informants are thinking, rather than follow a ready-made format of questions. Piaget, a researcher who has perhaps made the most of such interviews, offers a sense of his respect for good interview procedure:

> . . . it is our opinion that in child psychology as in pathological psychology, at least a year of daily practice is necessary before passing beyond the inevitable fumbling stage of the beginner. It is so hard not to talk too much when questioning a child, especially for a pedagogue. It is so hard

not to be suggestive. And above all, it is so hard to find the middle course between systematisation due to preconceived ideas and incoherence due to the absence of any directing hypothesis. The good experimenter must know how to observe, that is to say, to let the child talk freely, without ever checking or side-tracking his utterance, and at the same time he must constantly be alert for something definitive, at every moment he must have some working hypothesis, some theory, true or false, which he is seeking to check. (Piaget, 1976, pp. 8–9)

Types of questions which could be asked in interviews include the following:

1. Knowledge of semantics
   Why is a blackboard called a blackboard?
   What would you call a baby pig? Why?
   Could you call this fork a wug? Why or why not?
   What would a disher be? How do you know?
2. Knowledge of syntax
   Would it be right to say "The ice cream ate the boy"? Why not?
3. Knowledge of language as a system
   How do baby children in France learn to talk that way?
   Could you say _____ in French? Could you say it in English?
4. Knowledge of speech events. Asking children to explain a speech event, such as a game or a joke, gives you perspective on their knowledge of the intricacies of the structure of the event and how they view it.

RETELLING OR REENACTMENT   Children can be asked to recount or act out events to determine how they understand the original events (Piaget, 1976), how they handle narrative, how they take the listener's perspective, as well as many other things. One particularly interesting use of retelling was designed by Ferreiro and Sinclair (1971). Their subjects watched a two-stage situation—e.g., a girl doll washing a boy doll and then the boy doll going up some stairs. They were then asked to describe the second stage in the event before the first. The task was designed to test children's ability to describe events apart from the order in which they occur and their use of temporal words such as "after." (The normally developing children in this study were unable to do this before they reached the stage of concrete operations, around seven years of age.)

Reenactments are often easier than retellings, since the children act out a previously occurring event rather than talk about it. So, for example, showing how the table is set at home would be easier than describing to an adult how this is done. This is particularly true for the language-impaired child. Thus, one of our clinical cases, a Down's syndrome child named Mike, was able to enact an elaborate story using one-word utterances to speak for the characters and to narrate the event but could not describe the event verbally. Chapman and Miller (1980) have used this kind of evidence to show a gap in development between cognitive and linguistic understanding, in order to determine whether a child would be amenable to learning an alternative communication system.

LET'S PRETEND   Joining the child in pretending where roles or situations are enacted can reveal the child's contextual awareness. For example, James (1978) and Read and Cherry (1978) have elicited polite forms and indirect requests from children by asking them to pretend to talk to someone politely. Read and Cherry describe the task as follows:

> The task was introduced to each subject as a game that she was going to play with a puppet and the experimenter. The child was to request the puppet to provide a desired object, juice, cookie, or crayon. In each situation, the puppet took the desired object and announced that it would not share the object with the subject. Then the experimenter prompted the subject to produce a directive addressed to the puppet. The following prompts, which were phrased in neutral terms, were used: "You really want a cookie, too. Say something to Cookie Monster to get a cookie." In each situation the puppet failed to comply with the child's initial request for the desired object. After the child's second directive, the puppet produced a response—but not as requested in the directive. The puppet would substitute another object for the desired object. For instance, a child's directive such as "Please give me the cookie" was followed by the puppet handing the subject a paper cookie. Following the child's third directive, the puppet gave a response which indicated a postponement of compliance, e.g., "Just a minute." Once again, the puppet did not provide the desired object requested in the directive. After each subject had produced these directives, the puppet gave the child the desired object. (Read and Cherry, 1978, p. 235)

CONTINGENT QUERIES   Questions which are situationally related—questions about an ongoing situation or about what has just been said by a child—have been called contingent queries (Garvey, 1977). These queries can be used to elicit and to assess children's language. For example, Gallagher (1977) studied how normal children at three stages of language development responded when an adult pretended not to understand what they said and used the contingent query "What?" Using children classified according to Brown's Stages I–III (see Chapter 6), her results indicated that at all three stages children responded to "What?" by giving a revised version of their original utterance, but they differed in the type of revisions made. Stage I, the youngest children, tended to revise in two ways—by phonetic change (e.g., C: He kit ball A: What? C: He kick ball) or by elaborating on a constituent in the utterance (e.g., C: It ball A: What? C: It big ball). Stage II children had significantly fewer phonetic changes in revisions and often changed the grammatical structure of the original sentence by adding new constituents (e.g., C: big ball A: What? C: It big ball). They also frequently reduced constituents on revision (e.g., C: It big ball A: What? C: It ball). Stage III children displayed the same pattern of adding and reducing constituents and in addition substituted new words in a significant proportion of their revisions (e.g., C: He kick ball A: What? C: He kick it). Gallagher's use of the question-answer technique to study normal children's revision behaviors is obviously highly amenable to studying revisions in children whose language is not normal and can thereby be adapted as an assessment procedure for discovering strategies in children's approach to conversational breakdowns.

TRANSCRIPTION

After eliciting a sample of behavior, the next step in performing a structural analysis is to transcribe the sample in ways that will achieve the goals of the structural analysis. This will, of course, vary with different goals. If your purpose is to analyze the phonological system for its structural regularities, the phonological errors in the sample should be transcribed in narrow phonetics (see Chapter 4). In this case, there is less need for contextual transcription (if you already know what the child is saying). In contrast, when investigating aspects of a child's knowledge of pragmatics, you will want to transcribe the verbal production in standard orthography, and your transcript will have detailed notes or descriptions of contextual changes (see Chapter 3).

Not only will the goal of the structural analysis dictate the detail within various levels of language (phonology, morphology, syntax, semantics, pragmatics), it will also dictate which segments are selected for transcription at each level. If you want to investigate a child's difficulty with the production of spatial prepositions, a listing of the contexts which require the prepositions (obligatory contexts) and what the child says and does in those contexts would be all that is necessary for this analysis. This would be called a *listing transcript,* in which pertinent items in the sample are listed and perhaps described. Box 2.1 illustrates such a transcript.

Box 2.1   *Listing Transcript: Obligatory Contexts for Past Tense*

Mother talk	Child talk	Context
1. When did you give that to your teacher?	I do it yesterday.	
2. Did you see her leave?	No, go away. Me out of room.	
3.	He not there. Mommy there, and then come back.	About the teacher at school yesterday.
4.	He goed and she goed too.	

The most commonly used transcript is a *running transcript,* which includes a written version of most of the child's and adult's verbal productions. Usually it is presented in standard orthography with some commentary on the context accompanying the production. This is the type of transcript most useful for structurally analyzing the morphology or syntax of the sample (Bloom and Lahey, 1978). An example of such a transcript is seen in Box 2.2.

Box 2.2   Running Transcript

<table>
<tr><td rowspan="4" style="writing-mode: vertical">Sequential time</td><td>**Adult talk**</td><td>**Child talk**</td><td>**Context notes**</td></tr>
<tr><td>Do you want this now?</td><td>Uh-uh.</td><td>Adult offers milk to child.</td></tr>
<tr><td>What else do you like here?</td><td>Just a hamburger.</td><td></td></tr>
<tr><td>OK, but drink some of your milk first.</td><td></td><td>Child gets up from table.</td></tr>
</table>

Finally, in order to use the nonverbal and intonational aspects of behavior to study pragmatics, we use the *multilevel transcript*. This is a detailed transcription of a brief segment of behavior where descriptions of simultaneous behavioral changes are made. Condon and Sander (1974) have called these co-occurring changes *whiles*. The transcript involves more detail than can be assimilated in direct observation with note-taking; and because it includes nonverbal and behavioral synchrony information, it requires more information than is available from an audiotape. For these reasons, the multilevel transcripts require that videotaped samples be used as the data base. An example of such a transcript is given in Box 2.3.

Box 2.3   Multilevel Transcript: Levels Accompanying Points

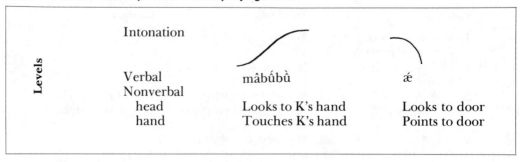

The multilevel transcript has been used to analyze for such things as nonverbal performatives (Dore et al., 1976), sensorimotor origins of first words (Carter, 1975), types of requests (Dore, 1977; Read and Cherry, 1978), self-synchrony in behavior (Condon and Ogston, 1967), and functions of echolalia in autistic children (Prizant, 1978; Prizant and Duchan, 1981).

DISCOVERING STRUCTURES

So far we have talked about selecting, recording, and transcribing language samples. Now we turn to the most important aspect of the structural approach to language assessment—analyzing the material to discover regularities. We are calling these regularities *structures*, hence the name for the overall approach *structural analysis*. We will present some general procedures for the discovery of structures here; in later chapters we are more specific as to how to proceed with structural analysis for the different aspects of children's linguistic and prelinguistic performance.

When analyzing running or listing transcripts for within-level regularities, you can approach each level either in terms of a *deviation* analysis or an analysis of the *correct forms* (or both). The deviation analysis can involve describing regularities in terms of how they differ from the adult target (e.g., he has difficulty with past tense) or in terms of the regularities themselves (e.g., she indicates past tense by adding a "did" form to the verb). The correct-form analysis can classify the forms which are correctly made (e.g., the child has stops and fricatives in the initial position) or can analyze for the conditions under which the correct forms occur (e.g., he produces "is" correctly in simple sentences). (See Muma, 1973, for his CORS analysis.)

Often you will find that productions seem to be inconsistent—they are produced correctly sometimes and incorrectly other times. This inconsistency calls for more detailed analyses. Linguistic and nonlinguistic contextual influences might be evaluated, as in our place + feature analysis in Chapter 4. An illustration of the success of this approach is a study by Ferguson and Farwell (1975), who analyzed the patterns involved in phonological inconsistency. First, they sought children who showed variation of pronunciation of particular words. Then, for each child, they listed all the productions of the initial consonants in the same word and ascertained the range of possible variation in the phonology of the child's initial consonant production (e.g., child says /pʌp/, /kʌp/, /tʌp/ for cup). The variations were studied for their consistencies, in this case all stop consonants.

Only after all conceivable influences producing the apparent inconsistency are considered should you conclude that children are inconsistent in their production. In other words, a good policy to follow is to assume consistency exists unless you have done the necessary work to prove yourself wrong.

When analyzing multilevel transcripts, regularities are examined across the levels rather than confined to a particular level of language. For example, you may find that during a prelinguistic child's production of grunts with question intonation, he or she looks at the conversational partner and points to an object. You might conclude from this multilevel behavioral pattern—from the grunt, the look, and the point, together—that this is a coherent, unified structure which functions as a request for the child (Garvey, 1975).

Once regularities are found in the sample, you will probably need to verify their existence by going back and eliciting new behaviors from the child. These might be behaviors which can be predicted from your hypothesized patterning, or they might be behaviors which would test a new idea you have for the regularities in the child's behaviors. This procedure of returning to the child for further testing we have called *deep testing,* after McDonald (1968). It should be used often, even after you have begun therapy, in order to help you keep track of changes in the patterns in the child's performance.

TESTING THE STRUCTURES— ARE THEY PSYCHOLOGICALLY REAL?

The structural analyst not only needs to discover and abstract regularities from the language sample but should also devise ways to determine whether or not the discovered structures are psychologically real for the child. Examples of times when they are not are

1. When the speakers respond to the task in routinized patterns but cannot use the structure in other situations
2. When they have memorized material
3. When they have learned linguistic segments as wholes and do not analyze them into the units that we may be investigating (e.g., "Once upon a time . . .").

There are several techniques in the psycholinguistic literature for determining the psychological reality of structures. One is to use evidence from *development.* The logic is that behaviors categorized as part of the same structure should develop or change together. If, instead, some elements in the category change while others do not, the category may have been the analyst's construction rather than the child's structure. For example, a child in our clinic substituted stops for fricatives. When he was taught to prolong the stops, he altered his production of all fricatives, except the θ and ð. This suggests that in his category system the unaltered sounds were not classified as fricatives.

The child's exhibition of generalization is also a useful kind of developmental evidence for verifying the reality of a category. The extension of a rule to a group of elements argues for the psychological reality of the category into which the elements are classified. For example, when children begin to use plurals, they can apply the plural ending to all nouns (including plurals such as "mans"), indicating that they have a noun category.

A second source of evidence for psychological reality is that the structure be *productive*—that is, that it extend to new knowledge or occur in diverse contexts rather than only in specific, unique environments. Bloom and Lahey (1978) consider a structure to be productive if it occurs in the sample in at least four different contexts. Thus, the category of "past tense" would not be considered by them to be psychologically real if it only occurred with one verb, even if that verb were used several times.

A third test for the appropriateness of a category for explaining children's knowledge is whether another, less complex explanation can be offered to account for the regularity. This simplicity or *parsimony* test has been used by researchers who argue against too "rich" an interpretation being made of child language data. For example, Bowerman (1973) contended that the category "subject" was not psychologically real for children in the early stages of two-word utterances because they only used subjects which were animate. They never spoke sentences with instrumental subjects, such as "The knife cut the bread." Bowerman (1973) said that the children knew about the semantic relation of agents but did not have the category of syntactic subjects. We have taken Bowerman's argument further and argued that semantic relations such as agents might also be too complex a category system to attribute to the child (Duchan and Lund, 1979). We asked children questions of the form "What do you _____ (verb) with?" and found their answers could be categorized into semantic relations but that they did not have to understand those categories to answer. Rather, all they may have been doing was answering with what was most needed to carry out the action (e.g., "What do you eat with?" "Food"). This is a more parsimonious explanation because it is a single strategy, while the other explanations assume the child has a complex set of knowledges. Thus, it is more plausible as a psychological construct than the more linguistically based notion of semantic realtions. (See also our example of Jimmy's two-syllable strategy [Chapter 4].)

Another basis for evaluating the psychological reality of a structural category, related to the parsimony criterion, is asking about its *explanatory adequacy*—that is, does the category account for what is important in the data? Bloom's classic argument against the psychological reality of the pivot-open categories is that they are inadequate to explain the relevant features of children's utterances (Bloom, 1971). Every occurrence of the utterance "Mommy sock" would be described as the same in a pivot-open grammar, which does not account for the fact that the child could say "Mommy sock" and mean at least two things: (1) That's mommy's sock or (2) Mommy, put my sock on me.

Equivalence is yet another way to show evidence that a category is a real one for the child. If, for example, linguistic units can be shown to substitute for one another in similar contexts, they can be regarded as units that the child categorizes together. A familiar example is the phoneme. A variety of sounds are categorized together as a simple, psychologically real unit despite the fact that they differ in actual production because they are regarded as functionally equivalent. Likewise, a phrase such as /wʌdʒawana du/ is functionally identical to its carefully articulated counterpart "What do you want to do?" if we are investigating questioning behavior.

Another source of evidence for functional equivalence is when elements we have assigned to a category all display change under changing conditions. For example, if children are asked to rearrange a sentence, they will typically move an entire noun phrase together, which argues for the psychological reality of noun phrase for them. They will also preserve predictable positions such as noun-verb and adjective-noun, which points to their knowledge of categories of parts of speech.

In summary, when you look for evidence that a structure is psychologically real for the children you are evaluating, you can

1. Teach the child to change one item in a category and see whether or not this change generalizes to other items in that category (Development)
2. Examine the language sample or get a new sample to see if the structure exists in different contexts (Productivity)
3. Try to derive a more parsimonious category which is closer to what the child is doing than it is to preexisting linguistic or cognitive categories (Parsimony)
4. Try to find a category that accounts for what the child is doing (Adequacy)
5. Get the child to express exemplars or manifestations of the structure in different ways, to see if he or she acts the same under conditions of change (Equivalence).

TYING THE RESULTS TOGETHER

Once you are confident that the structures are psychologically real for the child, you might find it fruitful to summarize everything from your analysis into a unified framework where knowledges at one level of analysis are reflected at other levels. It might be that you will have trouble finding such integration, in which case you can list the problem areas separately so that you can see them all at once. For example:

Phonology
   stops for fricatives
Morphology
   omits auxiliaries
   overregularizes past tense
Syntax
   only intonation questions
   single clause structures
Semantics
   overextensions of animal terms

The best place to start your inquiry into the psycholinguistic relationships between problem areas is with pragmatics, since some of these conceptualizations cross psycholinguistic levels. For example, you will discover from our discussion of pragmatics (Chapter 3) that children's problems with deictic terms in semantics, with subordination in syntax, and with discourse devices and polite forms in pragmatics might all be a reflection of their lack of listener perspective taking.

A second fruitful way to discover intermeshing between levels is to compare morphological and phonological deviations. For example, inflectional endings may be deleted by virtue of a problem with weak-syllable deletion, or as part of a larger problem with fricative omissions. It may also be the case that semantics of particular morphological forms are not yet acquired, such as those involving temporality, in which case the morphological and semantic levels are intertwined.

Finally, as the particular conditions under which the language occurs become more demanding, the language may change systematically. Sometimes called *style shifting*, other times *task constraints*, these coordinated shifts could be studied in terms of what occurs together. In rapid or excited speech, for example, there will be a greater likelihood for weak-syllable deletion, stop consonant underarticulation, syntactic simplification, and deletion of morphological forms. These areas can then be regarded as systematically related, and the relationship can be examined in further detail.

The goal in all of these steps is to give the clinician an understanding of how the child thinks about language and about the world, and of how these thought processes are expressed. A disjointed list does not capture the integration of the knowledge and the processes. Therefore, this final step is an attempt to construct a wholistic picture or model of the child's language and thought processes.

Box 2.4. *Summary of Steps in Structural Analysis*

The steps in structural analysis are

1. Getting a language sample
2. Eliciting particular structures
3. Transcribing relevant data
4. Discovering consistent structures
5. Discovering context influences
6. Verification
7. Testing for psychological reality
8. Tying results together

EXERCISES

1. Tape record an interaction with a child while you play and talk together using the principles discussed in this chapter. Transcribe the sample in standard orthography and include at least 50 of the child's utterances. Include your own utterances in this segment. Analyze your role in this interaction to determine what you did to facilitate or impede the child's responding. Indicate what you would do differently next time. Choose a child who is intelligible.

2. With the same child, try to elicit 15 negative forms (*no, not, nothing, none, never*). Notice how the interaction changes when you impose more structure. Describe the change in what you do and how this affects the child. Transcribe as you did above.

REFERENCES

BERKO, J. The Child's Learning of English Morphology, *Word,* 14, 1958, 150–77.

BLOOM, L. Why Not Pivot Grammar? *Journal of Speech and Hearing Disorders,* 36, 1971, 40–50.

BLOOM, L., AND M. LAHEY. *Language Development and Language Disorders.* New York: John Wiley, 1978.

BOWERMAN, M. *Early Syntactic Development: A Cross Linguistic Study with Special Reference to Finnish.* Cambridge, England: Cambridge University Press, 1973.

BROWN, R. *A First Language: The Early Stages.* Cambridge, Mass.: Harvard University Press, 1973.

BROWN, R., AND U. BELLUGI. Three Processes in the Child's Acquisition of Syntax, *Harvard Educational Review*, 34, 1964, 133–51.

BRUNER, J., R. OLVER, AND P. GREENFIELD. *Studies in Cognitive Growth.* New York: John Wiley, 1966.

CARTER, A. The Transformation of Sensorimotor Morphemes into Words: A Case Study of the Development of "More" and "Mine," *Journal of Child Language,* 2, 1975, 233–50.

CHAPMAN, R., AND J. MILLER. Analyzing Language and Communication in the Child, in *Nonspeech Language Intervention,* ed. R. Schiefelbusch. Baltimore: University Park Press, 1980.

CONDON, W., AND W. OGSTON. A Segmentation of Behavior, *Journal of Psychiatric Research,* 5, 1967, 221–35.

CONDON, W., AND L. SANDER. Neonate Movement Is Synchronized with Adult Speech: Interactional Participation and Language Participation, *Science,* 183, 1974, 99–101.

CRYSTAL, D., P. FLETCHER, AND M. GARMAN. *The Grammatical Analysis of Language Disability.* New York: Elsevier North-Holland, 1978.

DORE, J. Children's Illocutionary Acts, in *Discourse Production and Comprehension,* ed. R. Freedle. Hillsdale, N.J.: Lawrence Erlbaum Associates, 1977.

DORE, J., M. B. FRANKLIN, R. T. MILLER, AND A. RAMER. Transitional Phenomena in Early Language Acquisition, *Journal of Child Language*, 3, 1976, 13–28.

DUCHAN, J. Interactions with an Autistic Child, in *Language: Social Psychological Perspectives*, eds. H. Giles, W. Robinson, and P. Smith. New York: Pergamon Press, 1980, 255–60.

DUCHAN, J. Elephants Are Soft and Mushy: Problems in Assessing Children's Language, in *Speech Language and Hearing,* eds. N. Lass, L. McReynolds, J. Northern, and D. Yoder. Philadelphia: Saunders, 1982.

DUCHAN, J., AND N. LUND. Why Not Semantic Relations? *Journal of Child Language,* 6, 1979, 243–52.

FERGUSON, C., AND C. FARWELL. Words and Sounds in Early Language Acquisition: English Initial Consonants in the First Fifty Words, *Language,* 51, 1975, 419–39.

FERREIRO, E., AND H. SINCLAIR.   Temporal Relationships in Language, *International Journal of Psychology,* 6, 1971, 39–47.

GALLAGHER, T.   Revision Behaviors in the Speech of Normal Children Developing Language, *Journal of Speech and Hearing Disorders,* 20, 1977, 303–18.

GARVEY, C.   Requests and Responses in Children's Speech, *Journal of Child Language,* 2, 1975, 41–63.

GARVEY, C.   The Contingent Query: A Dependent Act in Conversation, in *Interactions, Conversation, and the Development of Language,* eds. M. Lewis and L. Rosenblum. New York: John Wiley, 1977, pp. 63–93.

GLEASON, J., AND S. WEINTRAUB.   The Acquisition of Routines in Child Language, *Language in Society,* 5, 1976, 129–36.

GLEITMAN, L., H. GLEITMAN, AND E. SHIPLEY.   The Emergence of the Child as a Grammarian, *Cognition,* 1, 1972, 137–64.

JAMES, S.   Effect of Listener Age and Situation on the Politeness of Children's Directives, *Journal of Psycholinguistic Research,* 7, 1978, 307–17.

KRAUSS, R., AND S. GLUCKSBERG.   The Development of Communication: Competence as a Function of Age, *Child Development,* 40, 1969, 255–66.

LABOV, W.   Methodology, in *A Survey of Linguistic Science,* ed. W. Dingwall. College Park, Md.: University of Maryland, 1971.

LEE, L.   *Developmental Sentence Analysis.* Evanston, Ill.: Northwestern University Press, 1974.

LONGHURST, T., AND S. GRUBB.   A Comparison of Language Samples Collected in Four Situations, *Language Speech and Hearing Services in the Schools,* 5, 1974, 71–78.

McDONALD, E.   *A Deep Test for Articulation.* Pittsburgh: Stannix House, Inc., 1968.

MUMA, J.   Language Assessment: Cooccurring and Restricted Structure Procedure, *Acta Symbolica,* 4, 1973, 12–29.

PIAGET, J.   *The Child's Conception of the World.* London: Routledge & Kegan Paul, 1929. (Reprinted Totowa, N.J.: Littlefield Adams, 1976.)

PRIZANT, B.   An Analysis of the Functions of Immediate Echolalia in Autistic Children. Ph.D. dissertation, State University of New York at Buffalo, 1978.

PRIZANT, B., AND J. DUCHAN.   The Functions of Immediate Echolalia in Autistic Children, *Journal of Speech and Hearing Disorders,* 46, 1981, 241–49.

READ, B., AND L. CHERRY.   Preschool Children's Production of Directive Forms, *Discourse Processes: A Multidisciplinary Journal,* 1, 1978, 233–45.

SLOBIN, D., ed.   *A Field Manual for Cross-Cultural Study of the Acquisition of Communicative Competence.* Berkeley, Calif.: University of California, 1967.

SNOW, C., AND C. FERGUSON, eds.   *Talking to Children, Language Input and Acquisition.* New York: Cambridge University Press, 1977.

TAYLOR, O.   Sociolinguistics and Communication Disorders, in *Speech Language and Hearing,* eds. N. Lass, L. McReynolds, J. Northern, and D. Yoder. Philadelphia: Saunders, 1982.

THOMAS, E.   It's All Routine: A Redefinition of Routines as a Central Factor in Language Acquisition. Paper presented at the Fourth Annual Boston University Conference on Language Development, Boston, Mass., 1979.

Tyack, D., and R. Gottsleben. *Language Sampling, Analysis and Training* (rev. ed.). Palo Alto, Calif.: Consulting Psychologists Press, 1974.

Von Raffler Engel, E. An Example of Linguistic Consciousness in the Child, *Orientamenti Pedagogici*, 12, 1965, 631–33. Reprinted in C. Ferguson and D. Slobin, *Studies of Child Language Development.* New York: Holt, Rinehart & Winston, 1973.

3

Pragmatics

Traditionally, researchers and clinicians have studied language as though form and meaning existed independent of the contexts in which language occurs. Recent research in the area of pragmatics has begun to show us the dramatic effect of contexts on the way language is used and interpreted, making it clear that we cannot assess language if we isolate it from what is going on with the speaker and listener. Pragmatics, or the effects of context, has been studied in a variety of ways, each offering us an approach to analyzing children's use of language. (See Rees, 1978, for a review of many of these approaches.)

The study of pragmatics has had different focuses. Some study it as a separate and separable level of language, along with phonology, morphology, syntax, and semantics (Miller, 1978; Prutting, 1979). Others regard pragmatics as much more important than other areas of language and in fact regard it as a determiner of the structures at those other levels (Bates and MacWhinney, 1979). These functionalists, as they are called, look at language structure as a way of carrying out communicative jobs dictated by the function. For example, speakers use language to express their intention, to track topics in conversation, and to manage their interactions.

A third way people have thought about pragmatics is as a combination of the first two ways—they study it as a separable domain as well as studying its influence on phonology, morphology, syntax, and semantics. We have taken this third approach in our book because it represents the evolution from a linguistic to a more functional approach.

We have chosen to organize this discussion of pragmatics into four areas, each describing one aspect of context and how it affects language production. Drawing from the literature on pragmatics, we will discuss how the contexts of situation, the speaker's intention, the listener, and the language itself affect what children say and what they mean. These four areas—situational context, intentional context, listener context, and linguistic context—have been chosen because they comprise most of the recent literature on pragmatics and because they can be studied by using structural analytic techniques with which we are now familiar: language elicitation and sampling, transcription, and analyzing for patterned regularities.

THE SITUATIONAL CONTEXT

There are various ways of characterizing a situation. We can think of a situation as a physical setting or as an event that is going on. There might be a sequence of events or a routine that typifies the event that is occurring; and usually there is a topic that participants are focusing on. Our awareness of each of these aspects determines our sense of the situation and in turn affects our language use in the situation. In this section we will discuss further the facets of "situation" and then suggest some techniques for structurally analyzing children's conceptualization of their situation context.

The Physical Setting

By physical setting, we mean the objects and people that are present and the activities that they are engaged in. The frequently referred to "context boundedness" of young children pertains to their inability to distance themselves psychologically from the physical setting of the here-and-now event; that is, before age two, children seem to think and talk about only those things which they are currently experiencing. Their first words have referents of familiar objects, people, and actions, and they utter them when those familiar events are physically present.

Children progress from a here-and-now reality to one involving thinking about remote events. Their progression is through a middle period in which they can think about events and objects that are not currently perceptible but are indicated within the physical setting—that is, children at first respond to what they see, hear, smell, etc.; they then come to anticipate objects and events from indicators, such as closed drawers, refrigerators, or someone getting a coat on. Such an indicator has been called an *index* (Piaget, 1926; Tanz, 1980) and is seen as a step toward representational thinking (see Chapter 9 for an elaboration of this stage).

Even when children can construct representations of noncurrent events (at around three years of age), much of their language is associated with ongoing activities. Thus, they talk about present objects, initiate verbal routines around their current play or playmate, and fail to understand or produce language that lacks some grounding in the present situation.

Bruner and his colleagues have illuminated another aspect of physical context in their descriptions of the role of mutual referencing in language acquisition (Bruner, 1975; Ninio and Bruner, 1978). For children to learn lexical items, they must know which referent is being labeled by their language partner. Thus, the role of pointing, showing, and giving in joint activity is to make clear what is being referred to by the language used. It enables both participants to look at the same object. Helen Keller's reported late understanding of the symbol-referent association can be understood as her inability, because of her blindness and deafness, to engage in mutual referencing with Anne Sullivan, her persevering teacher.

In addition to children's early development of the ability to participate with their language partner in mutual referencing within the current physical situation, they also learn early how to use mutual gaze as an indicator that their partner is paying attention to them. Thus, until children get the attention of their addressee, they do not move on in the interaction. They may accomplish this by tugging, making noises, repeating their beginning word, or through ritualized attention-getting phrases (e.g., "Know what?" "Lookit").

As we discuss in Chapter 7, the physical situation influences the language of all speakers and listeners, not just those who are beginning language learners. The physical placement of objects and people will influence the choice and interpretation of particular deictic terms used for referring to them (e.g., "this one," or "here"). The presence of other possible referents encourages the use of modifiers, such as "the big one" or "that red one."

The Speech Event

Another aspect of a situation besides the physical setting is the speech event. Speech events are the participant's overall sense of what the interaction is about. Thus, if you were to ask children "What's going on here?" in different speech events, they would answer differently. They might answer on different occasions "We're playing," "We're telling jokes," "We're in speech class." A speech event, then, is the participant's conceptualization of the kind of interaction he or she is having and, so, sets the scene for particular kinds of exchanges.

Happenings which are not speech events are those which are loosely organized, have little prearranged purpose, and give no sense of how things will progress. Instead participants may have a feeling that they are in a transition period between events. These periods might be characterized by the responses of participants asked what they are doing, as follows: "Oh, nothing"; or "Oh, we're just getting together"; or "I'm taking a break"; or "Riding on an elevator, what do you think!"

The speech event may or may not be the same for all participants. The adult may view a given exchange as "teaching," while it may be a conversation or play session for the child. Likewise, the adult may be conceptualizing a conversation speech event, while the child perceives the same exchange as a quiz where there are right and wrong answers.

Although it is probably often the case that speech event categories are not the same for children and adults, speech events are typically researched according to adult categories with the assumption that children regard the event in the same way as the adult. For example, Garvey (1977) has studied children's utterances under the speech event category of play, which she defines as the child's nonliteral orientation to the verbal material. Similarly, Ervin-Tripp and Mitchell-Kernan (1977) have grouped their research into the adult categories of talk-stories and instructional teaching.

Speech events can be distinguished from each other on the basis of the way in which they are structured. Typically, an event will have a detectable beginning, middle, and ending which the participants adhere to or noticeably violate or negotiate during their execution of the event. Openings such as

Let's pretend that . . .
Today we're going to . . .
Once upon a time . . .

generally mark the beginning of a new speech event, each of which will then proceed with certain regularities of turn taking and reach a termination that may be equally explicit:

And they all lived happily ever after.
Let's do something else.
That's all the time we have today.

Some speech events are characterized by one participant getting virtually all the "turns"—e.g., a sermon or lecture—and other participants getting a turn only if formally recognized—e.g., raising a hand to be called on. Other events require turn taking, either where both participants are equally free to initiate turns, as in an egalitarian conversation, or where one participant initiates and the other responds, as in quizzing or interrogation. These characteristics of each event make up its frame.

Speech event frames include those aspects which are predictable, expected, inviolable, and characteristic of that particular event. Events also have parts which are not characteristic of that type of event but just happen to occur in the particular instance. These circumstantial parts are not what we mean by frames. For example, Shank and Abelson (1977) describe a restaurant event as necessarily involving being seated, ordering food, eating, and paying for the food. They also talk about circumstantial instantiations of that generalized event, as when the waitress spills soup. In our conceptualization, the soup spilling would not be part of the event frame because it is not predictable nor expected, but paying the bill would be part of it.

Events differ in the type of frame and the degree to which the frame dictates the carrying out of the event. For example, the most tightly framed events are those that involve highly specified routines in which every part of the sequence is dictated. Less tightly framed events are, for example, scripts such as the restaurant script. These carry expectations, or what Shank and Abelson called stereotyped sequences of actions, but they also contain slots which can be filled in different ways in each new example of the event (Shank and Abelson, 1977, p. 41). Loosely framed events are those which have negotiated sequences as a large part of the contents. The sequences are not determined before the event takes place but occur as a result of the particular set of happenings in that particular happening. Unritualized play and conversation without a goal are examples of such sequences.

44

The Topic

The term *topic* has been used in several senses that are relevant to analyzing the situation in which language is occurring. When used in relation to a sentence, it pertains to what the sentence is commenting about. Hurtig (1977) has called this a sentence's "aboutness." The second sense of topic involves a group of utterances and describes what they are *all* about—as when we refer to a *topic of conversation.* Van Dijk (1979) has distinguished these by calling the first *sentence topic* and the second *discourse topic.* The essential difference is one of scope, in that one covers the sentence and the other has a wider scope—a set of utterances related to the same topic.

SENTENCE TOPIC   When we examine a transcript of dialogue, it becomes apparent that many utterances do not state their topic but rather are comments on an implicit topic. If we take these utterances out of context, we often cannot identify the topic. Sometimes it is the language that gives the context that makes the topic clear, which we will discuss as linguistic context. Other times it is the situational context. Imagine, for example, two people watching a game and the first saying to the second "Jerk." This is a comment on a topic that we assume is mutually understood by the participants but is unknown to us because we are not there to witness what the speaker is talking about. We do not know the situational context.

Sentence topics can be expressed syntactically or semantically in a variety of ways. While topics are usually expressed as agents or subjects in the surface sentence, they need not be, as can be seen in the following examples:

> There was this guy who was afraid of whistles. (Topic—*guy*)
> That's my book. (Topic—*book*)
> Don't run in the hall. (Topic—*you running*)

Also, determination of sentence topic can be difficult if there are embedded topics in the same sentence, as when subordinate clauses contain a second topic, for example:

> I'll do it when they get ready. (Topics—*doing something; they will get ready*)

DISCOURSE TOPIC   A topic that extends to two or more utterances can be identified as a discourse topic. It may cover only a two-utterance exchange.

> How do you like school?
> It stinks.

Or it can extend over many utterances, as in a lengthy discussion. It can be returned to after a short or lengthy interruption, usually with a transition to refocus on the topic:

> Now, what were you saying?
> Last time we talked about . . .

Bransford and Johnson demonstrate how a topic provides coherence to a set of utterances by first offering the following passage without such a topic:

The procedure is actually quite simple. First you arrange things into different groups. Of course one pile may be sufficient depending on how much there is to do. If you have to go somewhere else due to lack of facilities that is the next step, otherwise you are pretty well set. It is important not to overdo things. That is, it is better to do too few things at once than too many. In the short run this may not seem important but complications can easily arise. A mistake can be expensive as well. At first the whole procedure will seem complicated. Soon, however, it will become just another facet of life. It is difficult to foresee any end to the necessity for this task in the immediate future, but then one never can tell. After the procedure is completed, one arranges the materials into different groups again. Then they can be put into their appropriate places. Eventually they will be used once more and the whole cycle will then have to be repeated. However, that is part of life. (1972, p. 215)

The paragraph appears complex and confusing until the authors provide the topic around which the details make sense. The topic in this case is washing clothes.

TOPIC CHANGE AND TOPIC CONTINGENCY   Determining topic may appear to be a formidable task. It becomes more manageable when we focus on children's inappropriate departures from the topic or failure to specify the topic. Appropriate topic changes can involve a gradual fading from one topic to the next:

Jack went home from shopping.
He ate supper and then watched TV.
The show was his favorite, Johnny Carson.
Johnny was especially funny that night.

Abrupt changes in topic require a request or notification statement:

Can I change the subject?
This is totally unrelated, but . . .

Inappropriate changes are abrupt and unannounced departures from the ongoing topic. These are common in normal children's conversations before about four years of age. These exchanges have been described by Piaget (1926) as egocentric speech or collective monologues. Such changes often produce discourse breakdowns and listener requests for the sentence or discourse topic:

What do you mean?
Who are you talking about?

Several studies have been devoted to analyzing children's responses to determine if they are related to the topic of the previous utterance. Responses that are topically related are said to be contingent, with the result being discourse agreement or topic sharing. At the least contingent end of the topic contingency dimension, one finds non sequiturs, which are utterances not contingent at all to the immediately preceding utterance. Blank et al. (1979) report on a three-year-old child whose language was age appropriate when examined for syntax and semantic performance but who frequently responded to adult utterances in non sequiturs. Instead of sharing a topic with the adult, the child would introduce new topics. The authors give an example:

Father: (looking at stroller in a book) Who's there?
  John: Read it again.
Father: OK. What do you want to read?
  John: What's that?

John's utterances would have been an appropriate initiation of new topics if his father had not been asking him questions. Since John's utterances follow questions that they are not topically contingent with, however, they are inappropriate. It appears that John's utterances are an attempt to initiate a verbal routine. Blank et al. (1979) describe these routines as "highly specialized language-based routines which [are] tied to specific situations." They are clearly noncontingent on the utterance that precedes them.

Dore (1977) presents a few examples of responses in his two and one-half to three-year-old subjects which show somewhat more contingency but still lack full discourse agreement.

Teacher: Are you there?
  Child: I'm going to do this color.

Dore ventures this interpretation: "The teacher had been trying for some time to get the child's attention, but he had been ignoring her. Her final solicitation, 'Are you there?,' was not meant seriously—she knew where he was. The child finally conceded, but only to the extent of telling her what he was going to do" (Dore, 1977, p. 157).

Moving toward yet more topically contingent responses, one finds those that involve implications which the speaker assumes the listener can follow, and which are referred to as implicatures. Dore also describes this type of exchange:

Teacher: John, are you finished?
  John: They're out 'cause I'm sorting them.

Dore explains: "The teacher is presumably asking about the blocks that several children are playing with. The child's response, instead of a direct answer, is an explanation of why the blocks are out. He may even be explaining why he is not finished" (Dore, 1977, p. 160). In this exchange, the child understands, probably correctly, that the implied topic of the teacher's utterance is the blocks, and thus his response is contingent on hers.

Finally, at the most contiguous end of the continuum, one finds what Corsaro (1979) describes as topic relevant acts and topic relevant responses. These occur when there is an established topic and the act or response conforms to it. Topic-relevant acts follow either the utterance that initiates the topic or another topic relevant act, in either event adding substance to the previous act. Topic-relevant responses, on the other hand, acknowledge the previous utterance but do not go beyond it by adding any substance. Corsaro offers this example of dialogue between Buddy (B) and his mother (M):

B: Mom? (topic shift initiator)
M: What? (topic shift response)
B: (Chips) have blood on them. Do they have blood on 'em? (topic relevant act)
M: No, I don't think so (topic relevant response)
B: Kids and people do (topic relevant act)
M: Um-hum (topic relevant response)
B: And monsters (topic relevant act)
M: Yeah (topic relevant response)
B: Like Grover has blood in him (topic relevant act)
M: Well, Grover's a pretend monster. He's really a puppet, you know? (topic relevant act)
B: Yeah (topic relevant response)
(Corsaro, 1979, pp. 387–88)

THE INTENTIONAL CONTEXT

A second context which affects language is the context of the speaker's intention. Utterances do not occur as meaning units separate from the speaker but are entities which the speaker uses—that is, which the speaker says in order to achieve a particular goal. When the speaker says "That's too noisy," we can interpret the meaning of the utterance on two levels. First, the *propositional* meaning is a description of a noisy condition. However, we would also interpret the utterance to mean "Stop it," i.e., as a request by the speaker for someone to put a stop to the noisy condition. This second aspect of the meaning illustrates what is meant by *intention.* It is also referred to as a function, as an intentional act, as an illocutionary act, or as an illocutionary force, and has been studied in the pragmatics literature under the rubric of speech act theory (e.g., Austin, 1962; Searle, 1969) or use theory of meaning (Bates, 1976). Within this framework, every utterance, whether it be communicative or noncommunicative, has a function or intention (we will use these terms interchangeably).

Some utterances explicitly state their function by using verbs that name the speaker's intention. These are called *performative* verbs and include verbs such as *ask, tell, promise,* and *declare* which actually perform an act rather than describe it (e.g., "I ask you now to go with me"). Most utterances, however, do not have performative verbs, so we have to look at the context to derive the speaker's intention. Sometimes the intention is quite obvious, as in direct requests, such as "Give me a drink," "Gimme," "Drink," or even a grunt and a point. Less obvious would be requests expressed indirectly, such as "I'm thirsty" or "Do you have anything to drink?"

Classifications of Intention

Some researchers who have studied speech act functions have attempted to develop a classification system that would describe all the basic functions in child and adult language. Halliday (1975), for example, has described a list of general functions which he found expressed in his son Nigel's vocalizations at 9 months of age, and he traced the development of these functions through the child's 24th month.

At stage 1, from 9 to 16 months, Nigel expressed four functions by using vocables which seemed to have no external or internal referent but had as their meaning only those functions; that is, the vocables had no propositional content but only expressed intention. Halliday described the functions, giving them the following adult glosses:

> Instrumental—I want
> Regulatory—Do as I tell you
> Interactional—Me and you
> Personal—Here I come

At stage 2 (16½ to 18 months), Nigel developed from using vocables to using words. At first, each word corresponded only to a single function, just as the vocables did in stage 1. For example, "cat" expressed only the interactional function, as if Nigel were saying "Hello cat"; and "syrup" expressed only the instrumental function, equivalent to "I want syrup." Later, the same lexical item could express several functions, which demonstrated independence of the propositional meaning from the function.

Also in stage 2, Nigel developed a new intention—that of categorizing experiences through new words. Halliday described this as the child's attempt to learn about the environment and labeled this function

> Heuristic—Tell me why

Nigel distinguished utterances for learning about the self (personal) and the world (heuristic) from those involved in getting things (instrumental) or requesting actions (regulatory) by marking the first two with a falling intonation and the latter with a rising intonation. Halliday summarizes, therefore, that Nigel had two function classes—a learning or *mathetic* class, as distinct from demands for a response or *pragmatic* class.

At stage 3 (18 months), Nigel completed his functional development by adding two more function categories to his repertoire:

> Imaginative—Let's pretend
> Informative—I've got something to tell you

Halliday was working from his sociolinguistic theory to classify the child's utterances into abstract components. Dore (1974), working from another framework, studied communicative acts of children at this same single-word stage of development. He found them to be classifiable into nine types: labeling, repeating, answering, requesting action, requesting answer, calling, greeting, protesting, and practicing.

Dore has more recently (1979) presented a classification system that is more encompassing than his earlier formulation. It is also based on the utterances of older preschoolers. Dore fits intentions into a broader theory of conversational acts, which he has developed as a model incorporating speech act theory, characteristics of conversations—such as turn taking and topic changing—and also grammatical structure. He identifies three primary functions of conversational acts: conveying content, regulating conversation, and expressing attitude. The functions are modeled after Buhler's (1934) functions for children's utterances—the propositional, evocative, and expressive functions.

Dore subdivides the content-conveying function into *conversational initiation,* which is performed by requestive, assertive, and performative acts, and *conversational response,* which is performed by a responsive act. Each of these general content-conveying categories is divided into specific functions. *Assertives,* for example, are classified as assertives about perceived information, about internal phenomena, and about social phenomena. For each of these functions, there are particular conversational acts specified that perform that function. Assertions about internal phenomena, for example, are expressed as internal reports ("I like it"), evaluations ("That's good"), and attributions ("He wants to"). At this level there are twenty-six particular illocutionary acts derived through a five-level hierarchy from the content-conveying function of conversational acts. The other two general functions, regulating conversation and conveying attitude, are not as elaborate and together include only nine categories of particular acts at the terminal level. Conversational regulators act as discourse markers and ways to get in and out of conversations (e.g., attention-getting acts, such as "Look"). Acts which convey attitude are nonpropositional comments which either express an attitude (e.g., "Wow!") or repeat prior utterances.

Dore's system is different from Halliday's in its explicitness as well as in the types of data it includes. For example, a single category in Dore's system can entail in its defining criteria the syntactic form of the utterance (e.g., question vs. statement); its semantics (e.g., labeling objects vs. expressing emotion); its conversational and situational context (e.g., teasing vs. protesting); and the intention (e.g., requests for action vs. requests for permission). Surprisingly, Dore achieves an 82 percent agreement between two experienced coders on his category system. He does this by examining in detail utterances on which they disagree.

DIRECTIVE ACTS   A less ambitious and more controlled approach to examining utterances' functions is that done by Ervin-Tripp (1977). She confined her study to a particular kind of speech act—directives—and devised a taxonomy of six adult directive types whose use depends on the social and situational context. With one exception (the Hints category), the categories are syntactically based. They are

Need statements—I need an X
Imperatives—Give me an X
Embedded imperatives—Could you give me an X
Permissive directives—May I have an X
Question directives—Have you got an X
Hints—The X are all gone

Several research studies have examined children's directives using Ervin-Tripp's category system (Anderson, 1978; Ervin-Tripp, 1977; Mitchell-Kernan and Kernan, 1977). Ervin-Tripp (1977) summarizes these and other research findings about children's acquisition of directives by postulating a set of stages through which two to five year olds progress. According to her summary, two year olds express directives through attention-getting words along with gestures and rising intonation, request words (e.g., more, want, mine), problem statements (e.g., hungry), and verbal routines. At age three, children begin using modal forms (would you + request), and at age four, they mask the directive force of utterances by giving hints with statement of the problem (e.g., "He hurt me."). Finally, by about five years of age, children form requests which are so distinct from the intent that the desired goal is not even mentioned (e.g., "Pretend this is my car").

REQUEST ACTS   Garvey (1975) has studied acquisition of requests for action, following Searle's (1969) model in his work on speech acts. She first structurally analyzed the form and content which such requests can or must have for adults. She points out that a single request can extend over several sentences and turn-taking exchanges.

Speaker: You see the hammer there?
Listener: Yeah.
Speaker: Hand it to me.

She refers to the request domain, which coheres by virtue of having the request as its focus and having all utterances in the domain relate to that request. Some of the utterances are not required, such as those involved in restating the request, or elaborating on it by means of justification statements or clarification. What is required for a request to be completed is that a request statement be made by one party and some form of response or acknowledgment of it be made by another.

Garvey found that requests involve a set of conditions that are understood and obeyed by adult speakers and listeners. An adult request assumes that the speaker wants the listener to perform a reasonable act which the listener would not do were it not for the request. Further, the listener must be willing and able to carry out the request and is indeed obligated to carry it out unless there is a good reason not to, in which case the reason must be given for the refusal.

Indirect requests are like direct requests in that they specify that the speaker wants the listener to do something, but they differ from direct requests in that they are embedded in a "matrix clause," such as a question or statement (e.g., "Why don't you . . ."; "Don't forget to . . ."). Inferred requests, as opposed to direct and indirect requests, do not contain the core request clause which states what the speaker wants the listener to do; but rather, they rely on the listener to infer it, as in "I need the soap," which the listener must infer as a request for the soap even though the directive "Give me the soap" is not stated.

Besides analyzing adult requirements for different request types, Garvey studied three and one-half to five and one-half year olds' production of requests for action. In so doing she found that all the children made direct requests, that indirect requests did not emerge until four and one-half years, and that inferred requests were very infrequent at all ages.

CHILD-DERIVED CATEGORIES   None of the researchers discussed so far assume that children and adults—and structural analysts for that matter—can develop or discover new kinds of intentions in new contexts. Further, the researchers neglect to consider the fact that their categories may not be culturally invariable or a finite group but rather may be idiosyncratic and infinite. Further still, the researchers we have been discussing do not emphasize or show the worth of working from a detailed examination of a particular child's expression.

A notable exception to these objections is the work of Ann Carter in her study of a normal two year old, David. Carter's work (1975a, 1975b, 1978) entails a set of intricate analyses of the patterns in David's gestures and vocalizations. At age two, David produced eight vocable-action schemes in which each scheme contained a characteristic vocable and gesture. Carter ascribed functions to some of the schemes on the basis of David's productions and traced the evolution of the schemes over a series of play sessions occurring as he progressed from two to two and one-half years of age. David, like Dore's and Halliday's subjects, had different vocalization-gesture units for requests for objects (reach + "M") and attention to objects (reach + "I"). He also had a pleasure expression, which is comparable to Dore's express attitude category. Unlike Nigel, or Dore's young subjects, David had separate vocable-gesture units for attention to self: request for giving or taking objects; request to change an unpleasant situation (dislike and rejection); or request to remove something.

Prizant (1978) also performed a detailed study in which he examined echolalia in autistic children and found patterns in the echoes which suggested that they were serving different functions. Prizant (1978) and Prizant and Duchan (1981) studied the mode of expression and the situational context (antecedent and subsequent events) of the verbal echoes of four echolalic autistic children and found functions which do not fit into the a priori lists of Dore or Halliday. Had they classified the utterances according to Dore's system, they would all have simply been repetitions; they would not have fit at all into the classification system of Halliday. Indeed, they would not even have fit Carter's system because that too was idiosyncratic to Carter's particular subject.

In summary, attempts to classify children's intentions into a finite set have proved to be less than satisfactory. Investigators have generally derived these a priori categories from adult perspectives (e.g., Ervin-Tripp, Garvey) or from a previously evolved theoretical perspective (e.g., Halliday), neither of which allow for differences between children and adults or among children. The problem with fixed categories emerges both with very broad formulations, such as Dore's conversational model, and with more limited formulations, such as Garvey's request for action categories and Ervin-Tripp's directives. For this reason, the clinical approach we advocate does not follow a list of possible functions but rather is based on the method exemplified by Carter and Prizant to discover a given child's set of functions.

Agenda

Besides illocutionary force, there is a second kind of intentionality which has a strong influence upon meaning, one which has been typically neglected in speech act analysis. It is what we are calling *agenda*. This has to do with the goals of the speaker over more of a language segment than the individual utterance. For example, the speaker's agenda may be to persuade the listener that they should go to a movie together. This would likely be manifest in a number of sentences, possibly extending over a whole topic or speech event. The importance of agenda becomes clear when you experience an interaction wherein the goal of the interactant is different from yours. For example, language pathologists who use a game to teach a child a structure may be disappointed when the child describes the event only as a game, missing the "point" which was to learn the structure. The clinicians see the event as a way to carry out their teaching agenda; the child's agenda is to play the game. Agenda mismatches between interactants are a frequent source of breakdown, and because of this an agenda analysis of both speaker and listener is called for (Lubinski, Duchan, and Weitzner-Lin, 1980).

While the notion of agenda has not been focused on, there are allusions to it in the literature. Agenda as a general category has been discussed under titles of illocutionary domain (Dore, Gearhart, and Newman, 1978) and personal script (Shank and Abelson, 1977). As a specific category, agenda has been studied in terms of dispute resolution (Brenneis and Lein, 1977) and request domain (Garvey, 1975).

Agendas need not dominate interaction sequences. This is exemplified by the existence of "backchanneling," which describes a listener who is disengaged and is placing the burden of conversational responsibility on the conversational partner (Duncan and Niederehe, 1974; Lubinski, Duchan, and Weitzner-Lin, 1980). An agenda may span different units: entire speech events, as in a persuasive argument; a few sentences, as in the request domain; or a single sentence, at which point it would be identical to an illocutionary act.

THE LISTENER CONTEXT

Some of the intentions that children are found to express, such as requests, assume their ability to consider the perspective of the attending listener. This ability develops gradually and has been studied as part of *decentering*—that is, as part of the ability to assume the point of view of the other person and to understand the uniqueness of one's own temporal or spatial orientation (Flavell, 1968). As we have said, children's early utterances are not from a perspective of decentration but rather are egocentric in that children cannot understand that others do not experience what they themselves experience.

In order for children to understand the perspective of others, they must be able to assume another's point of view in the current context and to understand something about the listener's background knowledge. Further, they must know something about the role of the listener in relationship to themselves in order to use language appropriately. Each of these kinds of knowledge can be reflected in their language and can account for some of the pragmatic errors we find in their language use.

The Physical Perspective

The spatial orientation of the speaker relative to the listener is one aspect of the situation that must be recognized in order to use some of the deictic terms correctly. We are concerned here about those terms that reflect the speaker's sense of perspective. *Come* and *go* and *bring* and *take* are examples of such terms. *Come* and *bring* are generally indicators that the listener is distant from the speaker and approaches the speaker. These verbs thus reflect both the current position of the speaker and listener and the direction of motion. "Go outside," for example, implies both the speaker and the listener are inside, while "Come outside" would be appropriate if the speaker is already outside or on the way out. "Will you come in?" likewise presupposes that the speaker is in and the listener is approaching, but "May we come in?" is contrary to the rule that *come* implies that the listener is to approach the speaker since in this case the speaker is approaching the listener and not vice versa. This latter case is an example of taking the listener's perspective—that is, "come" would fit the rule if the listener were to say it. Listener perspective is also shown by the speaker who says from the top of the stairs to a listener on the level below "I'm *up* here."

Speakers and listeners often face each other in interactions, and this adds another dimension of potential difficulty for egocentric speakers, since their listener's perspective is opposite from their own. If there is a picture lying flat on a table between speaker and listener, the "top" and "bottom" of the picture might be ambiguous due to their different perspectives. "In front of" presents the same problem with objects placed between them. Likewise, "right" and "left" present confusion in this situation, even for sophisticated language users who attempt to take their listener's perspective.

Background Knowledge

A second type of decentering requires that children understand the background knowledge of the listener. When normal children first talk, they work to maintain listener attention by showing, pointing to, giving an object to the listener; and at the same time they verbalize about it. They also will repeat the communicative act until they get the listener's acknowledgment (Keenan, 1974, 1977). This suggests that they understand at the very beginning stage of language that they are often more successful in achieving their communicative intent when the listener is showing evidences of paying attention (Keenan and Schieffelin, 1976).

However, beginning speakers seldom paraphrase when listeners fail to understand them. It is only later, when they can assume the perspective of the listener, that they make attempts to patch up confusions by restating the utterance in different terms, by filling in background information, and by offering conversational cues which help the listener understand and keep track of what the child is talking about.

Among the things which can be indicators of the child's ability to take account of the listener's orientation are

1. *Existence of relative clauses.* Clauses which follow nouns serve the function of orienting the listener to a particular referent (e.g., "the boy, who is my friend . . ."; "the book which we read yesterday . . .").

2. *Presence of identifying adjectives.* These, too, inform the listener about the particular referent (e.g., "the *red* house").

3. *Use of orienting terms and transition indicators.* Terms and phrases such as "You know that X we saw yesterday . . . ," or "Remember when . . . ," or "As I was saying . . ." show the speaker's sensitivity to the need for the listener to be kept informed of the topic.

4. *Adjustment of language complexity.* When children are speaking to listeners whose language is not developed (e.g., younger children, dogs, etc.), they may need to adjust their language to a level which the listener can understand. Normal four year olds have been found to do this when speaking to two year olds (Gelman and Shatz, 1977).

In addition to structures which indicate how the child accounts for the listener, one can take particular conversational breakdowns as evidence of the child's inability to orient to the listener. Thus, when the listener asks questions such as "Which X?" or "Who?" indications are that the speaker did not appreciate the listener's point of view. This could have happened because he or she failed to consider the listener's (1) need to know pronoun antecedents or general noun references (e.g., "the boy"—Which boy? "she"—Who?); (2) difficulty with excessive ellipsis (e.g., "don't"—Don't what? "mine"—What's yours?); or (3) lack of specification of deictic terms (e.g., "that one" when said to someone on the phone).

Role Relationships

The listener's place in the situation and background knowledge are not the only important things that speakers must consider. There are also language forms which reflect power relationships between speakers and listeners. These relationships might be fixed ones where one is always more dominant, as in parent-child, teacher-student, or boss-employee relationships; or relationships might depend upon the situation, as when the speaker is asking a favor of the listener or when the listener is unlikely to comply with the speaker's request. Whether the dominant-subordinate relationships are fixed or variable, the general cultural rule for speakers is that the language becomes a more direct expression of the communicative intent to the degree that the listener is dominant over the speaker.

Normal children, perhaps because they tend to find themselves in subordinate roles, learn these rules fairly early (Bates, 1976; Ervin-Tripp, 1977; Garvey, 1975). The most studied of these patterns in children are those involved in directives—or utterances which express speech acts such as requesting, ordering, forbidding, or permitting. For example, as we have discussed in terms of speaker context for requesting, the most explicit expressions are imperatives, such as "Give me an X." Indirect forms are

1. Imperatives embedded in other structures, such as questions ("Why don't you give me an X?"), need statements ("I want you to give me an X"), or tag questions ("Give me an X, OK?").
2. Permission statements ("May I have the X?" "Please may I have the X?").
3. Hints or implicatures ("It's cold outside" as a hint for "Get me a sweater"; "Is X there?" implying "Get X"; "Mary's mother got her an X" implying "Get me an X"; "Have you got an X?" implying "Get it for me").
4. Manipulations ("I bet you can't get me an X," or "Let's pretend this is mine").

Ervin-Tripp (1977) describes an unpublished study by Lawson (1967) of a two year old who used different degrees of directness and politeness when issuing requests to peers as opposed to adults. For peers she used simple imperatives, for adults she formed directives by using desire statements or questions. Even more refined were her differentiations between her three-year-old and four-year-old peers. She used indirect and polite forms with the four year olds and direct forms with the three year olds. Finally, and revealingly, she used more polite and indirect forms when requesting from her father than from her mother.

Ervin-Tripp reports the results from another unpublished study, this time by O'Connell (1974), in which four year olds showed sufficient social sensitivity to request difficult-to-get items more politely. This is evidence that they have sufficient social savvy to assess the likelihood that their listeners will comply with the request. Ervin-Tripp's examples were that the children used embedded imperatives to obtain goods from other children, but direct requests when trying to control others' behaviors.

THE LINGUISTIC CONTEXT

We have seen that language is spoken not as a string of unrelated sentences but as a set of sentences which are woven together through their common topic, through their underlying frame, through their congruence with the ongoing situation, and through the shared knowledge held by the speaker and listener. In addition to this, and in accordance with it, sentences are tied together linguistically. They have meanings which reflect back to earlier sentences and which point to later sentences. Linguistic cohesion devices differ from other cohesion phenomena in that they rely on the information contained in the language rather than on the situation or background knowledge of the interactants. Sometimes the reference made by the device is to a general class of objects, sometimes it is to a particular object; sometimes what is referred to has already been mentioned in the conversation and therefore does not need to be mentioned again in each sentence; sometimes the speaker can prepare the listener for what will be referred to in the next sentence or sentences; and sometimes the referent needs to be distinguished from the one emphasized in previous sentences. We will describe these functions under the separate headings of *anaphora, ellipsis, cataphora,* and *contrastive stress.*

Anaphora is the linguistic means for referring to something that has already been identified linguistically. The article *the,* when referring back to an already mentioned noun, indicates that the speaker and listener agree on the particular referent of the noun. *The dog,* in its appropriate anaphoric use, obliges the speaker to have mentioned it earlier in the discourse so the listener knows which dog the speaker means. When it is first mentioned it is described with an indefinite article, as when the speaker says "A dog bit me." Similarly, pronouns used anaphorically in discourse must have a linguistically designated antecedent; otherwise, the listener will not know who or what the speaker is referring to.

Ellipsis is different from anaphora in that linguistic units are omitted and the listener forms a full understanding by remembering meaning from earlier sentences. For example, when one answers "red" to the question "What is your favorite color?" the listener can fill in the ellipsis by referring to the previous question to understand that red is the person's favorite color. Because ellipsis works by virtue of accumulating meanings across utterances, it qualifies as a discourse tie.

In a third discourse cohesion device, cataphora, the speaker indicates to the listener what is coming up in the discourse. Phrases or terms such as *this, these,* and *here* can refer forward—"*this* is the way to do it"; "*these* are what we'll make"; "*here* is what she said." Cataphorically used terms point forward in the narrative unlike anaphora and ellipsis which take their referential meaning from preceding sentences.

Finally, contrastive stress can serve as a discourse marker by emphasizing the new information in the sentence and thereby contrasting it with what has been said previously. Thus, a sentence such as "No, Mary hit Jane" in which both Mary and Jane are stressed would indicate that someone previously said something about Jane hitting Mary. If, instead, Jane received the strong stress and not Mary, one would assume the conversation had previously contained information about someone hitting Mary, and not Jane, or that Mary hit someone other than Jane. Our capability for making such presuppositions upon hearing the contrastive stress shows the use of such a linguistic device in building linguistic cohesion in discourse.

There have been many other devices which have been identified as functioning to tie discourse together (Halliday and Hasan, 1976). We have only taken a few and refer you to other sources and your own ingenuity for discovering what your children are or are not using to connect their language together.

Before we leave the discussion on linguistic contextual factors, we would like to mention the influence of the meanings of previous utterances in the interpretation of ambiguous sentences. For example, Shatz (1974) found children as young as two years old interpreted the illocutionary force of the same sentence differently depending upon the meanings set up in earlier linguistic context. In one context, the child was asked yes-no questions of the form "Can N V?" (e.g., "Can you talk on the telephone?") along with other questions, such as "Who talks on the telephone?" In the second context they were asked the same yes-no questions, but this time as part of a sequence of directives, such as "Come and get the telephone; push the buttons." In the first case, the children sometimes answered the question with a yes or no, in the second they responded by performing the act designated by the verbs, although in both cases the children had a predilection to perform the act. Ervin-Tripp (1977) commented from her observations of children, and from common sense, that the likelihood of the yes-no answer increases when the children are asked questions about an unfeasible act (e.g., Can you jump out the window?).

In sum, we have discussed four areas of pragmatics in this chapter. While these are not the only approaches to doing pragmatic analyses, they offer a suggested list for a beginning. The areas are as follows:

> The Situational Context
>   the physical setting
>   the speech event
>   speech event frames
>   the topic
> The Intentional Context
>   classifications of intention
>   agenda
> The Listener Context
>   the physical perspective
>   background knowledge
>   role relationships
> The Linguistic Context
>   anaphora
>   ellipsis
>   cataphora
>   contrastive stress
>   meanings of previous utterances

CONVERSATIONAL CONTEXT

So far we have developed means for analyzing children's sensitivity to the ongoing situational context, how they express their intentions, their ability to adapt to different listeners, and their use of linguistic context. We would like to test the usefulness of these analyses and ideas by looking at how children learn to engage in conversation. Conversations are speech events which have assumed a central place in the emerging literature on pragmatics. In addition they are a frequently used interaction form. For these two reasons, they offer us a fruitful way to exemplify how the analyses and ideas we have been discussing can apply to a particular kind of speech event.

Conversations usually occur between two or more people who are in a face-to-face interaction. They differ from other kinds of face-to-face talk in that they are free from a mutually agreed on agenda, in which case they would become meetings, games, or something other than conversations. They also differ from other speech events in that they contain turns whose order and size are not predetermined (Sacks, Schegloff, and Jefferson, 1974). Adult conversations often contain multiple turns which revolve around a particular topic. Topics are considered the main aspect of the conversation and can change repeatedly within a single conversation. There are parts of conversations which are not topic oriented in that they involve management of the conversation itself—that is to say, there are movement turns or turn sequences whose purpose it is to alter the conversation, such as those which change topic, which manage turn exchanges, which open, close, repair, or invite new members into the conversation.

Examples of conversational openings:
   Hi
   Do you have a minute?
   What are you doing?
Examples of closings:
   Well, I have to go now.
   Isn't your mother calling you?
Repairs:
   No, I meant _____.
   That one, not this one.
   I said that already.
New members invitations (or disinvitations):
   You can't play here.
   Hi Jack, we were just talking about you.

Conversations can contain narrative sequences in which one conversational partner produces a monologue or tells a story, but if there are too many of these prolonged units in a single conversation, the event becomes something other than a conversation and will be identified as such—for example, it might then be identified as a storytelling session, as listening to "X," or as a lesson.

Conversational Frames

Adult conversationalists often follow a fixed conversational frame by beginning the conversation in particular ways (Schegloff, 1968), by carrying out certain prearranged rituals for exchanging information, by acknowledging comments made by conversational partners, and by appropriately signaling the end of the conversation (Schegloff and Sacks, 1973).

Children's conversations are quite different from adults' until the children are age five or so, since they don't observe these schematic properties of adult conversations. In order to appreciate the differences, we will briefly outline the results of a recent literature on frames and characteristics of adult conversations and then discuss how children's conversations might be analyzed against the adult structuring process.

Many conversations, with telephone exchanges being the classic example, begin with greetings and an exchange of amenities which often refer to when the conversationalists last talked. The opening ends with a transition comment about why the initiator started the conversation (Schegloff, 1968).

The main part of the conversation might be about one topic, in which case the two (or more) conversational partners exchange information about it, taking turns in an orderly way. When one partner wants to change the topic, he or she should indicate this somehow, resulting in a second topic becoming the focus. Conversational etiquette dictates that partners should not allow too much time between turns, that no one monopolize the conversation or digress too much from the topic at hand, and that speakers should not lie, unless they so indicate (Clark and Clark, 1977; Grice, 1975). When one conversational partner makes a point, the other may acknowledge it by nodding or saying something which suggests affirmation, such as "uh-huh." This may be taken by the speaker as permission to continue. Turns are exchanged when the speaker looks at the listener and waits for him or her to talk.

Conversations end when one partner makes a preclosing gesture or statement, such as "Well" or "So." The other then accepts it and both engage in a final exchange wherein they may reinvoke the reason for the conversation, make arrangements for the next conversation, or wish one another well. Then the final closing statement occurs, such as "Bye" or "See you."

Young children's conversations are not so structured. The literature on conversational exchanges between children and adults and between two or more children points to this difference and suggests a sequence of stages in the development of children's conversational skills. The developmental progressions can be depicted as proceeding from preverbal volleys through beginning verbal exchanges containing a sequence of single volleys or two-volley exchanges and then to a stage of multiple-volley exchanges. We will describe each in turn, beginning with preverbal volleys.

PREVERBAL VOLLEYS   One type of preverbal volley is what Piaget has classified as a type of circular reaction (see Chapter 9) in which the adult or child initiates a vocal or movement gesture and the conversational partner imitates it or elaborates on it (Moore and Meltzoff, 1978; Trevarthan, 1977). A second early appearing preverbal volley is exchanges of vocalizations and looking patterns between caregiver and infant (Bateson, 1975; Stern et al., 1977). These exchanges occur after feeding, bathing, and dressing and are characterized by rhythmic sequences of vocal exchanges accompanied by changes in facial expression and mutual gaze. Stern et al. (1977) and Sander (1977) describe these interaction sequences as play and place their onset at three months for the normal child. Bateson (1975) and Trevarthan (1977) call them "protoconversations" and describe them as occurring as early as three weeks in the neonate. Brazelton et al. (1974) also describe these interactions in subjects as young as four weeks and find they have predictable cycles of attention and inattention occurring between the caretaker and the child. From the child's behavior they see these attention sequences as beginning with initiations and proceeding through orientation, state of attention, acceleration, peak of excitement, deceleration, and then ending with withdrawal. The whole period lasts for not more than a few seconds, especially in the younger infant.

In addition to the circular volleys which contain imitated exchanges, and to the reciprocal play interactions, preverbal children engage in sequences of exchanges characterizable as "games" or "routines," such as patty-cake, peekaboo, etc. (see Chapter 9). Cazden (1979) and Ratner and Bruner (1978) have delineated four special features of these early preverbal games, as follows: (1) a restricted format; (2) a clear and repetitive structure; (3) positions for appropriate vocalizations; and (4) reversible role relationships. In the early forms of these routines, the adult takes the initiative and carries the moves; later the child initiates (Cazden, 1979; Ninio and Bruner, 1978).

A fourth type of preverbal volley is communicative gesturing by the child, such as pointing, showing, and giving, which are responded to by others and thereby represent a turn exchange, or in this particular case, a single-volley adjacency pair (e.g., child points at object, adult names object). These can be accompanied by vocalizations and the vocalizations have been found to be differentially used with particular gestures. For example, Carter (1979) and Halliday (1975) found their young preverbal subjects used one set of vocables to accompany gestural points, a different set to accompany push away gestures, and so on. Unlike the other three interactions described earlier, these gestures and vocalization units typically involve manipulable objects. Trevarthan (1977) has noted from his detailed description of one child that before nine months of age she engaged in social interactions which did not involve objects, and only after nine months did she regard the object as well as the person in the same interactive event.

BEGINNING VERBAL EXCHANGES   Once children go beyond the vocable stage and reach the symbolic stage in which they use words to signify meanings, they enter a conversational period which has been depicted as one of single conversational volleys. That is to say, the children's words are responded to by the parent, whereupon the conversations about that topic end. Alternatively, their words may be in response to adult initiations and function to terminate the topic.

Because the situational context is changing continuously, because the child's focus is on these physical changes (Greenfield and Zukow, 1978), and because these changes are often not related to adults' definition of the topic, the child's conversational interactions appear to lack topic scope or coherence beyond that particular exchange. When such volleys are examined in light of the various contexts which support them, they no longer seem to be a series of topically unrelated volleys but rather cohere by virtue of dependence on a speech event or ongoing action sequences which are occurring in the situation. Said another way, the nature of these early conversational volleys differs from later types of volleys in that the situational context defines the topic or carries it for the child rather than the language context.

By definition, then, single-volley pairs begin either with the child's utterance—a child-initiated pair—or an adult utterance—an adult-initiated pair. Among the child-initiated pairs which have been studied most are requests made by the child for adult action, attention, an object, or permission (Garvey, 1975). Other types which occur are for labels of objects or events which occur in the situational context. These are typically responded to by repeating or expanding the utterance and in so doing affirming its correctness. Children in the one-word stage also use question intonation, which, if successful, results in an answer response; or they may have falling intonation, typically answered with an acknowledgment. To summarize, then, the types of child-initiated single volleys, we find the following:

Child: Single-word request
Adult: Response

Child: Single-word label
Adult: Repetition, expansion, affirmation

Child: Single-word and question intonation
Adult: Answer

Child: Single-word and falling intonation
Adult: Acknowledge (e.g., uh-huh)

Adult-initiated volley exchanges are most often question forms, and of those, frequently "what" questions (e.g., "What's this?") responded to by a single-word label naming the designated referent. These questions can occur as part of ritualized games, such as in speech events involving looking at pictures. Similarly, "Where's X?" occurs in hiding games. A second commonly occurring adult-initiated volley is the directive where the adult asks or tells the child what to do and the child responds verbally (Corsaro, 1979; Garvey, 1977; Shatz, 1974).

Finally, the adult may describe or label an object or event and the child will respond by repeating part of the adult's utterance. Keenan (1977) has analyzed the function of these one-word repetitions in her two-year-old twins and found, on the basis of context and intonation, that they can function for the child as clarification, requests, agreements, or self-information. We can summarize the adult-initiated pairs as follows:

Adult: WH-question
Child: Answer

Adult: Asks or tells child what to do
Child: Response

Adult: Describe or label
Child: Single word repeated

MULTIPLE-VOLLEY EXCHANGES   Two-volley (three-turn) exchanges are also common in child conversations at the single-word stage. Just as for single-volley exchanges, these may be child initiated, wherein the child takes the first and third turns, or adult initiated, wherein the child takes the second turn and may or may not have an awareness of the first and third.

Among the most interesting child-initiated two-volley sequences are those in which the stage is set in the initiation of the first turn for the termination or third turn. These sequences can involve attention-getting initiations, such as "you know what?" or "Look." Dore (1977) has called such sequences preparatory conditions; they are evidenced in the following exchange:

Child 1:   What are you making?
Child 2:   A zoo.
Child 1:   Put the animal in the zoo.

A second type of two-volley sequence is begun by the child but not necessarily intentionally. That is to say, the child is not mindful at the time he or she speaks the first turn that it will be followed by two more turns. Examples are breakdown-repair sequences, in which the conversational partner asks the child to clarify in some way (Gallagher, 1977; Mishler, 1975a); expansions, in which the partner elaborates on the child's imitation and the child responds to the elaboration (Bellugi and Brown, 1964); or prompts, in which the child reports on a topic and the adult prompts for more information whereupon the child offers it (Stoel-Gammon and Cabral, 1977).

Scollon (1979) describes an interesting third type of two-volley exchange in his data on vertical constructions in which children express aspects of a proposition across several utterances. The most frequently occurring and earliest version of this exchange is the two-volley sequence wherein the child says a word, repeats it until the adult acknowledges it, and then continues by saying a second word, thus completing a proposition initiated by the first word.

In an example from Scollon, one and one-half year old Brenda has the following exchange with an adult:

Brenda: Car (Repeated four times)
 Adult: What
Brenda: Go

Scollon states ". . . it is evident that Brenda intended to go on to the second word but was simply waiting for verification from the listener that he had understood" (Scollon, 1979, p. 221). In sum, types of child-initiated multiple volleys are

Child: Preparatory condition (e.g., question)
Other: Answer
Child: Follow-up

Child: Comment
Other: Classification request or elaboration
Child: Child responds to other

Child: First part proposition
Other: Acknowledgment
Child: Second part of proposition

A commonly occurring type of adult-initiated two-volley sequence is that in which the child asks for clarification of the initiation made by the conversational partner and the adult responds. A second type, and a commonly occurring one in didactic relationships between teachers and children (Fine, 1978; Garvey, 1975; Mishler, 1975a; Sinclair and Coulthard, 1975), is the question + answer + confirmation exchange, or the command + response + evaluation exchange (Cazden, 1979).

These two-volley structures can easily increase without too much additional complexity to three and four volleys by adding on well-formed adjacency pairs. In these sequences an attention-getting turn may be added to the question + answer + confirmation exchange: "Look," "What's that?" "It's an X," "Oh."

Moving along to more complex multiple-volley exchanges, we find that one way the complexity increases is that one turn in a volley can serve an initiation function for the next turn as well as a response function to the preceding turn (Fine, 1978; Mishler, 1975a). For example, Fine and Mishler report sequences such as question + answer + second question + answer to the second question. In this case, the second question ties to the answer of the first and at the same time initiates the next turn. Further, these multiple exchanges, unlike their linear precursors which we have been describing, are hierarchical in structure in that they need to be analyzed in nested units where the sequences and turns are part of embedded narratives, scripts, discourse topics, etc. To do this, one must be sensitive to points of change within those units, such as movement along scripts, turn taking, and topic shifts. Children will vary in their competence for managing such units, thus one may need to analyze how the larger conversations are framed by the participants, the cohesion devices used to build them, when and why the discourse breaks down, and how the breakdowns are repaired. The analysis, of course, will depend upon what seems to impair the communication of the child in question. Adult-initiated multiple-volley sequences are

Adult:	Says something
Child:	Asks for clarification
Adult:	Clarifies

Adult:	Question or comment
Child:	Answer or response
Adult:	Confirmation or evaluation

Adult:	Question
Child:	Answer
Adult:	Another question about first answer
Child:	Answer

Mother-Child Conversations

It is only in the last few years that the adult side of conversations with children has been looked at carefully with an eye to the role it plays in children's language learning. Transformational linguistics led researchers away from looking at language input and toward looking at children by contending that children had an innate set of knowledges about language which resided in a mentalistic device, labeled the *Language Acquisition Device,* or LAD, by Chomsky (1965). The assumption was that adults' talk to children is essentially the same as their talk to other adults, which is characterized by being complex and often ungrammatical. This assumption has been challenged and disproved by a spate of research in the last decade (e.g., Broen, 1972; Drach, 1969; Ferguson and Snow, 1977; Newport, 1976; Snow, 1972).

There is now little question that talk to children is characteristically different from the language directed to more mature, capable language users. The variant of language that is directed to children has been labeled "Motherese," although it is used by other adults and older children as well as by mothers. Some of the features of Motherese as compared to language directed talk to older listeners are

1. Shorter utterances
2. Highly intelligible; less dysfluent
3. Well-formed grammatical sentences
4. Slower rate
5. More restricted vocabulary
6. Greater repetition
7. Higher and more varied pitch
8. More questions and present tense verbs
   (Broen, 1972; Remick, 1976; Snow, 1972)

While there is general agreement on the form of Motherese, there is some controversy concerning the role this specialized dialect plays in helping children to acquire language. Newport, Gleitman, and Gleitman (1977) argue that the syntactic characteristics of Motherese are not particularly sensitive to changes in the child's linguistic capacities, and therefore not a powerful source of language instruction; that is, they find that the length of maternal utterances and the variety of sentence types do not change in predictable ways with small changes in the child's language over time. They feel that mothers speak to children the way they do because "mother and child are mutually engaged in an attempt to communicate about the here-and-now, trying to get the local situation managed at the moment, rather than trying to make a frontal attack on the language acquisition problem" (Newport, Gleitman, and Gleitman, 1977, p. 139). Thus, while Newport, Gleitman, and Gleitman acknowledge that the discourse features of Motherese may be important in teaching children how to talk about things, they do not feel it contributes to learning general language structure.

Cross (1977) also finds that mother's syntactic "fine tuning" to children's expressive language is not generally impressive, but it corresponds to children's language comprehension more closely. Further, she argues with Newport, Gleitman, and Gleitman's contention that the influence of Motherese should be evident at the syntactic level in order to be a significant tutorial mode. Looking at the language of mothers of linguistically advanced children, Cross (1977) finds a significant correlation between all measures of the children's language skill and the mother's utterances that are semantically contingent on the child's utterances. Semantically contingent utterances are important for the role they play in maintaining discourse rather than for their syntactic structure. They include

> *Maternal expansion.* The mother repeats the child's utterance, filling in missing words and grammatical morphemes.

>> Child: Daddy bowl
>> Mother: That's daddy's bowl

> *Semantic extension.* The mother stays with the same topic expressed by the child and adds additional information.

>> Child: Daddy bowl
>> Mother: It got broken

> *Imitation of child.* The mother repeats exactly or in part the child's utterance.
> *Maternal self-repetition.* The mother repeats exactly or paraphrases a previous utterance of her own.

Cross found that the least linguistically mature of the children in her study received the highest proportion of such utterances, often in combinations during a single exchange. She sees the use of semantically contingent utterances as particularly powerful in providing a language lesson for children. For example

> Child: Daddy bowl
> Mother: That's daddy's bowl   (Expansion)
>   Daddy's bowl is broken (Repetition with extension)

As children's language skills increased, the mother's use of the semantically related utterances, along with stock phrases used in routines, decreased. Cross also found that the mother's references to the child's activities—references which are most common with the youngest children—are gradually replaced by topics relating to others in the immediate situation and then to the nonimmediate situation as the child's psycholinguistic abilities increase.

The relationship between the semantic relations expressed by caregivers and children has also been studied (Snow, 1977; Van der Geest, 1977). These investigations reveal that the majority of mother's utterances express only semantic relations that the child has already expressed. For example, the mother significantly increases her expression of where objects are located after the child begins to increase his or her indications of location. This suggests that caregivers are sensitive to the kinds of meanings the child can understand. Van der Geest finds that adults express these meanings in syntactic frames that are slightly more advanced than the child's form, thus providing a meaningful linguistic model for the child since the adult expression relates to a message the child might also express. Thus, the child takes the lead semantically, with the adult leading syntactically.

It appears then that some features of adult language are more finely tuned to the language skill of the individual child than others. Syntax, while clearly adjusted to distinguish talk to children from talk to adults, appears to be less finely tuned to the child's changing abilities than some other aspects of input to children. The tightness of semantic contingency does seem to be more finely tuned, in that discourse with young children contains a great deal of redundancy through imitation, expansion, extension, and maternal repetition, with this redundancy gradually decreasing as the child becomes more linguistically capable. The referential aspect of language directed to children also changes predictably with changes in the child's language skills, with the references being first to the child's state or action and then to referents more removed in space and time. Likewise, the semantic relations adults express are tuned to those the child has demonstrated an understanding of. These patterns have been found to be generally characteristic of adults talking to linguistically typical and advanced children. Although we cannot be positive that they contribute to these children's language acquisition, we would hope that language-impaired children are likewise exposed to adult language adjusted for their abilities.

PRAGMATICS ASSESSMENT

We have outlined four types of context which influence language: situational context, intentional context, listener context, and linguistic context. Within each we have delineated various dimensions which can now offer us a guide for analyzing how context influences the language of children. The analyses are

FOR SITUATIONAL CONTEXT:

1. Physical setting analysis
2. Speech event and frame analysis
3. Topic analysis for sentences and discourse

FOR INTENTIONAL CONTEXT:

4. Analyzing for illocutionary force
5. Agenda analysis

FOR LISTENER CONTEXT:

6. Evidence for listener perspective taking

FOR LINGUISTIC CONTEXT:

7. Discovering discourse cohesion devices

The analyses that follow are by no means rigidly spelled out; they are instead designed to help you develop new and different ways to discover patterns. For pragmatic analyses there are no defined procedures; rather, it is necessary for you, the clinician, to uncover what it is in the context that the child ties his or her language to. We will present suggestions for elicitation and transcription procedures for each of the analyses, but first we will make a few general comments about those procedures.

Elicitation Procedures

The elicitation procedures you use will depend upon what you will be analyzing for. The sampling may need to involve contextual contrasts where the influence of context is manipulated in several ways. Thus, unlike a single language sample which was used as a base for analyzing syntactic or phonological structures, you may need several samples in pragmatics, each taken under different contextual constraints. The types of elicitation will vary—for example, you could (1) *interview* the children to learn their attitudes or ideas about the event; (2) engage them in *enactments*, in which they are asked to role play various situations; (3) participate in *structured interactions*, wherein you design and carry out an event to elicit particular prespecified behaviors; (4) design *structured situations*, or specific contexts in which the children will carry out a prescribed sequence of behaviors without your intervention; or (5) observe a *naturalistic interaction*, or sample the children's performance in a context familiar to them where they are allowed to simply "do their thing."

Transcription

The transcript will also vary depending upon what you are analyzing for (Braunwald and Brislin, 1979; Ochs, 1979). It has been our experience that the form and content of the transcript often needs to be changed dramatically after you have done some transcribing, because in the course of transcribing you become clearer about what it is you are looking for and how best to reveal it. In Chapter 2 we talked about three types of transcripts: the listing, running, and multilevel transcripts. These offer a format for transcribing, but for pragmatics analyses we will need to develop more formats for capturing the necessary contextual detail.

Situational Context

PHYSICAL SETTING ANALYSIS   This analysis will provide an index for context boundedness into the current physical setting. Its use would be pertinent for children whose language seems to be what people have called concrete or context bound and would provide an index of the degree to which it is bound to the physical context. This analysis can also be used to determine whether children's language is related to mutual referencing and whether they consider the attention of the interactant as an important factor in the situational context. Finally, their ability to use deictic terms requires study as part of how these terms articulate with aspects of the physical context.

Our approach to this analysis would be to elicit, record, and transcribe a sample and to examine it for references to events or objects either present or not present in the physical setting. Since any event offers data which can be analyzed for its here-and-now referencing, a sample selected for this analysis could be from any naturally occurring event. Deeper testing might be pursued which involves an elicitor participating in interactions or structuring situations which require cognitively distant responses (e.g., "What did we do yesterday?" storytelling, or pretending). The most direct approach would be to interview the child, asking about the non-here-and-now, for example "When did you go to the zoo?" or "Where do you buy groceries?"

The event is best videorecorded to capture behaviors such as distant points and looks; and the transcription would be a running transcript which can then be analyzed for its amount of here-and-now referencing. Each utterance in the running transcript can be examined for its degree of temporal or spatial separation from the here-and-now. For example, a scaling of cognitive distance could be developed with one point given for physically present referents, two points for nonpresent but indexed referents, and three for spatially or temporally distant referents. Three point referents would be apparent in linguistic forms for past or future indicators, such as "gonna," temporal adverbs, temporal connectives, when or where questions, and referents which are not triggered by the present physical context.

For children whose language seems not to be related to mutual referencing, a transcription can be made to describe the amount of mutual referencing going on between conversational partners. For example, a videorecording can be examined for whether the children respond to others' points or "what's that" questions and whether their verbalizations are related to the object they are looking at, an object of common regard between them and their interactants. Listing transcripts of the presence or lack of mutual referencing could be analyzed to measure the degree of success in achieving mutual regard.

Multilevel transcripts can be designed to show the relationship between mutual gaze and initiating interactions to determine whether or not the child considers the interactant's attention as an important factor and as license to proceed in the interaction. The transcript can indicate their attempts to get the attention of their social partner as well as breakdowns due to their lack of success in achieving mutual gaze.

Finally, the use of deictic terms that take as their meaning the present referent can be analyzed from multilevel transcripts where terms such as *here, there, come, go* and modifiers are examined for their appropriateness in the situation.

SPEECH EVENT AND FRAME ANALYSIS   Children's difficulty in understanding the speech event might be manifest in their inattentive behaviors, inappropriate responses, lack of initiative, or lack of cooperation. They may only be willing or able to respond to tightly framed familiar events, and inept or uncooperative in more negotiated events. Thus, an analysis of their sense of speech events and frames could lead to insight into their erratic or poor performance in particular events.

Children's as well as adults' ideas about speech events are impossible to divorce from their ideas about the event frame. Thus, their sense of the event frame will likely be elicited along with their ideas about the event. The most direct way to elicit their event and frame sense is through an interview procedure where they are asked to name the event or where they are asked about an event already named by you or them. This interview procedure is a common one in ethnographic analyses and has been used successfully with verbally competent and reflective children (Spradley and McGurdy, 1972).

The interview would involve asking the children about a particular kind of event, such as playing house—asking what the event is called, when it might occur, and what it entails in terms of action sequences, participants, necessary props, rules, etc. The interview, then, becomes one basis for the transcription. An analysis of such an interview would perhaps involve discrepancies between the child's conceptualization and that of other participants or that of the adults in the culture, or perhaps a comparison between what the children say about the event and their actual behavior when they participate in the event. They may have one rendition in the interview and another when they are in the event itself.

A second way to find out about children's conceptualization of events is to ask them to reenact them, perhaps inserting commentary along the way. For example, ask them to pretend they are in speech class. Comparisons of several reenactments would allow you to make some judgment about what is incidental and what is prescribed as necessary to the event. This is the distinction between frames and circumstantial aspects of the event structure. A variant of this reenactment + commentary technique is to allow children to observe a videotaped segment of the event and to comment on it (Emihovitz, in progress).

Finally, the most natural way to learn about children's sense of events is simply to observe them participating in the event and to analyze their perform-ance in relation to the culturally prescribed frame and in relation to previous and subsequent performances of the same event. From this you can extract the action sequences common to all enactments of the event and thereby determine its frame.

A running transcript with descriptions of most important actions would be the most obvious means for transcribing the event. If temporal issues seem important, or mutual gaze as in turn taking, then aspects of the event may be transcribed in a multilevel way. The transcript is most logically begun at the beginning of the speech event, for example a story or conversation. If there are shifts in the sample to singing, to a new conversation, or to a new activity, this could be indicated by designating it as a separate speech event and by specifying the defining features which led to its separate classification.

The event can be structurally identified by examining the transcript for statements or behaviors which could be typical beginnings and endings of the event. Possible indications of beginnings of new speech events are initiations made by the child or interactant (e.g., "Read me this story," "Let's play a game," etc.). Possible endings are postural shifts (e.g., child gets up or looks around), mutual gaze (e.g., child looks up expectantly at the interactant), or closing state-ments (e.g., "I don't want to play any more," "Let's do something else").

Some general procedures for examining events and frames are

1. Examine running transcripts of several speech events of the same type (jokes, stories) and look for structural similarities.
2. Analyze multisentence productions for how new utterances follow from or relate to old ones. (What is the temporal progression? Is the same

character doing different things? Are the events described in spatial order? Are all the utterances related to a single category, e.g., animals?)

3. Determine whether long narratives are made up of smaller units, such as verbal routines (e.g., Watson-Gegeo and Boggs, 1977).

From observations such as the preceding, we have discovered thematic frames in a normal four-year-old child's joke telling. The sequence we observed in all his jokes were (1) getting the attention of his mother; (2) telling a four to five sentence story which progresses in time to a point where there is a conflict between people which ends in a tragedy; (3) laughing; and (4) checking with his mother to get an evaluation (e.g., "Was that a joke, Mom?").

The structural patterns which we found in this series of events in the child's joke telling we take to be internal structures which are integrated and characteristic of joke telling situations for this child. Therefore, they qualify as the frames which he uses in the speech event of jokes.

TOPIC ANALYSIS FOR SENTENCES AND DISCOURSE   Children who have problems with topic management are those whose conversations might seem confused, whose utterances are not topically contingent with the sentence before, who do not sustain a topic in the speech event, and who seem rude, abrupt, or nonresponsive.

A topic analysis can reveal several things. One is what the child is interested in talking about. Second, it can indicate his or her cognitive sustaining power in following a topic through discourse. Third, it can provide a way to diagnose the breakdowns in conversations due to topic contingency or topic sharing problems. Fourth, it can reveal the child's ability to draw inferences from the situation or from the conversation. Finally, it can offer another indication for the degree and quality of the child's context boundedness to the physical rather than conversational context.

The procedure for eliciting data should be naturally occurring conversations, preferably with familiar and nondominant interactants, and about favorite as well as not so favorite topics. If the child is not a conversationalist, the elicitation could be done in a favorite speech event, but one which has a loose frame where the utterances are not dictated by the event but optional.

Transcriptions could be of the running format, perhaps with topic changes indicated in one column and topically contingent responses in another. For analyses related to topic sharing, the best transcription might be the traditional one: one person's utterances and behaviors in one column, the other person's (the child's) in a second column, and context notes in a third.

The analysis will depend upon the data and what you are analyzing for. If you are analyzing for the child's topic interests, the topic could be listed for each utterance in the context column, and a summary of what the child talked about could be made at the end. If sustaining power is the issue, the number of topic relevant acts and responses under each topic could be counted and averaged, or detailed for the longest sequences. Breakdown or topic contingency analysis could develop criteria for degrees or types of contingency (see Blank et al., 1979) or could analyze for places of breakdown with an attempt to account for the cause of each. For example, breakdowns can be caused by such things as the mother entering the room, the child being preoccupied with something, or not following the language of the preceding utterance. A listing transcript of apparent inferences could be made for an inference ability analysis and a topic selection analysis would detail where the topics of the child's utterances originate, thereby offering a sense of degree of context boundedness.

To summarize, we have presented three different types of analyses for determining the influence of the situation on a child's language. They are physical context analysis, speech event and frame analysis, and topic analysis. Each is flexible in terms of the elicitation procedure, the design of the transcript, and the analysis of the transcript, and each will differ depending upon what the particular child seems to be having difficulty with. Analyses will only be done for children who display symptoms which lead you to question their abilities in one of the designated areas. The suggested procedures can be outlined as follows:

PHYSICAL SETTING ANALYSIS

1. When to do it—presenting symptoms
   Context bound language
   Lack of mutual referencing and attention-getting devices
   Misuse or underuse of deixis
2. Elicitation procedures
   Observe naturally occurring event
   Participate in and direct interactions
   Structure situations non-here-and-now, pretend, storytelling
   Interview about temporally and spatially distant occurrences
3. Transcription
   Running transcript
   List presence or absence of mutual referencing instances
   Multilevel gaze + interaction initiations, deictic terms, and context transcript
4. Analysis
   Scale for degree of distancing
   Counts for mutual referencing
   Co-occurrence of gaze and interaction initiations
   Deictic terms, their relationship to context

SPEECH EVENT AND FRAME ANALYSIS

1. When to do it—presenting symptoms
   Inattentiveness in certain speech events
   Inappropriate responses throughout an event
   Lack of initiative or uncooperativeness unless event tightly framed (e.g., ritualistic behaviors)
2. Elicitation procedures
   Interview—name and characterize a designated event

Reenactments of an event
Comment on an event as it is happening
Observe naturally occurring events
3. Transcription techniques
Running transcripts
Listing of transition markers
4. Analysis
Transitions discovered (beginnings, closings)
Comparisons of similarities across like events
Discoveries of critical elements in frame common to different renditions of same event
Comparison between event markers of interview and actualization

TOPIC ANALYSIS FOR SENTENCES AND
DISCOURSE

1. When to use it—presenting symptoms
Conducts confused conversations
Frequent conversational breakdowns
Problems sustaining conversation
Rude, abrupt, nonresponsive
2. Elicitation procedures
Naturally occurring conversations with topics of varying interest or familiarity to the child
Loose speech event context, i.e., one with negotiated and undetermined frame
3. Transcription technique
Running transcript—topic changes in one column
Running transcript—people + context columns
Listing transcript—inferences
4. Analysis
Topics designated for each utterance, summary of different topics, how topics come up—context breakdown (Greenfield and Zukow, 1978)
Topic sustenance, how many volleys on particular topic
Topic contingency, a scale with criteria for degrees of relevance to previous utterance
Breakdowns—where and why they occur
Topic selection

Intentional Context

INTENTIONAL ACT ANALYSIS   As we have mentioned, we prefer analyses which do not begin with checklists, such as the particular functions found by Dore and Halliday, but rather which begin with the child's behavior and derive categories from the regularities found there. We take as our model, then, the approaches used by Carter (1975, 1978, 1979) and Prizant (1978). Their transcripts were multilevel descriptions of single communicative acts. They include nonverbal, intonational, and, when present, verbal levels. In addition, contextual notes should be made about the situationally relevant material preceding and following the communicative act in question.

The behaviors that accompany the utterance are important because intentions are often best revealed in the nonverbal aspect of the communicative act, such as points, shows, push-aways, or the direction of gaze. Intonation is also an important clue to intentionality. For example, if one hears a question intonation accompanying the word "drink," one would more likely classify it as a request rather than a show, which would be more likely to be said with a falling intonation.

Finally, the transcript should include what happens before or after the communicative act. One can imagine, for example, that responses to questions are likely to serve a different function than if they are initiations (e.g., Q: What does a milkman do? A: Drink). Utterances followed by the child's grasping an object may be classified as functionally different from those followed by his refusal of the object.

The analysis involves looking for repeated clusters of behaviors across the levels. For example, Prizant (1978) found with this type of analysis that autistic children's echolalia functioned in different ways for them. He discovered echo types were characterizable according to frequently occurring features, which he summarized in the following list:

1. Evidence of attention to a person or object as determined by gaze or body orientation
2. Some evidence of comprehension as indicated by a demonstrative gesture, action upon object or appropriate verbal response
3. Verbal or nonverbal response is initiated subsequent to the echoic utterance and after a short delay
4. Echoic utterance is most often not directed to the interlocuter as evidenced by a whisper and lack of gaze to the interlocuter. (Prizant, 1978, p. 112)

Carter (1979), with the same approach, describes her subjects' gesture vocalization schemata in terms of cross-level criteria. For example, the riddance schemata involved the following characteristics:

1. Object ridding action: bandy, push, strike, tap, nudge, rub, slap, toss, knock, pound, rap, flap
2. Crisp, explosive vocalization with initial /b/ (ba, bae, buh) and falling intonation
3. Goal of getting receiver's help in removing an object.

We have called this analytic procedure *multilevel functional analysis*. An example of this type of video transcription is described in Bloom and Lahey (1978); while they do not detail procedures for carrying out speech act analysis, one can elaborate on their transcription procedures and reexamine some of their findings in terms of speech act analysis.

Take, for example, their depiction of different types of negation. The first, *nonexistence*, can be a *no* said with rising intonation, accompanied by looking for something which would ordinarily be present. Thus, we have three levels which might be transcribed like this:

LEVELS	TIME 1	TIME 2	TIME 3
Verbal and intonation	"No cookie?"		
Nonverbal	Looks in cookie jar	Looks to mother	Extends hand to cupboard

The transcript suggests that the speech act force is a request because of the question intonation, the gaze to parent, and the gesture extended to the cupboard. Similarly, Bloom describes rejection as being accompanied by a push-away gesture, and we would assume, though she does not indicate it, a forceful intonation contour. Thus, the transcript might look something like this:

TIME 1	TIME 2	TIME 3
	(loud) "No cookie"	
Mother extends cookie to child	Looks at cookie	Pushes mother's hand away

The speech act force of this utterance is, as Bloom has indicated, one of rejection, and indeed seems to us to be characterizable as a pure performative.

The other forces of negation described by Bloom are disappearance, nonoccurrence, cessation, prohibition, and denial and have been classified into these semantic categories on the basis of contextual cues and the analyst's assumptions about what the child is thinking (see our discussion on p. 139). For example, negation utterances are classified as disappearance and cessation when something disappears from view or stops moving; as nonoccurrence when the child cannot carry out an attempted action; as prohibition when the child reprimands someone else; and denial, when she denies the truth (e.g., "Not truck, car"). Since these types of negation are not described in terms of intonational or nonverbal accompaniments, and since we would need to do so in order to assign them a speech act category, we cannot easily subject them to multilevel functional analysis. It may be the case that the various utterances which make up any one of the categories are said as different speech acts, thus suggesting that these children, like adults, are able to use the same propositions to express different intentions.

AGENDA ANALYSIS   An analysis of an agenda would best be done for those speech events where agenda questions are at issue, such as events involving persuasion, arguments, or conversations where one of the partners is inattentive. Thus, an elicitation procedure would be one of structuring situations, as did Brennis and Lein (1977) who asked children to argue with one another; or naturalistic interactions, where agenda or lack of agenda becomes a determining force (Lubinski, Duchan, and Weitzner-Lin, 1980). For those children who can evaluate an event, an interview where you ask what they or others were trying to do could lead to insight about their notions and enactments of agendas.

The transcription, at least at first, would be a running transcript which could then be evaluated, utterance by utterance, for whether the illocutionary force of each utterance is in concert and therefore a manifestation of a hypothesized agenda. For example, if the child wants to leave, one could imagine several utterances which would stem from that agenda and then perhaps a period which departs from that agenda where the child becomes diverted or gives up, only to return to it later. This "agenda tracking" could perhaps account for topic shifts; it could also reveal how well children can make their needs known and how well interactants can respond to their expression of agenda.

MULTILEVEL FUNCTIONAL ANALYSIS

1. When to use it—presenting symptoms
   Lack of initiative in communication
   Utterances which are not interpretable (jargon, unintelligible speech, echolalia, vocables)
   Unresponsive caretakers or teachers
2. Elicitation procedures
   Naturally occurring communicative acts; create "want" situations and don't fulfill the needs (especially for requests)
3. Transcription techniques
   Multilevel transcripts
4. Analysis
   Cross-level correspondence
   Recurrences of same sequences (e.g., Child does *this*, and *that* always follows)

AGENDA ANALYSIS

1. When to use it—presenting symptoms
   Lack of coherence in situations where agenda would be expected
   Hidden agendas where something else seems to be motivating utterances
   Preoccupation situations where agendas do not pertain to ongoing event
2. Elicitation procedures
   Direct children to achieve particular agenda
   Construct conflict situations where interactants must negotiate solutions
   Interview—"What was going on?" "What did you want to happen?" "What did the other(s) want to happen?"
3. Transcription
   Running transcript

4. Analysis
Topic shifts
Agenda tracking—analyzing for diversions and how agenda gets reinstated

Listener Context

What indicators do we have that the child we are evaluating can assume the perspective of the listener? We have mentioned three aspects of listener perspective taking which we can examine: (1) Are the children taking the point of view of the listener in the *physical setting*? (2) Are they adjusting what they say to be in keeping with the *listener's background knowledge*? and (3) Are they cognizant of the culturally defined *role relationships* between themselves and their listeners? If children have difficulty in these areas, we would expect them to misuse deictic terms, to lack linguistic devices for filling in the background knowledge that listeners need, and to lack or indiscriminantly use indirect request forms which are needed to signal deference in unequal role relationships.

The sample which offers these indicators would be natural interactions, and in this case we would need to compare samples of interactions with different interactants, such as unfamiliar adults, a younger child, and a familiar adult or older sibling. Special elicitation procedures might be needed for the deictic terms, procedures which create obligatory contexts for using such terms. For example, Piaget (1954) designed a well-known "three mountain" experiment in which the child is asked to show or tell what mountains look like from the perspective of the person sitting opposite them. A similar elicitation technique would be a version of Krauss and Glucksberg's (1969) communication game wherein one child is asked to give directions to someone seated opposite him or her and in so doing must reverse his or her own perspective when using terms such as right, left, top, and bottom.

The transcription could be a listing one, and those parts of the sample which indicate absence or presence of listener perspective taking would be indicated. In some cases, a diagram or multilevel depiction might be needed. In others, listing the existence of the structure, such as a relative clause which gives the listeners necessary background knowledge, would be sufficient. Some transcripts might need to be more detailed. For example, if you are asking what changes the child makes for different listeners, you will need to do a summary transcript to get a feel for what the child is doing in the way of code shifting. The analysis could be for the existence or use of one or several of the following indicators:

Deictic terms (see Chapter 7)
Relative clauses
Adjectives
Transition phrases
Changes in language complexity for different listeners
Breakdowns

Repairs
Changes in directives depending on listener

Linguistic Context

The basic question to be answered by this analysis is, What are the linguistic cohesion devices produced by the child? The question is only pertinent to children whose language is sufficiently advanced to string sentences together in some larger unity. The most obvious approach is to look for those cohesion devices which are typically used by competent speakers of the language. We have designated those as anaphora, ellipsis, cataphora, and contrastive stress.

The first approach might be to collect a naturalistic language sample, preferably a conversation, in which the child takes a strong part. Once this is examined for cohesion devices, you might want to go back to elicit those which did not happen to show up in the sample. For example, Maratsos (1976) tested children's expression of definite reference through a story and questioning procedure. One story Maratsos told the children was about a man who was walking through a jungle and who saw a monkey and a pig racing. The children were asked who won the race. If they had adult use of definite reference, their answer would contain the word *the* (*the* monkey, or *the* pig) because particular animals had been previously (anaphorically) designated. Contrastively, there are instances where previous reference does not designate a particular object, as in the sentence "I rode in *a* car." In this case, the procedure used by Maratsos was to tell about a man who went into a jungle to find a tiger or a zebra. Later the man looked up and "Who do you think came running out at the man?" The child's answer should contain an indefinite article (*a* tiger or *a* zebra).

Maratsos (1976) also found that an imitation with expansion procedure was useful in that it predicted the children's responses on the more naturalistic tasks. The crucial utterance to be imitated was part of a sensible story and had in it an article omission. The child, for example, was asked to imitate each sentence as the story was told, one of the sentences being "So he took monkey home." Children typically fill in the article, if they have articles in their spontaneous language.

Finally, Maratsos cleverly designed a game procedure where he varied the number of objects in a category (one boy and one girl vs. several boys and several girls). In one game, the child was asked to select a toy to be placed in a car which was then rolled down a ramp to the child. The child should ask for "the boy," when there was only one and ask for "a boy" when there were several to choose from.

A listing transcript with contextual indicators showing the linguistic referencing would be appropriate for assessing children's use of cohesion markers. The analysis might be a detailed one if the child appears inconsistent, or simply one which indicates presence, absence, or misuse of the indicators.

The Conversational Interaction

Along with assessment of the child's language, it is also important to describe the nature of the child's interactions with others. Observing the child with one or both parents (or primary caregivers) provides an opportunity to assess the adult's input to the child as well as other aspects of their interaction. The adult utterances can be transcribed along with the child's for this analysis to see how they are related. Since it appears that input that is finely tuned to the child's language abilities has a positive effect on language acquisition, there is not a "best" way to talk to all children, but rather the style and content of input should ideally be tailored to the child at a particular point in development. While it appears that normally developing children can tolerate input that is less than ideal and still develop language, language-impaired children are further handicapped by adult language that does not suit them. There are many different parameters of the talk to children that can be described. Some of these will be more relevant for particular dyads than others. Some general parameters to look at in your transcripts or in live observation include those that follow.

JOINT FOCUS   Young children assume that the language they hear is related to whatever they are thinking about. If both participants in a conversation are focused on the same object or event, the language that is used will most likely be understood correctly. Mothers of young children typically talk about whatever the children are doing or looking at, thus focusing with the child and providing a model for how to talk about the object or event in focus. This understandably makes the adult's talk very here-and-now oriented. Most language-impaired children can benefit from a great deal of adult modeling based on joint focus, so the extent to which the language directed to the child involves joint focus is important to assess.

SEMANTIC CONTINGENCY   Semantically contingent utterances relate to the meaning of the prior utterance. This contingency might be expressed through repetition of another's utterance, expansion to include missing forms, or extensions to include new information. Answers to questions and questions related to the previous utterance are also semantically contingent. The adult's utterances can be analyzed for semantic contingency with their own or with the child's prior utterances. Conversations that are semantically contingent are easier to understand than those that are not. Contingency between conversational partners also indicates there is joint focus between them.

SYNTACTIC COMPLEXITY   While parents generally adjust the length and complexity of the sentences they direct to children, there may be marked discrepancies between the adult's utterances and the child's ability to comprehend. Some parents actively resist using "baby talk" with their children and try to use sentences of the same length, complexity, and vocabulary as they would use with adults. While the normally developing child can usually handle this, it may present a problem for the child with language learning difficulty. On the other hand, some adults talk to young or language-impaired children in telegraphic speech to match the child's own structure. It is not clear that this facilitates comprehension; there is some evidence to the contrary (Duchan and Erickson, 1976).

The importance of looking not only at the child but also at the interaction with a conversational partner was highlighted by Weitzner-Lin (1981) in a study of requests made by language-impaired children. She examined not only the child's expression but also looked at whether or not the conversational partner was jointly focused before, during, and after the request and at how the child's partner responded to the request. With this analysis, it was apparent that different requests involve different kinds of interactions, not simply different intentions. Weitzner-Lin also found that the conversational partner makes a difference. Requests directed to another child more often caused a breakdown in the interaction in that they were not responded to by the child partner, compared to fewer breakdowns with an adult interactant. The language-impaired children were more likely to attempt repairs of these breakdowns with the other children than they were when such breakdowns occurred with their adult partners. These and other patterns can only be discovered by looking at the interaction as a unit rather than at the child's utterance or response as an isolated event.

EXERCISES

1. Given the following sentences in the first column, pick the sentences in the second which (a) are highly contingent to the first; (b) follow the first with implicature; (c) are non sequiturs to the first. Defend your answers.

   a) I have a new cat

   1) _____ I saw a man.
   2) _____ By the way, did you hear about my car?
   3) _____ What breed is it?
   4) _____ Have your eyes been itching?

   b) I'm moving to California

   1) _____ I lived there.
   2) _____ Do you like smog?
   3) _____ I broke my leg yesterday.
   4) _____ Did you know I bought a new house?

2. Write an imagined conversation (five volleys, ten turns) which is highly bound to the context, and another which is decontextualized. Include in your contrast the differences in degree of binding to the physical setting, the temporal here-and-now, the speech event, and the speaker perspective. Indicate for each turn where it adheres to or departs from the context.

3. Indicate which form of linguistic discourse cohesion device is implicated in the following italicized segments; some may have more than one. Your choices are anaphora (a), ellipsis (e), cataphora (c), and contrastive stress (cs).
   a) _____ That man is my friend. *He* came home yesterday.
   b) _____ *Yes.*
   c) _____ Now hear *this.*
   d) _____ No, not the red book, the *blue* one.
   e) _____ I see a red book, but I don't want *it.*
   f) _____ *Mabel?* I don't believe it.
   g) _____ Is *it* true that blond men have more fun?
   h) _____ *This* will blow your mind.
   i) _____ Mary hit Paul, then *he* hit *her.*

j) _____ Anaphora, cataphora, what's *it all* for, huh?
k) _____ *Huh?*
l) _____ *No,* I don't think I'll go.
m) _____ *No.*
n) _____ *Why?*
o) _____ *Naturally.*

4. The answers to the following questions show that the listeners either regard the question as a request for information or as a request for action. Indicate which is the case (information = I, action = A).

a) Is Mary home?   _____ Yes. So is Jane.
                                           _____ I'll get her.

b) Do you have my comb?   _____ Here it is. (Gives comb)
                                           _____ Yes. I use it every day.

c) How many do you have?   _____ How many do you want?
                                           _____ You can have more than two.

d) Can I go in?   _____ No.
                                           _____ (Person steps aside).

e) How are you?   _____ Fine, how are you?
                                           _____ Better, want to see my scar?

f) Why do you always answer me   _____ Why not?
   with another question?   _____ Sorry. I'll try to do better next time.

g) Which dessert is mine?   _____ This one.
                                           _____ Here. (Gives dessert)

h) How much longer do I have to put   _____ Three more days.
   up with that?   _____ OK. I'll stop.

5. Can you take a hint? Below are examples of hints. Decide what they might be hints for, and analyze why you think so.
   a) What are these toys doing here?
   b) Mary's parents let her go to camp for three weeks.
   c) I can't read.
   d) The floor was clean an hour ago.
   e) Want to see my etchings?
   f) The last person who did that has two broken legs.
   g) I'll make you an offer you can't refuse.
   h) Are you thirsty?

6. What speech events do you engage in daily? weekly? annually? once in a lifetime? What speech events are not engaged in by adults but are by children? What speech events are idiosyncratic to interactions between language clinicians and their clients?

7. Analyze the following sample for indicators of listener perspective taking. It is a monologue from a conversation between two lawyers. Indicate what linguistic devices are used including orienting terms, relative clauses, identifying adjectives, and identifying prepositional phrases. Give as many examples of each as you can find.

Do you remember the Bird vs. Lyons case, the one which involved the sale of that old white mansion over on Fulton Street? Well, I met Garcia, the assistant D.A. to Stockwell who prosecutes real estate fraud cases, at a party for Judge Stone last week—you know the one at the Statler Hilton across from the bank. Dominic told me that the case has been reopened because the people who sold the house to the present owners were basing their ownership claim on the will signed by their father, and there is new evidence that the will was forged. Do you know the case I'm referring to?

REFERENCES

ANDERSON, E.   Will You Don't Snore Please? Directives in Young Children's Role-Play Speech, *Papers and Reports on Child Language Development*, 15, 1978, 140–50.

AUSTIN, J.   *How to Do Things with Words.* Oxford, England: Oxford University Press, 1962.

BATES, E.   *Language and Context: The Acquisition of Pragmatics.* New York: Academic Press, 1976.

BATES, E., AND B. MACWHINNEY.   A Functionalist Approach to the Acquisition of Grammar, in *Developmental Pragmatics*, eds. E. Ochs and B. Schieffelin. New York: Academic Press, 1979.

BATESON, M. C.   Mother-Infant Exchanges: The Epigenesis of Conversational Interaction, in *Developmental Psycholinguistics and Communication Disorders*, eds. D. Aaronson and R. Rieber. Annuals of the New York Academy of Sciences, Vol. 263, 1975.

BELLUGI, U., AND R. BROWN, eds.   The Acquisition of Language, *Monographs of the Society for Research in Child Development*, 29, 1964, Serial number 92.

BLANK, M., M. GESSNER, AND A. ESPOSITO.   Language without Communication: A Case Study, *Journal of Child Language*, 6, 1979, 329–52.

BLOOM, L., AND M. LAHEY.   *Language Development and Language Disorders.* New York: John Wiley, 1978.

BRANSFORD, J., AND M. JOHNSON.   Contextual Prerequisites for Understanding: Some Investigation of Comprehension and Recall, *Journal of Verbal Learning and Verbal Behavior*, 11, 1972, 717–26.

BRAZELTON, T., B. KOSLOWSKI, AND M. MAIN.   The Origins of Reciprocity: The Early Mother-Infant Interaction, in *The Effect of the Infant on Its Caregiver*, eds. M. Lewis and L. Rosenblum. London: Wiley, 1974, 49–77.

BRAUNWALD, S., AND R. BRISLIN.   The Diary Method Updated, in *Developmental Pragmatics*, eds. E. Ochs and B. Schieffelin. New York: Academic Press, 1979.

BRENNEIS, D., AND L. LEIN.   "You Fruithead": A Sociolinguistic Approach to Children's Dispute Settlement, in *Child Discourse*, eds. S. Ervin-Tripp and C. Mitchell-Kernan. New York: Academic Press, 1977.

BROEN, P.   The Verbal Environment of the Language Learning Child, *Monograph of the American Speech and Hearing Association*, no. 17, December 1972.

BRUNER, J.   The Ontogenesis of Speech Acts, *Journal of Child Language*, 2, 1975, 1–19.

BUHLER, K.   *Sprach Theorie: die Darstellungsfunktim der Spraehe.* Jena, Germany: Gustav Fischer, 1934.

CARTER, A.   The Transformation of Sensorimotor Morphemes into Words: A Case Study of the Development of "Here" and "There." *Stanford Papers and Reports on Child Language Development*, 10, 1975a, 31–47.

CARTER, A.   The Transformation of Sensorimotor Morphemes into Words: A

Case Study of the Development of "More" and "Mine," *Journal of Child Language,* 2, 1975b, 233–50.

CARTER, A.   From Sensorimotor Vocalizations to Words: A Case Study of the Evolution of Attention-Directing Communication in the Second Year, in *Action, Gesture, and Symbol: The Emergence of Language,* ed. A. Lock. New York: Academic Press, 1978.

CARTER, A.   The Disappearance Schema: Case Study of a Second Year Communicative Behavior, in *Developmental Pragmatics,* eds. E. Ochs and B. Schieffelin. New York: Academic Press, 1979.

CAZDEN, C.   Peekaboo as an Instructional Model: Discourse Development at Home and at School, *Papers and Reports on Child Language Development*, 17, 1979, 1–29.

CHAPMAN, R., AND J. MILLER.   Analyzing Language and Communication in the Child, in *Nonspeech Language Intervention*, ed. R. Schiefelbusch. Baltimore, Md.: University Park Press, 1981.

CHOMSKY, N.   *Aspects of the Theory of Syntax.* Cambridge, Mass.; M.I.T. Press, 1965.

CLARK, H., AND E. CLARK.   *Psychology and Language.* New York: Harcourt Brace Jovanovich, Inc., 1977.

CORSARO, W.   Sociolinguistic Patterns in Adult-Child Interaction, in *Developmental Pragmatics,* eds. E. Ochs and B. Schieffelin. New York: Academic Press, 1979.

CROSS, T.   Mothers' Speech Adjustments: The Contributions of Selected Child Listener Variables, in *Talking to Children,* eds. C. Snow and C. Ferguson. Cambridge, England: Cambridge University Press, 1977.

DORE, J.   A Description of Early Language Development, *Journal of Psycholinguistic Research,* 4, 1974, 423–30.

DORE, J.   'Oh Them Sheriff': A Pragmatic Analysis of Children's Responses to Questions, in *Child Discourse,* eds. S. Ervin-Tripp and C. Mitchell-Kernan. New York: Academic Press, 1977, pp. 139–64.

DORE, J., M. GEARHART, AND D. NEWMANN.   The Structure of Nursery School Conversation, in *Children's Language,* ed. K. Nelson. New York: Gardner Press, 1978.

DORE, J.   Conversational and Preschool Language Development, in *Language Acquisition,* eds. P. Fletcher and M. Garman. Cambridge, England: Cambridge University Press, 1979, pp. 337–62.

DRACH, K.   The Language of the Parent: A Pilot Study. Working Paper 14, Language-Behavior Research Laboratory, University of California, Berkeley, 1969.

DUCHAN, J., AND J. ERICKSON.   Normal and Retarded Children's Understanding of Semantic Relations in Different Verbal Contexts, *Journal of Speech and Hearing Research,* 19, 1976, 767–76.

DUNCAN, S., AND G. NIEDEREHE.   On Signalling That It's Your Turn to Speak, *Journal of Experimental Social Psychology,* 10, 1974, 234–47.

EMIHOVITZ, C.   An Ethnography on Race Relations in Early Childhood, Ph.D. dissertation, S.U.N.Y. Buffalo, in progress.

ERVIN-TRIPP, S.   Wait for Me Roller-Skate, in *Child Discourse,* eds. S. Ervin-Tripp and E. Mitchel-Kernan. New York: Academic Press, 1977.

FERGUSON, C., AND C. SNOW, eds. *Talking to Children.* Cambridge England: Cambridge University Press, 1977.

FINE, J. Conversation, Cohesive and Thematic Patterning in Children's Dialogues, *Discourse Processes,* 1, 1978, 247–66.

FLAVELL, J. *The Development of Role Taking and Communication Skills in Children.* New York: John Wiley, 1968.

GALLAGHER, T. Revision Behaviors in the Speech of Normal Children Developing Language, *Journal of Speech and Hearing Research,* 2, 1977, 303–18.

GARVEY, C. Play with Language and Speech, in *Child Discourse,* eds. S. Ervin-Tripp and C. Mitchell-Kernan. New York: Academic Press, 1977.

GARVEY, C. Requests and Responses in Children's Speech, *Journal of Child Language,* 2, 1975, 41–63.

GELMAN, R., AND M. SHATZ. Appropriate Speech Adjustments: The Operation of Conversational Constraints on Talk to Two Year Olds, in *Interaction, Conversation, and the Development of Language,* eds. M. Lewis and L. Rosenblum. New York: John Wiley, 1977.

GREENFIELD, P., AND P. ZUKOW. Why Do Children Say What They Say When They Say It? An Experimental Approach to the Psychogenesis of Presupposition, *Papers and Reports on Child Language Development,* 15, 1978, 57–67.

GRICE, H. Logic and Conversation, in *The Logic of Grammar,* eds. I. Davidson and G. Harmon. Encino, Calif.: Dickenson Press, 1975.

HALLIDAY, M. A. K. *Learning How to Mean: Explorations in the Development of Language.* London: Edward Arnold, 1975.

HALLIDAY, M. A. K., AND R. HASAN. *Cohesion in English.* London: Longman, 1976.

HURTIG, R. Toward a Functional Theory of Discourse, in *Discourse Production and Comprehension,* ed. R. Freedle. Norwood, N.J.: Ablex Publishing Corporation, 1977.

KEENAN, E. Conversational Competence in Children, *Journal of Child Language,* 1, 1974, 163–83.

KEENAN, E. Making It Last: Repetition in Child Discourse, in *Child Discourse,* eds. E. Ervin-Tripp and C. Mitchell-Kernan. New York: Academic Press, 1977.

KEENAN, E., AND B. SCHIEFFELIN. Topic as a Discourse Notion: A Study of Topic in the Conversations of Children and Adults, in *Subject and Topic,* ed. C. Li. New York: Academic Press, 1976.

KRAUSS, R., AND S. GLUCKSBERG. The Development of Communication: Competence as a Function of Age, *Child Development,* 40, 1969, 255–66.

LAWSON, C. Request Patterns in a Two-Year-Old. Unpublished Manuscript, Berkeley, California, 1967.

LUBINSKI, R., J. DUCHAN, AND B. WEITZNER-LIN. Analysis of Breakdowns and Repairs in Aphasic Adult Communication. Proceedings of the Clinical Aphasiology Conference, Bar Harbor, Maine, 1980.

MARATSOS, M. *The Use of Definite and Indefinite Reference in Young Children.* Cambridge, England: Cambridge University Press, 1976.

MILLER, J. Assessing Children's Language Behavior: A Developmental Process Approach, in *Bases of Language Intervention,* ed. R. Schiefelbusch. Baltimore: University Park Press, 1978, 269–318.

MISHLER, E.   Studies in Dialogue and Discourse: An Exponential Law of Successive Questioning, *Language in Society,* 4, 1975a, 31–51.

MISHLER, E.   Studies in Dialogue and Discourse II: Types of Discourse Initiated and Sustained Through Questioning, *Journal of Psycholinguistic Research,* 4, 1975b, 99–121.

MITCHELL-KERNAN, C., AND K. KERNAN.   Pragmatics of Directive Choice Among Children, in *Child Discourse,* eds. S. Ervin-Tripp and C. Mitchell-Kernan. New York: Academic Press, 1977.

MOORE, K., AND A. MELTZOFF.   Object Permanence, Limitation, and Language Development in Infancy: Toward a Neo-Piagetian Perspective of Communicative and Cognitive Development, in *Communicative and Cognitive Abilities—Early Behavioral Assessment,* eds. F. Minifie and L. Lloyd. Baltimore: University Park Press, 1978.

NEWPORT, E.   Motherese: The Speech of Mothers to Young Children, in *Cognitive Theory,* Vol. II, eds. N. Castellan, D. Pisni, and G. Potts. Hillsdale, N.J.: Lawrence Erlbaum Associates, 1976.

NEWPORT, E., L. GLEITMAN, AND H. GLEITMAN.   Mother, I'd Rather Do It Myself: Same Effects and Non Effects of Maternal Speech Style, in *Talking to Children,* eds. C. Ferguson and C. Snow. Cambridge: Cambridge University Press, 1977.

NINIO, A., AND J. BRUNER.   The Achievement and Antecedents of Labelling, *Journal of Child Language,* 5, 1978, 1–15.

OCHS, E.   Introduction: What Child Language Can Contribute to Pragmatics, in *Developmental Pragmatics,* eds. E. Ochs and B. Schieffelin. New York: Academic Press, 1979.

O'CONNELL, B.   Request Forms as a Measure of Social Context. Unpublished Manuscript, Berkeley, California, 1974.

PIAGET, J.   *The Language and Thought of the Child.* London: Routledge & Kegan Paul, 1926.

PIAGET, J.   *The Construction of Reality in the Child.* New York: Ballantine, 1954.

PRIZANT, B.   An Analysis of the Functions of Immediate Echolalia in Autistic Children. Ph.D. dissertation, State University of New York at Buffalo, 1978.

PRIZANT, B., AND J. DUCHAN.   The Functions of Immediate Echolalia in Autistic Children, *Journal of Speech and Hearing Disorders,* 46, 1981, 241–49.

PRUTTING, C.   Process/prắ/, ses/n: The Action of Moving Forward Progressively from One Point to Another on the Way to Completion, *Journal of Speech and Hearing Disorders,* 44, 1979, 3–30.

RATNER, N., AND J. BRUNER.   Games, Social Exchange and the Acquisition of Language, *Journal of Child Language,* 5, 1978, 391–402.

REES, N.   Pragmatics of Language, in *Bases of Language Intervention,* ed. R. Schiefelbusch. Baltimore: University Park Press, 1978.

REMICK, H.   Maternal Speech to Children during Language Acquisition, in *Body Talk and Infant Speech,* eds. W. von Raffler-Engel and Y. Lebrun. Lisse, Netherlands: Swets and Zeitlinger, 1976.

SACKS, H., E. SHEGLOFF, AND G. JEFFERSON.   A Simplest Systematics for the Organization of Turn-Taking for Conversation, *Language,* 50, 1974, 696–735.

SANDER, L.   The Regulation of Exchange in the Infant-Caretaker System and

Some Aspects of the Context-Content Relationship, in *Interaction, Conversation, and the Development of Language,* eds. M. Lewis and L. Rosenblum. New York: John Wiley, 1977.

SCHEGLOFF, E. Sequencing in Conversational Openings, *American Anthropologist,* 70, 1968, 1075-95.

SCHEGLOFF, E., AND H. SACKS. Opening Up Closings, *Semiotica,* 8, 1973, 289-327.

SCOLLON, R. A Real Early Stage: An Unzippered Condensation of a Dissertation on Child Language, in *Developmental Pragmatics,* eds. E. Ochs and B. Schieffelin. New York: Academic Press, 1979.

SEARLE, J. *Speech Acts.* Cambridge, England: Cambridge University Press, 1969.

SHANK, R., AND R. ABELSON. *Scripts, Plans, Goals and Understanding.* Hillsdale, N.J.: Lawrence Erlbaum Associates, 1977.

SHATZ, M. The Comprehension of Indirect Directives: Can Two-Year Olds Shut the Door? Paper presented at summer meeting of Linguistics Society of America, 1974.

SINCLAIR, J., AND R. COULTHARD. *Towards an Analysis of Discourse: The English Used by Teachers and Pupils.* Oxford, England: Oxford University Press, 1975.

SNOW, C. Mothers' Speech to Children Learning Language, *Child Development,* 43, 1972, 549-65.

SNOW, C. Mothers' Speech Research: From Input to Interaction, in *Talking to Children,* eds. C. Ferguson and C. Snow. Cambridge, England: Cambridge University Press, 1977.

SPRADLEY, J., AND D. MCGURDY. *The Cultural Experience: Ethnography in Complex Society.* Chicago, Ill.: Science Research Associates, 1972.

STERN, D., B. BEEBE, J. JAFFE, AND S. BENNETT. The Infant's Stimulus World during Social Interaction, in *Studies in Mother-Infant Interactions,* ed. H. Schaffer. New York: Academic Press, 1977.

STOEL-GAMMAN, C., AND L. CABRAL. Learning How to Tell It Like It Is: The Development of the Reportative Function in Children's Speech, *Papers and Reports on Child Language Development,* 13, 1977, 64-71.

TANZ, C. *Studies in the Acquisition of Deictic Terms.* Cambridge, England: Cambridge University Press, 1980.

TREVARTHAN, C. Descriptive Analyses of Infant Communicative Behavior, in *Studies in Mother-Infant Interaction,* ed. H. Schaffer. New York: Academic Press, 1977.

VAN DER GEEST, T. Some Interactional Aspects of Language Acquisition, in *Talking to Children,* eds. C. Ferguson and C. Snow. Cambridge, England: Cambridge University Press, 1977.

VAN DIJK, T. Relevance Assignment in Discourse Comprehension, *Discourse Processes,* 2, 1979, 113-26.

WATSON-GEGEO, K., AND S. BOGGS. From Verbal Play to Talk Story: The Role of Routines in Speech Events among Hawaiian Children, in *Child Discourse,* eds. S. Ervin-Tripp and C. Mitchell-Kernan. New York: Academic Press, 1977.

WEITZNER-LIN, B. Interactive Request Analysis. Unpublished Ph.D. dissertation, State University of New York at Buffalo, August 1981.

4

Phonology

While pragmatics has emphasized how language changes in different contexts, phonology, or the study of the sound system of language, has traditionally been studied as having a fixed structural organization whose contextual variability is regarded as an aberration. There is strong evidence from various sources, however, against this fixed view of phonology. One set of studies is of style or code shifting. It documents the fact that the sounds you use can depend upon the person you are talking to and the formality of the situation. A second influence of context on phonology is that of linguistic context. For example, a well-known phenomenon to speech pathologists is that children's speech sounds vary depending upon the phonological and syntactic difficulty of the surrounding language. This influence of adjacent sounds on one another is studied under the titles of *coarticulation* and *assimilation*. Finally, there is evidence from the developmental literature that children's early language forms are highly context bound. They are closely intertwined with the accompanying action in both timing and form and also are tightly related to the accompanying intonation pattern.

Some of the following discussion about phonology is context focused, such as our sections on context sensitive analysis and context sensitive rules. Other parts ignore the role of context and leave it to you to keep in mind that children's performance will vary depending upon the person they are talking to, the situation, and the phonological and syntactic environment of the particular sound in question.

PHONOLOGY AND WHAT IT INCLUDES

Phonology, as an area of linguistics, has to do with the way the sounds of a language are organized. It can include the documentation of what the sounds are (the sound inventory), their component features, how the sounds are strung together, and the various underlying rules or processes which operate to influence how the sounds change when they are produced under certain circumstances and in certain contexts. Sometimes intonation is included as an aspect of phonology, probably because it too can be heard and measured acoustically, using such instruments as sound spectrographs. However, components of intonation are at least as closely tied to meaning and sentence structure as they are to the sound system of the language. Therefore, we see the treatment of intonation as an aspect only of the phonological system as a mistake; the same mistake, incidentally, which is made when we think that the study of speech sounds is only the study of what we hear.

Let us elaborate this idea by filling in some background information. Our account will lead to our view that the sounds of a language, and of any child's speech, come from a nonobservable or underlying set of structures, instead of to the mistaken view that you can determine what the sound system of a language is by studying the sound waves which it produces.

Phonemes

We, as speakers, readers, writers, and listeners of the language have an elaborate and abstract sense of what the sounds are that make up the language. However, we develop this sense as much from our meaning system as from the way the words sound. That is, we learn in English that /p/ and /b/ are different because we use the difference to distinguish words with different meanings. It is also the case that speakers of English produce /p/ sounds differently, but when they do it does not result in a word of a different meaning. Said another way, /p/ and /b/ are contrastive, and the various /p/ sounds are not. It is usual, therefore, to refer to /p/ and /b/ as *phonemes* and the different /p/ sounds as *allophonic variants* of the same phoneme.

Because we know that /p/ and /b/ make a meaning difference, we as adult native listeners ignore the subvarieties of each and treat what we hear as an abstract category or phoneme. A phoneme, then, is like a concept, and not an observable phenomenon. As speakers of English, we would agree, for the most part, on what the phonemes of English are. Linguists who have listed our phonemic inventory of English conclude that there are over forty in number.

Distinctive Features

The abstract phonemes which speakers and listeners of English have as categories differ from one another along particular dimensions. Some are prolonged, some are quick; some are hissing in quality, some are not. These differences are ones of *manner*. Phonemes also differ in where they are said in the mouth, a difference of *place;* and whether or not they are said with laryngeal vibration, a difference in *voicing*. These three features—manner, place, and voicing—can characterize the basic distinctions which make a difference in English—that is, each phoneme differs from every other phoneme along one or more of these three dimensions.

Table 4.1 outlines the distinctive features of English consonants along these place, manner, and voicing dimensions. The various place features have to do with the articulators and the place involved in creating the narrowest point of constrictions as the sound is said. Thus, for bilabial, the narrowest point is between the lips; for labiodental, between the lips and teeth, etc. The manners have been subclassified in Table 4.1 into six types: stops, fricatives, affricates, glides, liquids, and nasals. In other classification systems, there may be more manners distinguished. Finally, there are sounds which contrast only in that one is voiced and the other is voiceless. The table follows the format used by Fisher and Logemann in their Test of Articulatory Competence (1971).

We have picked this feature system as our frame because it is easier to work with in doing structural analysis and has, in our experience, captured the essence of most of our children's phonological problems. That is to say, it is psychologically real to children (see Chapter 2 for more on psychological reality). Other feature systems can be borrowed from when needed. One is the system of Chomsky and Halle (1968) which consists of a classification based on data from acoustic phonetics rather than having the articulatory focus of our place, manner, and voicing classification. That is, Chomsky and Halle derived their features from differences portrayed in an examination of physically measured aspects of the sound waves. Those subscribing to any feature system agree that the distinctions between phonemes are not clear cut, and the features, like the phonemes themselves, operate as abstract categories which are used by speakers, listeners,

Table 4.1   Manner, Place, and Voicing of English Phonemes

PLACE IN MOUTH FROM FRONT TO BACK	MANNER OF PRODUCTION					
	Stop	*Fricative*	*Affricate*	*Glide*	*Liquid*	*Nasal*
Bilabial	p[a]	hw				
	b			w		m
Labiodental		f				
		v				
Tip dental		θ				
		ð				
Alveolar	t	s				
	d	z			l	n
Blade-prepalatal		ʃ	tʃ			
		3	dʒ			
Front-palatal				j		
Central-palatal					r	
Back-velar	k					l
	g					ŋ
Glottal		h				

[a] The top line within a category is voiceless; bottom line is voiced.

and structural analysts to distinguish the sounds for their use as linguistic entities.

Phonological Rules

So far, we have been concentrating primarily on sound and feature inventories and pretending that once these inventories are discovered they are stable, and all is said and done about phonology. However, as we will see throughout this book, nothing is so easy. Rather, phonemes and features are different when they are produced together. They combine in prescribed ways, since not all sounds can be next to one another, and once the allowable combinations are made at an abstract level, the abstract plan of production can be changed in its execution. The entities which describe and govern these combining and changing processes have been called *rules*.

There are a number of phonological rules which have been found to occur in languages of the world as well as in the language of developing children. For example, an assimilation rule which occurs in English is that the plural morpheme becomes voiced, voiceless, or syllabic depending upon features of the last sound of the word they attach to. Thus, the plural is said as [z] in dogs because the /g/ is voiced; it is said as [s] in cats because the /t/ is unvoiced; and it is said as [ɪz] in dresses because the /s/ is a fricative.

The assimilation rule we have mentioned is based on what phonemes or distinctive features surround the changed element. Other rules depend not on phoneme or feature influences but upon the syllable structure, or consonant-vowel relationships in the word. For example, if a voiceless stop such as /p/, /t/, or /k/ occurs at the beginning of a syllable, it becomes aspirated [pʰɑt]. This rule, as well as the assimilation rule, is context sensitive; but with this rule the relevant context is the syllable and not the feature or phoneme.

Not only do rules differ in whether they depend on phoneme, feature, or syllable structure, they also differ in how abstract they are. This difference would distinguish rules variously identified as abstract, high, or phonological level rules from those produced on a surface, low, or phonetic level. This abstract versus surface level distinction is made by generative phonologists who look for underlying structure of sound patterns and is different from that of descriptive linguists who describe what it is they hear.

Generative phonologists have developed a multilevel model for understanding phonological knowledge. In it, words are indexed in several ways. First, they are organized according to their abstract phonemic characteristics—that is, they are classified into abstract phonemes. Thus, the prefix *in* meaning "not" is abstractly indexed as I + nasal. At this abstract level, the surface versions of this prefix which occur as /I + n/ in *innocuous,* /I + m/ in *impossible,* and /I + ŋ/ in *incongruous* are depicted as the same. A second indexing procedure for the lexicon is by number and location of syllables and syllable boundaries. Third, the individual phonemes within the words are indexed according to their distinctive features. In the case of *in*, feature indexing /n/ could be [+ nasal]. The features used in the indexing will differ depending on the system used.

The lexical items are then "processed" through a set of phonological rules, and they are transformed in ways specified by those rules. The result of the operation of such rules is that they achieve a phonetic output, still abstract, but more detailed and less abstract in their distinctive feature representation. For example, once the assimilation rule is applied to the abstract [I + nasal], the particular place for the nasal becomes specified as either /m/, /n/, or /ŋ/.

The phonetic level is where linguists stop in their analysis but cannot be where we stop as speech pathologists who are concerned about motor production as well as linguistic conceptualizations. Parker (1976) has pointed out this difference clearly and advocates, as we do, the addition of a set of production rules which transform the phonetic forms to motor commands.

In sum, the generative model, plus Parker's addition, has several levels that can be depicted visually (see Figure 4.1).

Phonologists are not particularly concerned with specific individuals, but, rather study the language in general. Psycholinguists and language pathologists, however, have been influenced by the generative model and have borrowed pieces of it to describe normal and abnormal acquisition of the sound system of the language. There are problems with doing this. One is that it assumes that language learners have an adult lexicon or dictionary which they then transform to produce patterns which do not conform to an adult model. A second is that it is a model which focuses on production and says little about perception of the sounds of the language. Third, the model assumes that the units are morphemes or words and has no place in it for children learning individual phonemes or features. This makes it difficult to show why or how new knowledge of features spreads from one word to another. Finally, it is a model of language knowledge and does not consider psychological factors involved in processing that knowledge, such as those which would be present if the child had memory problems, hearing loss, motor difficulty, or cognitive limitations. We will be discussing these factors as we move on now to the literature on how normal children learn the phonological system of their language.

PHONOLOGICAL DEVELOPMENT

Perceptual and Phonological Discrimination

Apparently children are born with the ability to distinguish complex sounds along the lines that languages of the world are organized. That is, when infants as young as one month are presented with a repetitive stimulus, they first

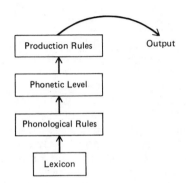

Figure 4.1

adjust to the repetition and ignore it. When that stimulus is changed only slightly, say, in place-feature changing a /ba/ to a /da/, or in voicing changing a /pa/ to /ba/, the babies take note as evidenced by a change in their heartbeat or in their sucking rate (Morse, 1972). What is also true, however, is that they do not understand these changes as meaningful phonological contrasts, since they do not yet have the ability to understand or produce words. These distinctions, then, are not linguistic, but are perceptual ones that are later applied to language learning.

The linguistic distinctions between minimal difference pairs of monosyllables have been studied by Schvachkin (1973) and Garnica (1973). When Schvachkin studied 10 to 21 month old children, he taught them meanings for what at first were nonsense syllables. His subjects were comparable in the order in which they learned distinctive features. Garnica (1973), on the other hand, found considerable variability among her 17 to 22 month old English-speaking subjects, with a tendency for voice-voiceless distinctions to be late in acquisition.

Barton (1976, cited in Menyuk and Menn, 1979) found that children's familiarity with a word aided them in their performance on discrimination tasks, suggesting that Schvachkin and Garnica's results are conservative, since the words they used were new to the children. Barton's results for children distinguishing meaningful and familiar words were that children between 27 and 35 months were able to distinguish between two words with single feature contrasts for all the features of English.

Menyuk and Menn (1979) summarize this sparse literature on children's acquisition of phonetic and linguistic distinctions between similar sounding syllables and words as follows:

> The human infant at age 1 month is capable of discriminating between some acoustic parameters that mark speech sound differences; by age 9 to 13 months, the infant appears to be able to comprehend the meaning of phonological sequences in certain contexts; that is, gestalt comprehension of phonological sequence plus context, rather than phonological differentiation of sequences; the child is able to learn to associate objects and nonsense syllables that contrast many of the initial consonant features during the period of 10 to 22 months; the child can distinguish between minimal pair words that contain most English singleton phonological contrasts by 35 months. (Menyuk and Menn, 1979, p. 52)

Menyuk and Menn (1979) continue in their summary to warn against our believing that children at this age are making their distinctions on the basis of single feature discriminations. Instead, based on naturalistic rather than laboratory studies, children appear to be attending to the phonological sequence as a whole and are using situational cues in assigning meaning to the words they hear. Thus, although infants can hear the differences between syllables which contrast on features of voicing or place, they do not use this fine a distinction until later in their language development, when they become more analytical and can separate sounds from one another and from the linguistic and situational contexts in which they occur. The rich interpretation fallacy which Menyuk and Menn warn us against would have its parallel in visual perception where we would jump from watching children distinguish the written letters *b* and *p* to assuming they could read words containing this distinction.

Prelinguistic Stages in Sound Development

Just as for sound perception, it is not obvious how a child's vocalizations before language relate to their acquisition of language. Despite controversy around this issue, a sequential progression can be described. Typically, one finds a sequence of stages on the way to language described as follows:

1. Cooing—containing back sounds, both back consonants and vowels, done in pleasure situations, and emerging at about two months of age.
2. Babbling—with more of a diversity of back sounds including clicks and grunts, progressing from long strings of sounds and syllables unlike those in the native language, to a final period with the sequential strings containing phonemes and syllable structures comparable to morphemes in the native language. This period lasts from three months through the emergence of first words, around ten or fifteen months.
3. Jargon—a vocalization which is more interactive in focus than babbling, with eye contact and communicative gestures, and with the intonation contours characteristic of the adult language (Menn and Haselkorn, 1977).
4. Vocables—isolated single sounds or one or two syllable segments which are phonetically consistent and context specific. They often are accompanied by identifiable gestures (Carter, 1979), and occur as part of ritualized games (peekaboo), emotional states ("uhoh"), or frequently occurring communicative acts ("hi" + greeting; reach + grunt; point + "da"). The vocables do not qualify as words because they are not used apart from the contexts and appear to be one component of the action sequence rather than a symbol which can stand in its stead (Carter, 1979; Dore et al., 1976; Ferguson, 1978; Halliday, 1975).

Phonological Stages Accompanying First Words

At about ten months, most normal children start producing their first words. These tend to be words whose referents are familiar objects or events. The words have a simple consonant + vowel syllable structure (e.g., da) which may or may not be reduplicated (e.g., dada). The consonants are typically front stops or nasals, although children vary in their choice of favorite sounds and syllable structures. Some children confine their choice of words to fit their phonology, only saying words whose adult forms conform to their structural competences. These children avoid words which they cannot produce. Other children are more imperialistic in their productions and make adult words conform to their limited phonological capabilities. Menyuk and Menn (1979) call these children the "modifiers."

Another phenomenon reported for this period is that the first words can for some children fluctuate considerably in how they are said, suggesting that for these children the phonemes and features are still in broadly circumscribed categories (Ferguson and Farwell, 1975). One view of this phenomenon is that these children have large overlapping phoneme categories with considerable allophonic variability within each. Within their systems this fluctuation could be seen as phonetic variability (Ferguson and Farwell, 1975). The problem with this view is described by Menyuk and Menn (1979) who have noticed that, for their subjects, some words vary much more than others and that the variability may be more related to the lexical item than to the sounds which make it up. Menyuk and Menn (1979, p. 63) put it this way: "In such a state of affairs, a feature bundle (phonemic) specification is inadequate; lexical (word particular) specification is necessary. Near the onset of speech, we may find many forms which similarly do not decompose into entities which are comparable across words." These two renditions of what is going on have been called the "across the board" versus the "lexical diffusion" hypotheses (Fletcher and Garman, 1979). In the first, a feature or phoneme will be rendered the same way across lexical items; in the second, the pronunciation will vary depending upon the lexical item. What all this says about first words, perhaps, is that for some children they are highly rule constrained phonologically; for other children, there is a tendency toward a high degree of phonetic variability which is not rule governed but depends upon the particular word being produced.

In sum, this early word stage is different for different children. Children vary in their sound and syllable structure preferences; they vary in the degree to which they impose these preferences on adult forms; and they vary in whether they organize their phonological systems by rules which work across words, or by memorizing individual lexical items. What seems to be common to all children is that this is a stage where their phonological ability is highly restricted, and it is a stage which is followed by another which is qualitatively different and one of rapid phonological progression (Ferguson, 1978; Ingram, 1976; Menyuk and Menn, 1979).

Phonological Rules and Processes

As we described earlier, generative phonologists have devised techniques for discovering sound changes and phonological environments in which these changes occur. The changes or phonological processes may be (1) *substitution,* where segments are modified often depending upon their position in a word; (2) *assimilation,* where adjacent phonemes or features become more alike; or (3) *syllable structure changes* where the number of syllables or the consonant-vowel patterns of syllables is systematically changed. Stampe (1969), in an influential article, forwarded the hypothesis that children are born with an adultlike knowledge of phonological processes which are common to all languages. The processes make up "an innate system ... revised in certain ways by linguistic experience" (p. 441). The child then revises the innate processes by suppressing some, partially limiting others, and ordering others, as he or she proceeds to learn the native language.

Stampe's theory differs from other theories of phonological development in that he sees the child's phonological knowledge as consisting of phonological processes, rather than seeing phonological development as acquiring context sensitive rules, or acquiring an inventory of individual phonemes (Templin, 1957), features (McReynolds and Engmann, 1975), or feature opposition (Jakobson, 1972).

While Stampe's (1969) formulation was made at a highly abstract level and began with phonological universals from languages of the world, Ingram (1976) used his idea of phonological processes in a more descriptive way to characterize error patterns in phonological acquisition. The processes which Ingram lists as characteristic of normal children are

SUBSTITUTION PROCESSES:

Stopping—substituting stops for fricatives

Fronting—substituting alveolars for velar and palatal consonants

Gliding—substituting glides for liquids

Vocalization—substituting vowels for syllabic consonants (*m,n,l,r*)

Vowel neutralization—changing vowels to oral and central position

ASSIMILATION PROCESSES:

Voicing—consonants tend to be voiced before a vowel and unvoiced at the end of a syllable

Consonant harmony—two consonants tend to become more alike when they are near one another

Progressive vowel assimilation—unstressed vowels become like a nearby stressed vowel

SYLLABLE STRUCTURE PROCESSES:

Cluster reduction—consonant clusters are reduced to a single consonant

Deletion of final consonants—consonant-vowel-consonant (CVC) syllables become CV syllables

Deletion of unstressed syllables—unstressed syllables are deleted

Reduplication—a syllable is repeated in a multisyllabic word (wawa for water)

PHONOLOGICAL ASSESSMENT

Assessment of phonology has traditionally been called "articulation testing," and the most common testing procedure is to administer an articulation test which requires the child to say each sound in the beginning, middle, and end of words. The objective of such a procedure is to identify mismatches between the child's sound production and the correct or *target* phoneme.

Problems with this approach have long been recognized by clinicians. For example (1) it is a common phenomenon to see children who have many more misarticulations in connected speech than are revealed in test samples; (2) describing a production of a sound as a distortion does not capture the fact that it is still a substitution, but one where a nonstandard allophonic variant is used in place of a standard allophone of the target sound; (3) the traditional approach tends to operate with broad or phonemic transcription and does not recognize errors which fall within the phoneme class, such as a production of the aspirated /t/ in *butter* ([bʌtʰɚ/bʌt̬ɚ]); (4) there is no focus on patterns of consistency across substitution errors with this approach (the child who devoices all final consonants would appear to have many errors if all substitutions were simply listed, and the critical interaction of voicing and position in the word might be missed); (5) there are frequent error-to-target matching problems where the number of segments in the child's production are not the same as the number in the target production, and it is unclear which elements are omitted and which are substituted or distorted (e.g., /tʌpaɪ/ for *butterfly*); and (6) children who are "inconsistent" defy description in substitution analysis with a single sampling approach—no test captures accurately the variety of productions they have for a given target phoneme in their nontest speaking situations.

There have been several alternatives to this traditional approach described in the literature in recent years. Recognition that single productions of sounds are not representative of the sound in all contexts has been highlighted by McDonald (1968), as well as by studies of coarticulation (Daniloff and Moll, 1968; Liberman, 1970; MacNeilage and de Clerk, 1969).

Feature approaches, such as those suggested by McReynolds and Engmann (1975) or Fisher and Logemann (1971), have become a commonly used alternative which meets some of the criticisms of the traditional approach. The feature approaches are based on the recognition that sounds can be analyzed in bundles of features and that any given feature can occur in a number of sounds. Application of this approach to defective articulation has taken the form of identifying the features that are not used or are used incorrectly. The focus is thus on the pattern of consistency. The feature approach is an improvement over traditional analysis because it requires moving away from single sample testing and because it may reveal a consistent error pattern related to features. However, as generally used, it has many of the same disadvantages of the traditional approach in that it does not allow within-phoneme error detection, it does not treat distortions, it does not solve the error-to-target matching problem, and it fails to reveal consistencies which are not related to features.

Recently a broader based approach has begun to be used—one which we have been describing. As we have said, it derives from the linguistic literature on generative phonology (Chomsky and Halle, 1968; Hooper, 1976; Hyman, 1975; Schane, 1973) and has been applied to the study of language acquisition (Ferguson, 1978; Ingram, 1976) as well as to language assessment (Ingram, 1976; Lund and Duchan, 1978; Shriberg and Kwiatkowski, 1980; Weiner, 1978). It has been called the phonological process approach. We prefer calling it the multifaceted approach, since we would like it to do more than discover phonological processes. It incorporates analyses from traditional and feature approaches and adds to them analysis of deviations which are not mere substitutions of the child's production of the adult form. In cases where the phonological context is the relevant determinate of the deviation, *context sensitive analysis* captures the consistency. *Syllable structure analysis* is appropriate when the child's errors are alterations of consonant-vowel relationships within a syllable, or are additions or reductions in the number of syllables in a word. Finally, for those patterns which remain and which are idiosyncratic to the child, *idiosyncratic analyses* can be devised.

SUBSTITUTION ANALYSIS

Feature Analysis

Substitutions can be analyzed in terms of features that reveal regularities in the child's phonology. The feature analysis should be flexible enough to discover features which not only describe the variation across phoneme boundaries, usually called *substitutions,* but also describe the allophonic variations in the child's production, usually called *distortions.* Narrow transcription of the child's production is necessary to record the allophonic variations and reveal the significant feature substitutions—that is, those features which make the child's articulation deviant.

A feature system developed by Fisher and Logemann (1971) uses narrow transcription, thus providing for analysis of the allophonic variations within a phoneme as well as substitutions of one standard phoneme for another. Using the features of place of production, manner of production, and voicing, the child's misarticulation is precisely described. For example, if a child produces a voiced bilabial fricative [b̬] in place of a bilabial stop [b], this is described as the substitution of manner (frication for stop) rather than as a distorted /b/.

Referring back to Table 4.1 (p. 89), we can see that errors which are substitutions of sounds in one column for those in another are described as *manner* errors—that is, sounds of one manner are substituted for sounds of another manner. Often these errors are consistent across several sounds. For example, when there is a pattern where stops are substituted for fricatives of like voice and place, the pattern is *stopping* (refer back to Ingram's list given earlier). Similarly, fricatives for stops can be described as a problem of *frication,* nasals for like stops is *nasalization,* and affricates for like fricatives, *affrication.* The common pattern of w/r and j/l is *gliding.* It is often accompanied by substitution of a rounded vowel or w for final r and l. This is referred to as *vocalization.*

Substitution errors of sounds in one row for another are *place* errors. In this case, as we have said, sounds made in one place in the mouth are substituted for sounds made somewhere else in the mouth. Sometimes these place errors are patterned across several substitutions, as t/k, d/g, in which case front or alveolar sounds are substituted for velars. This is an example of *fronting. Backing* is, as one would guess, the tendency to substitute back sounds for those more forward. Often children have preferences for a particular articulatory position, such as the alveolar ridge, in which case they substitute alveolar sounds for those made in other places, as t/k, t/p, d/g, d/b. This has been called *tetonism* but could more descriptively be called *alveolarizing.* One can easily imagine, then, what the patterns would be for children who display *labializing* or *velarizing.*

Examining Table 4.1 again, a within-cell substitution pattern can also occur where voiced sounds are substituted for their voiceless cognates, or vice versa. In the first case, the problem is one of *voicing,* in the second a *devoicing* error.

Position plus Feature Analysis

Children often have feature substitutions that are specific to a particular position of a sound in a word. The child who, for example, omits final stop consonants while producing them in initial position may appear inconsistent. Consistencies can be found through an analysis which lists substitutions according to their position in the word.

Traditionally, sound positions are classified as initial, medial, and final. These categories can lead to inaccurate classification. For example, words such as "faster" and "sister" contain two consecutive consonants in the position which would be identified as medial in traditional analysis. This identification fails to distinguish a medial cluster or blend from two adjacent consonants, one terminating the initial syllable and the other initiating the final syllable. Description of the position of consonants in relation to vowels in the syllable unit leads to more precise classification. If the child produces two sequential consonants as a cluster, the cluster can be classified as a postvocalic unit (*rest* + ing) or prevocalic unit (re + *store*). If the child separates the consonants by a juncture (si*s* + *t*er), the first consonant would be classified as postvocalic, the second as prevocalic. Thus a child may say "sister" correctly but omit the fricative in the clusters in "resting" or "restore." Position plus feature analysis advocates that the position be determined by listening to the child's production and listing the feature error by where it occurs in the syllable.

Summary

Traditional substitution analysis has here been adapted to describe more accurately children's misarticulations. Using narrow transcription allows one to view "distortions" as allophonic substitutions. Once a comparison is made between different error and target sounds, the manner, place, or voicing features can be discovered which characterize the within-phoneme as well as across-phoneme substitutions. Manner errors could be those of stopping, fricating, or nasalizing. Place errors could be fronting, backing, alveolarizing, labializing, or velarizing. Voicing errors could be voicing or devoicing. A position and feature analysis reveals consistency in patterning where children have different feature substitutions depending upon where the consonant is located in the syllable unit.

CONTEXT SENSITIVE PATTERNS

While adaptation of substitution analysis helps to circumvent some problems, there remain some inherent difficulties with the substitution procedures which cannot be remedied without going to a different kind of analysis. One such problem is that misarticulations are often produced because of the influence of sounds and syllables on one another. For example, later sounds can affect earlier ones in a word or a syllable, and vice versa. These *context sensitive* effects cannot be discovered by an error segment to target segment match. For example, although a child's production of *pup/cup* looks like a /p/ for /k/ substitution, it is possible that the final /p/ in *cup* is affecting the production of the initial /k/, especially if the initial /k/ is produced correctly in other contexts. Context sensitive analysis abandons the error-to-target matching procedure and instead looks for patterns in errors which might be due to the sequential relationship of sounds and syllables to one another within or across word boundaries.

Assimilation

Assimilation or harmony describes the phenomenon wherein sounds in a word change under the influence of other sounds. When a child said *pup* for *cup*, as mentioned before, it was suspected that the initial /k/ in *cup* was influenced by the final /p/. On reexamining the data, it was found that in words where /p/ occurred, the /p/ influenced other stops and fricatives. For example, the child produced /pɪpɚ/ for *zipper*, /pʌmpɪ/ for *jumping*, /pəpæmʌz/ for *pajamas*, as well as /pʌp/ for *cup*. Thus, the concept of assimilation of adjacent sounds to /p/ explains the child's misarticulations, which might have appeared to be inconsistent substitutions when using substitution analysis.

Assimilation in which an earlier sound influences a later one may occur—for example, /dɑdi/ for *doggy*, and /daɪdɪ/ for *diaper*. We will call this *perseverative assimilation*. Assimilation can also occur in which a later sound influences an earlier one—for example, /gɔg/ for dog. We are calling this *anticipatory assimilation*. Ingram (1976) has described a child's production wherein the liquid becomes a stop through anticipation, as seen in the production of /dɑdo/ for ladder, /tɛto/ for letter, /taɪt/ for *light*, and /tɪp/ for *lamp*. In some cases, the influenced sound is not completely assimilated, but only some of its features are—for example, /gʌk/ for *duck*, where the place feature of a final voiceless stop influences the initial voiced stop, but the initial stop maintains its original voicing feature. Smith (1973) describes his son, who through assimilation produces velar stops in place of fricatives when the target word has a velar stop. Thus /s/ and /θ/ appear as /g/ initially in *thank you, sing,* and *sock;* medially in *glasses;* and finally in *kiss* and *cloth.* This child displays both velar perseveration and anticipation. We would call his overall problem *bidirectional assimilation.* This means that the influence of a sound can operate in both directions. It can influence sounds which occur before as well as after it in a word.

Coalescence

Children's misarticulations which have fewer syllables than the target word may also be the result of syllables coalescing. Menn (1971), for example, found such productions in her two-year-old child, exemplified by /mɛn/ for *melon,* where the single syllable retains /m/ from the initial syllable in the target word and /n/ from the final; /æʃ/ for *radish,* where /æ/ is derived from the initial syllable and /ʃ/ from the final; and /gæʒ/ for *garage,* where /g/ is retained from the initial and /ʒ/ from the final. A more familiar example is sketi/spaghetti, where the /s/ from the first syllable is coalesced with the second syllable.

Transposition

When children change the order of sounds from the target word, we say they are transposing. A common example of transposition is /ækst/ for *asked.* Other examples would be /ful/ for *flu* or /bɛts/ for *best.* Phonological transposition may occur across syllables as well as within syllables. For example, /pɑsgɛti/ for *spaghetti* maintains all the phonemes and syllables in the word but reorders the elements.

Summary

Context sensitive analysis leads to the discovery of how phonetic context influences error patterns. It will reveal patterns of feature or of whole phoneme *perseveration* and *anticipation,* syllable *coalescence,* wherein two syllables are coalesced into one, and *transposition,* wherein elements are reordered.

SYLLABLE STRUCTURE PATTERNS

Words have characteristic syllable structure in that the consonants and vowels must be ordered in prescribed ways and there must be a predetermined number of syllables in a word. Some types of phonological errors reflect a problem with the syllable structure of words rather than with individual phonemes. The earlier example of syllable structure change was described as *coalescence.* Here, the number of syllables are reduced as well as sounds being coalesced across syllables.

Weak-Syllable Deletion

Certain multisyllabic words are often misarticulated by children and adults alike, resulting in familiar forms such as bʌflo/Buffalo, or membɚ/ remember. Children with phonological problems might have an abundance of such errors. Since the sounds omitted will vary with the word (/ri/ in remember; /ə/ in Buffalo), it is inappropriate to characterize the errors by listing them as sound omissions; instead, what is common to all the errors is that the weakest syllable in the word is being dropped, thereby warranting the description of *weak-syllable deletion.* For example, Moskowitz (1970) noted that Erica, a two year old, omits unstressed syllables when they are followed by stressed syllables, as seen in her production of /tɑtɑ/ for *potato,* /dʒæmʌs/ for *pajamas,* /meitos/ for *tomatoes,* and /nɑnɑ/ for *banana.* Ingram (1976) found weak-syllable deletion for a three and one-half year old with a language problem. This was seen in the child's production of /tʌpo/ for *telephone,* /tʌtʌt/ for *elephant,* and /tʌpɑɪ/ for *butterfly.*

Reduplication

Another example of a problem which acts on syllable structure is that of reduplication, often exhibited by normally developing children. The most common form of reduplication occurs when the child repeats the initial consonant and vowel for a two-syllable word, as in *mama* and *dada,* or as in Waterson's (1971) examples of her one and one-half year old son's production of /pupu/ for *pudding,* and /tɪtɪ/ for *kitty.* It would be inaccurate to think of his production of

/tɪtɪ/ as a t/k substitution. Rather, he selects a syllable from the target word and duplicates it.

Restricted Syllable Structure

Sometimes children's words can be described as having a particular consonant-vowel patterning, and this patterning in turn can account for children's sound and syllable omissions. For example, children who say /tɑ/ for *star* and /tɑ/ for *bottle* may be displaying a pattern of producing a consonant + vowel syllable for all their productions. Children who operate in this way may be said to have *strong syllable retention* or consonant-vowel (CV) structuring. We would predict, then, that these children would also reduce blends or consonant clusters to a single consonant—e.g., /tɔɪ/ for *story*—a phenomenon called *cluster reduction* and that they would consistently omit final consonants.

Final consonant omission has been described as the "open syllable" by Renfrew (1966). Panagos (1974) has expanded the open syllable notion to account for consonant reduction in other positions besides final position of the morpheme. In Panagos's example of a child's production of /pi dɪ mi ɪ nɑ/ for *please give me it now,* the initial /pl/ is reduced to /p/ as well as omission of /z/, /v/, and /t/. It can be postulated that this child's phonological system is based on *CV structure,* which would account for both his consonant cluster reduction in *please* and omission of final consonants. We do not know from this sample of his speech what he would do with a two-syllable word. He might reduce the entire word to one CV structure (such as /sɪ/ for *sister*) or preserve the two syllables and make the utterance into a CVCV form as /sɪ tə/ for *sister.* We can indicate the first as CV structuring and the second as CVCV structuring.

Syllable Addition

Finally, changing the syllable structure of words can involve *adding syllables,* as when children add /i/ to a word, producing a diminutive form. While many conceive of these forms as adult-to-baby talk, they can be productive for the child, as was noted in our observation of a one and one-half year old child who said /buki/ for *book,* a form unlikely to have been produced by the adult. The same child, for a one week period, added /jɑ/ to the base form of words designating animate objects, as in /mɑmɪjɑ/ for mommy and /dædijɑ/ for daddy. This again suggests that baby talk to children is not necessarily how this child learned the syllable addition but that the addition is a productive phonological rule in that she applied it to particular forms to generate combinations she had never heard.

Summary

Syllable structure deviations are those which involve changes or restrictions in the consonant-vowel relationships in a word. They can take several forms: *coalescence, weak-syllable deletion, reduplication, syllable addition,* and restriction of sounds within a syllable as evidenced by *restricted consonant-vowel structure, cluster reduction,* and *final consonant omission.*

IDIOSYNCRATIC STRUCTURES

In many of our examples, the target forms are more varied than the child's productions. The similarity with which the morphemes are produced by children suggest that children are taking the adult form and making it fit their own phonological structures. The structural consistencies can be manifested in ways other than those previously mentioned under context sensitive analysis.

Waterson (1971) described five specific structures which her one and one-half year old child used in his word production. These structures had a characteristic number of syllables and consonant-vowel sequences that usually did not correspond to the adult configuration. For example, the child's *nasal structure* included /ŋẽːŋẽ/ for *finger*, /ŋeːŋe/ for *window*, /ŋaŋa/ for *another*, and /ŋaŋo/ for *Randall*.

One seven-year-old child with multiple articulation problems presents a striking example of this phenomenon. He has a *two-syllable structure*, that is, a consonant-vowel-consonant-vowel pattern, with the medial consonant always being the glottal stop (ʔ). This pattern underlies his production of two-syllable words as disparate as *zipper, feather, scissors,* and *fishing*. Their productions in this child's structure become /wʌʔĩ/, /hʌĩʔĩ/, /dʌʔĩ/, and /wʌʔĩ/, respectively. The productions are not determined by the features of the phonemes in the target words, so much as by their bisyllabic configuration; so it is clearly erroneous to assume his productions are phoneme-for-phoneme substitutions.

ANALYZING FOR PHONOLOGICAL STRATEGIES

So far, we have been presenting ways to discover patterns in children's sound production and to cast them as separable phonological rules. Once you have a set of rules formulated, you may find that they seem similar; that is, for example, maybe the effect of cluster reduction, final consonant omission, and weak-syllable deletion all work together to produce a CV structure. These rules can be seen as being in *conspiracy* with one another (Kisseberth, 1973) and can be thought of as rules fulfilling a child's phonological strategy to simplify to a CV form.

The notion of "strategy" is perhaps too rich in the sense that it implies consciousness on the part of the child. We find it a useful way to think about how rules work together for the child and do not intend to imply that the child is thinking in any conscious way about what he or she is doing.

It pays, then, to ask yourself what strategies or general processes may be operating for children you are evaluating. Strategies which have been found by those studying normal children are (1) avoidance of words with unattainable phonological structures, and (2) favorite sound strategies, wherein sounds are used either instead of others or words are learned because they have those favorite sounds in them (Ferguson, 1978).

STEPS TO PHONOLOGICAL
ASSESSMENT

When working with this multifaceted approach to phonology, one can discover regularities in deviations which have traditionally been characterized as inconsistencies. When a child appears to be phonologically inconsistent, further analysis of the results of standard articulation tests as well as language sample analysis can reveal consistencies. Following is a suggested set of steps for carrying out such an analysis. However, not all of the patterned regularities that occur in children's speech production can be discovered through using these steps. They are meant to be suggestive of an analytic approach to phonological analysis rather than an exhaustive list of procedures. Using this approach, clinicians will no doubt discover new kinds of patterns in the speech production of children and become aware that most children are not phonologically inconsistent.

First, when administering an articulation test, it is suggested that the clinician transcribe in narrow transcription the child's production of the whole word rather than recording only the particular sound being tested. Further, if the child is prompted on some items, this should be indicated so that differences between imitated and spontaneously produced utterances can be revealed. Some symbols to facilitate narrow transcription are given in Table 4.2. Other symbols can be found in Fisher and Logemann (1971) or Trager (1972) or can be created by the clinician as the need arises to describe a distinctive production. If the word is produced correctly, it need not be transcribed phonetically but simply marked as correct.

Second, a narrow phonetic transcription of a sample of the errors in a child's spontaneous language should be made so that production of the sounds in connected speech can be displayed. The addition of the adult translation of the child's utterances and notes on the situation can facilitate analysis.

Third, a search for the effects of context on misarticulations should be made by looking for instances of assimilation and coalescence. Look for instances where the sounds affected by assimilation or coalescence are produced correctly and compare the contexts of correct and error productions. These analyses should be done prior to substitution analyses to avoid erroneously classifying misarticulations as substitutions where there is, in fact, a lack of one-to-one correspondence between the child's error and the adult form of the word.

Fourth, examine the errors for syllable structure patterns such as weak-syllable deletions, instances of reduplication, CV or CVCV structuring, or syl-

Table 4.2 Modifiers for Allophones

∩ —lateral	[ŝ]	x —fricative	[b̽]
⊓ —dental	[t̪]	· —stop	[z̩]
◡ —rounded	[r̫]	h —aspirated	[pʰ]
⋔ —unrounded	[w̜]	= —unaspirated	[p⁼]
⌄ —lax	[f̬]	: —lengthened	[aː]
		~ —nasal	[ã]

103

lable additions. For a deviation to be judged as due to syllable structure restriction (CV or CVCV), you should find many examples that fit the pattern. One or two words do not warrant identification of this structure.

Fifth, note instances of whole word configurations that appear to have distinctive elements in common, such as a characteristic syllable structure or sound or feature patterning which depart in unusual ways from the adult form. By listing these together, a child's idiosyncratic structures might be discovered.

Specific examples of possible context sensitive, syllable structure, and idiosyncratic errors should be accumulated in lists in order to discover the existence and strength of the patterns. The following list offers such an organization.

> Context sensitive errors
>> Perseveration
>> Anticipation
>> Coalescence
> Syllable structure errors
>> Coalescence
>> Weak-syllable deletion
>> Reduplication
>> Restricted syllable structure
> Idiosyncratic structures

Sixth, an inventory of what sounds the child has can be taken by marking them in the appropriate columns of a phonemic inventory chart such as Figure 4.2. For such an *inventory analysis*, mark the sound if it occurs—even if it does not match the target word. For example, if an /s/ is made in the initial position when the child says *sue* for *shoe*, place an E in the prevocalic /s/ column. If it occurs in the correct context, place a check in the column. Similar charts can be made for consonant clusters and for vowels. Consonant clusters can be grouped by the elements they contain, and correct and error productions can be compared.

Table 4.3 Substitution Analysis

	PREVOCALIC	INTERVOCALIC	POSTVOCALIC
Manner			
Stopping			
Fricating			
Nasalizing			
Other			
Place			
Fronting			
Backing			
Other			
Voice			
Devoicing			
Voicing			

Seventh, a *substitution analysis* can be done on the remaining errors by entering misarticulations in a chart such as Table 4.3. Here the specific occurrences of manner errors, place errors, and voicing errors are listed together. Some will involve more than one feature in which case it is entered in several places.

The advantage of a structural analysis such as the multifaceted one presented in this chapter is that remediation can be geared to work simultaneously on all the sounds entailed in a particular pattern. For example, McReynolds and Huston (1971) have suggested that a child who has a stopping problem in which he or she substitutes stops for fricatives be taught the feature of continuancy. The notion is that all fricatives be worked on at once. Before this

		Prevocalic	Intervocalic	Postvocalic
Stops	p			
	b			
	t			
	d			
	k			
	g			
Fricatives	hw			
	f			
	v			
	θ			
	ð			
	s			
	z			
	ʃ			
	ʒ			
	h			
Affricates	tʃ			
	dʒ			
Glides	w			
	j			
Liq.	r			
	l			
Nasals	m			
	n			
	ŋ			

Figure 4.2

assumption of equal teachability of all fricatives is accepted, we suggest the child be given a stimulability test, wherein he or she is given cues for producing the new sounds. A procedure for approaching stimulability within the multifaceted phonological framework has been developed where patterns of sounds are examined for their amenability to correction (Duchan, Holt, and Ritter, 1979).

EXERCISES

1. Match the category in the left column with the deviation in the right column. Some deviations match more than one category.

Context sensitive patterns
___ perseveration of alveolars
___ anticipation of velars
___ coalescence
___ bidirectional alveolar assimilation

a) mɪtɚ/mister
b) gɔg /dog
c) dɔd /dog
d) lɪŋ /lightning

Syllable structure patterns
___ coalescence
___ weak-syllable deletion
___ reduplication

e) pei /paper
f) kʌ /cup
g) resɚ /eraser

Restricted CV patterning
___ cluster reduction
___ CV structure
___ final consonant omission
___ CVCV Structure

h) pæpæ /pacifier
i) wɑwɑ /water
j) tɔ /story
k) nɪstet /mistake

2. Identify the deviations as place, manner, or voicing substitutions, or a combination of these, or none of these.

a) s/ʃ
b) m/b
c) t/s
d) nasalization
e) w/m
f) velar anticipation
g) f/v
h) r/l
i) gliding
j) g/all stops
k) k/m

l) weak syllable deletion
m) b/p
n) cluster reduction
o) velar perseveration
p) tʃ/ʃ
q) dædæ/daddy
r) n/ŋ
s) bidirectional alveolar assimilation
t) ð/s
u) ð/voiced fricatives
v) pos/police

3. Identify one pattern which describes all the deviations in each of the examples that follow:

a) fef/safe
   fɛf/chef
   fif/thief
   nɑɪf/knife

   sen/sane
   guf/goof
   gofɚ/gopher
   fef/face

b) dædɚ/ladder   tɛt/let
   dɛd/red   gæg/rag
   dɪd/read   wægn̩/wagon
   wɪndo/window   dalɚ/dollar
   saɪd/side   dor/door
   tatn̩/rotten   ræŋ/rang
   torɪd/torrid   tɛlɪŋ/telling

c) tar/star   kaɪ/sky
   pun/spoon   slip/sleep
   blu/blue   flaʊɚ/flower
   trit/street   fæt/fast

4. How would a child with the following patterns say the "Twinkle, Twinkle Little Star" poem? Fill in the changes that would occur for each line of the poem. A few have been done for you. If you need more specification of the pattern, indicate how you would specify it.

	TWINKLE	TWINKLE	LITTLE	STAR
cluster reduction	tɪŋkl̩			
CV structure			lɪ	
bidirectional alveolar assimilation	twɪntl̩			
w for all semivowels			wɪtow	

	HOW	I	WONDER	WHAT	YOU	ARE
cluster reduction						
CV structure						
bidirectional alveolar assimilation						
w for all semivowels						

	UP	ABOVE	THE	WORLD	SO	HIGH
cluster reduction						
CV structure						
bidirectional alveolar assimilation						
w for all semivowels						

LIKE	A	DIAMOND	IN	THE	SKY

cluster
reduction

CV structure

bidirectional
alveolar
assimilation

w for all
semivowels

REFERENCES

BARTON, D.   The Role of Perception in the Acquisition of Speech. Ph.D. dissertation, University of London, 1976.

CARTER, A.   Prespeech Meaning Relations: An Outline of One Infant's Sensorimotor Morpheme Development, in *Language Acquisition,* eds. P. Fletcher and M. Garman. Cambridge, England: Cambridge University Press, 1979, 71–92.

CHOMSKY, N., AND M. HALLE.   *The Sound Pattern of English.* New York: Harper & Row, Pub., 1968.

DANILOFF, R., AND L. MOLL.   Coarticulation of Lip Rounding, *Journal of Speech and Hearing Research,* 11, 1968, 707–21.

DORE, J., M. FRANKLIN, R. MILLER, AND A. RAMER.   Transitional Phenomena in Early Language Acquisition, *Journal of Child Language,* 3, 1976, 13–28.

DUCHAN, J., L. HOLT, AND D. RITTER.   Phonological Approach to Stimulability Testing. Paper presented at New York State Speech and Hearing Association, April 1979.

FERGUSON, C.   Learning to Pronounce: The Earliest Stages of Phonological Development in the Child, in *Communicative and Cognitive Abilities: Early Behavioral Assessment,* eds. F. Minifie and L. Lloyd. Baltimore, Md.: University Park Press, 1978, pp. 273–97.

FERGUSON, C., AND C. FARWELL.   Words and Sounds in Early Language Acquisition, *Language,* 51, 1975, 419–39.

FISHER, H., AND J. LOGEMANN.   *The Fisher-Logemann Test of Articulation Competence.* Boston: Houghton Mifflin Co., 1971.

FLETCHER, P., AND M. GARMAN.   *Language Acquisition.* Cambridge, England: Cambridge University Press, 1979.

GARNICA, O.   The Development of Phonemic Speech Perception, in *Cognition and the Acquisition of Language,* ed. T. E. Moore. New York: Academic Press, 1973, pp. 215–22.

HALLIDAY, M.   *Learning How to Mean: Explorations in the Development of Language.* London: Edward Arnold, 1975.

HOOPER, J.   *An Introduction to Natural Generative Phonology.* New York: Academic Press, 1976.

HYMAN, L.   *Phonology: Theory and Analysis.* New York: Holt, Rinehart & Winston, 1975.

INGRAM D. *Phonological Disability in Children.* London: Elsevier North-Holland, 1976.

JAKOBSON, R. *Child Language, Aphasia and Phonological Universals.* The Hague: Mouton, 1972.

KISSEBERTH, C. The Interaction of Phonological Rules and the Polarity of Language. Mimeographed. Indiana University Linguistics Club, 1973.

LIBERMAN, A. The Grammar of Speech and Language, *Cognitive Psychology,* 1, 1970, 301–23.

LUND, N., AND J. DUCHAN. Phonological Analysis: A Multifaceted Approach, *British Journal of Disorders of Communication,* 13, 1978, 119–26.

MCDONALD, E. *A Deep Test of Articulation.* Pittsburgh: Stannix House, Inc., 1968.

MACNEILAGE, D., AND J. DE CLERK. On the Motor Control of Coarticulation in CVC Monosyllables, *Journal of the Acoustical Society of America,* 45, 1969, 1217–33.

MCREYNOLDS, L., AND D. ENGMANN. *Distinctive Feature Analysis of Misarticulation.* Baltimore, Md.: University Park Press, 1975.

MCREYNOLDS, L., AND K. HUSTON. Distinctive Feature Generalization in Articulation Training, *Journal of Speech and Hearing Disorders,* 36, 1971, 155–66.

MENN, L. Phonotactic Rules in Beginning Speech, *Lingua,* 26, 1971, 225–51.

MENN, L., AND S. HASELKORN. Now You See It, Now You Don't: Tracing the Development of Communicative Competence. Unpublished paper, Boston University, 1977.

MENYUK, P., AND L. MENN. Early Strategies for the Perception and Production of Words and Sounds, in *Language Acquisition: Studies in First Language Development,* eds. P. Fletcher and M. Garman. Cambridge, England: Cambridge University Press, 1979.

MORSE, P. A. The Discrimination of Speech and Non-Speech Stimuli in Early Infancy, *Journal of Experimental Child Psychology,* 14, 1972, 477–92.

MOSKOWITZ, A. The Two-Year-Old Stage in the Acquisition of English Phonology, *Language,* 46, 1970, 426–41.

PANAGOS, L. Persistence of the Open Syllable Reinterpreted as a Symptom of a Language Disorder, *Journal of Speech and Hearing Disorders,* 39, 1974, 23–31.

PARKER, F. Distinctive Features in Speech Pathology: Phonology or Phonemes, *Journal of Speech and Hearing Disorders,* 41, 1976, 23–39.

RENFREW, C. Persistence of the Open Syllable in Defective Articulation, *Journal of Speech and Hearing Disorders,* 31, 1966, 370–73.

SCHANE, S. *Generative Phonology.* Englewood Cliffs, N.J.: Prentice-Hall, 1973.

SCHVACHKIN, N. The Development of Phonemic Speech Perception in Early Childhood, in *Studies of Child Language Development,* eds. C. Ferguson and D. I. Slobin. New York: Holt, Rinehart & Winston, 1973, pp. 91–127.

SHRIBERG, L., AND J. KWIATKOWSKI. *Natural Process Analysis of Continuous Speech Samples.* New York: John Wiley, 1980.

SMITH N. *The Acquisition of Phonology: A Case Study.* Cambridge, England: Cambridge University Press, 1973.

STAMPE, D. On The Acquisition of Phonetic Representation. Papers from the Fifth Regional Meeting of the Chicago Linguistic Society, 1969, Chicago, Illinois.

TEMPLIN, M.   *Certain Language Skills in Children.* Minneapolis, Minn.: University of Minnesota Press, 1957.

TRAGER, G.   *Language and Languages.* San Francisco: Chandler Publishing Company, 1972.

WATERSON, N.   Child Phonology: A Prosodic Review, *Journal of Linguistics,* 7, 1971, 179–211.

WEINER, F.   *Phonological Process Analysis.* Baltimore, Md.: University Park Press, 1978.

5

Morphology

There are a set of words, usually little words, and a set of word endings that convey subtle meaning and serve special grammatical and pragmatic functions in language. These words have been called *grammatical morphemes* to distinguish them from the more direct meaning-carrying words, the *lexical morphemes*. This distinction can be seen by comparing two segments such as "rabbits hop" and "the rabbit hopped." The major elements of meaning are the same in these two sentences, namely the entity "rabbit" and the action "hop." What distinguishes these utterances in meaning is the variations of the particular words expressed—"rabbit" can refer to one or several animals, depending on whether the singular or plural grammatical morpheme is chosen; "hop" can be in the present or the past, as indicated by the grammatical morpheme marking tense.

The study of the meanings of lexical morphemes has been called *semantics,* while the study of the more subtle carriers of meaning has been called *morphology.* Morphology is closely related to semantics—a particular meaning may be conveyed by a word in one language and by a grammatical morpheme in another language. Even within a language we have some choice as to how to express some meanings, as can be seen by comparing "Tomorrow I go" with "I will go." The future is more central to the point being made in the first expression and is conveyed with the lexical morpheme "tomorrow"; in the second expression, the future is in its less focused manifestation, with the grammatical morpheme "will." Likewise, the concept of plurality is part of the lexical meaning of words like "two" or "bunch" which have central focus. It can also be expressed by the less emphasized plural grammatical morpheme.

The function of some of these grammatical morphemes has been described pragmatically as a "keeping track" function, or a point-sharing function (Bybee, 1980; Talmy, 1980; MacWhinney, 1981). That is to say, speakers use certain grammatical morphemes to remind or inform their listeners about what is already established, or where one is located in the discourse, or what nuance of meaning is being conveyed. At the same time, the speakers can go ahead and tell their listeners through lexical morphemes the main or focused part of their ideas.

Our discussion of grammatical morphology will de-emphasize this point-sharing function and instead center on helping you recognize grammatical morphemes and understand the way the English grammatical system dictates their use.

We have organized this chapter to reflect developmental progressions, since this is how morphology is generally presented in the literature. When we move into analysis, however, we recommend analyzing children's morphology according to word classes, while keeping usual developmental sequence in mind. The word classes we will consider in this chapter are nouns, verbs, adjectives, and adverbs, because these are the words that can change their form to give grammatical information.

Nouns are generally easy to recognize by their ability to be modified by an article (*the book*) and/or be made plural (*books*) or possessive (*book's cover*).

Verbs can be categorized in a number of ways. We choose to distinguish among three types of verbs.

Lexical verbs: These add something to the content of the sentence; they specify the action or state of the sentence subject (*run, give*). There are subcategories of lexical verbs which we will discuss under syntax.

Copulas: These are forms of *be* and add no content information to the sentence (*am, is, are, was, were*).

Auxiliary verbs: These accompany a lexical verb to indicate tense or mood (*can* sleep, *is* going, *might* eat).

Adjectives are descriptive words that can either precede a noun (a *good* man) or follow certain verbs (he is *good*).

Adverbs are typically more difficult to identify, so we have included a discussion of types of adverbs and how to recognize them, as well as presenting the morphological variations.

The morphological system is not mastered all at once. Some grammatical morphemes begin to appear early in development, generally about the time children begin to put three words together. Others are typically not fully mastered until well into the school years. Further, a given morpheme is not suddenly learned. Longitudinal studies of normally developing children have traced the acquisition of individual morphemes over periods of several months, from the time they first occur until they are used consistently. Therefore, one would expect to find that children are not perfectly consistent in their use of grammatical morphemes—some will likely be mastered, others will not yet have emerged, and still others will be present in some instances and absent, or incorrect, in others. Structural analysis will be utilized to specify the rules that account for these various occurrences.

The most impressive evidence that children do in fact formulate rules of language usage is their tendency to apply these rules more broadly than adults do. This is particularly apparent in morphology. Children who say "goed" for *went* or "childs" for *children* are demonstrating their knowledge of English rules for past tense and plural formation. They show their recognition that a verb plus *-ed* indicates past action, while a noun plus *-s* means more than one of the nouns named. What they have failed to recognize at this point is that "go" is an irregular verb and "child" is an irregular noun and thus do not conform to the regular rule. Instead, they apply the rule for regular vocabulary items and "overregularize" in their productions. These should be seen as "good" errors at early stages of development, since they show a child is formulating a morphological rule system. Once a rule is well established, children begin to be aware that there are exceptions to the rule, and thus begins their distinction between regular and irregular classes of nouns and verbs.

EARLY APPEARING GRAMMATICAL MORPHEMES

Roger Brown (1973) has presented an extensive discussion of fourteen morphemes and the course of their acquisition by normally developing children. Twelve of the fourteen are presented here in the order they typically appear, but it must be expected that a given child's acquisition may differ somewhat from this sequence. The prepositions *in* and *on* are not included here as they are in Brown's list but will be discussed with other prepositions in Chapter 7.

1. Present progressive verb (*-ing*). To indicate that an activity is in progress and is of temporary duration, the adult English speaker adds two parts to the verb—an auxiliary verb and the *-ing* ending to the lexical or main verb; that is, we distinguish between a continuing or repeated activity ("I play tennis") and an actual occurrence of an activity ("I *am* play*ing* tennis") by adding two grammatical morphemes. Children express the progressive verb first by using only the *-ing* ending without the auxiliary verb, resulting in statements like "he sleeping."

2. Plural noun (*-s*). There is no grammatical morpheme to indicate the singular form of a noun so an uninflected noun is generally taken to be singular in form. The plural ending *-s* on regular nouns is an early means of making the distinction between one instance of an object (*dog*) and more than one (*dogs*). Learning all the exceptions to the regular plural rule takes considerably longer and is largely dependent on the frequency of occurrence of the irregular plural. The overregularized "childs" will change to "children" long before "indexes" becomes "indices."

3. Past tense—irregular. Irregular past tense verbs in English, unlike irregular plural nouns, are much more frequent than their regular counterparts. These include past tense verbs that are formed in ways other than by adding the *-ed* ending to the present tense of the lexical verb. Most common verbs in English are irregular and have wide variability in their formation—for example, *go-went, have-had, think-thought, run-ran*. It is not surprising, therefore, that children first learn some irregular past tense verbs before they discover the rule for forming regular past tense.

4. Possessive noun (*'s*). Children first express the possessive relationship between two nouns through word order—the first noun is clearly the possessor and the second the possessed when the child says "Daddy chair." Adding the grammatical morpheme to the first noun ("Daddy's chair") thus is really adding redundant information. Frequently possession will be expressed with pronouns (*my, your*) before the possessive noun form is mastered.

5. Uncontractible copula. The "be" verb has three present tense forms—*am, are,* and *is*—and two past tense forms—*was* and *were*. These forms can function grammatically in two ways: as a *main verb* or as an *auxiliary verb*. When a form of *be* is the main verb (or only verb) in a clause, it is called the copula. In the sentence "John is tall," *is* functions as the copula—it is the only verb in the sentence. In the sentence "John is sleeping," *is* functions as the auxiliary verb and *sleep* is the main verb that expresses the action. The course of development of these two types of verbs differs. The first type to appear is generally the copula, but only in those contexts where the copula cannot be contracted. Our distinction between contractible and uncontractible forms is made on the basis of what would be permissible in adult language. When asked, for example, "Who is hungry?" the answer must be "I am," and not the contracted form "I'm." Likewise, in asking the question "What is it?" it would not be grammatical to use the contraction "What's it?" Thus, in these cases the copula is said to be uncontractible.

6. Articles (*a* and *the*). It is often difficult to tell from children's pronunciation whether they are producing the indefinite article ("I want *a* cookie"—meaning any one of several will do) or the definite article ("I want *the* cookie"—meaning the last one there on the plate). It is quite likely that their first articles are undifferentiated, with the definite-indefinite distinction coming later, and hence the phonetic similarity. Still later, they learn the phonological distinction between the use of *a* and *an*.

7. Past tense verb-regular (*-ed*). When children learn the regular past tense rule and form verbs such as *walked* and *wanted,* they frequently can be observed to apply incorrectly their new rule to irregular verbs, resulting in forms like *goed, falled,* and *satted.* This may appear to be a regression, since correct irregular past tense forms appeared earlier. As we said in the preceding section, however, these overregularized forms instead are evidence that the child has discovered a regularity in the language, indicating a growing sophistication as a language producer. Later comes the discovery of which verbs fit into the regular pattern and which do not. Correct irregular verbs again become more consistent.

8-9. Third person singular verb—regular (*-s*) and irregular. Although this is an inflection of the verb, its presence is governed by the person and number of the subject noun. In the present tense, verbs in English are not inflected except when the subject is third person (i.e., not *I* or *you*) and singular. Thus, we add the verb inflection in "He jog*s*," but not in "I jog" or "They jog." No comparable inflection is added in past tense. Since the number and person is generally clear from the subject, this inflection typically conveys redundant information. (Exceptions are cases such as "The sheep eats," wherein the same noun form expresses singular or plural.) There are only a few English verbs that form the third person singular in an irregular way. Most notable are *do-does* and *have-has.*

10. Uncontractible auxiliary. The only auxiliary verbs considered by

Brown are the forms of *be*. As noted previously, if these verbs are the main verb in a clause, they are copulas; if they precede another verb in the *-ing* form, they are auxiliaries.[1] Uncontractible auxiliaries, like uncontractible copulas, are judged by the possibility of contraction. Uncontractible auxiliaries are most frequent in past tense—e.g., the contraction of "She was" to "She's" would be unacceptable because it would lose the element of past tense.

11. Contractible copula. Most present tense copulas are contractible whether or not they are actually in a contracted form. Thus, both "*he's* big" and "he *is* big" are considered contractible. It can be noted that contractible copulas are unnecessary to convey the meaning of a sentence.

12. Contractible auxiliary. The same observations can be made regarding contractible auxiliary verbs as were made regarding contractible copulas. Both "I'm eating" and "I *am* eating" would be considered contractible auxiliaries. They differ from the copula verbs by their relation to another main verb in the clause.

OTHER GRAMMATICAL MORPHEMES

These morphemes have not had the systematic study of the morphemes detailed by Brown. Thus, we know less about their order of acquisition and course of development. They generally are later appearing than those already discussed and indicate the child's increased facility with unscrambling the myriad regularities and irregularities of the language.

1. Perfective verb (*have* and past participle). *Have* as an auxiliary requires the past participle form of the main verb. This is referred to as the *perfective* tense. The past participle of most verbs is identical to the past tense. Others are formed with either the present or past tense verb plus the *-n* ending. Still others have a root that differs in the vowel from both the present and past tenses and may or may not have an *-n* ending. These options are illustrated in Table 5.1.

Understandably, it takes considerable time for children to master this system, and regularities in their errors can be observed. Participles may all initially be treated as identical to past tense (e.g., "I have went"). Then, when the *-n* participle ending is discovered, it may be applied to the past tense, producing forms such as *aten, gaven, roden, sawn,* and *wroten.* Zwicky (1970) observed this sequence with exceptions being phonologically determined in that the participles that did not conform involved vowel changes between present and past tense (*sing, sang; blow, blew*). Other patterns may emerge for other children.[2]

2. Passive verb (*get* or *be* and past participle). Sentences are said to be in

[1]The only exception to the rule that *be* auxiliaries take *-ing* forms is the passive form, which will be discussed in the next section.

[2]The idiomatic "have got" appears to be increasingly common in adult speech along with the use of *got* as a present tense verb in place of *have* as a main verb. The distinction between these verbs may eventually disappear in "good" English, as have distinctions between *will* and *shall* and possibly between *can* and *may*. While teachers and clinicians may not be ready to accept "I got it" as grammatical, it probably would be inappropriate to view it as a language-learning problem.

Table 5.1 Past Participles

ROOT			SUFFIX			
Present	Past	Vowel Changed	-ed	-n	Unmarked	Perfective
walk	walk		ed			have walked
eat	eat			-n		have eaten
run	run				✓	have run
choose		chose		-n		have chosen
feed		fed			✓	have fed
ride		ridd-		-n		have ridden
ring		rung			✓	have rung

the passive voice (as opposed to the active voice) when the action of the verb is not being carried out by the referent for the grammatical subject of the sentence—e.g., "The letter will be written by me"; "The window got broken." Clearly, the letter and the window are not the actors in these sentences but rather the passive recipients of action. Passive verbs are formed with either a *get* or *be* verb followed by the past participle form of the main verb. An actor is implied and in some cases specified with *by,* as in the first sentence above.

3. Modal verbs. Some auxiliary verbs have been identified as modal verbs, in that they indicate something about the attitude or mood of the speaker. Lyons (1968) has described three such moods that are conveyed with modal verbs. The earliest mood to be expressed by children is *wish or intention,* which appears first as "gonna" or "wanna." Later, children indicate their future intentions through use of "will" or "shall" as modal verbs. The second mood expressed is *certainty and possibility.* Typically, this appears first as the negative "can't." Later, "can" develops, followed by the expressions of various degrees of possibility: "may," "might," "could," "would." The last mood to be expressed is *necessity and obligation.* Early forms that indicate necessity are "gotta" and "hafta." Later, the child learns "must" and "should" and "ought."

Verbs that involve more than one auxiliary verb convey increasingly subtle shades of meaning and develop slowly. These forms always involve a *have* or *be* auxiliary, or both, along with a modal auxiliary. The English auxiliary verb system has been described by Chomsky (1957) as

$$C + (M) + (have + en) + (be + ing) + verb$$

This specifies the order in which various auxiliaries can occur, with *M* representing modal verbs, *have + en* indicating the perfective form, and *be + ing* indicating the progressive form. The *C* indicates tense and number, which is expressed by the first occurring verb. The items in parentheses do not all have to be included before the main verb, but those present must occur in this order. To illustrate, consider the following sentences where *C* represents present tense and singular number:

He runs	C + verb
	—no auxiliary verb
	—tense and number indicated by main verb
He is running	C + be + ing + verb
	—tense and number indicated by *be* auxiliary
	—*ing* attached to next verb (*run*)
He has been running	C + have + en + be + ing + verb
	—tense and number indicated by *have* auxiliary
	—*en* attached to next verb (*be*)
He may have been running	C + M + have + en + be + ing + verb
	—tense and number indicated by modal

INFINITIVES AS MODAL VERBS   As we have indicated, some of the earliest occurring modal verbs are forms such as "gonna," "wanna," "hafta," and "gotta." If we expand these forms for an "adult" translation, we find we have the infinitive form following another verb:

> Going to eat
> Want to play
> Have to go
> Got to do it

The first verb in the infinitive form functions in the same way as the early contracted forms—that is, to modulate the meaning of the lexical verb. Because of this similarity of function, and because it is frequently difficult to judge which form the child is using, we include these verb + infinitive constructions as modals. In some cases, this modal also includes a *to be* auxiliary, as in

> I *am going to* take it.
> You*'re supposed to* help me.

These modal forms are not to be confused with infinitives that do not occur after verbs, as in

> I told the boy *to eat* his dinner.
> *To slide* on the snow is fun.
> I'm afraid *to look*.

or infinitives that express an action distinct from the verb that precedes the infinitive.

> I stopped *to watch*.
> He helped *to put* out the fire.

4. *Do* forms. *Do*, like *have* and the *be* forms, can either be a main verb in a sentence ("I do the dishes") or occur along with another verb ("I do run fast"; "Do you like it?"). When it occurs in a statement along with another verb, the *do* form acts to emphasize the speaker's affirmation of the statement ("I *do* run fast" vs. "I *don't* run fast"). This is called the *emphatic do.* In other cases, it acts as an auxiliary verb but does not convey any grammatical information or mood, as do true auxiliaries. Rather, it "stands in" to form questions ("Do you like it?") when there is no auxiliary in the underlying statement. We call this the *dummy do* to distinguish it from true auxiliaries and will discuss it further in relation to questions. *Do* forms in both statements and questions can take negative forms (don't) and can be inflected for tense (did) and person (does).

5. Adjective forms. We will discuss ordering of adjectives in noun phrases under syntax, but it is appropriate to include adjective forms in our discussion of morphology. While many adjectives have only one form, some can take the comparative (*-er*) and superlative (*-est*) forms. Other are modified by including the adverbs *more* and *most*. A small class of adjectives changes completely in the comparative and superlative forms (*good, better, best; less, little, least*).

For the most part, choice of an adjective form is lexical rather than grammatical—that is, saying "The big girl" instead of "The bigger girl" is not grammatically incorrect but rather reflects something about the feature of the situation the speaker is focusing on. The only context where these forms are grammatically required appears to be with "than" in the form "I am _____ than you," which calls for the comparative, and with "of all," where the construction calls for the superlative, as in "I am the _____ of all." Errors on adjective forms consist of applying endings to words that should have the adverb ("beautifuler," for "more beautiful") or to the irregular adjective ("gooder" for "better"). Occasionally, children mark the form twice, sometimes for increased emphasis, as in "It got hotter and more hotter."

6. Adverb forms. Adverbs are described in a multitude of ways by different grammarians. In all descriptions, several types of modifiers are grouped together in this class. Rather than attempting to define adverbs at this point, we offer a structural approach borrowed from Strang (1969) to help the clinician recognize them. We will then discuss the morphology of adverbs. An adverb can be identified as a stressed form that is not an object noun and that can immediately follow a verb—that is, an adverb can fill in the slot in the form "I ran _____." It can be seen that a variety of word types can go in this position—for example, time indicators (*yesterday*), place indicators (*outside*), manner indicators (*fast*), number indicators (*twice*), and degree indicators (*all the way*).

It should be noted that adverbs do not *have* to occur in this frame, but rather they *can* occur in this frame. They can occur in other positions ("Quickly I ran") or with verbs that have object nouns ("I rode my bike quickly"), but they can be recognized as adverbs by their capacity to fit the test frame ("I ran quickly in the race"; "I rode quickly on my bike"). Adverbs generally do not occur after copula verbs except if they are locations ("I am *home*"), or if they modify an adjective ("I am *very* tired").

Most adverbs have only one form—that is, they are always uninflected and do not have variable morphological forms. Some of these *invariable* adverbs have no other function. They are always adverbs; *now, often, seldom, perhaps, still, once, twice,* and *always* are examples of this type. Other invariables can have other functions and are adverbs only if they modify a verb, adjective, or other adverb (or fit into our test slot). Thus, *yesterday* is an adverb when it modifies the verb by stating the time of action ("I went yesterday") but not when it serves as an identity with a copula ("Yesterday was Monday").

Other invariable adverbs are derived from other word classes by addition of prefixes or suffixes. The most common of these *derived* forms are the adjective + *-ly* forms (e.g., *timidly, carefully*). Adverbs are also derived from combinations of *some-, any-, every-,* and *no-,* with *how, way, where,* and *time.*

Only the *variable* adverbs have different morphological forms. These express comparisons and have forms that correspond to the comparative and superlative adjective forms (*faster, fastest; better, best*) as well as the uninflected form (*fast, well*).

Learning to use adverbs is a complex activity and probably does not develop as a unitary system. We shall discuss adverbial construction further in relation to syntactic and semantic development.

DOING MORPHOLOGICAL ANALYSIS

Of all the systems involved in language, the morphological system is the easiest for the clinician to assess. Although we have generally argued against using a checklist approach to assessment, this seems to be the most efficient way to proceed with morphological analysis. The reason for our shift on this point is that there is a finite set of grammatical morphemes that modulates the meaning of the major word classes. Children we have seen either use these inflections—correctly or incorrectly—or do not use them; they do not create new inflections or appear to create new categories of information to express with inflections. This is not to say that their use of grammatical morphemes is necessarily consistent, either within their samples or with adult usage. We have not found the need, however, to go beyond the description of conventional morphology to capture children's productions. There is always the possibility, of course, that the next child we see will be the exception and will present a new challenge for structural analysis.

The Children

Morphological analysis is most appropriately carried out with children who have relatively intact language systems, since inflections are essentially refinements in conveying content. If a child has no syntactic structure, that is, if he or she is using primarily one- and two-word utterances, we would not be concerned with morphology. Likewise, if a child shows pragmatic problems, such as echoing or inappropriate dialogue structure, morphology would take on lesser importance in terms of interference with communication. Finally, if a child has severe phonological problems, morphological competence again would be of secondary importance, since most inflections would probably not be produced intelligibly even if they were part of the child's linguistic structure.

The Sample

We generally make a running transcript of a naturalistic language sample for morphological analysis, using standard orthography. If only one or a few inflections are of interest, it is possible to do a listing transcript by listening to a sample for the specific structure(s). Since the grammatical morphemes used in any sample may be restricted by the topic or speech event involved, it is usually necessary to use elicitation procedures to get evidence of the child's competence with a wide variety of inflections. These techniques may be incorporated into the initial sample for assessment, as when the clinician asks questions or shifts topics to elicit particular structures. Or, further elicitation techniques may be used after analysis of the initial sample, with the techniques designed to elicit structures that were not sampled.

The Analysis

Typically the clinician is interested in assessing the child's entire repertoire of grammatical morphemes. It is helpful, then, to analyze each utterance for presence or absence of grammatical morphemes in obligatory contexts. A worksheet, such as Table 5.2, can be helpful for utterance analysis. From worksheets we can summarize the morphological regularities displayed in the sample. A summary chart, such as that found in Table 5.3, can be helpful in assuring that the most common inflections have been considered. We feel it is preferable to summarize according to the major word classes rather than by developmental order. We suggest the following protocol for use with this table (you will find adaptations and short cuts that work for you as you work through several analyses):

1. Structures that are consistently correct or absent and occur at least three times in the sample are simply noted as correct (√) or absent (X).
2. Exceptions or inconsistencies are noted by listing the specific words in question.
3. Consistent errors are described (e.g., overregularizes irregular verbs).
4. If a structure is sampled less than three times, or if it takes several

Table 5.2 Morphology Worksheet

For each utterance, identify grammatical morphemes that are present by underlining them. Indicate those missing or incorrect with a slash (/).

UTTERANCE	MORPHEMES PRESENT	DEVIATION
1. /Boy/runnin	progressive	article, auxiliary
2. I wanna apple	article ?	
3. /Dog's hungry	copula (is)	article
4. I wanna go in/car	modal (wanna)	article
5. /Boy was sleepin	auxiliary (was) progressive	article
6. I needs mittens	plural	third person singular (overregularizing)

Table 5.3 Summary of the Morphological Forms of the Major Word Classes

NOUN FORMS	VERB FORMS	ADJECTIVE FORMS	ADVERB FORMS
singular	Lexical verbs:	uninflected	uninflected
plural	uninflected	comparative	comparative
possessive	third person singular	superlative	superlative
definite	simple past—regular		
indefinite	irregular		
	With auxiliary verbs:		
	progressive (be + ing)		
	auxiliaries used		
	auxiliaries omitted		
	perfective (have + en)		
	passive (get or be + en)		
	modals		
	do forms		
	Copula verbs:		
	present (am, are, is)		
	past (was, were)		

different forms, such as the copula, auxiliaries, and modals, the individual words are listed.

5. If the structure is not called for anyplace in the sample, indicate not sampled (NS).

The clinician should pay particular attention to structures that are inconsistent. There may be regularities that are not immediately apparent. We suggest looking at various contexts to determine if the variable performance can be explained by such differences as phonetic context, syntactic complexity, intent of the child, materials presented, type of event that is going on, or different listeners.

The results of sentence-imitation testing or other elicitation procedures, or of a subsequent natural sample can be included on this chart (with appropriate designation, such as entry in a different color) to aid in the comparison of the child's performance in a different task, in a different setting, or at a different time.

EXERCISES

1. Match the utterance in the first column with the description in the second column that best describes the morphological error.

_____ I see mommy bike.	a) Missing copula
_____ Who has tooken my book?	b) Overregularized past
_____ Boys running.	c) Two comparative morphemes
_____ I doed it.	d) Incorrect stem for participle

_____ See all the childs!
_____ The girl run fast.
_____ Drive fastlier.
_____ I tired.
_____ I might could do it.
_____ Mine's more better than yours.

e) Two modal verbs
f) Overregularized plural
g) Missing possessive
h) Missing auxiliary
i) Incorrect adverb form
j) Missing third person singular morpheme

2. For each statement indicate the grammatical morphemes that are present and correct and those that are missing or in error. To begin, _underline_ correct forms and indicate with a slash (/) incorrect or missing morphemes.

PRESENT AND CORRECT   MISSING   ERROR

a) I gonna buy big dog.
b) She was there when we was.
c) Jimmy eated all my Cheerios.
d) Daddy picking up baby toy.
e) I walked really fast.
f) Balloon gots big and big and big.
g) I runned over it with bulldozer.
h) I hafta get some new marbles.
i) Red car drives on road.
j) I could had do it.

3. Summarize the morphological patterns displayed in the sentences in exercise 2. Indicate which forms are present and correct (√), which are missing (X), and which error forms are present. Indicate forms not sampled (NS) as well. List the specific words used for forms sampled less than three times.

NOUN FORMS

plural regular
plural irregular
possessive
articles

VERB FORMS

Lexical
    third person singular
    past regular
    past irregular
Auxiliary + verb
    progressive
    perfective
    modals
    do form
Copula
    am
    are
    is
    was
    were

ADJECTIVE FORMS

uninflected
comparative
superlative

ADVERB FORMS

uninflected
comparative
superlative

4. Most grammatical morphemes have a semantic basis in that they convey meaning. Try to determine for each of the grammatical morphemes in exercise 3 the specific concept that the child must know in order to understand the morpheme. Which grammatical morphemes do not seem to have semantic meaning or are redundant?

REFERENCES

Brown, R.   *A First Language.* Cambridge, Mass.: Harvard University Press, 1973.

Bybee, J.   What's a Possible Inflectional Category? unpublished manuscript, SUNY/Buffalo, 1980.

Chomsky, N.   *Syntactic Structures.* The Hague: Mouton, 1957.

Chomsky, N.   *Language and Mind.* New York: Harcourt Brace Jovanovich, 1968.

Lyons, J.   *Introduction to Theoretical Linguistics.* London: Cambridge University Press, 1968.

MacWhinney, B.   Point Sharing, in *Communicative Competence: Acquisition and Intervention,* eds. R. Schiefelbusch and J. Pikar. Baltimore, Md.: University Park Press, 1981.

Strang, B.   *Modern English Structure,* 2nd ed. London: Edward Arnold, 1969.

Talmy, L.   Lexicalization Patterns: Semantic Structure in Lexical Form, in *Language Typology and Syntactic Field Work,* Vol. III, ed. T. Shopen. 1980.

Zwicky, A. M.   A Double Regularity in the Acquisition of English Verb Morphology, *Papers in Linguistics,* 3, 1979, 411–18.

6

Syntax

In the last chapter, we discussed combining grammatical morphemes into words. In this chapter, we will be discussing *syntax,* which has to do with the structural regularities for combining words into larger meaningful units. Combining words involves combining ideas, and different kinds of ideas are communicated with distinctive syntactic structures. If we wish to indicate a specific entity (e.g., the pencil on the desk), we combine a noun that names the general class of the entity (*pencil*) with words that identify the specific object (e.g., *this, blue*). The structure of the resulting statement ("this blue pencil") is a noun phrase. If we wish to comment on the pencil rather than simply identify it, we need a different syntactic structure—that is, we need a clause, such as "Hand me the pencil" or "The pencil fell on the floor." We have added a comment to the topic; or in syntactic terms, we have a clause consisting of a subject and a predicate. Noun phrases and clauses are the basic units that result from word combinations.

Syntax is closely related to pragmatics in that the specific syntactic structure of an utterance is determined by the intention behind the utterance and the context in which it is spoken. Asking a question is the most direct way to request information ("What is this?") or confirmation ("Is this yours?"). Less direct expression may be chosen because of the particular situation or conversational partner. A statement imparts information ("This is mine"), while an imperative conveys a command ("Give it to me"). The intent to reject ("I don't want it") or deny ("It's not true") is conveyed with negatives. Less direct expression may be chosen for any of these intentions because of the particular situation or conversational partner ("Do you suppose you could hand that to me?"). It is likely, however, that learning these syntactic systems is motivated by the need to express intention directly.

Awareness of listeners and their need for information is also reflected in syntactic structure. Along with elaborating noun phrases to aid the listener's identification of the topic ("that little blue box"), we can combine clauses to clarify referents for the listener ("I need the box that I gave you for your birthday"). We highlight new information for listeners by position in the clause ("The pencil is *blue*" vs. "The *blue* pencil is broken"). We tend to reduce redundancy that listeners do not need by use of elliptical structures ("What do you want to eat?" "*Clams*") and pronouns ("Give *it* to me").

Children obviously do not begin to use syntactic structures that are like adult syntax with their first combinations. While it is relatively easy to recognize phrases and clauses, statements, imperatives, and the like in adult language and to describe their syntactic structure, word combinations in children's early speech often do not fall into these familiar categories. It thus becomes important to discern the regularities displayed in their combinations and to ascertain the communicative intent behind their utterances in order to know how their syntactic regularities function for them pragmatically.

We begin this chapter by discussing adult syntactic systems, since understanding these systems is helpful in describing regularities in children's productions as well as identifying children's deviations from adult grammar. Next, we will summarize syntactic development and then discuss doing structural analysis for syntactic regularities. Some other descriptions of English syntax that may be helpful can be found in Crystal, Fletcher, and Garman (1976), Quirk et al. (1972), and Stockwell (1977).

We will not emphasize abstract syntax in our descriptions of syntactic structure; that is, you will not find a distinction made between deep and surface structure syntax in our discussions, although we do feel there is some evidence that the generative model developed by Chomsky has psychological reality for children and adults (see Chomsky, 1965). Our reason for not emphasizing abstract syntax is that we find its use as a clinical assessment approach to abnormal language impractical (see Crystal, Fletcher, and Garman, 1976, for a discussion).

SYNTACTIC SYSTEMS

Learning syntax involves organizing utterances on several different levels. Any one utterance can be analyzed for its conformance to the regularities of several different systems. One such system is *clause structure*. The utterance may consist of one or more clauses, and clauses may be of different types, each requiring different syntactic rules to execute it correctly. Another syntactic system operates in the formation of *noun phrases,* dictating the kind of words that can be combined with nouns, and permissible word order. *Pronouns* refer to the same entities as nouns but have different rules. We recognize some utterances as *questions* because of their characteristic syntactic structure; likewise, the *negative* system operates to convey the intention of some utterances. We will discuss analysis of each of these systems separately, but it should be clear that they may all be contained in the same utterance.

SIMPLE CLAUSE STRUCTURE

Word combinations that contain verbs are clauses; for every verb or verb phrase in an utterance, there is a separate clause. We distinguish between clauses formed with copulas and those consisting of lexical verbs because these two types of clauses convey different kinds of information, and we want to look at them separately.

Clauses with Copulas

Copulas, which are forms of *be* (*be, am, are, is, was, were*), are used as the main verb and do not add content information to the utterance. They simply relate the subject of the clause to some additional element called the *complement*. Complements are used with "state of being" verbs as well as copulas (e.g., *seem, feel, appear, look, become*). We treat these as copulas syntactically. Complements may be nouns, pronouns, adjectives, adverbials, participles, or infinitives.

I'll be *the mother*. (Noun)
He is *it*. (Pronoun)
I am *happy*. (Adjective)
He was *on time*. (Adverbial)
She seems *interesting*. (Participle)
She is *to run*. (Infinitive)

Clauses with Lexical Verbs

Lexical verbs, in contrast to copulas, add content to the clause—they specify the action or state of entities referred to. They cannot be omitted and still be implied, as copulas can, because each lexical verb conveys unique information. Clauses formed with lexical verbs can be subdivided into two types, depending on whether or not the verb is followed by an object. Clauses without objects have lexical verbs that express actions or states that do not need an object to be carried out:

Mary fell.
He is sleeping.

Clauses with objects have lexical verbs that express an action or state that do need an object in order to be carried out. The object can be from various word classes but can generally be seen as answering the question, What does the _____ (subject) _____ (verb)? as in "What does the girl eat?" for the sentence "The girl eats dandelions."

John reads *the book*. (What does John read?)	Noun
John reads *it*.	Pronoun
John liked *eating* alone. (What did John like?)	Gerund
John liked *to paint*.	Infinitive

Clauses may also contain elements that add other kinds of information. A subclass of lexical verbs that take objects can also be used with elements which answer the question, To or for whom is the action done? This question will be answered with a noun, noun phrase, or pronoun, which we call the *dative* element.

Mary gave *the dog* a bath.	Noun phrase
He showed *her* the book.	Pronoun
She promised *him* to go home.	Pronoun

The difference between the object and the dative element in these sentences can easily be seen by asking

What did Mary give?	A bath. (Object)
To or for whom?	The dog. (Dative)
What did he show?	The book. (Object)
To or for whom?	Her. (Dative)
What did she promise?	To go home. (Object)
To or for whom?	Him. (Dative)

Clauses with either copulas or lexical verbs can also contain elements that answer the questions, Where, When, How, How many? If these elements are single words, they will be *adverbs:*

Mary walks *home.*	Where?
Mary walked *yesterday.*	When?
Mary walks *quickly.*	How?
Mary walked *twice.*	How many?

Prepositional phrases also serve to provide the same kinds of information:

Mary walks *to the bus.*	Where?
Mary walks *with a cane.*	How?
Mary walks *in the morning.*	When?

We will refer both to the simple adverbs and to the prepositional phrases used in this way as *adverbials.* A clause can have more than one adverbial.

Mary walks *quickly to the bus stop everyday.*
Twice he hit the ball *over the fence yesterday.*

One last element that can be part of a simple clause is the *object complement.* Just as the complement that occurs with the copula relates to the subject of the clause, the object complement relates to the object of the clause as though there was a copula conjoining the object and its complement. This element implies a second underlying clause, and thus is more involved than are other simple clauses. Complements may be of various forms:

I'd call him *a hero*.	Noun complement
You get your fingers *hurt*.	Adjective complement
We made her *it*.	Pronoun complement
She told Ed *to go home*.	Verb (infinitive) complement
There's a bear *sleeping* on the pillow.	Verb (participle) complement

When they are of the verb complement type, we treat them as subordinate clauses, as discussed in the section that follows.

Although these clauses look similar to those with dative elements, they can be distinguished. It may be useful to do so, since use of object complements would be an indicator of different and probably more complex syntactic rules.

COMPLEMENTS	DATIVE ELEMENTS + OBJECT
I'd call him *a hero*.	I'd call *him* a taxi.
	(I'd call a taxi for him.)
She told me *to go home*.	She promised *me* to go home.
	(She promised to go home for me.)

Clauses with No Subjects

Generally, when the subject of a clause is not given, the subject "you" is implied. This type of clause, which is grammatically correct, can be identified as an imperative. The intention of imperatives is usually a direct request. For example,

Give it to me.	V
Don't do it.	V

Sometimes children omit the subject of a clause when a subject other than "you" is implied. This is described as a syntactic deviation in contrast to imperatives, which are correct clauses. We distinguish between them in our notation by showing the missing obligatory subject in this way:

(I) don't like it.	$VO
(He) can't get up.	$V

MULTIPLE CLAUSES

Utterances with more than one clause are used when a speaker wants to relate more than one event or state of affairs. This involves using more than one verb. Again, we are guided in our identification of the component clauses by locating the verbs—for every verb there is a clause. We still distinguish between copulas and lexical verbs in our notation, but our primary interest in looking at multiple clauses is to determine the variety and complexity of such utterances a child can

Box 6.1 Summary of Simple Clauses

Clauses will be one of the following types:
Subject + Copula + Complement	SVC
Subject + Lexical Verb	SV
Subject + Lexical Verb + Object	SVO

Clauses may also contain the following elements:
Dative (D): To or for whom action is done		SVDO
Adverbial (A): Where, When, How, How many		SVCA
	or	SVA
	or	SVOA
Object Complement (C)		SVOC
	or	SVCC

Parallel clause types can occur with no subject stated:
V (A)	Run! (faster)
VO (A)	Throw the ball (here)
VC (A)	Be nice (now)
VDO (A)	Give him a drink (before bed)
VOC (A)	Make him an assistant (next year)

use. We will identify three ways clauses are combined in one sentence, hence three types: compound clauses, subordinate clauses, and relative clauses.

Compound clauses are two or more simple clauses of any type joined together with a coordinating conjunction (*and, or, but*). They are each structurally complete by themselves and could be stated as separate sentences. This can be shown with the following notation:

We could go to the movie (or) we could go home.	SVA + SVA[1]
I'd like to go (but) I can't.	SV + SV
I went to the store (and) I spent all my money.	SVA + SVO

Some compound clauses are complete without a conjunction:

These aren't shoes; they're clogs.

When the subject of both clauses is the same, it can be deleted in some cases. We then refer to the sentence as having compound predicates:

I fell down and skinned my knee.

The conjunction can be omitted in compound predicates in a few constructions:

I'll go get it.

It is possible to produce compound subjects or objects as well as compound predicates:

[1]Conjunctions are indicated by +.

> *The boy and the dog* ran home.   (Compound subjects)
>
> The dog chases *cats and birds*.   (Compound objects)

In these cases, however, there is only one verb in the sentence. We are considering them simple clauses.

Subordinate clauses are part of the structure of the main clause of the sentence and depend on the main clause for their occurrence. In our examples illustrating the possible forms of a clause, the elements (S, V, O, C, D, A) were represented as single words or phrases. Any of these elements (except the verb) can also take the form of a·complete clause, which is identified as a subordinate clause. This can be seen in the following examples:

It is obvious	(Simple subject)
That she is happy is obvious.	(Subject clause)
I like *chocolate*.	(Simple object)
I like *how you did it*.	(Object clause)
This is *mine*.	(Simple complement)
This is *what I ordered*.	(Complement clause)
She drank it *quickly*.	(Simple adverbial)
She drank it *like it was water*.	(Adverbial clause)

Subject, object, or complement clauses cannot be removed from the main clause without destroying the sense of the clause, because they are an integral part of it. Grammatically, these clauses are necessary to make the main clause a whole sentence; i.e., "is obvious," "I like," and "this is" in the preceding examples have a sense of incompleteness without the subordinate clauses.

Adverbial clauses, however, like all simple adverbs, can be removed without destroying the sense of completeness. This may make them somewhat harder to recognize, so it helps to remember that they answer the questions, When, Where, How, How many, and Why? These adverbial clauses are not distinguished from compound clauses by some researchers; structurally they are very similar.

Subordinate clauses will be introduced by a subordinate conjunction (e.g., *that, what, when, because, how, since*) or will have *that* implied. We suggest the following notation system, with the subordinate clause elements written over the element of the main clause which they function as:

Subject:
```
         +   S   V   C
        ─────────────────
              S            V      C
        That she is happy  is   obvious
```

Object:
```
                    S  V  C
             S   V  ─────────
             ─   ─      O
             I  think  she is here
```

Complement:
```
                       +    S    V
              S    V  ────────────────
              ─    ─       C
             This  is   what I ordered
```

$$\text{Object:} \quad \underset{\text{I'll}}{\underline{S}} \quad \underset{\text{tell}}{\underline{V}} \quad \underset{\text{you}}{\underline{D}} \quad \overset{+ \; \underline{S} \; \underline{V} \; \underline{O}}{\underset{\text{how I did it}}{\underline{O}}}$$

$$\text{Adverbial:} \quad \underset{\text{She}}{\underline{S}} \quad \underset{\text{drank}}{\underline{V}} \quad \underset{\text{it}}{\underline{O}} \quad \overset{+ \; \underline{S} \; \underline{V} \; \underline{C}}{\underset{\text{like it was water}}{\underline{A}}}$$

Relative clauses specify something about an element in the main clause rather than taking the place of an element, as in the preceding examples. Relative clauses are generally introduced by relative pronouns (e.g., *that, who, which*). These clauses can be removed from a sentence without leaving it grammatically incomplete. They generally answer the question, Which one?

> The book *that I like* is gone.
> The book   is gone.
> Which book?   *that I like*

> The book I like is gone.
> The book   is gone.
> Which book?   (that) *I like*

> That is the man *who fixed my bike.*
> That is the man.
> Which man?   *who fixed my bike*

Notation for relative clauses should indicate which element in the main clause they refer to, since those that refer to subjects typically develop later in children than those that refer to objects or complements.

> S   (R S V) V C
> The book *that I like* is gone.[2]
> S   (S V) V C
> The book *I like* is gone.
> S V C (R V O)
> That is the man *who fixed my bike.*

Box 6.2. *Summary of Multiple Clauses*

Compound Clauses:	More than one simple clause
	Joined by *and, but, or*
Subordinate Clauses:	Subordinate clause acts as S, O, C, or A of main clause
	Usually introduced by a subordinate conjunction
Relative Clauses:	Relative clause specifies something about the S or O of the main clause
	Indicates, Which one?
	Usually introduced by a relative pronoun

[2]R indicates relative pronoun; the relative clause is enclosed in parentheses.

We now shift from clause structure description, in which our intent was to identify the type of clause, to looking at other syntactic systems that operate within the various clause types and also in utterances that are not clauses. That is, in addition to identifying the variety and complexity of clause types a child can use, we also want to know how the child specifies and describes entities with noun phrases and identifies them with pronouns; how the child asks questions; and how he or she conveys negative intent. We will discuss each of these systems separately.

NOUN PHRASE STRUCTURE

In discussing clauses, we indicated that some of the elements, notably the subject, object, or complement, might be a noun. We will now focus on these nouns and the words that refer to them as we investigate noun phrase structure. Nouns identify the entities that utterances are about—the people, the objects, the places, the mental operations, and so on. While we sometimes use simple nouns to refer to those entities (e.g., "*Milk* is good for you"), we generally use modifiers to specify something about the entity, or to identify the specific referent for our listener. These modifiers precede the noun in English and with it comprise a noun phrase. We have already discussed one kind of element that precedes a noun in a noun phrase when we looked at the morphology of definite and indefinite articles. We will briefly describe the other elements that can be part of a noun phrase.

DETERMINERS   The *articles* are part of the class of words called determiners. Other determiners are the *genitive articles* (*my, our, your, her, his, its, their*); *demonstratives,* which also may act as pronouns, but as determiners occur before a noun (*this, that, these, those*); and *qualifying terms* (such as *any, each, either, enough, much, neither, no, some, such*). Determiners are mutually exclusive—that is, only one can occur in a phrase.

		but not	
We can have	a book		*a my book[3]
	my book		*this either book
	this book		*this my book
	either book		*the any book

INITIATORS   Determiners are usually the first elements in a noun phrase; the only elements that can precede them are called initiators. The most common initiators are *all, both, half,* and *only,* along with qualified forms of each, such as *not quite all* or *almost half.*

ADJECTIVALS   The largest class of words that can occur before a noun are the adjectivals. Along with descriptive *adjectives* (*big, old, red*), this class includes *ordinals* or terms of relative position (*first, second, last, next*) and *quantifiers* (*one, two, several, many*). A noun phrase can include more than one adjectival as

---

[3]Asterisk before utterance indicates it is not grammatical.

well as combinations of an initiator, a determiner, and adjectivals. The order in which all these elements can occur is restricted. A sentence generally does not "sound right" if we deviate from this order, as follows:

> initiator—determiner—ordinal—quantifier—adjective—noun
> e.g., Only the first two little boys

This phrase can be expanded further by including more adjectives:

> e.g., Only the first two tired, cold, dirty, hungry little boys

Most adjectives seem to have a "right" place in a sequence—we say "big old house" and not "old big house." The usual sequence seems to be

> characterizing adjective—size—age—color
> as in "lovely big old red house"

The ordering of prenominal adjectives has been described by Vendler (1968) and Martin (1968) as dependent on the "nounlike" qualities of the adjective, with the most nounlike adjective being closest to the noun in the phrase. Thus a substance adjective like *metal,* which can easily occur as a noun as well as an adjective, must come closer to the noun than a color adjective, which in turn is seen as more nounlike than size. For example, *red* can function as a noun as in "Red is my favorite color" or "Give me some red" more readily than can *old* or *small* ("Old is my favorite age"; "Give me some small").

PRONOUNS

Pronouns also refer to entities and in this sense function like nouns. Unlike nouns, however, they are not explicit labels; they depend exclusively on the context in which they occur for interpretation. Pronouns cannot be modified as nouns can to specify something about the entity referred to, to identify it or comment on its characteristics. Pronouns also involve shifting reference—the referent for "me" or "you" shifts continually, depending on who is speaking, unlike a name which stays "attached" to a person or object. Correct use of *personal pronouns* involves a significant amount of knowledge that is not needed when using nouns. This is because in English these pronouns are inflected for person, number, case, and gender, while nouns are inflected only for number and then in a relatively consistent way. The inflectional possibilities for pronouns as shown in Table 6.1 include

> Person: first (speaker), second (addressee), third (others)
> Number: singular, plural
> Case: subjective, objective, possessive, reflexive
> Gender: masculine, feminine, neuter

Table 6.1 Pronouns

	SINGULAR				PLURAL			
	Subj.	*Obj.*	*Poss.*	*Reflex.*	*Subj.*	*Obj.*	*Poss.*	*Reflex.*
1st person	I	me	mine	myself	we	us	ours	ourselves
2nd person	you	you	yours	yourself	you	you	yours	yourselves
3rd person	he	him	his	himself	they	them	theirs	themselves
	she	her	hers	herself				

Another group of pronouns are the *indefinite pronouns.* We have already referred to demonstrative pronouns, which are part of this class. Like personal pronouns, indefinite pronouns also take the place of a noun, thus eliminating the name of the referent, or object referred to. Unlike personal pronouns, they are not inflected, so they have only one form regardless of their syntactic role. (The exception to this is *it* when the referent is given human qualities, as in "This plant takes care of itself.") Some demonstrative pronouns have a singular referent (*it, this, that*), while others have plural referents (*these, those*). Other indefinite pronouns are *something, somebody, no one, anything, anyone,* and *everybody.*

PREPOSITIONAL PHRASES

A noun phrase or pronoun can be used to comment on where, when, or how an event or state occurs by introducing it with a preposition. It then becomes part of the prepositional phrase. Prepositions are a limited class of words that indicate the relationship between two nounlike items. They can be classified according to the nature of the relationship they specify, with most prepositions expressing space and time relationships and fewer expressing relations such as cause, manner, or origin. See Chapter 7 for examples of prepositions.

Prepositions always precede an object or an implied object; and they may follow other nouns that they refer to:

The man *in* the middle

They may also serve as adverbials as illustrated earlier and thus appear in a variety of positions in a clause.

Some prepositionlike words occur along with specific verbs and without an object noun, such as *turn on, think over,* and *set up.* These are *particles* and are properly considered part of the verb and not prepositions. Particles, unlike prepositions, change the meaning of the verb and can be separated from it by a noun or pronoun but cannot be followed by a pronoun. Conversely, prepositions can be separated from the verb by adverbs while particles cannot be.

Compare the sentences that follow and determine why those marked with asterisks are ungrammatical:

PARTICLE	PREPOSITION
He ran up the flag.	He ran up the hill.
He ran the flag up.	*He ran the hill up.
He ran it up.	*He ran it up.
*He ran up it.	He ran up it.
*He ran quickly up the flag.	He ran quickly up the hill.

QUESTIONS

There are two types of questions that can be asked—those that call for a yes or no answer and those that require further content information. The latter are called wh- questions because they include a specific question word, most of which begin with wh- (*who, what, where, when, why, how*). *Yes-no questions* can be asked in four ways, as follows:

1. Intonation. Rising intonation on the end of a word, phrase, or sentence conveys a questioning attitude:
    That's your dog?
    Milk?
2. Inversion. Beginning a sentence with an auxiliary verb or copula verb instead of the subject produces a yes-no question. This is referred to as inversion because the presumed underlying structure is a subject-verb-object statement that is transformed into a question by inverting the subject and verb. Notice that only the first auxiliary verb precedes the subject:
    Can I do it?
    Should I have been there?
3. *Do* Insertion. As mentioned in Chapter 5, the "dummy do" acts as an auxiliary but adds no meaning to the verb. It is used before the subject to ask yes-no questions where no other auxiliary verb is used. The *do* form used reflects the tense of the sentence:
    Do you want to go?
    Did you go?
4. Tag Questions. Tag questions involve making a statement that is presumed to be true and then requesting verification. The earliest forms of this, which might be called pretags, are the addition of "right?" "huh?" or "okay?" after a statement. True tags involve an auxiliary verb which is either negative or nonnegative to contrast with the main clause verb:
    You will go, won't you?
    You can't go, can you?
    You saw it, didn't you?   (dummy do)

Wh- questions involve a question word that specifies the kind of information being requested, such as location (*where*), time (*when*), and so on. These words usually are at the beginning of the sentence but when asking for clarification or repetition of something previously said may occur in the position of the missing information. These are called occasional questions (Brown, 1968) and involve emphasis on the question word:

> John will read *what?*
> John will read *where?*

Some wh- questions occur along with a form of yes-no questions. These are one kind of embedded question (Brown, 1973):

> Know where my games are?

NEGATIVES

We first want to distinguish *syntactic negation* from pragmatic and semantic notions of negation. An utterance is considered to have syntactic negation if it contains the negative morphemes *no, not,* or contractions of *not* with auxiliaries, e.g., *can't, don't, wouldn't.* Syntactic negatives function to negate an affirmative proposition within the statement. We distinguish this from *nonsyntactic negation,* which is a single-word response, usually *no,* to a prior speaker's utterance:

Q: Do you want this?
A: No.

These responses are of interest pragmatically because they demonstrate discourse cohesiveness and proposition sharing between speakers, but they reveal nothing about the speaker's syntactic system. Semantically, there are other morphemes besides *no* and *not* that express negation, such as *none, nothing, gone,* and *empty,* but these operate as lexical items rather than as syntactic devices to negate affirmative propositions.

The basis of all syntactic negation is rejecting or denying an assumed or explicit affirmative statement. When we say "I'm not hungry," we are responding either to someone's suggestion that we are hungry, or to an assumption that we generally are hungry at this time of day. Volterra and Antinucci (1979) distinguish four types of negation, each with a different underlying assumption.

In type A, the speaker presupposes the listener is doing or about to do something that the speaker does not want the listener to do.

> e.g., Don't drop it.

In type B, the speaker presupposes that the listener believes something that the speaker does not want the listener to believe.

> e.g., It's not broken.

In type C, the speaker presupposes the listener wants the speaker to do something that the speaker does not want to do.

e.g., I don't want to go.

In type D, the speaker presupposes the listener wants confirmation or disconfirmation of a statement.

e.g., Q. Did you eat yet?
Speaker: No, I didn't.

In this last example, we see both a syntactic negative ("I didn't") and a nonsyntactic negative ("No"). Like all questions, there is also the presupposition here that the person to whom the question is addressed knows the answer; this is frequently negated.

e.g., Q. Is this yours?
Speaker: I don't know.

The presence of a syntactic negative in a sentence does not in itself indicate which element of the statement is being negated.

The man is not giving the award to the boy.

This sentence can be interpreted in a variety of ways, depending on which element we perceive as negated.

Not the man, the woman
Not giving it, selling it
Not the award, the package
Not to the boy, to the girl

Unless the meaning is clear from context, we generally stress the word to which the negative applies. Read the above sentences with stress on different words to see how the meaning seems to change. If the negative is stressed, the implication is that our presumption that the man is giving the award to the boy is false; but no other information is implied.

SYNTACTIC DEVELOPMENT

Most of the research in child language from the mid 1960s through the early 1970s was directed to studying syntactic development of young children. Thus there has been a vast amount of data collected and reported, and much is known about the patterns children display, at least up until about age five, which was the upper limit of most studies. There are still many unknowns, however, and several controversies exist about the nature of what children learn and how best to represent children's linguistic knowledge. Our intent in this section is to summarize some of the observations generally made about syntactic development—

and to highlight acquisition of particular syntactic systems—so as to give some guidance in assessing children's regularities within these systems.

Stages of Syntactic Development?

Many researchers and writers have described syntactic development in terms of stages. The best known of these schemes is that of Roger Brown (1973). Brown identified five stages of development, each named "either for a process that is the major new development occurring in that interval or for an exceptionally elaborate development of a process at that stage" (Brown, 1973, p. 59). Brown does not imply that stages are discrete, but rather that development is continuous and stages are arbitrary divisions of that continuum. Brown's study consisted of longitudinal data from three children—Adam, Eve, and Sarah. When he found that the age and rate at which syntactic milestones emerged was very different for each of the three children, he used the average number of morphemes per utterance, or mean length of utterance (MLU), for comparison among them; that is, he described their syntactic development relative to their MLU, rather than their age. The stages evolved out of points on the MLU distribution at which the children were compared, with the points becoming intervals. Brown's stages are referred to by Roman numeral designations, as follows:

Stage I	Semantic roles and syntactic relations	MLU 1.0–2.0
Stage II	Grammatical morphemes and modulation of meaning	MLU 2.0–2.50
Stage III	Modalities of simple sentences	MLU 2.50–3.25
Stage IV	Embedding	MLU 3.25–3.75
Stage V	Coordination	MLU 3.75–4.0+

Brown notes the stage in which each of the three children mastered the early morphomes and notes the regularities observed. Although Brown does not present his data as discrete or prescriptive stages, they have frequently been treated in this manner by researchers and clinicians who use MLU to determine therapy goals.

Other authors have presented stages that are built on criteria other than MLU, with the stages being used to set goals for therapy. Crystal, Fletcher, and Garman (1976) use chronological age to identify seven stages. Stage I goes from 9 months to 1.6 years; the remaining stages are in 6-month intervals, with stage VII having no specified upper limit (4.6+). Lee and Canter (1971) describe eight stages that are based on specific forms identified in language samples of normally developing children. Eight stages of development are described for each of the following morphological and syntactic systems: indefinite pronouns, personal pronouns, verbs, secondary verbs (i.e., infinitives, gerunds, and participles), negatives, yes-no questions, wh- questions, and conjunctions. The various forms within a system that occur at a given stage are thought to correspond in normal development with forms in other systems at that stage (e.g., stage III negatives and stage III verbs).

We do not attempt to establish stages of syntactic development, as these and other authors have done, because it seems to lead to the erroneous assumption that language acquisition does in fact progress in stages and that children can be assigned to stages of development. There is little evidence that we can accurately predict for a given child the forms that will have been acquired in one system from knowing the forms acquired in another system. For example, knowing which question forms the child uses is not a particularly good predictor of his or her use of pronouns, at least not reliable enough for us to want to plan our therapy around this relationship.

There is another approach to stages that has been taken by researchers who attempt to identify natural stages children go through in the acquisition of a particular form or construct. Klima and Bellugi (1966), for example, found children had distinctive stages in their acquisition of questions. These stages may be identified as typically occurring at particular ages or MLU levels, but the boundaries of the stages are identified by observed changes in children's behavior rather than by arbitrary cutoff points (such as age or MLU). These stages are perceived as arising from different rules or mental constructs on the part of the child, with early rules giving way to later rules as the child moves to a new stage. Klima and Bellugi are not seeing development as simply adding new forms, as in the Lee and Canter stages.

We have taken this latter approach to stages of development. Thus, we have not tried to summarize all of the syntactic systems according to MLU or age, since the variability across children and across different conditions is too great to have confidence in generalizations. We do, however, report stages for specific structures when they are provided by the researchers of the studies we refer to. Further, we can identify some general progression in the sequence of syntactic development.

SEQUENCE OF SYNTACTIC DEVELOPMENT

One-Word Syntax?

It has been argued that syntax begins at the one-word stage, with the word acting like a whole sentence. The term *holophrase* is often applied to convey this idea of single words that express ideas adults would say in a sentence. McNeill (1970) argues that children have something like a sentence in mind but use single words at the onset of speech because they are limited by memory and attention. Ingram (1971) feels that the limitation is lack of linguistic knowledge to translate the relatively complete ideas into sentences, so only single words are expressed. Bloom (1973) and Dore (1975) among others have argued against a holophrastic notion, pointing to the lack of evidence that children at this stage have any grammatical awareness. Interpreting children's utterances to mean the same as adult utterances and thus attributing adultlike meaning and categories to children has been called "rich" interpretation. Giving rich interpretation to single-word utterances to derive syntactic categories seems to lead us away from looking at the child's meaning for those words. Thus, at the beginnings of speech, when a child is producing mostly single-word utterances, we feel it is more appropriate to analyze these utterances pragmatically and semantically, and not syntactically.

Transition to Syntax

Toward the end of the single-word period some changes occur that appear to be indications that the child is moving toward word combinations. This might first be signalled by the child using the same word with different intonation patterns or accompanying gestures to express different intentions. This would indicate that the referent for the word is separate from the sought-after consequences of the utterance for the child. For example, the child may use "cup" both as a request for a cup and for an expression that the cup is not in its usual place, using different intonation and/or accompanying gestures with each expression. Leopold (1939) and Halliday (1975) among others report observations such as this during the first half of the second year. This separation of the referent (cup) from intention (request for cup; request for information about cup) seems to be a fundamental step to the use of syntax in expressions such as "want cup" or "where cup?"

Another indication of the transition to syntax is that multiple single words are thematically related. Prior to this, each single word typically refers to a different event. Bloom (1973) reports that near the end of her subject Allison's seventeenth month she began using successive single words that related to the same event. At first, the order of the words reflected the order of actions in the event, with as many as six separate single words referring to a sequence of actions. A short time later, the successive words referred to the entire event rather than to discrete parts or steps. Bloom describes these as holistic successive utterances. Scollon (1974) found a similar progression of single words referring first to unrelated events and then to the same event. He also presents evidence of a psychological difference for children when he finds that the phonetic representation of words in holistic successive utterances are often regressions of less mature forms as compared to the same words when unrelated to successive words. For example, he noted that a child omitted the final consonants from "tape" and "step" when they referred to her threat to step on the tape recorder but on the same day correctly included the final sounds when the words were said as isolated utterances. This would argue that the holistic successive utterances involve more effort on the part of the child, diverting concentration from another part of the system.

Two-Word Combinations

Shortly after holistic successive utterances are observed, first true word combinations are common (Bloom, 1973; Leopold, 1949). The primary difference is intonation—that is, while successive single words each have separate intonation contours and sound separate even though spoken close together, word combinations are said together in a single intonation contour. While early combinations may have level stress on each word (Leopold, 1949), these combinations typically involve stress and pitch difference between the component words. Children are generally described as beginning to combine words around age eighteen to twenty months, or when they have acquired a single-word vocabulary of about fifty words. There have been various characterizations of children's two-word combinations, each demonstrating that children display predictable regularities and not random combinations of words from their single-word vocabulary.

An early characterization of children's presentence utterances was to describe them as *telegraphic*. Brown and Bellugi (1964) described children's utterances as consisting of the content-carrying words—nouns, verbs, and adjectives—with omission of "functors," or low-information words, such as pronouns, articles, prepositions, and auxiliary verbs, along with inflectional morphemes. The analogy is drawn from the language used by adults when brevity is important, as in a telegram. The content words tend to correspond to stressed words in an utterance, which led to the speculation that differential stress is a factor in children's retention of content words. Telegraphic speech was used as a general description of presentence utterances that deviated from adult grammar, and not just two-word productions.

Several researchers in the 1960s independently described two word classes used by children in these early combinations (Braine, 1963; McNeill, 1970; Slobin, 1968). These word classes are most commonly described as *pivot* words and *open class* words. Pivots are a small class of frequently used words, generally in combination with many other different words. Some pivots may always be used in the first position of a two-word combination by a particular child, for example:

> *allgone* milk
> *allgone* kitty
> *allgone* light

Other pivots may always be in the final position, as in:

> me *down*
> kitty *down*
> shoe *down*

Some children will use a particular pivot word in the first position of two-word combinations, while other children may use the same word in the second position, but each pivot typically has its fixed position for a given child.

Open class words consist of most words in the child's vocabulary and are the major additions as vocabulary grows. Whereas pivots rarely occur alone or with other pivots, open class words can occur as single words, in combination with other open class words, or with pivots. For example:

> milk   open
> more milk   pivot + open
> baby milk   open + open

The possible types of utterances that can be represented with pivot-open grammar can be summarized in the following manner:

1. P_1 + O (Pivot + Open)
2. O + P_2 (Open + Pivot)
3. O + O (Open + Open)
4. O (Open)

For example, if a child says

> shoe off
> blanket off
> light off

each of these utterances would be designated O + P_2, with "off" identified as a pivot by its combination with several open class words, always in the second position.

It has been argued that pivot-open grammar is an inadequate description of these two-word utterances on two grounds. First, all children do not display these patterns in their two-word utterances but tend to show greater variety than that implied by pivot-open depictions (Bowerman, 1973). Second, the classification of all words as either pivots or opens obscures the variety of meanings children express. Bloom (1970), borrowing from case grammar depiction of adult language (Fillmore, 1968), proposed a description of two-word utterances to indicate the function that words serve in the presumed underlying sentence. She emphasized the importance of context to determine the sentence. In her most famous example, Kathryn, one of the children being studied, says "mommy sock" twice in one day—once when she picked up her mother's sock and again when her own sock was being put on her by her mother. Bloom describes the first utterance as *possessive,* and the second as *agent-object* on the assumption that the child is describing the agent of an action (*mommy*) and the object acted upon (*sock*). In a pivot-open grammar, both of these utterances would have been described simply as O + O. Brown proposed a similar and more extensive list of these grammatical function categories, referring to them as *semantic relations.* Bloom and Lahey (1978) have more recently enumerated twenty-one categories which they identify as semantic-syntactic relations, applying them to one-word and multiple-word utterances in addition to two-word combinations. (See Chapter 7 for further elaboration of these categories.)

Using semantic relations to characterize early words and word combinations has also been criticized on several grounds. Braine (1976) found that the patterns of *other* + X, *big* + X, and *two* + X develop independently in children and argued that it is inappropriate to ascribe to children knowledge of the broad semantic relations category of modifier + noun. Howe (1976) also has argued against this rich semantic relations interpretation of children's utterances. Her arguments are based on her assessment of children's cognitive capabilities, which she contends are not developed enough to understand the classifications attributed to them. In addition, she casts doubt on the validity of semantic relations referred to in the literature by showing evidence of arbitrary classification. Duchan and Lund (1979) also found categorization of children's responses into a priori semantic relations to be arbitrary and argue that it is possible to derive children's categories from structural analysis of their responses, without relying on preconceived linguistic categories.

It does not seem appropriate to analyze children's two-word utterances according to adult syntactic categories. Instead, our preference is to describe the structure of these word combinations in terms of the words or word classes the child combines. An example of this word class description is detailed in Crystal et al. (1976) who found children at the two-word stage who used primarily noun phrases, some with predominant patterns such as preposition + *here* or *there* (e.g., "in there," "on here"); and other children with a predominance of rudimentary clause structures with verbs expressed or implied (e.g., "carry it," "sit here"). Examination of a child's two-word utterances may reveal these or other patterns.

Multiword Combinations

Longer utterances of three or more words typically begin to appear when children produce about equal numbers of one-word and two-word utterances (MLU 1.5). When children formulate clauses, we can begin to compare the structure of their utterances to adult grammar—they are beginning to use conventional means of word order and inflectional morphemes to convey information. Simple clauses become more expanded as articles, adjectives, adverbs, and other modifiers are added. Simple clauses also combine to form multiclause utterances. We can best describe the development of multiword utterances by tracing the development of clauses and other syntactic systems.

CLAUSE DEVELOPMENT

SIMPLE CLAUSES   Children seem to use simple clauses to express the same kinds of intentions and ideas they previously expressed with gestures, single words, and two-word combinations at successive points in time. What is added is the organization of content into conventional forms that approach adult structure. The earliest clauses, which lack morphological refinement, are typically of the forms

SVO	Eden make man
SVA	I sit chair
V O	Make a couch
V A	Sit daddy chair

Bloom, Lightbown, and Hood (1975) report from their study of four children that the first verbs to appear were simple action verbs, such as "eat," "read," "do," and "fix"; followed later by verbs that indicate a change in location, such as "put," "go," and "sit"; and then by verbs indicating the state of the subject, such as "want," "have," and "know." Copulas (*to be*) generally are not present at this stage, resulting in clauses with implied verbs.

e.g., I Eden

Demonstrative pronouns (e.g., *this, that, it*) may appear frequently as the subject of these sentences.

> e.g., That a cow.
> It my book.
> There shoe.

As we indicated in Chapter 5, copulas appear to develop as grammatical morphemes rather than as lexical items, and their appearance is generally delayed until after other grammatical morphemes have emerged. We therefore consider the subject-complement utterance a clause when it occurs in a sample along with other clauses with explicit (lexical) verbs.

MULTIPLE CLAUSES Sometime between two and three years of age, generally as length of utterance moves beyond MLU of 3, multiple-clause utterances appear. The earliest of these complex forms may have no connective but may consist of two parallel clauses:

> You take that one; I take that one.

or an object subordinate clause:

> I hope *I don't hurt it.*
> I don't want *you read that book.*

Brown (1973) and Limber (1973) identify these object clauses as the most frequent complex form to appear first. Along with the absence of a conjunction, it can be noted that these subordinate clauses have the form of a simple sentence.

Brown (1970) observes that conjunctions begin to appear in early speech at about MLU 3.5. The earliest connective form expressed by virtually all children is *and.* Bloom et al. (1980), in a comprehensive study of four children's acquisition of connectives up through age 38 months, found all four used *and* productively between 25 and 27 months of age, before the emergence of any other connectives. (By *productively* they mean the form is used at least five times in two successive observations.) The children used these early *ands* syntactically, and they used them also to chain an utterance to events occurring in the situation:

> (Eric picks up puppet, puts it in box with other puppets)
> E: And I close them.

Syntactically, *and* is used in two ways—to connect words within a phrase and to connect two clauses. When the connective is used within a phrase, it results in a compound element of a clause. Most typically, young children produce compound objects or complements:

> I want *this one and this one.*

Compound subject phrases are less common for young children:

> *Mommy and Becky* drink coffee.

As we have noted, simple object subordinate clauses appear as early multiple-clause utterances. Connectives in subordinate clauses, along with more variety in their position in the main clause, appear somewhat later. There is less consistency in the order of age of acquisition of these connective forms than is found for *and.* Bloom et al. (1980) found considerable variation in the age at which each of the four children studied used subordinate conjunctions productively. *Because, what,* and *when* were used frequently and were produced by all four children between age 27 and 36 months; *and then* was also acquired during this period but was less frequently used. *So, then,* and *where* were used by some of the children as young as age 30 months but were not productive by at least one child until after age 38 months, where analysis stopped. *But* was productive for all children between 32 and 38 months of age. *If* also appeared for some but not all of the children in this period. *How* as a connective did not emerge for any of the children until after 34 months of age.

Brown (1973) and Limber (1973) distinguish subordinate clauses introduced by wh- words (*what, where,* etc.) from those introduced by other subordinate conjunctions. They identify these former clauses as indirect or embedded questions and indicate that they develop first, with Dale (1976) reporting that clauses referring to location or time seem to emerge before other wh- clauses. For example,

> I remember *where it is.*
> *When I get big,* I can lift you up.
> Mommy know *what Roy do.*

This sequence is in contradiction to the findings of Bloom et al. (1980). They found that connectives that also have other meanings (such as *which* or *what* functioning as question markers or *that* as a demonstrative pronoun) are learned later than those with only one function (*and, then, because,* etc.). They also note that with one exception (*when*) these words are used first as nonconnectives—that is, with their alternative meanings:

> *What* is that?   before   I know *what* that is.
> It is *like* a hat.   before   *Like* I said, it's too small.

In addition to use of varied subordinate conjunctions, subordinate clauses become more complex through modification of the simple sentence structure used in early clauses. This generally involves the infinitive form of the verb:

> I don't want you *to read* that book.
> It bothers me for you *to do* that.

We can thus identify types of subordinate clauses that seem to correspond to levels of complexity and developmental sequence. Since it is unclear whether embedded questions or other subordinate conjunctions are simpler, we do not order them but do distinguish them from each other.

1. Object clause—simple complete sentence as object.
   e.g., I want *you read that book*
2ª. Embedded question—wh- word plus simple sentence.
   e.g., Mommy know *what Roy do*
2ᵇ. Clause with other subordinate conjunction.
   e.g., You can have it *if you want it*
3. Modifications of simple sentence structure.
   e.g., I want *you to read that book*

Relative clauses appear slightly later than the early occurring subordinate clauses. *That* was the only relative pronoun found in the Bloom et al. (1980) samples of children up to 38 months of age, with *it* appearing after 34 months for all the children. The sequence of other relative pronouns and deleted pronouns is not clear. Relative clauses are first produced to modify objects or complements:

That a box *that they put it in.*   (Complement)
I show you the place *we went.* (Object)

Menyuk (1977) reports that relative clauses referring to subjects develop after five years of age and are still relatively rare at age seven:

The boy *who hit the girl* ran away.

More common would be expansion of the sentence object:

I saw the boy *who hit the girl* and ran away.

Relative clauses with implied pronouns and verb forms are also rare until later childhood (Menyuk, 1977):

The bird *sitting in the tree* flew away.

NOUN PHRASE DEVELOPMENT

Children begin to produce noun phrases by prefacing nouns with an article or an adjective:

A doggy
Big truck

They generally have a small repertoire of modifiers at first and only gradually learn the different elements and rules for combination or ordering. They may display some difficulty with appropriate use of modifiers, such as using two determiners:

> A my book

or using an article with mass nouns:

> A soup

Occasionally, children display difficulty with appropriate ordering of elements in a noun phrase:

> A green big snake

DEVELOPMENT OF QUESTIONS

Children begin to ask questions with single words by using rising intonation, so the first questions they ask are typically yes-no questions. Klima and Bellugi (1966) describe the development of questions in the three periods that correspond to MLU.

Period 1:	Nucleus + intonation	See hole?
(MLU 1.75–2.25)		I ride train?
	What NP (doing)[4]	What's that?
		What man doing?
	Where NP (go)	Where horse?
		Where horse go?

The wh- words are used only in a few routines that generally ask for names of objects, actions, or locations of previously present objects. At this stage, Klima and Bellugi found the children did not respond appropriately to wh-questions.

Period 2:	What ⎫	What book name?
(MLU 2.25–2.75)	Where ⎬ NP + (VP) + (NP)	Where my mitten?
	Why ⎭	Why you smiling?

In period 2, yes/no questions are still only indicated by intonation. Wh-questions are generally answered appropriately.

Period 3:	aux + NP + VP	Will you help me?
(MLU 2.75–3.5)	do + NP + VP	Does lions walk?
	wh- + NP + VP	Where the other Joe will drive?

[4]Optional elements are enclosed in parentheses.

At this stage, children are developing auxiliaries, beginning with the negatives "can't" and "don't" and then other *do* forms. They use them in the inverted order to ask yes–no questions but do not make this inversion in wh- questions when it is needed. We will add a final stage to describe this step in question formation as follows:

$$\text{wh-}+\overset{do}{\underset{aux}{}}+\text{NP}+\text{VP}$$

What can the baby eat?
Why don't you talk?

Tag questions and truncated questions (e.g., "Did he?") were found by Brown and Hanlon (1970) to occur later than other question forms, with truncated questions occurring after truncated answers (e.g., "He did," "He didn't") and before tag questions.

DEVELOPMENT OF NEGATION

The acquisition of negation has extensively been studied in different languages (Japanese: McNeill and McNeill, 1968; Finnish, Samoan, and Luo: Bowerman, 1973; English: Bellugi, 1967; Bloom, 1970; Bowerman, 1973, 1975; Lord, 1974). Attempts have been made to determine both the syntactic form and the sequence of acquisition of various types of negation.

The earliest negative to appear for most children is the nonsyntactic *no*. This has been reported in the single-word stage, below MLU 1.5, by both Bloom (1970) and Bowerman (1973). This early *no* suggests children have the concept of negation and use it to reject or deny someone else's statement or action.

Syntactic negation appears slightly later, when *no* or *not* are combined with other words, as in "no milk." Bellugi (1967) characterizes this stage of negation as

neg + X, where X is the sentence nucleus.

That is, the negative utterance is characterized as the same as a nonnegative utterance, with the addition of an initial negative. She found this form in children's samples from MLU 1.17–2.25. Bloom (1970) argues against this characterization of the negative outside of the sentence nucleus, since the nucleus in negative sentences tends to be less complex than that in nonnegative sentences. She also identifies some of these neg + X utterances as nonsyntactic *no* + affirmative statement in response to a previous statement or situation:

D: Can Daddy do it?
Child: No Mommy.

Bellugi did not find this kind of discourse tie with negation until between MLU 2.0 and 2.6.

Bellugi (1967) describes three periods of syntactic development of negatives. The first (MLU less than 2.25), as we mentioned, is neg + nucleus, where negatives are "no" and "not."

The contractions "can't" and "don't" along with "no" and "not" appear within clauses in period 2 (MLU 2.25–2.75):

> I can't catch you.
> He no bite you.
> Don't leave me.

The other auxiliary verb forms, besides "don't" and "can't," and the copulas occur in period 3 (MLU 2.75–3.5), as well as the corresponding negative forms:

> I didn't do it.
> Donna won't let go.
> I am not a doctor.

DEVELOPMENT OF PRONOUNS

Several investigators have reported two dominant patterns in children's early utterances with regard to use of nouns and pronouns (Bloom, Lightbown, and Hood, 1975; Huxley, 1970; Nelson, 1973, 1975; Ramer, 1976). There appear to be some children who use a wide variety of nouns in combination with other word classes in their early word combinations.

> Put all (in) box.
> Put cookie (on) table.

Other children use a predominance of pronouns in early expressions.

> Fix it.
> Broke this.

Bloom, Lightbown, and Hood (1975) report that all the children they studied used similar numbers of nouns, so the use of pronouns in word combinations does not reflect limitations in vocabulary. Differences between the children disappeared when MLU was about 2.5, when they seemed to shift from either the predominant noun or pronoun pattern to use of both forms as equivalent.

Huxley (1970) observed the development of pronouns in two children—one started out with a predominantly nominal strategy, and the other used a predominantly pronominal strategy. The child with the nominal strategy, who learned nouns first and then substituted pronouns, developed pronouns in the following sequence:

it (obj.)	prior to	*them*	prior to	*I*	prior to	*they*
				you (sub.)		
				it (sub.)		

The other child, who began reference primarily with pronouns, followed this sequence:

I				*you* (sub.)		*we*
it (sub.)	prior to	*them*	prior to	*she*	prior to	*you* (obj.)
it (obj.)				*they*		
				me		

It as an object was learned early for both children. The child with the pronominal strategy also used subject pronouns early (*I, it*), while the other child did not use subject pronouns at all until several developed together somewhat later (*I, you, it,* followed by *they*). The plural object (*them*) was learned before the plural subject (*they*) by both children. Other pronouns were rare or not observed by Huxley.

DOING SYNTACTIC ANALYSIS

All children with language problems do not have syntactic problems, and those who do may not need to have all aspects of syntax analyzed. In this section we suggest some steps to guide you through initial syntactic analysis. As you develop your familiarity with the elements to look for, it will become possible to choose those aspects of syntax that are most relevant for a particular child and thus find short cuts to carrying out the analysis. We are interested primarily in describing problem areas, so the analysis might focus only on those. A more comprehensive analysis might be desirable to show development of language over time as new structures emerge or to find evidence of more complex structures than the child typically displays. Thus, the clinician will choose to analyze the aspects of syntax that are relevant for a particular child. The steps we suggest for your initial analysis are not intended to be dictates, but merely guidelines. If a child shows regularities in systems to which we have not referred, develop your own approach. Structural analysis is a discovery procedure—we can alert you to some common patterns, but children are infinitely creative in showing us new ones.

Doing a syntactic analysis involves first looking for regularities in the use, misuse, and omission of forms within the various syntactic systems in spontaneous productions. Working from a running transcript, indicate which utterances are questions, which are responses to questions or prompts, which are imitations, and which are stereotyped patterns, such as greetings, memorized sequences, idioms, rituals, or interjections. The stereotyped patterns will not be used at all for syntactic analysis, since they do not reveal anything productive about a child's syntactic system. They may be of interest, however, in pragmatic analysis.

Imitated utterances often have different syntactic structures from spontaneous utterances and will be analyzed separately if it appears that this analysis could provide information in addition to analysis of spontaneous utterances. We take as imitations any utterance wherein the child repeats all or part of someone else's utterance. This includes elicited imitation, or telling the child to imitate ("Say, I'm a big girl" "I big girl"), echoed responses ("What's this?" "What's this") and repetitions as questions ("Give me the ball" "The ball?"). If any element is added or changed in the child's utterance, it is not counted as an imitation ("Give me the ball" "Give you the ball"). The child may be imitating an utterance that does not immediately precede the imitation. The best indication that such an utterance is in fact an imitation is if it does not conform to his or her usual pattern of production.

Responses to questions and other prompts are eliminated from clause structure analysis unless they are complete sentences because typically they are elliptical—that is, they are incomplete because part of the information has already been supplied by the question. When a child is asked "What are you painting?" the usual answer is the elliptical "A house," and not the implied statement "I am painting a house." Thus, syntactically, responses are likely to differ from spontaneous utterances. Crystal, Fletcher, and Garman (1976) suggest classifying responses by their completeness and appropriateness and by type of stimulus (question or "other"). These categories could be useful in finding regularities within the response utterances.

Likewise excluded from clause-structure analysis but included in other syntactic analysis are questions. It generally does not add new information to do detailed clause-structure analysis on questions, since clause structure in nonquestions is likely to be at least as advanced as the structure in questions. You may want to note, however, any questions that have compound or complex clause structure, as these are indications of increased control of syntax.

1. IDENTIFY CLAUSE STRUCTURE OF SPONTANEOUS STATEMENTS   You have now identified all spontaneous nonquestions in the sample. This will be the group of utterances on which you will do clause-structure analysis. If most of the child's spontaneous utterances are one or two words in length, they probably will not have many clauses. If this is the case, we suggest you group the child's utterances together with others of the same length and look for patterns based on common words or word types and see how multiword categories differ from one another.

In doing clause analysis, it will be helpful initially to circle each verb or indicate missing verbs to determine how many clauses each utterance contains. At this point, also make a notation as to the verb type so you can easily make a listing transcript of similar clauses. We make a note in the margin of our transcript to distinguish copulas (SVC), verbs with no objects needed (SV), and verbs that require objects (SVO). Utterances with one main verb (present or missing) are simple clauses; those with more than one verb are multiple-clause sentences. Using appropriate notation, these multiple-clause utterances can be identified and grouped into compound clauses, subordinate clauses of various types, and relative clauses.

Our purpose in separating clause types is to determine if the child uses a variety of clause types. Also, we may find that patterns emerge regarding the kind of information children convey with different clause types, such as using complements only with pronoun subjects, or expressing locations or time markers only with certain lexical verbs. This information is helpful in planning remediation, since it gives us clues to ways children organize their language.

Table 6.2 shows a sample worksheet we use to find regularities in clause structure. It is filled in with sample utterances to illustrate how it is used. This worksheet includes some categories created for utterances that do not fit the

Table 6.2 Syntactic Worksheet

UTTERANCE	S	C	A
SVC			
That's mine	Dem(onstrative)	PN(pronoun)	
It's broken	Dem	adj	
It's here	Dem	adv	
SC			
*Mommy gone	N(oun)	adj	
*Doggy hungry now	N	adj	now (when)
*Button here	N	adv	
ASV			
There it is	Dem		there
Here it goes	Dem		here
SV			
I can't	PN		
He won't go	PN		
I didn't	PN		

SVO	S	O	D	A
I want that book	PN	NP		
Give me that one		NP	PN	
You take it now	PN	PN		now (when)
*I want get that one	PN	NP		

Other Simple Clauses

I have to   incomplete infinitive

MULTIPLE CLAUSES

Compound Clauses	Clause Type	Conjunction
He came down and broke his arm	SV + VO	and

Subordinate Clauses

I want you to get it for me   SV $\frac{\text{S Inf O D}}{\text{O}}$

I mean it's broken   SV $\frac{\text{SVC}}{\text{O}}$

Relative Clauses

You know, the one that I showed you   SVO(RSVD)   that

Other Multiple Clauses

I'm bigger than him   SVC+S(incomplete)

I think you know what I mean $\frac{+SV}{\frac{SV\ O}{SV\quad O}}$

predetermined categories, such as "Mommy gone" (SC). Indicate, as with an asterisk, utterances that do not follow clause-structure rules. Utterances that are unique in their structure should be listed separately. They will generally be of three types—those that may be correct but incomplete constructions, those that are more complex than the clause structures given, and those that do not follow adult patterns and indicate different syntactic rules. These three types should be analyzed separately.

When each clause has been categorized, regularities of the following types can be described for each clause type:

VERBS

1. Is there a variety of this verb type expressed, or are there a restricted number of different verbs?
2. What errors occur on these verbs?
   a) Verbs missing
   b) Verbs incomplete
   c) Other errors

SUBJECTS

1. What can serve as clause subjects for this child? Some examples could be
   a) Names (including own)
   b) Nouns
   c) Personal pronouns (which ones?)
   d) Indefinite pronouns
   e) Compound subjects
   f) Subjects implied
2. What errors are present?
   a) Subject missing where obligatory
   b) Name or noun used where pronoun is obligatory
   c) Wrong pronoun used

POSTVERB ELEMENTS

1. What objects or complements follow the verb? (SV *what?*) Some examples could be
   a) Names
   b) Nouns
   c) Personal pronouns
   d) Indefinite pronouns
   e) Adjectives
   f) Adverbs
   g) Prepositional phrases
   h) Compound objects
2. What dative elements occur? (SVO *to* or *for whom?*)

ADVERBIALS

1. Do adverbials occur? (*how, where, when, how much, why?*)

COMPOUND CLAUSES

1. What coordinating conjunctions are present?
2. Do clauses have same or different subjects and verbs?
3. What errors are present?
   a) Conjunction missing
   b) Wrong conjunction

SUBORDINATE CLAUSES

1. What kind of subordinate clauses are present?
   a) Object sentence (I know *you did it*)
   b) Embedded wh- question (That's *why I did it*)
   c) Adverbial (*Before you came,* I did it)
   d) Modification of simple sentences (I want *you to get it for me*)
2. What errors are present?
   a) Needed conjunction missing
   b) Wrong conjunction
   c) Other

RELATIVE CLAUSES

1. What do relative clauses identify?
   a) Object (That takes the piece *that's over there*)
   b) Complement (She is the girl *who did it*)
   c) Subject (The girl *who did it* went home)
2. What errors are present?

The following are sample summary statements regarding clause structure:

Clara's statements in this sample consisted primarily of simple clauses, with a wide variety of nouns, names, and pronouns serving as both subjects and objects. She used copulas as well as lexical verbs, with most complements being adverbs of place. All four of her multiclause sentences were compounds with duplicate subjects and verbs.

Tom uses few Subject-Verb-Object (SVO) statements in this sample, and no Subject-Verb-Complements. He used a variety of correct Subject-Verb clauses, as well as some Verb-Object clauses with missing subjects. All SVO clauses had the verb "get."

Gina used a number of multiclause statements in this sample as well as appropriate use of SV (Adv), SVO (Adv), and SVC simple clauses. She used several object clauses, such as "She said that I could do it"; and one relative clause modifying the sentence object ("I want the one that's over there"). Adverbials included several clauses and prepositional phrases as well as simple adverbs.

2. IDENTIFY QUESTIONS   Classify yes-no questions and wh- questions separately and look for patterns within each class. Note nonoccurrence of either kind of question as well as errors that occur. Table 6.3 is a worksheet for listing questions.

Sample summary statements regarding questions follow:

Bob used no wh- questions in this sample. Yes-no questions are indicated only with intonation, typically with a two-word or three-word nucleus.

Juan used frequent yes-no questions in this sample, displaying correct use of both auxiliary inversion and *do* insertion. Wh- questions are either "What's that?" or "Where's NP?"

Paula used no yes-no questions in this sample, but she has been observed to correctly use these questions on other occasions. She used frequent and varied wh- questions, generally with no inversion of auxiliary or *do* insertion. She used one complex wh- question ("What's the name of the one you have?").

Table 6.3   Worksheet for Questions

YES-NO QUESTIONS

Intonation Type:
  You want to ↑
  That's yours ↑

Auxiliary Inversion:
  Can I help you
  Will you go

Do Insertion
  Do you like it
  Does it work

Pretag
  I can have it, okay ↑
  It's fixed, right ↑

Tag
  You'll do it, won't you
  It's not here, is it

WH- QUESTIONS

What you doing	Missing auxiliary
Why I can't	No auxiliary inversion
What's that	

MULTIPLE-CLAUSE QUESTIONS

When my birthday come, you on a diet?   Missing auxiliary and verb

---

3. LOOK FOR NOUN PHRASES   Include questions and responses as well as spontaneous statements for this and remaining analyses, since complete utterances are not necessary for noun phrases, negatives, or pronouns to occur. First underline noun phrases and prepositional phrases in the running transcript. Then list together phrases with the same elements modifying the noun (i.e., initiators, determiners, ordinals, quantifiers, adjectives). Find the length of the child's longest noun phrase and typical noun phrase. Describe any errors or omissions of noun modifiers. Include reference to use of prepositional phrases.

Sample summary statements regarding noun phrases follow:

> Kim used primarily two-word, and occasionally three-word, noun phrases. The single modifier is always an indefinite or genitive article (*a* or *my*). Three-word phrases add either a color or size adjective following the article. In prepositional phrases using either *in* or *on,* the article is inconsistently omitted.

> Roger used extensive noun phrases, including initiators, determiners, articles, and a variety of adjectives, with a maximum length of four modifiers. Ordering of adjectives is occasionally inappropriate. A number of prepositional phrases are used with elaborated noun phrases.

4. LOOK FOR NEGATIVES   List all negatives, indicating both correct and incorrect usage. If there are incorrect negative forms, group them together to find patterns of use. Note also any obligatory contexts where negatives are missing. The following are sample summary statements regarding negatives:

> Dawn used negatives of the form *no* + verb, *I can't,* and *don't* + verb.

> Nicky used a variety of negative forms. *Can't* and *don't* are consistently used correctly, but other negatives show confusion such as double negation or self-correction.

5. LOOK FOR PRONOUNS   Summarize which personal pronouns are present, missing, incorrect, or not sampled. It may help to work from a chart such as the one presented in Table 6.4 to make sure all forms are considered. Check forms that are used correctly, and write in incorrect forms. Also indicate whether indefinite pronouns are used appropriately, incorrectly, or are not present. Sample summary statements regarding pronouns follow:

> Hector does not use *I* as a subject pronoun and instead refers to himself by name. Second and third person subject pronouns are used correctly, and all object pronouns are correct, including *me.* The only plural pronoun used in this sample is *them,* which was correct. No possessive pronouns were sampled, although the genitive article *my* was common. The indefinite articles *it, this,* and *that* were frequently used as clause subjects and objects.

Table 6.4 Worksheet for Pronouns

PERSONAL PRONOUNS

	Singular			Plural		
	Subj	Obj	Poss	Subj	Obj	Poss
1st						
2nd						
3rd F.						
M.						

INDEFINITE PRONOUNS

	Singular		Plural	
	Subj	Obj	Subj	Obj

Carla showed consistent object-subject confusion of personal pronouns, using *me*, *her*, and *him* as subject pronouns. The only object pronoun used was *it*. The possessive *mine* was frequently used as a single-word request; no other possessive pronouns were used.

EXERCISES

1. Following are some simple clauses to give you practice in identifying different clause types. Use the steps immediately following to help you identify these types:

   Circle each verb.

   Find each clause that contains a copula or other state of being verb. Designate each constituent as S, V, or C.

   For each remaining clause, determine if the verb has an object (SVO), no object (SV), an object and a dative element (SVDO) or (SVOD), or an object and a complement (SVOC).

   Locate adverbials; indicate where they occur in each clause (A).

   a) This is mine.
   b) He was under the tree.
   c) I saw it.
   d) Sammy gave it to me.
   e) I went by myself.
   f) Make a fence.
   g) It looks funny.
   h) The sun is coming back.
   i) I don't know.
   j) I can't remember it.
   k) They're all right now.
   l) He didn't give me something.
   m) We just work quietly with our coats on.

2. The following utterances were taken from a child's language sample. Some of them are given a gloss, or supposed intended meaning, to make the meaning clearer. Identify the constituents in each utterance to derive the clause type as you did in exercise 1. Asterisk clauses that are not grammatically correct. Show missing elements with a slash (/).
   a) I talk in there.
   b) I don't know.
   c) Eric give a man. (I'll give you a man.)
   d) Eric mix them up. (I want to mix them up.)
   e) Talk on telephone.
   f) Stick it to the page.
   g) I Eric.
   h) Make a boy.
   i) Eric make a boy.
   j) He sick.
   k) Eric show mommy.
   l) You a piggy.
   m) Felt on my tummy and my back. (The doctor felt . . .)
   n) Eric make it red.
   o) Lady put glue on. (You put the glue on)
   p) Eric give mommy. (I'll give it to mommy)
   q) Eric push.
   r) Boy walk up on top.

3. The following are multiple-clause sentences from different children's language samples. Use the steps immediately following to help you analyze the clause relations:

   Circle the verbs in each sentence.

   Asterisk ungrammatical sentences.

   Identify each element in the clauses by filling in the line below it with one of the following designators:
   S—subject
   V—verb
   O—object
   D—dative
   A—adverbial
   R—relative pronoun
   +—coordinate or subordinate conjunction

   Put parentheses around relative clauses.

   In the margin, identify each sentence according to the type of multiple clauses it contains, that is, as compound (C), subordinate (S), and/or relative (R). The first two are completed.

C   a) He   ran   and   go down   like that.
       S   V   +   V   A

S   b) I   hate   owls   cause   I   can't read.
       S   V   O   +   S   V
                                          A

    c) It   's   time to go home   when   we   finish   our spelling.
       _   _   _____   ____   __   ____   _____
                                         _____

d) I   think   she   's   upset.
_   ___   ___   _   ___
_____

e) A   palace   is   where   a king   lives.
_   _____   _   ___   ____   ___
_____

f) What   is   inside   are   wires   that   control   this.
____   _   ____   __   ___   (___   _____   ___)
_____

g) Try to eat   them,   you   see.
_____   ____   ___   ___
_____

h) This   is   a powder   we   put on   after baths.
____   _   _____   (__   ____   _____)

i) I   know   something   you   don't know.
_   ___   _____   (___   _____)

j) It   's   like   the sky   is.
_   _   ____   _____   _
_____

k) I   didn't want to   but   I   can't.
_   _____   ___   _   ___

l) I   don't know   if   I   can get   it   back.
_   _____   _   _   _____   __   ___
_____

m) In summer   I   no have go   school   cause   it   gonna be   very hot.
_____   _   _____   _____   _____   __   _____   _____
_____

n) I   will   if   you   want   me   to.
_   ___   _   ___   ____   __   __
_____

o) That   not mine   you   gave   me.
____   _____   ___   ____   __

p) It   's   the one   that   got broke.
_   _   _____   (___   _____)

4. Referring back to exercises 2 and 3.
    a) Group together all utterances in exercise 2 that have the same clause structure. Asterisk those that are ungrammatical.
    b) Identify each grouping you come up with, and specify what parts of speech are used for each element in the clause, as shown in Table 6.2.

c) Group together similar sentences in exercise 3, indicating the clause structure and conjunctions used.

d) Summrize the patterns observed in each group and across groups with each exercise.

5. Underline the noun phrases and bracket prepositions in each utterance. Indicate which elements are present in each. List each preposition. The first two examples are already done for you.

a) We get lots of candy.   quantifier + noun
b) It go [in] the water.   article + noun; in
c) It's a little car.
d) My big wheel go faster than her big wheel.
e) Put my piece of paper in.
f) Clown has a red nose.
g) All the fur.
h) My own seat.
i) I wanna blow my nose bathroom.
j) For my cold.
k) Come in my van when my daddy pick me up.
l) I like that part.
m) He go through the wall.
n) A funny one.
o) Look at this little one.
p) We don't play very much games.

What is the longest noun phrase in this sample? Which of the following modifiers are present? Which are used incorrectly?

a) Initiators
b) Articles
c) Demonstratives
d) Qualifiers
e) Ordinals
f) Quantifiers
g) Adjectives

Which prepositions are used?

6. Identify all negatives in the following utterances, and indicate any errors you detect. The first two are already done for you.

a) It looks funny, doesn't it?
b) I don't see nothing else.   double negation
c) I not know.
d) I not went and saw that.
e) I no walk.
f) I'm not do that.
g) I can't make no fuzzy snowman.
h) No, he eat.
i) Not on my birthday.
j) We don't play very much games.
k) We didn't do a whole lot.
l) I got nothing to play with there.
m) No inside, outside
n) It won't kill you.
o) In summer, I no have go school cause it gonna be very hot.

7. Assume for this analysis that the utterances in exercises 1 through 6 were all said by the same child. Summarize pronoun usage, indicating which pronouns are present and correct, which are missing or incorrect, and which were not sampled.

PERSONAL PRONOUNS							
Singular				*Plural*			
subj	obj	poss	ref	sub	obj	poss	
1st							
2nd							
3rd F.							
M.							

INDEFINITE PRONOUNS			
Singular		*Plural*	
subj	obj	subj	obj

8. Construct a list of sentences that contain all possible morphological inflections and syntactic forms discussed. One sentence may have more than one relevant form, so there should not be a separate sentence for each form. Use vocabulary suitable for a young child. When you have completed this exercise, you will have your own instrument for assessing syntax and morphology through elicited imitation, which we discuss in Chapter 10.

REFERENCES

BELLUGI, U. The Acquisition of Negation. Ph.D. dissertation, Harvard University, 1967.

BLOOM, L. *Language Development: Form and Function in Emerging Grammars.* Cambridge, Mass.: The M.I.T. Press, 1970.

BLOOM, L. *One Word at a Time.* The Hague: Mouton, 1973.

BLOOM, L., AND M. LAHEY. *Language Development and Language Disorders.* New York: John Wiley, 1978.

BLOOM, L., M. LAHEY, L. HOOD, K. LIFTER, AND K. FIESS. Complex Sentences: Acquisition of Syntactic Connectives and the Semantic Relations They Encode, *Journal of Child Language,* 7, 1980, 235–62.

BLOOM, L., P. LIGHTBOWN, AND L. HOOD. Structure and Variation in Child Language, *Monographs of The Society for Research in Child Development,* 40 (serial no. 160), 1975.

BOWERMAN, M. Cross-Linguistic Similarities at Two Stages of Syntactic Development, in *Foundations of Language Development* (vol. 1), eds. E. Lenneberg and E. Lenneberg. New York: Academic Press, 1975.

BOWERMAN, M. *Early Syntactic Development: A Cross-Linguistic Study with Special Reference to Finnish.* Cambridge, Mass.: Cambridge University Press, 1973.

BRAINE, M. D. S. The Ontogeny of English Phrase Structure: The First Phrase, *Language,* 39, 1963, 1–13.

BRAINE, M. D. S. Children's First Word Combinations, *Monographs of The Society for Research in Child Development* (serial no. 164), 1976.

BROWN, R. The Development of Wh-Questions in Child Speech, *Journal of Verbal Learning and Verbal Behavior,* 7, 1968, 277–90.

BROWN, R. *A First Language.* Cambridge, Mass.: Harvard University Press, 1973.

BROWN, R., AND U. BELLUGI. Three Processes in the Child's Acquisition of Syntax, *Harvard Educational Review,* 34, no. 2, 1964, 133–51.

BROWN, R., AND C. HANLON. Derivational Complexity and Order of Acquisition in Child Speech, in *Cognition and the Development of Language,* ed. John R. Hayes. New York: John Wiley, 1970, 155–207.

CHOMSKY, N. *Aspects of the Theory of Syntax.* Cambridge, Mass.: The M.I.T. Press, 1965.

CLARK, E. V. On the Child's Acquisition of Antonyms in Two Semantic Fields, *Journal of Verbal Learning and Verbal Behavior,* 11, 1972, 750–58.

CRYSTAL, D., P. FLETCHER, AND M. GARMAN. *The Grammatical Analysis of Language Disability.* New York: Elsevier North-Holland, 1976.

DALE, P. *Language Development: Structure and Function,* 2nd ed. New York: Holt, Rinehart & Winston, 1976.

DORE, J. Holophrases, Speech Acts, and Language Universals, *Journal of Child Language,* 2, 1975, 21–40.

DUCHAN, J. F., AND N. J. LUND. Why Not Semantic Relations?, *Journal of Child Language,* 6, 1979, 243–52.

FILLMORE, C. The Case for Case, in *Universals in Linguistic Theory,* eds. E. Bach and R. Harms. New York: Holt, Rinehart & Winston, 1968.

HALLIDAY, M. A. K. *Learning How to Mean: Explorations in the Development of Language.* London: Longman, 1975.

HOWE, C. The Meanings of Two-Word Utterances in the Speech of Young Children, *Journal of Child Language,* 3, 1976, 29–47.

HUXLEY, R. The Development of the Correct Use of Subject Personal Pronouns in Two Children, in *Advances in Psycholinguistics,* eds. G. B. Flores d'Arcais and W. J. M. Levelt. New York: Elsevier North-Holland, 1970.

INGRAM, D. Transivity in Child Language, *Language,* 47, 1971, 888–910.

INGRAM, D., AND J. EISENSON. Therapeutic Approaches in Congenitally Aphasic Children, in *Aphasia in Children,* ed. J. Eisenson. New York: Harper & Row, Pub., 1972.

KLIMA, E., AND U. BELLUGI. Syntactic Regularities in the Speech of Children, in *Psycholinguistic Papers,* eds. J. Lyons and R. J. Wales. Edinburgh: Edinburgh University Press, 1966, 183–208.

LEE, L. L., AND S. M. CANTER. Developmental Sentence Scoring: A Clinical Procedure for Estimating Syntactic Development on Children's Spontaneous Speech, *Journal of Speech and Hearing Disorders,* 36, 1971, 315–38.

LEOPOLD, W. *Speech Development of a Bilingual Child: A Linguist's Record.* Vol. 1, Vol. 3. Evanston, Ill.: Northwestern University Press, 1939, 1949.

LIMBER, J. The Genesis of Complex Sentences, in *Cognitive Development and the Acquisition of Language,* ed. T. Moore. New York: Academic Press, 1973.

MCNEILL, D. *The Acquisition of Language: The Study of Developmental Psycholinguistics.* New York: Harper & Row, Pub., 1970.

MCNEILL, D., AND N. MCNEILL. What Does a Child Mean When He Says "No?" in *Language and Language Behavior,* ed. E. Zale. New York: Appleton Century, 1968.

MARTIN, J. E. A Study of the Determinants of Preferred Adjective Order in English. Ph.D. dissertation, University of Illinois, 1968.

MENYUK, P. Comparison of Grammar of Children with Functionally Deviant and Normal Speech, *Journal of Speech and Hearing Research,* 7, 1964, 109–22.

MENYUK, P. *Language and Maturation.* Cambridge, Mass.: The M.I.T. Press, 1977.

NELSON, K. Structure and Strategy in Learning to Talk, *Monographs of The Society for Research in Child Development,* 38 (serial no. 149), 1973.

QUIRK, R., S. GREENBAUM, G. LEECH, AND J. SVARTVIK. *A Grammar of Contemporary English.* London: Longman, 1972.

RAMER, A. Syntactic Styles in Emerging Language, *Journal of Child Language,* 3, 1976, 49–62.

SCOLLON, R. One Child's Language from One to Two: The Origins of Construction. University of Hawaii: Working Papers in Linguistics, 6, no. 5, 1974.

SLOBIN, D. I. Imitation and Grammatical Development in Children, in *Contemporary Issues in Developmental Psychology,* eds. N. S. Endler, L. R. Boulter, and H. Osser. New York: Holt, Rinehart & Winston, 1968, 437–43.

STOCKWELL, R. *Foundations of Syntactic Theory.* Englewood Cliffs, N.J.: Prentice-Hall, 1977.

VENDLER, Z. *Adjectives and Nominalizations.* The Hague: Mouton, 1968.

VOLTERRA, V., AND F. ANTINUCCI. Negation in Child Language: A Pragmatic Study, in *Developmental Pragmatics,* eds. E. Ochs and B. Schieffelin. New York: Academic Press, 1979.

7

Semantics

Semantics refers to meaning of words and word combinations. While we alluded to meaning in our discussion of morphology and syntax, the emphasis there was on the form rather than on the objects, events, and ideas being expressed with those forms. It is not easy to separate form and meaning, and it is probably making an artificial distinction to do so. Likewise, a distinction between cognition and meaning seems artificial. Thus, the relationship of semantics to syntax and cognition cannot be disregarded in our attempt to understand a child's semantic regularities.

The nature of meaning has long been debated (see Clark and Clark, 1977, for an introduction to theories of meaning). We will not go into these debates but will distinguish among several ways "meaning" is used and show how they relate to different aspects of semantics. The most familiar sense of meaning relates to the characteristics of the category to which a word applies. We call this *lexical meaning*. When we hear a new word and ask what it means, we are asking for its lexical meaning—that is, we are asking what class of beings, objects, events, or characteristics it applies to. These are the referents for the word. Some words do not have identifiable referents, but rather express a relationship between beings, objects, and/or events. Words such as *and* or *in* have as their meaning particular relationships—they have what we call *abstract relational meaning*. Some words are described as having abstract relations to other words in a sentence as well as lexical meaning. An important aspect of meaning is its reliance on context. Most words are interpreted in light of the situation or linguistic event they are a part of. Some words have a particular reliance on context for their meaning because their referents shift with context. Words such as *you* or *here* have primarily *contextual meaning*. A discussion of meaning must also take into account *nonliteral meaning*, or words' relation not to their usual referents but to some characteristic of those referents. Finally, an aspect of meaning that goes beyond individual words is the way words have meanings in common. We say they share *conceptual domains*. We all feel that certain words "go together" because of some common conceptual tie. Word pairs that are described as synonyms or opposites or associates are among those that share conceptual domains. The effective language user not only has meaning for individual words but knows how those words relate to the meaning of other words.

LEXICAL MEANING

Children's lexical meaning has been studied most extensively at the early stages of language development, with the intent being to characterize the meaning of children's first words and characterize how they are represented in the child's *lexicon* or mental dictionary. We will first present some presumed characteristics of lexical meaning and then discuss some ways child meaning differs from adult meaning.

Meaning as Prototypes

Rosch (1973) introduced the idea that a category or concept can be defined by a prototypic or "best" example of the category. Referents are included in the category based on their resemblance to the prototype, with some being very central because of their strong resemblance and others being more peripheral. Referents do not necessarily resemble each other and may in fact be quite different, but each shares some of the "family" characteristics with the prototype. This prototype view of category formation is in opposition to the more traditional "critical attribute" model which defines members of a category in terms of one or several critical attributes that each must have. If we attempt to define the meaning of *dog*, for example, in terms of critical attributes, we would have difficulty explaining how we know a hairless, tailless, or nonbarking animal is in fact a dog, since having hair and a tail and barking would be considered part of the set of attributes that define *dog*. Using a prototype model, we could explain this inclusion in the category by noting the strong resemblance between the animal and our prototype dog, even though it lacks one or more of the features typical of a dog.

Adults seem to work from an abstract prototype that is composed of the most typical features of referents in a category. This can easily be demonstrated by having adults rate members of a class on how typical they are of that class. They will consistently find *robin* to be a "better" example of *bird* than *owl* or *stork*, for example. Some referents, such as *chicken* or *penguin*, will be very "poor" bird examples and may in fact lead to disagreements about whether they belong in the class. This demonstrates that typical features of the class which the prototype seems to contain are not critical attributes. Having few of the features accounts for some referents, such as penguins being at the periphery of the category. Referents that are most similar to the prototype are most similar to each other, while those nearing the boundaries may be quite dissimilar to each other and most susceptible to exclusion from the category under certain circumstances. For example, colors that are closely related to our prototype *red* will all be similar to each other, but those at different boundaries of the *red* category—those that approach purple or orange—will be perceived as very different from each other. Those at the boundaries are also more likely to be put into another category, depending, for example, on surrounding context of background color.

Some concepts, such as colors and shapes, have been described as natural categories (Palermo, 1978; Rosch, 1973) and have been demonstrated to have relatively stable prototypes across cultural and age groups (Mervis, Catlin, and Rosch, 1975; Rosch, 1973). Other categories appear to have the prototype determined more by experience. The concept of *clothing*, for example, would have a different prototype for individuals living in the arctic and the tropics. Children typically derive prototypes from the first referents they encounter (Rosch and Mervis, 1975). If their first experience with *bird* is the family canary, that will be their prototype against which the "birdness" of other objects is judged.

Meaning as Semantic Features

We have discussed the prototype in terms of the "features" of members of the class. By this we mean the perceptual and functional characteristics shared by some or all members of the class, such as, in the case of birds, feathers, wings, two legs, movement in a certain manner, and so on. Describing the lexical meaning in terms of semantic features involves portraying word meaning as a composite of such defining features. The meaning of *man,* for example, might be described as consisting of the features of "human," "adult," and "male." The feature of "human" would contain such features as "animate" and "mammal." The sense of different words can be described in terms of feature differences. Thus, the meaning of *woman* differs from *man* by including the feature of "female" rather than "male."

It appears that children's first referential words are based on dynamic functional features—that is, children are attentive to how objects act or can be acted on (Nelson, 1973). Later, the stable perceptual features such as shape and size appear to be more critical to the children's decisions on which referents will be included in the concept. Thus, *ball* may be an early word because the dynamic features of a ball make it interesting to the child—it can be picked up, thrown, bounced, rolled, and so on. It is likely to be the stable perceptual features, however, such as shape, that lead the child to identify a new referent as belonging to the ball category.

CHILDREN'S LEXICAL MEANINGS

There are some predictable patterns that children follow in the development of their semantic systems. There are other patterns that are less predictable because they are unique for a particular child. Through structural analysis, we look at the way children use words to try to determine the meaning they have at the time we are doing our assessment. Meanings change as children increase their experience with words, so we cannot take the semantic system to be stable. Some of the characteristics of children's early meanings will persist well beyond the development of complex syntax; others will be short-lived.

Overextension of Meaning

It has frequently been observed by investigators of child language that young children often use words to apply to a wider range of referents than adults do. An example of this is the child whose referents for "doggy" include cats, cows, sheep, and a variety of other four-legged animals. This type of confusion has been called *overextension* by Eve Clark (1973), and her hypothesis is that it results from children's creation of a category based on limited semantic features. In our example, it appears that the child's sense of "doggy" consists only of the features "animal" and "four-legged," but not the other features that distinguish dogs from other animals (such as size, sound, way of moving, and so on). Such overextensions have been reported to stem from a variety of features. Clark (1973, 1974) gives examples of overextensions from many different children learning different languages and concludes that these overextensions are based on a selected perceptual property that the newly named object has in common with the original referent. Shape is the most frequently reported basis for overextensions, as, for example, in the use of *ball* for all round objects. In this case, it can be assumed that a ball was the original referent for the word *ball,* so other round objects are called "ball." The properties of size, sound, movement, texture, and taste have also been reported to be relevant properties in overextensions. Notably absent from this list is color—that is, children do not make errors such as calling all red objects "apple." This leads us to speculate that certain perceptual properties are salient to children because they affect the way objects can be acted upon. Shape is salient because it determines whether the object can be rolled or stacked, for example. Size identifies objects that can be put in one's pocket or sat on. Color rarely makes a difference in the way an object acts or is acted upon until we get into activities such as card games, in which color is arbitrarily assigned significance.

In addition to those instances wherein a child overextends on the basis of one or two critical properties, it has also been observed that children will use the same word for diverse new objects that share different properties with the original object. Bowerman (1976), for example, gives the illustration of Eva using "kick" in connection with (1) herself kicking a stationary object, (2) a picture of a cat with a ball near its paw, (3) a fluttering moth, (4) cartoon turtles on TV kicking their legs, (5) throwing an object, (6) bumping a ball with her trike wheel, and (7) pushing her chest against a sink. While these situations do not share a set of common features, all of them are characterized by one or more features of the original situation which involved waving a limb, sudden sharp contact, and an object propelled. Clark and Clark (1977) refer to this as *mixed overextension.* We could also say each of these referents bears a "family resemblance" to the original, or prototype.

Underextension

Overextension can be seen as using a word for too wide a variety of reference; *underextension* (or *overrestriction*) refers to use of a word for only a subset of the referents in the adult category. Bloom (1973) provides the example of Allison at age nine months using *car* only for cars moving on the street below her window, not for cars standing still, pictured cars, or cars she rode in. While overextension can be explained as incomplete acquisition of semantic features, underextension can best be understood as children's prototypes derived from limited experience. As they learn that a word applies beyond the original referent, they may progress from underextension to overextension. For example, the child in our example may have learned "doggy" first in reference to the family pet, Jake. While the child used "doggy" exclusively for Jake, it was underextended. When the child began to apply "doggy" to other animals that shared some features with Jake, such as those having four legs, the word was overextended to include not only other dogs but nondogs as well.

Wrong Referent

Sometimes children's meanings are different from adults' because they pertain to the wrong referent. Upon first hearing a word, a child may take it to refer to the wrong referent. For example, Clark and Clark (1977) relate these observations made by E. E. Maccoby:

> A mother said sternly to her child: "Young man, you did that on purpose." When asked later what *on purpose* meant, the child replied, "It means you're looking at me."

> A nursery school teacher divided her class into teams, spread a small blanket on the floor at one end of the room and said, "This team will start here," and then put another blanket at the other end of the room, saying "This team will start here." At home, later, a child put down a blanket and set her baby brother on it. He crawled off and the child complained to her mother: "He won't stay on my team!"

These examples clearly demonstrate the role that context plays in the acquisition of meaning.

Word Deficit

We frequently find evidence in children's language samples that they have the meaning of a word but *lack the adult phonological form* to match it. In these cases, they may invent their own form or create one out of known adult elements, such as referring to yesterday as "last day," probably as a parallel form to "last night." They may also rely heavily on *proforms,* such as the pronouns "it" or "those," general descriptive terms, such as "this thing" or "the thingamajig," or pro-verbs such as "do" or "make" in place of more specific verbs. Also common is the use of related words or descriptions to convey their meaning, such as "those things on your shirt" to refer to buttons. In some cases, it appears that the child simply has not learned the phonetic form of the word; in others, it seems the form has been temporarily forgotten. Both of these cases are referred to as having *word-finding difficulty.* If this is the case, the child may actively "search" for the word by trying several descriptions and will recognize the word immediately if it is offered (e.g., Q: Do you mean buttons? A: Yes, that's it—buttons.).

ABSTRACT RELATIONAL MEANING

So far, we have been discussing meanings of words that have objects, events, or qualities as their referents. Meanings of these words, which convey the primary content of language, can be conceptualized in terms of the prototype and/or features that characterize their referents. There are other word classes, however, that have abstract relational concepts as their meanings—that is, they indicate the relationships among the objects, beings, or characteristics of events referred to. Attempts have been made to specify these relationships in various ways. Brown and Fraser (1963) identified a class of *functors* that includes prepositions and conjunctions which express such relationships as well as grammatical morphemes that reflect grammatical structure.

Case Grammar

Fillmore (1968) describes the semantic role of nouns in relation to other elements in the sentence, calling his description *case grammar*. Drawing from descriptions of adult language, he has identified a set of "presumably innate" concepts expressed in all languages. His basic list of cases along with definitions and examples is shown in Table 7.1. In the sentence "The boy plays the piano," *boy* not only has a lexical meaning, it also indicates the actor or agent in the activity and would thus be considered to be in the agentive case. *Piano* would be in the objective case as the noun whose role depends on the meaning of the verb. Each noun is thus seen as expressing abstract relational meaning in addition to its lexical meaning.

Semantic Relations

Several investigators of children's language have also described the abstract relational meanings between words, focusing on those relations expressed in children's early word combinations (Bloom, 1971; Brown, 1973; Schlesinger, 1971). These taxonomies are not restricted to nouns but include

Table 7.1

CASE	DEFINITION	EXAMPLE
Agentive	Instigator of action	*Sam* cut the bread
Instrumental	Force or object causally involved in state or action	*The knife* cut the bread
Dative	Animate being affected by the state or action	Ken murdered *Bob*
Factitive	Object/being resulting from state or action	God created *woman*
Locative	Location or spatial orientation of state or action	I ran *to school*
Objective	The semantically most neutral case; anything representable by a noun whose role in the state or action named by the verb depends on the meaning of the verb itself.	Helen opened *the door*

Source: From *Universals in Linguistic Theory* edited by Emmon Back and Robert T. Harms. Copyright © 1968 by Holt, Rinehart and Winston, Inc. Reprinted by permission of Holt, Rinehart and Winston, CBS College Publishing.

other word classes children use frequently. Schlesinger's list of semantic relations, along with examples of each, follows:

Agent + Action	airplane go; daddy bye
Action + Object	see hat; throw ball
Agent + Object	mommy soup (mommy is eating soup)
Modifier + Head	dirty soap; more milk
X + Dative	throw daddy (throw it to daddy)
(X is any variable)	
Introducer + X	see book; there kitty
X + Locative	sit chair; baby chair (baby is in the chair)

It can be observed that Schlesinger's noun categories of Agent and Object cover several of Fillmore's categories.

Semantic-Syntactic Relations

Bloom and Lahey (1978) have described an extensive list of "semantic-syntactic" relations in the following manner:

Possession—Refers to objects within the domain of different persons, such as "baby cap" or "my block."

Locative Action—Indicates movement to or from a location, as when the child says "away picture."

Locative State—Indicates a relationship between a person or object and its location, such as "dolly up there."

Dative—Indicates the recipient of an object or action, as "for mommy."

Causality—Indicates an implicit or explicit cause and effect relationship between two verb relations. This may be expressed with "because" or "so."

Coordination—Indicates two events and/or states that are independent of each other but are bound together in time and/or space. They may be joined with a conjunction.

Antithesis—Indicates a dependency between two events and/or states exists and is a contrast between them. This may be expressed with "but."

Bloom (1970) and Bloom and Lahey (1978) have also described various usages of negatives and see these as relational meanings. They have identified three meanings of syntactic negation, each with a different pattern of development.

Nonexistence occurs when the referent is not manifest in the context and is correspondingly negated in the linguistic expression. Bloom and Lahey (1978) find nonexistence in single-word utterances and two-word combinations at MLU under 1.5. For example

G: (Gia reads book; closing it) No more
K: (Kathryn not finding pocket in mother's skirt) No pocket

Rejection means that the referent actually exists or is imminent within the contextual space of the speech event and is rejected or opposed by the child. Rejection also is expressed at the one-word stage:

G: (Lois starts to put blocks away, Gia stopping her) No

Bloom and Lahey do not find rejection syntactically expressed until MLU 2.5 to 3.0, when children use the form "don't" + action:

Don't touch my blocks

Some children express rejection with "no" in two-word combinations.

K: (Kathryn pushing away a worn piece of soap) No dirty soap

Rejection also includes things the child does not want others to do:

E: (Eric to mommy after using toilet) No flush

Denial refers to a negative utterance which asserts that an actual (or supposed) prediction is not the case. The negated referent is not actually manifest in the context but is manifest symbolically in a previous utterance. Denial, as a negative answer to questions, may also appear as a single word "no" at an early point in development. Expression of denial syntactically is not described by Bloom and Lahey until MLU 3, then taking the form of two-word and three-word utterances, at first with "no" and later with "not." Examples of denial follow:

M: (Mommy offering car to Kathryn) There's the truck
K: No truck

M: You're just tired
K: I not tired

In many instances negatives have pragmatic function but no relational meaning. Rejection appears to be purely performative—that is, it performs the activity of expressing an obvious intention ("I don't want that"; "Don't do that"). Nonexistence statements may also be performatives when they function as a request for something (e.g., saying "No milk" while holding out an empty cup); or they may be relational when they indicate how implied or stated referents are related (e.g., "No pocket" [on skirt]). Denial statements, too, can be thought of as primarily expressing an intention (e.g., when we disagree or correct).
        Other semantic-syntactic relations identified by Bloom and Lahey also seem to have primarily performative functions. These include the following:

Existence—Indicates that some object is in the situation and has the child's attention. The child may say the name of the object or some form of a demonstrative pronoun or may use a routine "what" question.

Recurrence—Indicates some object exists in the context and either (1) it disappears and it or an equivalent object reappears, or (2) another equivalent object is brought in relation to the first object as another instance of the object. Children may say "more" or "again."

Notice—Refers to the direction of attention to a person, object, or event and includes a verb of notice, such as "see" or "look."

Also included in Bloom and Lahey's relations are several categories that appear to have lexical meaning as their basis. These include

Attribution—Refers to properties of objects, expressed by the child with adjectives.

Action—Refers to movement when the goal of the movement is not a change in location. Action is expressed with verbs.

State—Refers to states of affairs, which might be internal states ("want," "need"); external states ("cold," "dark"), temporary possessions ("my chair") or attributive states.

Quantity—Designates number of objects or persons with plural marker or word such as "some" or number.

Still others included in Bloom and Lahey's semantic-syntactic relations appear to be indicated primarily by specific grammatical forms. These include

Specifier—Indicates a specific person, object, or event by use of demonstrative pronouns or definite article "the."

Epistemic—Indicates a relationship between two states or events that is marked by certainty or uncertainty, as indicated by modals such as "may" or "will."

Mood—Indicates the attitude of the speaker about an event by use of modal verbs such as "should" or "must."

Time—Some references to time are made with grammatical morphemes such as *-ed* and *-ing* or by modal verbs such as "gonna" or "will." These seem to be primarily syntactic relations. Other utterances refer to time with adverbs such as "now"; these seem to have a lexical basis.

In a later report, Bloom and Lahey and their colleagues (Bloom et al., 1980) described several relations expressed with connectives, thus adding to and refining some of the previously identified relations. The relations they specified as expressed by connectives are as follows:[1]

Additive—When two events and/or states are joined without a dependency relationship between them.
e.g., Kathryn: Maybe you can carry that and I can carry this.

Temporal—When there is a dependency between events and/or states which involve temporal sequence or simultaneity.

[1](Examples from Bloom et al., 1980, pp. 244-245 unless otherwise noted.)

e.g., Kathryn: Jocelyn's going home and take her sweater off.

Causal—When there is a dependency between two events and/or states which is most often intentional.

e.g., Peter: She put a band-aid on her shoe and it maked it better.

Object Specification—When the two clauses combined describe an object

e.g., Kathryn: It looks like a fishing thing and you fish with it.

Epistemic—When certainty or uncertainty is expressed.

e.g., Eric: I don't know *what* her name is.

Notice—To call attention to a state or event named in the second clause.

e.g., Kathryn: Watch *what* I'm doing.

Adversative—When the dependency between two clauses is a contrast between them.

e.g., Kathryn: 'Cause I was tired, *but* now I'm not tired.

Spatial Relations

Quirk et al. (1972) have looked at adult usage of prepositions and have identified several relations expressed by this word class. The three broad types of relations most often expressed by prepositions are spatial relations, temporal relations, and manner. Within each type, specific relations have been identified. Spatial relations identified for adults are

1.	Static location	*at* the door
		on the wall
		in the box
2.	Negative location	*away from* the door
		off the wall
		out of the box

With the prepositions that are designated "negative," we do not know where the object or action is, we know only where it is not—thus, the designations as negatives.

3.	Destinations	(walk) *to* the door
		(stick) *on(to)* the wall
		(put) *in(to)* the box
4.	Negative destination	(walk) *from* the door
		(pull) *off* the wall
		(take) *out of* the box

The destination prepositions all involve movement to or away from a static location or destination, while the static locations can be viewed as a result of such movement. For example, compare the following:

I walked to the store	I am at the store
I stuck it onto the wall	It is on the wall
I put it into the box	It is in the box

5. Dimension of the prepositional object

0 dimension	*at* home
	at the bus stop
1 dimension (line)	*on* the road
	on the boundary
2 dimensions (surface)	*on* my face
	on the table
3 dimensions (bounded areas)	*in* the park
	in the state
4 dimensions (containment)	*in* the box
	in the house

Using "at" implies a dimensionless location—a spot that could be located on a map or diagram with no specification of physical properties. "On" indicates a location either on a line (one dimension) or on a surface (two dimensions). "In" implies either a three dimensional space that has volume and can contain matter or an area that is defined by boundaries, even though there may be no physical barrier. "On" can also relate to three dimensional objects, but only to the surface of those objects, and not their inner space:

> The ring on my finger
> The shoe on the foot

The same space can be referred to as either a surface or a bounded area, depending on how we are viewing it:

> There's a smudge on the mirror (surface)
> There's a face in the mirror (bounded area)

6. Relative position

vertical position:	above
	over
	on top of
	———————
	below
	under (underneath, beneath)

horizontal position:	behind	in front of
	in back of	

proximal position:	by, beside, near, between, among

All of these prepositions indicate spatial relation relative to some specified point or object. "Above" and "below" differ from "over" and "under" in that they seem to be broader terms, indicating simply higher or lower than something else.

"Over" and "under" tend to indicate a direct vertical relationship. Compare, for example

>Hold it over the flame (directly in line)
>Hold it above the flame (higher than)

"On top of" generally implies contact with a surface of another subject, which "over" may or may not, and "above" does not. "Beside," "by," and "near" seem to indicate progressively less proximity to the named object. "Between" and "among" both imply multiple objects, with "between" being more specific as it indicates position relative to two other objects.

7.   Passage

0 dimension	*past* the door
2 dimensions	*across* the floor
2–3 dimensions	*through* the wall
	through the park
	run *over* the hill
	fly *above* the clouds
	crawl *under* the table

The perceived dimension of passage is specified with "past" for no dimension or shape of the object:

>We went past the house
>We went past London

"across," which implies passage over a surface:

>The ball rolled across the grass

and "through," which adds the dimension of depth:

>The ball rolled through the grass

8.   Direction of movement

vertical	up
	down
horizontal	along
	across
	around
	toward

"Up" and "down" in this sense express absolute directions and are independent of the starting position of the object. "Along" implies a directional path from one end toward the other of a reference item, while "across" in this case denotes passing over the reference point from one side to the other. Compare, for example

> It rolled across the grass (passage over a surface)
>
> He ran across the road (movement over a reference point)

"Around" indicates a circular or angled path of direction, while "toward" specifies moving in the direction of the reference object.

9. Orientation of the speaker

   Most of the prepositions of relative position and direction of motion can be used in a static sense to indicate the position of the speaker.
   He lives across the road (from here)
   Her office is up the stairs (from here)

10. Pervasive meaning

    throughout the country
    all over my dress
    all through the garden

These prepositions can convey either a pervasive state ("He had mud all over him") or a pervasive action ("they drove all over town").

Temporal Relations

Temporal relations are the second broad type of relation expressed by prepositions. They include the following:

1. Time of occurrence   *at* eight o'clock
                          on Monday
                          in September

"At" is used for points of time, usually clock time or holiday seasons ("at Christmas"). "On" generally refers to specific days, while "in" usually indicates a period of time, such as a month, year, season, etc. While there are these regularities, the semantic distinctions are not clear, and these prepositions frequently give children more difficulty than their spatial counterparts. Inconsistencies such as "*in* the evening" but "*at* night" must complicate the learning.

2. Duration   *for* the summer
                over the summer
                through the holidays
                from June *to* September

Compare: We camp *in* the summer (at some point)
 We camp *for* the summer (for the duration of)

3.   Relative time   *before* the war
 after school
 since June

These can be conjunctions as well as prepositions.
Compare to above: *before* the war started
 after school is over
 since June turned cold

4.   Relational time   *between* lunch and dinner
 by four o'clock
 around noon
 up to last week

Other Relations

In English we also have prepositions of *cause or purpose*, which can generally be seen as an indication of why something is done:

because of the rain
for fun
for fear of a storm

Finally, prepositions of manner specify the manner in which something is done or the instrument it is done with:

manner	Do it *with care* It happened *without trouble* Come to school *by bus*
instrument	Hit it *with a hammer* Draw it *without a ruler* It was hit *by a bus*

Prepositions of *accompaniment* or *support* are also expressed by *with:*

with his friend
with you, not *against* you

The most common English preposition, *of,* has an extensive range of meanings and seems to be in a class of its own. We will simply give some examples to illustrate its versatility.

door of the car	glass of water
house of my family	one of my favorites
envy of the neighborhood	people of the desert
trial of the accused	girl of my dreams
arrival of the train	flock of geese

DEVELOPMENT OF ABSTRACT RELATIONAL MEANINGS

There have been only a few studies of children's abstract relational meanings. While many investigators have looked at acquisition of prepositions, they have tended not to examine the relational meanings expressed by these prepositions. Eve Clark's (1973) description of meanings attached to "in," "on," and "under" is a beginning in this direction. Her findings, as we will discuss in Chapter 8, indicate that earliest relational meaning is highly context bound.

Bloom et al. (1980) have looked at four children's development in their investigation of relational meanings expressed by connectives. They found the children expressed several relations with "and," with the additive meaning emerging first for all four children at about age 26 months. The age range of appearance for the other meanings was more variable but followed a general progression of temporal (mean age 28 months) followed by causal (mean age 31 months). Use of "and" for object specification and adversative meaning was productive for two out of the four children prior to age 36 months.

No other connective was found to express as many meanings as "and." Others noted, in general sequence of productivity, were

> "And then" and "when," expressing a temporal relationship, both emerging about age 31 months.
>
> "Because" and "so," expressing a causal relationship, emerging about 32 and 33 months of age, respectively.
>
> "What," to express epistemic relationship and notice relationship. The epistemic meaning was noted about age 32 months, with notice appearing productively for two children about age 35 months.
>
> "Then," expressing a temporal relationship emerged for two out of the four children about age 33 months.
>
> "If," as an epistemic expression, was used productively by two children about age 34 months.
>
> "But" was used by all the children to express an adversative meaning; it appeared about age 35 months.
>
> "That," as a relative pronoun to express object specification, appeared about age 36 months.

CONTEXTUAL MEANING

As we emphasize throughout this book, context affects our use and interpretation of all aspects of language. In relation to semantics, we can identify several specific ways that context relates to lexical meaning. First, we will discuss how context can affect the prototypic meaning for a category; and second, we will present some word classes which have shifting referents, dependent upon context.

Shifting Meanings

Both linguistic and nonlinguistic context can affect the prototypic meaning of a word. For example, the prototype of *man* will be different in the linguistic contexts of *old man, young man,* or *ancient man.* It can be noted that modifiers, such as adjectives and adverbs, specify a particular and unpredictable variation on a protoype. The features which are most characteristic of the prototype are not ordinarily mentioned. Palermo (1978) speaks to this issue in the following way:

> . . . in discussing dogs, one would not ordinarily mention the fact that they have four legs because that is presumably a part of the core meaning of dog. On the other hand, attributes of the core are likely to be made explicit in language when they involve transformations of the core, i.e., "collie dog." (Palermo, 1978, p. 247)

Nonlinguistic context can likewise shape our prototype. We may have an abstract "best" table, for example, but in the context of looking for a place to set our picnic lunch, the flat-surface feature of the table would be most central to the protype and might lead us to identifying a flat rock as a table.

These examples illustrate shifts in the prototype meaning or sense of words based on different contexts. In other cases, words have more than one meaning, and the context alerts us to which sense or prototype is intended.

Words with Multiple Meanings

There are many words in English that share the same pronunciation and sometimes the same spelling as other words. Thus, while we call these *multiple meaning words,* they are in reality different words that are said the same. These are often called *homonyms.* These include words that are unrelated in meaning, such as *bear* and *bare,* or *can* (auxiliary verb) and *can* (noun). For the prereading child, of course, difference in spelling is not a clue to which meaning is intended.

Many of these words have related meanings that are distinguished by the syntactic role they play. Without context, we cannot tell whether words such as *brush, hammer, pump,* and *building* are nouns or verbs. It becomes clear which meaning is appropriate when embedded in a sentence such as "I see a _____" or "Watch me _____."

When two homonyms are from the same word class, linguistic context alone will not make meaning clear—that is, the statement "The nail broke" is still ambiguous, since we cannot tell which meaning of nail is intended. We need some additional context—we need either something physically present to direct us to one or the other meaning or some knowledge of the topic under discussion. Sometimes ambiguity comes from not knowing which word class words belong to and how to fit words together, such as in the classic example, "Visiting relatives can be a nuisance." Here the ambiguity comes from not knowing whether *visiting* is a verb form, in which case the relatives are being visited, or an adjective form, in which case the relatives are doing the visiting. Within a conversational context the meaning may be clear.

Context, then, can direct us to one of several meanings or prototypes associated with a given phonetic form or word, and further, we are led to formulate or alter our prototype based on "best" meaning for a given situation. Thus, words that can be conceptualized as having prototypes, i.e., those that convey the content of language, are heavily dependent upon context for interpretation.

SHIFTING REFERENTS

Context plays a different role with word classes that have fairly stable meaning but have shifting referents. A word with shifting referents always means the same thing (or approximately so), but the object, person, or event to which it refers changes. We can determine the referent only by knowing what was previously said or experienced, the perspective of the speaker and/or listener, and what comparisons are being made.

Shared Reference

The statement "He can't have it" is impossible for you to interpret because of two words that have no referents for you. While you may know that *he* means male person, and *it* means single inanimate object, you do not know who *he* is or what *it* is. This is because these words lack previous reference. One way to establish the referents is to state them prior to using the pronouns, e.g., "Jack wants my cookie."

We now have *anaphoric reference,* or previous linguistic reference, that establishes the referents for *he* and *it.* The demonstrative pronouns *this* and *that* and the locative adverbs *here* and *there* can also be anaphoric in that they refer to something previously stated. For example

I took it to school and left it *there.*

I saw a movie *that* was really disgusting.

Lakoff (1974) and Tanz (1980) discuss "forward" reference, using the terms *discourse deixis* and *cataphora* respectively. They point out that the word *this* can be used to refer to portions of discourse that follow it as well as precede it:

Now this is what's happening. We must pick up the papers and then . . .

Articles are also influenced by anaphoric reference. If a referent has previously been named or made explicit, the speaker uses the definite article *the* in subsequent references to it, as opposed to the indefinite *a.* For example, if a discussion is taking place about a dog, after the first reference, the participants in the discussion would refer to *the* dog rather than *a* dog.

Related to anaphoric reference is *exophoric* reference, wherein the speaker and listener have participated in a common experience so the referent is clear from the nonlinguistic context. Pronouns and articles are influenced by exophoric reference in much the same way as they are by linguistic reference. Thus, as a muddy dog appears before the conversational partners, the referent for "He's dirty" would be clear and would elicit comments about *the* dog, rather than *a* dog.

Perspective Taking

Sometimes the referents for words shift depending on who is speaking, where the speaker or listener is, or the time the utterance is said. These words are described as *deictic*. The use of personal pronouns always involves person deixis, in that the referent (person) for *I* or *you* (or *my, him,* etc.) shifts, depending on who says it. Likewise, verbs of transfer (e.g., *give* and *take*) and kinship terms (*mother, aunt*) involve person deixis. Place deixis is involved in distinguishing pairs of words like *here-there, come-go,* and *this-that* and are chosen according to the proximity to the speaker and/or direction of motion relative to the speaker (contrast for example, "Bring it here" with "Take it there"). Time deixis is involved in use of tense markers and words such as *today* and *yesterday* and *next* for which the reference in time depends on the moment they are spoken. "Today" is Monday, but in twenty-four hours "today" will be Tuesday and "yesterday" will be Monday. It should be noted that there are nondeictic time references, such as calendar time (July 4, 1776) and clock time (3:00 P.M.). Likewise there are nondeictic uses of terms such as *that* and *there,* other than to denote speaker perspective, as in "I know that" and "There you go."

Comparisons

There are certain descriptive terms for which the referent likewise shifts with different contexts. These are words like *big, little, fat, hard,* and *cold* where there is an implied comparison to a "standard." We call these relative terms because they express a relative judgment. A ten-pound cat is a *big* cat relative to most cats; it is a *small* cat relative to a tiger.

DEVELOPING AWARENESS OF CONTEXTUAL MEANING

There have been numerous studies reporting on aspects of early language in relation to the child's developing awareness of context. We will summarize some of these briefly to illustrate work that has been done. While some patterns can be seen, there are still unanswered questions regarding children's awareness of context as revealed in word choice and comprehension. Current and future research will no doubt shed further light on this process.

Anaphoric References

Bloom, Lightbown, and Hood (1975) found that children's early use of pronouns, at about 2 years of age and when MLU was about 2.5, did not have anaphoric reference—that is, children used pronouns when there was no linguistic situational context available to allow the listener to identify the referent. At the same time, they used nouns in situations where the referent was clear and a pronoun would have been appropriate. It has been demonstrated that by three years of age, children understand the pronoun *it* when used anaphorically (Tanz, 1977); but it is unclear when they begin to use pronouns in a way that demonstrates their awareness of the requirements for previous mention or otherwise indicating the referent.

Warden (1976) found that children under five years of age used the definite article more than the indefinite, but without regard for previous reference. Indefinite articles were not used to introduce new referents until sometime between five and nine years of age.

Bloom (1970) describes the anaphoric *no* that relates back to something previously said or implied. She found that when *no* preceded the subject in children's early utterances (e.g., "No Lois do it"), the *no* negated an alternative previously specified action. An affirmative statement ("Lois do it") was actually being made.

Deixis

Children's first use of deictic terms has been described as beginning with first words, as for example, "da," "this," and "that" (e.g., Leopold, 1939; Nelson, 1973). Deictic terms are also reported to be common in early two-word utterances in a variety of languages (e.g., Bates, 1976; Bellugi and Brown, 1964; Bowerman, 1973; Braine, 1976). This early use of these terms does not, however, appear to be truly deictic, i.e., recognizing speaker perspectives, but rather serves as attention-directing or quasi-referential (Atkinson, 1979; Lyons, 1975). Snyder (1974) observed that a child aged 2.5 who used "that" indicated the distinction between two objects by gesture rather than by appropriate use of deictic terms. Huxley (1970) found no deictic distinction between two children's use of "this" and "that" as late as age four years. Slobin (reported in Clark and Sengul, 1978) found children as old as 4.8 used "there" equally as often to indicate a close object as a distant object.

It is more likely that *pronouns* are the first deictic terms used by children. Tanz (1980), in a study of several deictic forms with children from 2.7 to 5.3 years of age, found that the youngest children already knew the personal pronouns *I, you,* and *he,* while other forms were still unknown to most of them. It appears that the concept of speaker and listener is basic to all deictic systems and must develop first. Tanz offers some reasons why the personal pronoun system might be simpler to master than other deictic systems. She points out that boundaries between pronouns are all clearly defined. Speakers are always "I" and can never refer to self as "you" or "she" in direct discourse. It is never necessary to accompany "I" with a pointing gesture to clarify whom it refers to. Also, the contrast between persons is central to the meaning of pronouns unlike other deictic terms, such as *give* and *take* or *come* and *go,* which have meaning independent of person. These factors help to clarify the meaning of pronouns when used in context.

The other deictic systems seem to be less predictable in order or age of acquisition. Most studies have investigated contrasts within one deictic system, which makes comparison of the different systems difficult. In her investigation of children's comprehension of several contrasts, Tanz (1980) found general trends of development but much variation among children, except in the common development of personal pronouns. She found the spatial contrast between the prepositions *in front of* and *in back of* generally develop next (after personal pronouns), with the contrast being understood by most children around four years of age. Her four year olds also understood *at the side of*. These results are generally consistent with other investigations that report development of *in front of* and *in back of* around age four years (Kuczaj and Maratsos, 1975). Cox (1979) found that at four years of age children may understand one of these terms and be confused about the other but know they both refer to the same dimension in space. It is not clear how children's understanding is affected by use of the terms *in back of* versus *behind* or *at the side of* versus *beside*. There are some indications that *behind* and *beside* are not understood as early as their more descriptive counterparts *in back of* and *at the side of* (e.g., Bangs, 1975).

It must be pointed out that *in front of, in back of,* and *at the side of* have nondeictic meanings if the object being referred to has an intrinsic front and back, as is the case with a person, chair, or television set, for example. With these "fronted" objects, the preposition relates to the named object and not to the position of the speaker—that is, "Put this behind your mother" has a "right" position regardless of where the speaker, the addressee, or the mother are positioned. There are situations, however, where there might be a conflict between the deictic and nondeictic interpretation of these terms, as when the listener is situated between the side of the fronted object and the speaker. The listener is then *beside* the object in a nondeictic sense but *in front of* the object from the speaker's perspective.

Use of nonfronted objects to study children's understanding of these deictic prepositions leads to some problems of interpretation. If a child is asked to "put the ball in back of the spool" and puts the ball on the far side of the spool, the closest side of the spool is assumed to be its "front" (see Box 7.1 [a]). Most but

Box 7.1.

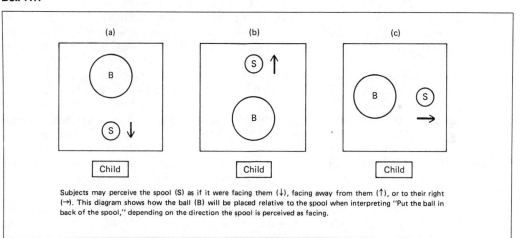

Subjects may perceive the spool (S) as if it were facing them (↓), facing away from them (↑), or to their right (→). This diagram shows how the ball (B) will be placed relative to the spool when interpreting "Put the ball in back of the spool," depending on the direction the spool is perceived as facing.

not all American adults would agree with this interpretation of *in back of*. If, however, the ball is placed on the near side of the spool, the assumption seems to be that the spool is "facing" the same direction as the child is (see Box 7.1 [b]). Hill (1978) refers to this as the in-tandem prototype and notes that it is the prevalent perspective in some cultures as well as that taken by some American adults. Tanz (1980) suggests a third perspective that can be taken, wherein the spool is seen as facing at a 90 degree angle to the right or left of the speaker, in which case the ball would be placed in the opposite direction to carry out the request to place it *behind* the spool (see Box 7.1 [c]). Interpretation is further complicated when we introduce speaker perspective. If we are seated across a table from each other and I ask you to "Put the ball in back of the spool," you must decide whether to take my perspective or to stay with your own perspective. It is also possible to take the perspective of some other person or force, as in "Let's take shelter behind the tree," when speaker and addressee share the same position. Tanz suggests that children's consistency of placement be taken as evidence of understanding these terms deictically, and not "correctness" as judged by the examiner—that is, *in front of* and *in back of* should consistently be represented in opposite positions by the child.

Children learn the nondeictic meaning of *front, back,* and *side* with fronted objects before they understand them deictically (Kuczaj and Maratsos, 1974; Tanz, 1980). Tanz found, however, that there is generally not much of a lag before the deixis of these terms is learned, with both senses being understood around four years of age.

Unlike pronouns, which have absolute boundaries, and unlike the deictic prepositions, which can be learned from concrete frontness-backness features of objects, the demonstrative *this* and *that* and the locative adverbs *here* and *there* indicate spatial relations that are relative and abstract. These terms relate to distance from the speaker, with *here* and *this* indicating proximity and *there* and *that* indicating distance. Distance is relative, however, and the boundary between close and far is not clearly defined, making it unclear in some situations whether *here* or *there* (or *this* or *that*) is the appropriate locater. As Fillmore (1971) points out, *here* can mean anything from "at this point" to "in this galaxy," while *there* can be as close as our own body as in "There's the spot that hurts." There are also no features of objects that make these distinctions easier—that is, there is no inherent "hereness" or "thereness" of objects in the same way there is "frontness" and "backness."

As we have mentioned, these terms may appear among a child's first words as indications of notice or instruments for directing attention; it is not until considerably later that they are deictic. By three years of age, deVilliers and deVilliers (1974) found, children could comprehend *here, there, this, that, my, your, in front of,* and *behind* in a situation wherein the adult sat on one side of a low wall and gave instructions to a child on the other side (e.g., "The M & M is on *this* side of the wall"). Thus, perspectives of speaker and addressee were opposite, and the locative terms could have been interpreted like the pronouns (i.e., on the side close to me versus the side close to you).

Understanding these terms as expressing relative distance from one point appears to be somewhat more complicated. Tanz investigated comprehension of *here, there, this, that,* and *close, far* and found that the proximal (closest to the reference point) member of each pair was most often correct across ages 2.6 to 5.3. Her data suggest that children learn *close* before *far,* since five out of nine of the youngest children (mean age 36 months) knew *close,* while *far* was not known by over one-half of the children until age 60 months. There is a strong tendency for children to learn the deictic *this* before *that.* There is less difference between the order of *here* and *there,* with children being equally likely to learn either first. Over one-half of the children knew both *this* and *that* contrastively at age 52 months; understanding of contrast between *here* and *there* and *close* and *far* was shown by most of the five year olds. Tanz argues that only knowledge of both members of these pairs should be taken as evidence that the child knows the deictic contrast, since correct performance in response to one member of the pair does not demonstrate the contrast is understood. Both Tanz and deVilliers and deVilliers found children tend to choose the option closest to themselves for point of reference. If the examiner makes this closest option the distance terms, as in the deVilliers and deVilliers study (*that* side and over *there* referred to the child's side), it appears they "know" the distance terms first; if this option is identified with the proximal terms (*this* one; *here*), the proximal terms appear to be "learned" first. Thus, it is only when children can demonstrate understanding of both members of a pair that we can be sure they understand either of them.

The verbs of motion, *bring-take* and *come-go,* involve direction of movement. The simplest deictic use of these terms relates to movement toward (*come, bring*) or away from the speaker (*take, go*):

> Bring it here.   Take it over there.
> Come here.   Go over there.

Interpretation becomes more complex when listener position must be considered. For example, "Come upstairs" and "Go outside" involve knowledge of where the listener as well as the speaker is located. A destination or reference point other than the speaker is possible. If these statements refer to past or ongoing events, they still generally indicate the speaker's perspective or "home base" at the time of occurrence.

> "She went to school," said her mother.
> "She came to school," said her teacher.

If the statement refers to future events, there may be more option on choice of verb:

> Everyone is going to the party tomorrow.
> Everyone is coming to the party tomorrow.

Come and *bring* can also be used to indicate accompaniment by the speaker or addressee, in which case direction of movement is not relevant:

> Come upstairs (with me).
> I'll bring it with me.

The results of investigations of children's acquisition of these verbs of motion are somewhat contradictory, but some commonalities can be found. Tanz (1980) studied these verbs by having children choose one of several dolls to be the speaker and another to be the addressee of imperatives containing these verbs. She used the child's ability to identify the speaker as the criterion for understanding the deictic meaning. She found that across the age range of 2.11–5.3, the best performance was on *go*, followed by *take*, with both *come* and *bring* being more often in error. There was no clear relationship between age and acquisition of these verbs, but it was clear that full knowledge of the deixis of *come, go, bring*, and *take* is not complete by age 5. Tanz's findings seem to contradict those of Clark and Garnica (1974) who found *come* and *bring* to be understood before *go* and *take*. Clark and Garnica do note, however, that when the speaker was identified, as was required in Tanz's task, it was easier with *go* or *take*. It was only when the speaker was clearly specified and the addressee had to be identified that *come* and *bring* elicited superior performance. For example, Clark and Garnica had items such as the following where identification of the addressee requires knowledge of deixis:

> The pig says, "Can I come/go into the barn?"
> Which animal is he talking to? (Lion is in barn and monkey is outside of barn)

It was in these cases that utterances with *come* and *bring* were more frequently correct than those with *go* and *take*—i.e., they led more often to choosing the correct addressee. It may be in these cases, as suggested by Tanz, that children have an overriding pragmatic rule that the "person" occupying a space is the one to ask permission from in order to enter it, thus accounting for "Can I come in?" and "Can I bring it in?" being correct, since they fit this rule, and "Can I go in?" and "Can I take this in?" being incorrect, since they do not.

Tanz found that when children were asked to identify the toy to which an utterance was addressed, there were few errors. She noted that the addressee could be identified as the one that was not in the position named. For example, "Go upstairs" must be addressed to someone who is not already upstairs. It is not necessary to understand deixis in order to choose the correct addressee. Identifying the *speaker* of "Go upstairs," however, involves knowing the deixis of "go."

The verbs of possession are similar to these verbs of motion in that they indicate both person and direction of action, but rather than involving overt movement, they describe a more subtle transaction. Gentner (1975) found the simplest of these verbs to be *give* and *take*, which were understood by children in this study by age three and a half; *pay* and *trade* were mastered somewhat later, and *buy, spend*, and *sell* were still not understood consistently by most eight year olds.

In sum, it becomes apparent as we review studies of deixis that it clearly is not mastered all at once. There appears to be a strong tendency for children to acquire first the person deixis involved in pronouns. Spatial deixis of the prepositions *in back of* and *in front of* usually develops next, probably emerging from children's knowledge of the nondeictic *back* and *front*. Spatial deixis is also involved in *here-there* and *this-that*, but in these cases acquisition is not aided by features of objects, which may account for the somewhat later emergence than the spatial prepositions. The verbs of motion can involve the spatial relationship between the speaker and addressee as well as the position of the object or destination in addition to direction of movement. Thus, mastery of these verbs is likely to extend over considerable time. The abstractness of the verbs of transfer account for the still later mastery of these forms.

Another observation that must be made about acquisition of deictic terms is that the specific context in which they are used and/or tested greatly affects children's displayed "knowledge," at least at young ages before mastery is complete. We must be cautious about comparison with "norms" or between children unless we are sure that conditions are comparable.

NONLITERAL MEANING

When we say things such as "It's raining cats and dogs," "The lake is glass," and "A stitch in time saves nine," we are being nonliteral in our meaning. In a different context (e.g., "He's feeding cats and dogs"), the same words have a literal meaning. These examples illustrate several forms of nonliteral meaning. The first is an *idiom*—that is, an expression for which the meaning (there is a lot of rain falling) cannot be derived from the meaning of the component words. The second example is an illustration of *metaphor*, wherein a word for one referent (glass) is applied to a different referent (lake) to make the point of similarity on some feature. Metaphors may be marked by words indicating similarity (referred to as *similes*):

> *As* white *as* snow
> Fly *like* a bird

or be unmarked, as in

> The lake is glass.

Proverbs are a third form of nonliteral meaning. These "wise sayings" are meant to imply a meaning more general than the literal meaning of the component words. While we generally put "all our eggs in one basket" in a literal sense, we may try to avoid situations where too much is at stake in a single unit or operation and thus follow this maxim in a nonliteral way.

Nonliteral language is related to multiple meanings of words, but it signals more than simply a different meaning—it requires the user to disregard the literal interpretation in order to get beyond it to the implication of what is not stated.

Jokes and riddles are similar to idioms, metaphors, and proverbs in that they require us to suspend our usual literal meaning and appreciate the unexpected. These forms of humor often depend on an incongruity or a sudden shift of perspective.

Jokes have been characterized in a variety of ways. Bever (1968, reported in McGhee, 1971a) distinguishes between deep structure and surface structure jokes, based on transformational theory. Surface structure jokes involve alternative segmenting of the words in the sentence:

Q: What kind of flower likes to be kissed?
A: A tulip (two-lip).

Deep structure jokes involve alternative interpretations of the same surface structure:

Q: What animal can jump higher than a house?
A: Any animal. Houses can't jump.

Shultz and Horibe (1974) elaborated on Bever's categories and added two others: lexical and phonological jokes. Lexical jokes involve ambiguity in a single word:

Q: What's black and white and red (read) all over?
A: A newspaper.

Phonological jokes involve focus on similar sounding words or sequences:

Gladly, the cross-eyed bear (Gladly the cross I'd bear)

Metalinguistic jokes have been included in a categorization system of Fowles and Glanz (1977). These focus on the form of the language, rather than the meaning:

Q: What's at the end of everything?
A: The letter *g*.

Some jokes have no "trick" involved beyond creating an expectation for something other than the obvious:

Q: Why did the chicken cross the road?
A: To get to the other side.
Q: One horse was in the barn and another was in the pasture. Which one was singing "Don't fence me in"?
A: Neither one; horses can't sing.

Some jokes involve more than one technique to create ambiguity. They may also involve idioms or metaphorical meaning.

Q: Why did the little boy throw the watch out the window?
A: He wanted to see time fly.

DEVELOPMENT OF NONLITERAL MEANING

Metaphor

Using or understanding a metaphorical meaning of a word that has been learned with a literal meaning is a more complex task than learning two literal meanings. The best studied of these dual-function words are adjectives which refer to both physical and psychological properties. Children first learn adjectives such as "cold," "sweet," and "crooked" as descriptions of physical properties. They gradually begin to apply these terms to personal characteristics. Asch and Nerlove (1960) found that before age six, children understood these terms only in relation to objects or physical characteristics of people, such as

The ice is cold.
Her hands are cold.

Between seven and ten years of age, they may understand the use of these terms when applied to a personal characteristic but give two separate and totally distinct meanings to the same term, as in

The ice is cold.
She is a cold person.

It is not until children are between ten and twelve years old that they understand and verbally describe the relationship between application of the term to objects and to people. For example, "she is cold like ice means she isn't friendly."

In another study of this same class of adjectives used metaphorically, Winner, Rosenstiel, and Gardner (1976) asked six to fourteen year olds to explain sentences such as

After many years of working in the jail, the prison guard had become a hard rock that could not be moved.

Again, it was found that children below ten years of age could not appreciate the dual-function term (*hard*). While ten and eleven year olds understood that a psychological trait was the topic (the guard's character in this example), it was only the adolescents who could identify the mutual characteristics (e.g., the guard is stubborn, unyielding, stern, cruel, set in his ways).

This was part of a series of studies of metaphor that have been conducted by Gardner, Winner, and their colleagues. They have also found that when the task is simplified, younger children show evidence of understanding metaphors. Children as young as eight years old can match the appropriate picture to a verbal metaphor, e.g., the metaphor "He has a very heavy heart" (Winner, Krauss, and Gardner, 1975). Gardner (1974) found that preschoolers are able to match adjectives across modalities (e.g., *bright, soft, loud,* in relation to color or texture) and interpreted this as metaphoric matching. An alternative explanation would be that the literal meaning of these terms is more general for children, perhaps translating as degree of intensity and thus applicable across modalities. This matching then seems nonmetaphorical.

Looking for evidence of nonliteral language in children's production is likewise confounded by possible alternative interpretations of what young children mean by what they say. When a three year old calls a chimney a "house hat," as reported by Gardner et al. (1978), or describes a bald man as having a "barefoot head" (Chukovsky, 1968), we might see these as metaphors. Alternatively, we can explain them as overextensions due to lack of awareness of restrictions on these words or due to making do with limited vocabulary. Winner (1979) suggests that metaphors in early language can be identified by one of several criteria:

1. The child has also used the literal name for an object, demonstrating that it is not lack of knowledge of the conventional name that leads to the unusual word choice.
2. A familiar object is used in a novel way and is renamed accordingly (e.g., putting a basket on the foot and calling it "boot").
3. Familiarity with the literal name is assumed based on familiarity with the object and high probability of having frequently heard its name, even though it is not produced.
4. Utterances expressed in the form of similes (e.g., "This looks like a moon").

Winner thus distinguished metaphors from anomalies, which she identifies as having no apparent overlap (e.g., calling the moon "piano"). She also distinguishes them from overextensions, which arise from the child's understanding that the objects in question belong to the same class and thus can be called by the same name.

Using these criteria, Winner examined unconventional word usage in the spontaneous language samples of Adam, one of the children studied by Brown (1973). She found the majority of Adam's utterances to be metaphors rather than overextensions or anomalies, with most metaphors being renamings of physical objects. The samples taken when Adam was between 2 and 3 years old showed primarily "pretend-action" metaphors, wherein he performed a pretend action on an object, treating it as if it were something else and renaming it accordingly. For example, he held a pencil as if it were corn on the cob and called it "corn."

By age four, most of his metaphors were non-action related but were based on similarities between the properties of two objects, such as shape, configuration, color, size, and so on. He also produced at ages two, three, and four, a few nonpretend action metaphors, in which object renaming is accompanied by an appropriate action, such as "I'm putting on your clothes, crayon," while replacing the paper cover on a crayon. Also, none of the metaphors at age two years were marked as metaphorical with "like," but rather took the form of using the copula—e.g., "This is a boot." By age four, the marked forms were more than twice as frequent as the unmarked (e.g., "This is like a moon"). Winner suggests that this change reflects an increasing sensitivity to the needs of the listener as well as the metalinguistic awareness that language is being used in a somewhat special way.

Using an experimental approach, Gardner et al. (1975) elicited metaphors from three to nineteen year olds by asking them to complete vignettes concluding with segments such as "It was as quiet as _____." They found the preschoolers produced more "imaginative" endings than any other group. Unlike Adam's spontaneously produced metaphors, however, many of these elicited metaphors were anomalous:

> Weather as cold as "the Indian."
> Sad as "a pimple."

They also were more complex than the renamings Adam displayed, which were restricted in form and topic and always referred to present objects. The school age children in this study showed very few imaginative endings, preferring conventional comparisons such as

> A noise as loud as "thunder."
> Weather as hot as "the sun."

It was only the oldest group, who were college students, who approached the preschoolers in frequency of imaginative responses. By this age, subjects formed metaphors based on a converging set of properties rather than on a single characteristic in common and conveyed an understanding of the affective or psychological realm.

This "literal" stage between preschool and adolescence, when metaphoric language virtually disappears, has been noted by other investigators (e.g., Billow, 1977; Pollio and Pollio, 1974; Winner et al., 1976). Not only are school age children less likely to produce their own metaphors, they frequently resist attempts to engage in figurative language—e.g., "A tie can't be loud"; "Cloth doesn't make noise" (Gardner et al., 1978).

This progression from imaginative forms in early childhood, conventional forms at school age, and imaginative forms at adolescence has been described as a U-shaped curve by Gardner and Winner and their colleagues, with the implication that resistance to being nonliteral emerges at about age six and subsequently declines as adolescence is approached. A possible explanation for this resistance is that school-age children are concentrating on learning society's literal meanings and are reluctant to consider violations to the conventions they are acquiring. As they become more confident of their literal knowledge, they can explore nonliteral alternatives.

Another explanation could be that the imaginative responses of the youngest children are not metaphorical at all but rather represent their lack of conventional associations and/or lack of understanding of the syntax. They may, for example, perceive this task as "Say something funny when it's your turn to talk" and not relate it to the form "as X as a Y" (as in "as pretty as a picture"). Young school-age children may likewise be largely ignoring the form and responding with a conventional association to the adjective presented (e.g., "hot sun"; "loud thunder"). Only by age ten or eleven do children appear to understand both the syntax and the concept of metaphoric comparison, as they are able to paraphrase metaphors appropriately. They are also able to produce some figurative language at this age but may not do so spontaneously. With adolescence comes the cognitive and linguistic abilities needed to understand and produce metaphors based on a variety of links between domains. It has been suggested that this precise use and understanding of metaphor is related to attainment of formal logical operations (Elkind, 1969; Inhelder and Piaget, 1958).

Proverbs

It is also not until adolescence that proverbs are understood. This is not surprising, since these nonliteral forms are more abstract than metaphors because the domain that is the topic is not mentioned at all. While preadolescents may or may not be able to paraphrase proverbs, they have consistently been found unable to interpret them in any generalized sense (Billow, 1975; Piaget, 1926; Richardson and Church, 1959). Thus we might expect preadolescents to explain proverbs literally—e.g., "Don't put all your eggs in one basket means you shouldn't put them all in one basket because you might drop it." We would not expect them to generalize this wisdom beyond eggs or even to other breakable objects.

Children's Humor

Children often reveal interesting things about their semantic knowledge—and lack of knowledge—through the jokes and riddles they understand and tell. The source of humor in puns, jokes, and riddles is largely semantic, often involving multiple meanings and metaphor. Comprehension depends on understanding multiple meanings, as well as on perceiving the incongruity among them. In addition, with riddles there is a particular form that is appropriate that is different from most verbal exchanges, which signals this as a particular kind of speech event wherein the surface form of language is important.

Prior to about age six, children's "jokes" are largely nonlinguistic. Children may appreciate the incongruity in a picture or story, or find the pie-in-the-face episodes in cartoons funny, but they are not able to appreciate humor created with language alone. Certain topics or words may be funny in themselves for young children, but this is different from the humor that comes from the manipulation of language that is involved in linguistic humor.

The development of verbal humor may be tied to concrete operational thinking, as suggested by a series of studies by McGhee (1971a, 1971b, 1972, 1974). Other investigators (e.g., Brodzinsky, 1975; Prentice and Fathman, 1975;

Shultz, 1974) also documented that six year olds, who are generally preoperational in their thinking, exhibit little appreciation for joke structure and enjoy "jokes" just as much when there is no incongruity or punch line. For example

Q: What do giraffes have that no other animal has?
A: Long necks.

is appreciated just as much as when the answer is a twist on the expected:

Q: What do giraffes have that no other animal has?
A: Little giraffes. (Prentice and Fathman, 1975)

Our own observations indicate that children often acquire the frame for riddles and jokes before they have the semantic and metaphoric knowledge to understand them. It is not uncommon for young children to tell riddles or jokes that are formally correct but totally nonsensical from an adult perspective. We know of a six year old, for example, who loved to tell a "scary" story, complete with appropriate intonation, with a punch line that involved a mysterious noise made by "wrapping (rapping) paper." In his version, however, the culprit became "paper towels," which was just as funny to him as the original version. We also have observed older children who clearly have the format but not the sense (or nonsense) of riddles, as shown in their attempts to create novel riddles:

Q: What kind of animal likes to be picked up?
A: A cat.   (John, age 8)

At this stage, children are likely to have "near misses" in retelling riddles they have heard:

Q: What's green and has wheels?
A: A garbage truck.   (Steven, age 7)

Riddle buffs will recognize this as an attempt at "What has four wheels and flies?" Since Steven didn't appreciate the ambiguity of "flies" when he originally heard the joke, it became unnecessary in its retelling. At the same time, the form of the exchange is recognized as important in making a riddle, and children will often adhere rigidly to this frame, usually telling the riddle in exactly the same way (although not necessarily the "right" way). Children recognize that slight changes make a difference, even though they do not yet understand which changes make a difference and which do not. In the same joke-telling session, Steven retold a joke he had previously heard from someone who was not following joke-telling rules, but he did not recognize this since the frame was correct.

Steve: What did the Chinese man say to the robber?
Adult: What?
Steve: I'm not going to tell you!
Adult: Why not?
Steve: That's it! That's the answer: I'm not going to tell you.

John also attempted a retelling of a joke, again a near miss, but revealing a possible reliance on phonological cues in recall:

Q: What kind of flower likes to be kissed?
A: A toilet (instead of tulip, i.e., two-lip)

   Fowles and Glanz (1977) also found this stage wherein children understand the frame but not the linguistics of riddles in a study of six to nine year olds. A prior stage that they identified was characterized by a vague, confused retelling of riddles with no evidence of the riddle frame. Explanation of riddles was confused and reflected no awareness of what made them funny. At the next stage (which is what we have been describing), children could coherently retell the riddle but changed the form, deleted portions necessary for a coherent interpretation, or added sections to make it informative rather than a riddle. Children's explanations at this level involve identifying something as funny in the riddle but not seeing that it is the language rather than the situation that makes it funny:

Q: How do you keep fish from smelling?
A: Cut off their noses.
Explanation: [It's funny] because I don't think fish really have noses. (Fowles and Glanz, 1977)

At the third level, riddles are retold verbatim or nearly so. Explanations focus on the attributes of language rather than on the situation. In response to the above riddle, one child explained "It means smelling like sniffing instead of smelling like stinking." Prior to this third stage, children often attempt to answer the question, usually in a literal way, indicating they are still having difficulty recognizing the uniqueness of this speech event. They have not yet understood that the intent is not to exchange information, not to attempt to answer a question. Fowles and Glanz also found that children's ability to recall and retell riddles was not necessarily predictive of their ability to explain them. Their findings did not indicate that level of competence with riddles was clearly related to age but did indicate some relation to reading ability. This would suggest that riddles might be useful for identifying children who are having difficulty dealing with language metalinguistically.
   Fowles and Glanz identify some factors that make riddles difficult for children to explain or retell. These include difficult vocabulary, stilted syntax, length, abstractness, or metaphorical meaning. They further found that some riddles seem to have a setup question that strongly favors one interpretation of the ambiguous segment, and this seemed to increase difficulty. If this is generally the case, riddles that have the ambiguous segment in the answer rather than the question would be easier:

Q: Why didn't the skeleton cross the road?
A: It didn't have the guts.

In a study of children aged eight, ten, and twelve years, Shultz and Horibe (1974) found children up to age nine to be most sensitive to jokes based on phonological structure. For example

Man:	What is this?
Waiter:	It's bean soup.
Man:	I don't care what it's "been," what is it now?

Between nine and twelve years of age, children also developed appreciation for jokes depending on dual interpretation of a single word:

Q: What has eighteen legs and catches *flies*?
A: A baseball team.

Not until after age twelve did children understand jokes that involved alternative deep-structure interpretation of the same surface structure:

Q: What makes people baldheaded?
A: Having no hair.

or jokes that involved alternative grouping of words in a sentence:

Q: What happened to the man who fell from a ten story window?
A: Nothing. He was wearing a light fall suit.

CONCEPTUAL DOMAINS

So far we have been talking about meanings of single words. However, our sense of what a word means cannot be isolated from how that word relates to other words. Semantic relatedness accounts for our feeling that certain words "go together." Word meanings are related to each other in different ways, depending on how we conceptualize the relationship between the referents for those words. "Cold" is related to "hot" in a different way than it is to "white." We conceptualize "cold" as opposite to "hot." "Cold" and "white" may seem unrelated until we think about qualities of snow. *Opposition* and perceived *qualities* are examples of *conceptual domains* within which we organize and relate individual word meanings. We will describe several of these to illustrate their role in semantic relatedness.

Qualities

There are several domains that apply to the attributes or qualities of objects that we perceive as related. Some of these qualities are *sensory* and thus have a general relationship with other sensory qualities, such as color with taste. We also have subcategories within sensory qualities that relate to only one sense, such as salty, sweet, and sour relating to the domain of taste; or subcategories that relate to one dimension of one sense, such as red, orange, and green relating to the color dimension of vision, while light, bright, and dim also relate to vision but are brightness qualities. We would agree that all of these qualities go together in a general way in that they are all sensory, but the conceptual domain in which we are operating will determine which specific qualities seem most related in meaning. If we are thinking about taste, "green" and "sour" are related, while if our domain is color, we are likely to relate "green" and "blue." Thus, we would not say that any word belongs to any one domain but rather that domains organize the way that the word relates to others.

We relate objects on the basis of other qualities in addition to sensory attributes, which we might group together as *logical* qualities in that these attributes require some integration of sensory input. Qualities of size, shape, substance, number, and spatial relations, among others, can be thought of as generally related to each other as well as to sensory qualities of objects. That is, "round" is related to "square" and "triangle" in the conceptual domain of shape. It is related to "big" and "hard" in the domain of logical qualities. It is also related to "red" in the domain of all physical properties.

Other properties of objects have to do with their *function* or activity. We might think of objects together because of what they do or what can be done to or with them. We thus see "car" and "airplane" related in meaning because of their common function of carrying passengers. Pencils and crayons are related because we perform the same kind of action with them.

People have *affective* qualities, which can be thought of as a conceptual domain. We tend to think of "happy," "sad," "friendly," and "cruel" as related in meaning because they refer to affective qualities. The first two ("happy," "sad") may seem more closely related to each other than to the latter two because both relate to feelings, which could comprise a separate domain from "friendly" and "cruel" which might imply one person's judgment of another's behavior or character.

Time

The conceptual domain of time involves much more abstract thinking than domains related to qualities of objects or people, since it does not relate to our senses or affective state. One point in time does not look or feel any different from another point in time if we separate out what we characteristically do at certain times. As adults, we frequently comment that it "feels like Friday" or "feels like midnight" because we have learned to associate certain events or bodily states with linguistically designated points in time. If we lacked the words for Friday and midnight, we would not be likely to have concepts of "Fridayness" or "midnightness," since we can experience the events and states typically associated with those points in time at other times. We contend, therefore, that the conceptual domain of time is developed only through the development of the language that relates to time. We use clocks and calendars, for instance, to teach the language and thus the concept of time, since we cannot give children direct experience with time as we can with elements of other cognitive domains. The time domain may be structured into clock time (one o'clock, noon), sequential time (morning, afternoon, night, before, after), and near time (yesterday, tomorrow) versus far time (historical past, distant future) among other possibilities. As we have mentioned, some of the time domain also involves deixis.

Specific Relationships

Many conceptual domains are given cohesiveness by a specific kind of relationship between referents within that domain. This cohesiveness is represented in the *superordinate* category to which all the referents belong. Apples, oranges, and kumquats, for example, all belong to the superordinate category of fruit, while carrots, cucumbers, and cauliflower are part of the vegetable domain.

Whole-part relationships operate in other domains. For example, tires are related to cars in a way that places them within the same domain. *Attributes* are similarly related to objects that possess them, as illustrated by the relatedness of "cold" and "snow."

Possession is a particular kind of relationship that, like attributes, expresses specification or modification of an object. Possession might be divided into two domains: *alienable possession* and *inalienable possession*. Inalienable possessions are those that always belong to a person—possession cannot be given up or taken away, as is the case with body parts and kinship (e.g., John's nose; Mary's mother). Alienable possessions are those that can be less permanently within the possession of one person (e.g., John's car; Mary's milk). We could also draw a distinction between alienable possessions that are relatively stable in their ownership and those that are transient. For example, "This is my chair" could be an expression of ownership or it could express a temporary state of occupying a particular chair. We generally do not include all these senses within the same domain.

Opposition likewise can be thought of as several particular relationships that are related. There are binary opposites, wherein the presence or absence of a single factor relates two states. There are relatively few of these "pure" opposites, but they would include life-death, on-off, and light-dark (in the absolute, not relative sense)—absence of life is death, absence of on is off, absence of light is dark.

With *polar opposites,* two qualities are highly related in that they refer to the same dimension but are described as opposites because they are taken as the extremes of that dimension. We have many examples of polar opposites, such as tall-short, fat-thin, young-old, hot-cold. It can be seen that each characteristic has much more in common with its "opposite" than with a member of a different pair (i.e., "cold" is much more similar to "hot" than it is to "tall"), so it is not accurate to think of these characteristics as maximally dissimilar; rather they should be thought of as differing only in the degree of some quality, such as heat, height, width, or age.

Finally, some "opposites" are actually mutually exclusive categories. We divide up some domains in an either-or fashion and then may think of them as opposites. People are either male or female; they cannot be in both categories at the same time, so we say these are mutually exclusive categories. We can classify trees as deciduous or conifers and animals as wild or domestic. These categories differ from binary opposites in that they are not based on the presence or absence of a single feature, but rather each category involves different features. We would not say, for example, that "male" is the absence of "female." We can also see that the way we divide up these domains is arbitrary—people could be classified as child or adult instead of male-female; likewise, we can divide trees into flowering and nonflowering, and animals into two-legged and four-legged. In other words, I can say the opposite of "man" is "boy" and not seem wrong. These categories depend on learning of specific mutually exclusive categories rather than on learning a principle of opposition.

We have not intended to be inclusive in our discussion of conceptual domains. There are other domains that have conceptual cohesiveness and thus relate different word meanings to each other—"sister" and "friend," for example, are related in meaning because both involve a relationship between people. Nor do we mean to imply that the meaning of a word relates to only one conceptual domain. Rather, the meaning of a word depends in part on the conceptual domain within which we are operating. "Sister" and "friend" may share a meaning if we are thinking in terms of people who we have a particular kind of relationship with; "sister" and "aunt" may share a different meaning, and "sister" and "brother" different still.

Common Context Categories

The context in which words and referents are frequently encountered also contributes to our sense that certain words go together. Words that refer to objects and actions that frequently occur together in our experience are related through situational context. For example, plates, cups, knives, napkins, and placemats are all part of our on-the-table context and thus are related even though they do not all fall under the same superordinate category. Some words occur together frequently and thus are related through *linguistic* context. This may be because the referents for the words have a common situational context (e.g., salt and pepper) or because of convention (e.g., ladies and gentlemen). In the latter case, it is not the common situational context of being together that leads us to use this expression to address a group of people, but rather social convention, since we might otherwise refer to the same group as "women and gentlemen" or "ladies and males" or even "talls and shorts." Expressions such as "tall, dark, and handsome" likewise fall within a conventional linguistic context. In some cases, we linguistically pair words that cannot occur situationally together, such as "night and day." This illustrates that all words that are related by linguistic context are not necessarily related by situational context. The reverse is also true. For example, most people would agree that "putter" and "golf" are related in meaning, but we do not typically talk about a "golf putter" or otherwise linguistically pair these words. Thus, it seems that it is the situational rather than the linguistic context that contributes to the relatedness of these two words.

SYNTAX AND CONCEPTUAL DOMAINS

When we look at the manner in which conceptual domains are expressed, we can see that the different syntactic classes tend to express particular kinds of concepts. Awareness of these relationships can assist us in doing structural analysis. We will discuss the major categories and some associated conceptual domains.

ADVERBIALS   Adverbials, which might be simple adverbs, prepositional phrases, or subordinate clauses, can express several conceptual domains. Most frequently, they express time, location, and manner but can also relay information on causality and recurrence. Stated in another way, adverbs supply information as to when, where, how, why, and how many times something occurred. The same adverb may express different concepts, so we want to think about the meaning, not just the word. For example, *once* in the utterance "I did it once" can refer either to time (sometime in the past, I did it) or number of occurrences (I did it only one time).

The following are examples of temporal adverbials:

three o'clock	tomorrow	before bed
on Saturday	next week	after dinner
during the summer	last night	the next day
on my birthday	now	since Friday

We can note that the first column lists definite points in time that do not shift, while the second column lists points in time that are all deictic—i.e., they have different referents at different times. The third column relates to sequencing of events more so than to points in time.

Spatial adverbials can also have possible patterns, such as definite vs. indefinite place:

in the chair	near the chair
under the bed	somewhere round my school
on the table	along the road

or static place vs. expression of motion

it's in my pocket	put it in(to) your mouth
it's at home	take it to her
it's on the wall	get it from her

Manner adverbials can relate to how the action is done in a number of ways—for example

1. A characteristic of the action
   slowly
   quickly
2. The instrument with which the action is done
   with a hammer
   with a brush

3. An accompanying person or object
   with my mom
   with my blanket
4. The state of the actor
   with pleasure
   in a fit

Other adverbials can likewise be identified and analyzed for the kind of information they convey. For example, *why* the action is done may be answered with either adverbs of causality or motivation:

because the rope broke (causality)
since you didn't do it

because he wanted to (motivation)
because I'm tired

How many times the action is done or the state occurs relates to whether it occurred one or more times. This may be indicated quantitatively, for example

once, twice, . . .

or with a general expression of recurrence:

over and over
again
a lot more times

ADJECTIVALS   Adjectivals express various kinds of qualities and particular relationships. The major qualities expressed can be grouped in the following manner:

SENSORY QUALITIES

Vision (e.g., blue, bright)
Sound (e.g., shrill, loud)
Touch (e.g., smooth, cold)
Taste (e.g., sweet, yucky)
Smell (e.g., stinky, delicious)

LOGICAL QUALITIES

Shapes (round)
Size (big)
Number (three)
Substance (wooden)
Condition (broken)

AFFECTIVE QUALITIES

Feelings (happy, sad)
Bodily states (hungry, sleepy)
Judgments (friendly, cruel)

Some of the specific relations expressed with adjectives are

Possession (my, mommy's)
Exclusivity (only, this)
Qualification (enough, many of)
Relative position (first, next)
Comparison (more, bigger)
Opposition (this one's big; this one's little)
Disappearance (all gone)

VERBS   To analyze the conceptual domains expressed by verbs, we are interested primarily in the lexical verbs, since the copula expresses existence, along with time, as shown in tense. The lexical verbs, on the other hand, can show many different domains. We will list only some of these.

1. *Change of state verbs* describe action that changes the state of material or person—e.g., *cut, bake, kill.*
2. *Action verbs* that need no object—e.g., *sleep, sit, run.*
3. *Causative verbs* are verbs that mean to cause the event or state of affairs to come about—e.g., *drop, kill, bring.*
4. *Motion verbs* express a manner of moving—e.g., *run, walk, skip.*
5. *Sensory stative verbs* relate to passive sensory experiences—e.g., *hear, see, feel, know.*
6. *Sensory process verbs* relate to active sensory experiences—e.g., *listen, look, touch, think.*
7. *Deictic verbs* depend on placement and direction of movement of the speaker and listener—e.g., *bring-take; come-go.*
8. *Pro-verbs* state a general action that could be applied in several situations—e.g., *do, go, fix.*

NOUNS   The domains covered by nouns are too numerous to begin to enumerate. Some basic categories within which to explore conceptual domains are as follows:

1. *Animate nouns,* which refer to people and animals—e.g., my *sister,* the *cat.*
2. *Inanimate nouns,* which refer to all others—e.g., *book, tree.*
3. *Concrete nouns,* which refer to tangible referents—e.g., the *cat,* a *tree.*
4. *Abstract nouns,* which refer to nontangible referents—e.g., *love, success.*
5. *Place nouns,* which name a location—e.g., Central Park, Buffalo.

Within each of the categories, there could be numerous conceptual domains expressed with nouns.

DEVELOPMENT OF SEMANTIC RELATEDNESS

Development of semantic relatedness has been studied primarily through various experimental procedures, with few attempts to study expression of conceptual domains in naturally occurring situations or to explain the nature of acquisition of semantic relatedness. One area of investigation that is tied to a theoretical formulation of acquisition of meaning is polar adjectives. More typically, performance on specially formulated tasks, such as word association tests or tests of specific relationships, are described with few attempts made at explaining the nature of what children are doing when they perform these tasks.

Polar Adjectives

Polar adjectives are "opposites" in that the two members of a pair denote opposite ends of a scale of a single dimension. Thus, *hot* and *cold* are related by the dimension of temperature but differ in placement on a temperature continuum. These pairs of adjectives have been related to a phenomenon called *markedness* (H. Clark, 1969; Lyons, 1968; Sapir, 1944; Vendler, 1968), by which one member of each pair is taken to be the neutral or positive characteristic of the scale, while the other member is seen as the negative or "marked" counterpart. The nonmarked member is seen as describing the whole scale and the "normal" condition of the dimension. Thus, we say "How tall is it?" or "How old is he?" when we have made no prejudgment about the height or age. Asking "How short is it?" or "How young is he?" implies that we already have judged height or age to be less than normal. *Tall* and *old* are thus described as unmarked, while *short* and *young* are marked.

Children are generally described as learning positive or unmarked dimensional terms before the marked term. We would thus expect them to know *tall* before *short, big* before *little, more* before *less, high* before *low,* and so on. It has been suggested that the two opposites may first mean the same thing for children, being either the positive end of the scale or a more general concept. Donaldson and Balfour (1968) suggest that children first understand *more* and assume *less* means the same thing. Clark and Clark (1977) suggest that both terms initially mean *some.* While the patterns observed generally follow the development of the unmarked term first, we cannot be sure that it is the positive nature of the concept that is salient rather than particular cognitive strategies or preferences that shape this sequence, or the way questions are framed to elicit responses consistent with the adult sense of unmarked.

Word Associations

Word association tests have been used for years as an experimental procedure. As early as 1916 (Woodrow and Lowell, 1916), it was noted that children below the age of about seven years typically respond to such tasks differently than older children and adults do in that their responses tend to be from a different word class than the stimulus word. More mature subjects generally give a within-class response. This is often referred to as the syntagmatic-paradigmatic shift, after Ervin (1961). A *syntagmatic* response is one in which the response forms a syntactic relationship with the stimulus word (e.g., stimulus: "hot"; response: "water"). A *paradigmatic* response forms a semantic relationship (e.g., stimulus: "hot"; response: "cold"). McNeill (1966) has suggested that young children's syntagmatic responses occur because the semantic features of words are not yet well enough established for them to stay within word class. This semantic explanation is consistent with other observations that not until around age seven years are children able to deal with more abstract language. Muma and Zwycewicz-Emory (1979), with a variation of a word association test, however, observed that when children were asked to fill in a blank before and/or after a stimulus noun, repeating the noun along with the added words, the results were reversed; that is, the youngest children (five years old) gave other nouns to fill in the blanks, while older children (age nine years) and adults gave other word classes to make a syntactic unit, such as adjectives before a noun and verbs following a noun. The difference is apparently in the perceived task, but this demonstrates that young children can make paradigmatic responses in this task. There would seem to be an element of syntactic awareness that is also being tested here, so results are difficult to interpret.

Analogies

Analogies are closely related to association tasks but involve embedding the stimulus word into a format to elicit a particular kind of association, such as

> *Boy* is to *girl* as *man* is to _____.

The relationship being elicited here is one type of opposite. If the item were

> *Boy* is to *man* as *girl* is to _____.

a different semantic domain, i.e., age, would be elicited. The relationship in analogies can be from any of a number of conceptual domains. Some examples follow:

> Subordinate-superordinate: *Apple* is to *fruit* as *chair* is to _____.
> Whole-part: *Apple* is to *peel* as *body* is to _____.
> Object-function: *Apple* is to *eat* as *water* is to _____.
> Object-attribute: *Apple* is to *red* as *grass* is to _____.

Research with children's analogies has been confined largely to older children. Achenbach (1970), using an original test of associations with children from grade 5 to grade 8, found that some children at all ages respond to analogies as though they were free association tasks.

Gentile and Seibel (1969) developed a rating scale of semantic relatedness, and in subsequent studies Gentile and his colleagues (1970, 1977) found degree of semantic relatedness to be highly correlated with analogy solutions. This suggests that analogic reasoning for both children and adults is largely association, i.e., they respond with another word that comes from the same conceptual domain as that they most frequently attribute to the stimulus word. For example, the child who completes an item such as

> Grass is green; sugar is _____.

with "sweet" is not wrong semantically but has responded with sugar in the taste domain, which is more usual, rather than in the color domain which is required by the analogy stem. Eventually, individuals learn to use the analogy to identify the conceptual domain rather than responding with that which is most frequent or otherwise most salient for them.

Analogy items appear on several standardized tests, generally for older children, but some with items for children as young as two years old (Kirk, McCarthy, and Kirk, 1968). At this age, it is improbable that children identify the domain of the analogy, and it can be observed that they respond to the second part of the item (sugar is _____) the same, whether or not the first part is given (grass is green). It is not clear when most children begin to recognize the domain and thus begin to treat the pair as an analogy, but it appears from the research that many cannot do this into late childhood. Unfortunately, the studies that have been done have generally not analyzed the items used for the kind of domain they signal, and thus they reveal little about the knowledge of semantic relatedness ideas of the children responding to them. This would be our interest in observing the analogies that children can and cannot solve. Familiarity of vocabulary is certainly a factor in recognizing the domain, so children may be able to solve some analogies within a domain with familiar vocabulary but miss the relationship between words they have had less experience with.

Verbal Absurdities or Anomalous Statements

Verbal absurdities are characterized by statements such as

> Mary stood under the flower to get out of the rain

wherein the proposition cannot be true. Anomalous sentences cannot be judged true or false because they are nonsensical, for example

> Colorless green ideas breathe furiously.

Recognizing the strangeness of both of these types of sentence depends on understanding not only the individual words but also recognizing the lack of semantic relatedness between words. Carr (1979) found that children as young as 2.3 could respond to her set of questions of the type

> Can rabbits fly?

This would indicate that at least by this age, children recognize that words are related to some words but not other words. The youngest children in this study relied on their own experience to judge the trueness or falseness of such questions—that is, they rejected statements they could not verify with their own experience. It is not until considerably later that children can explain the perceived absurdity in statements.

Children's awareness of anomalous sentences has been studied by comparing their imitation of these nonsensical sentences with their imitation of meaningful sentences and also of nonsyntactic strings of words (Entwistle and Frasure, 1974; McNeill, 1970). Children from six to nine years old listened to sentences of each type with superimposed noise; they then repeated them as heard. The six year olds showed little difference on the three types. By age seven, performance was better on meaningful sentences than on anomalous ones, indicating that children were utilizing semantic relatedness to aid recall. The gap between recall of anomalous and meaningful sentences widened with age, indicating the ability to recognize and use semantic cues continues to develop at least through age nine.

Definitions

Perhaps an obvious way to study what words mean to children is to ask them to define them. While this might be a reasonable approach with older children, it requires metalinguistic awareness that young children do not have—that is, defining words requires the ability to think about language analytically rather than simply to use it. Early definitions that children give are totally related to concrete actions. Werner and Kaplan (1963) report Barne's (1896) finding that 82 percent of six year olds' definitions are of this type. For example

Bird is "something that flies in the sky."

Around age eight, most children begin to show evidence of semantic relatedness in their definitions by including comparisons and distinctions:

Stool is "like a chair but it doesn't have a back."

By about age twelve years, definitions produced show the prototypic features that would also characterize most adult definitions:

Cup is "a round container that's open on one end and has a handle, and it is made out of something that will hold liquids."

Summary

Developing semantic relatedness begins early in children's linguistic experience and continues throughout childhood and possibly longer. Even for adults, learning new vocabulary entails learning how the new word fits together with previously learned words. There has been relatively sparse research on how children acquire various senses of semantic relatedness and how these senses relate to each other. There is a fairly consistent pattern, however, of changes occurring in children's semantic organization around seven to eight years of age and again around adolescence. These changes appear to correspond to changes in cognitive abilities, but we do not know specifically why or how they occur.

SAMPLING AND TRANSCRIPTION
FOR SEMANTIC ANALYSIS

It is possible when doing phonological, morphological, or syntactic analysis to work from a single spontaneous sample. In doing semantic analysis, however, there is rarely enough information in one sample to draw conclusions about the child's semantic knowledge. When we are attempting to determine what a child means by a given word, we must have multiple examples of the production of that word to formulate a hypothesis about its meaning. When we investigate the conceptual domains that the child talks about, we must be aware that the situation and the topic have a great influence on the domains expressed, and thus we need to look across several sessions with the child to get a representative sampling. Initially, we may want to let the child take the lead in conversation to determine the natural mode of expressing ideas. Later, we will want to ask leading questions in our interactions with the child to encourage expression of particular meanings. We may also want to use more structured procedures to elicit specific semantic operations. We have previously described some procedures used by various researchers and have included here some other possible elicitation procedures.

A listing transcript, with context included, can be used for semantic analysis. The categories which words or utterances are listed under will depend upon the type of analysis we do. If we are analyzing deviations from adult usage, we will list together those utterances that appear to reflect the same kind of semantic deviation, as in the following:

OVEREXTENSIONS

kitty	(points to stuffed lamb)
mʌk (milk?)	(reaches for bottle of juice)
beep	(holding up toy truck)

DOING SEMANTIC ANALYSIS

Analysis of all areas of semantics is generally not appropriate for a single child, so the clinician should not feel compelled to carry out unnecessary analysis in the name of being thorough. The child with limited expressive vocabulary would not be expected to display nonliteral language, for example. The older child who expresses a variety of ideas with rich vocabulary may show inappropriate word choice, calling for analysis of this error. We have suggested some characteristics of children's language that would lead clinicians to particular areas of analysis, but clinicians must use some clinical judgment in deciding which seems most appropriate. We will discuss assessment of the following semantic areas, paralleling the discussion presented earlier:

Assessment of lexical meaning
Assessment of abstract relational meaning
Looking for the influence of context

Assessment of nonliteral meaning
Assessment of word relatedness

ASSESSMENT OF LEXICAL MEANING

Assessment of lexical meaning should be carried out with the child whose word choices seem inappropriate or who appears to be having word finding difficulty.

Working from Language Samples

We begin by working from the language sample, looking through the transcript for instances where the child uses a word or phrase differently than an adult would. We then try to determine the nature of the difference. If the word is used more than once in the sample, we look at all instances to try to determine what it means for the child. We look for evidence of

1. Overextension, wherein the child extends the meaning of a word, probably based on semantic features—e.g., calls an orange "ball."
2. Underextension, which is probably based on a restricted prototype. These errors are difficult to find because the child never uses the underextended word inappropriately. Other words may be used inappropriately, however, in place of the underextended word—e.g., calls truck in book "truck," but real trucks are "car."
3. Wrong referent or wrong word. Words that seem to have the wrong referent should be examined in context to see if the sense is correct for another word—e.g., calls toy "tractor" rather than "barn."
4. Missing word for known meaning, where a filler is used—e.g., calls objects "that thing" instead of using name.

Elicitation Procedures

ALTERNATIVE REFERENTS   When we find an apparent semantic error in the child's language sample, we sometimes can deep test by presenting the child alternative referents to determine the boundaries of the word used inappropriately. For example, if we find our child calls an orange "juice," we would want to determine what else is "juice" for that child. If we have present several other foods, or pictures of foods and juices, we may find that only the orange is "juice." This would appear to be a case of using the wrong word for the referent—i.e., "juice" means orange and not the adult "juice." If "juice" applies only to a whole orange and not to one that is cut or sectioned, it appears to be underextension as well. If on the other hand, it applies not only to oranges but to other fruits, there may be overextension. Another possibility is that the child distinguishes between "juice" and "orange" when both are present.

DEFINITIONS   One type of interview procedure is asking a child what a word means when it appears that the word is used inappropriately. We would not expect children below about age six to give definitions, and not until about age twelve will most children give adultlike definitions that characterize meaning according to features of prototypes. The nature of young children's definitions is of interest because of what is revealed about their metalinguistic abilities and perhaps about the organization of their conceptual domains, but these definitions are difficult to interpret in terms of lexical meaning. For example, a child was asked "What does chair mean?" and responded "You sit on it." When asked whether a couch was a chair, she responded negatively, adding "But you can sit in it like a chair." The child's lexical meaning for chair clearly and typically went beyond her verbal definition.

ASSESSMENT OF ABSTRACT RELATIONAL MEANING

Assessment of abstract relational meaning would be appropriate for the child who shows difficulty with specific abstract relationships or with the general operation of expressing relationships. This may show up as using wrong forms or evidencing lack of forms for particular relations that tie together the content of an utterance such as coordination, spatial relations, or time reference.

Working from Language Samples

We examine the language sample for evidence of inappropriate expression or lack of comprehension of relational terms. The forms most likely to express these relations are conjunctions, negatives, and prepositions—for example

I eat *with* soup
I don't like her *but* she can't play
Milk (said while looking in empty cup)

When these deviations are discovered, an attempt is made to uncover what they mean for the child. This is done by grouping together any similar utterances and looking at the context in which they occurred to find commonalities. Often we have only a single utterance in a sample, so we can only form a tentative hypothesis to be further deep tested. Structural analysis of those forms may derive some of the same categories of meaning as were discovered by other investigators (Bloom et al., 1980 for conjunctions; Quirk et al., 1972 for prepositions). Do not be bound by these categories, however, since they do not reflect the performance of children with language impairments. Further examination of the preceding samples might result in the following descriptions:

1. *With* is used following the verb whenever the object that it precedes is something that must be introduced specifically for the activity. It does not imply accompaniment or instrument for this child.
2. *But* is used whenever there is a negative construction in a compound sentence. If there is no negative, *and* is used.

3. Commenting on absence of milk with no negative expressed is typical of this child's sample. Negatives are used, however, pragmatically to reject something or stop an action.

Elicitation Procedures for Assessing Abstract Relational Meaning

For some forms that express relational meaning, both their production and comprehension can be deep tested through various elicitation procedures. For example, to elicit production of spatial prepositions, the child can be asked where various objects are located (e.g., *in* the X; *on* the X, etc.). Comprehension can be evaluated in a similar task in which the child is to find objects when the clinician describes their placement. Other forms which are difficult to elicit, such as conjunctions, can be assessed for comprehension.

The child is given items corresponding to pictures, such as:

He will do it *and* she will do it.
He will do it *or* she will do it.
Who will do it?
What do we eat soup with?
What do we eat with soup?

LOOKING FOR THE INFLUENCE OF CONTEXT

One place we look for the influence of context is with reference to words with shifting referents.

Working from Language Samples

Children's understanding of context is displayed through their correct use of articles and pronouns that relate to shared reference and deictic terms, i.e., pronouns such as *this* and *that, here* and *there, come* and *go, bring* and *take*, etc.:

I'll take this one and you take that one.
Go over there.

Identify deviations by looking through language samples for evidence of the following:

1. Failure to recognize need for anaphoric or shared situational reference for certain words, particularly pronouns and articles—

Child says "She said that . . ." without identifying "she."

2. Use of incomplete sentences without anaphoric reference to make them understandable. Examine incomplete sentences to determine if they are

true ellipses and thus appropriate in context or are inappropriate because of lack of previous reference—

Q: What are you doing?
A: Ball.

3. Failure to recognize shifting referent quality of certain words. There might be problems specifically with person, time, or space referents—

Refers to self as "you" or by name (Person reference error)
"We'll go yesterday" (Time reference error)
"Put it here," pointing to distant spot (Space reference error)

Elicitation Procedures for Assessing Influence of Context

SHARED REFERENCE   If the child's sample shows lack of awareness of the need for anaphoric or situationally shared reference through inappropriate pronouns and articles, a task such as the following can be used. Show the child a picture with one girl and one boy. Describe what is happening in the picture without referring to the girl and boy. Ask the child "Who has the X?" or "Who is doing X?" This should elicit either a definite article ("*the* girl") or an appropriate pronoun ("*she* does"). Then present a picture with two girls and two boys, repeating the procedure. This time the task calls for either an indefinite article ("*a* girl") or a modifier ("the *big* girl"; "*one* of the girls").

DEICTIC TERMS   Using several dolls or animals and having the child identify which one is the speaker and/or listener makes it possible to assess several forms—

This cup has milk in it and *that* cup is empty.
Can I *come* in? Will you *go* in?
Go *there* and do X.
It's over *here*.

Listener-speaker perspective can also be addressed by using nonfronted items in directions such as

Put it *behind* the stool.
Put it *in front of* the ball.

Fronted objects can be used to assess the nondeictic use of these same directions.

Put it *behind* the chair.
Put it *in front of* the TV.

Use of pronouns and ability to shift pronouns to new referents can be assessed by asking the child to perform verbal tasks with a third participant, such as

> Tell him to give it to her and then to me.
> Ask her to tell you what I did.

Role playing and pretending are also excellent ways to observe the child's awareness of context—

> e.g., Pretend you are on the roof and need help. What would you say to tell people where you are?

ASSESSMENT OF NONLITERAL AND OTHER MULTIPLE MEANINGS

It is not necessarily significant if children do not show any spontaneous use of nonliteral meaning or other multiple-meaning words in their language samples. Our concern is primarily with the older child who uses such forms incorrectly or shows an inability to deal with multiple meanings receptively. If we suspect difficulty, we begin by looking through the language samples for evidence of both correct and incorrect use of multiple-meaning words and then move on to elicitation procedures if indicated by absence or inappropriate use of these forms.

Working from Language Samples

Multiple meanings of words can be shown through the child's use of the same phonetic form to mean different things:

> You *brush* with a *brush*.
> It's *in* my pocket; it's *in* your hair.

Older children's samples may contain jokes and riddles or puns which generally involve multiple meaning. Confusion over multiple-meaning words or nonliteral language may be revealed in the sample:

Adult: This is a hard book.
Child: I can bend it.

> *Nonliteral meaning* is likely to be shown first with early metaphors:

> This is a shoe. (Putting bag on foot).
> (And later) This is like a shoe.

Still later, we see evidence of metaphorical meaning of words previously used only literally:

> He's like a brick wall.

MULTIPLE MEANINGS   One of the most delightful ways to assess children's understanding of multiple meaning is through joke telling. Since children's appreciation of jokes does not always correspond to their understanding, you should ask the children to explain jokes they find amusing. Fowles and Glanz (1977) present a set of riddles they used in their research. You can also use any children's joke book to put together your own "test" items, choosing from a variety of types, some of which will be more difficult than others. Finding which jokes and riddles the child understands gives the clinician insight into that child's ability to deal with the ambiguities of the language.

METAPHORICAL LANGUAGE   Asch and Nerlove (1960) suggest an interview procedure to assess children's understanding of dual-function adjectives. After establishing that the child knows the literal meaning of *sweet, soft, cold, hard,* and *warm,* ask the child "Are people sweet? Do you know any sweet people? How do you know they're sweet?" Below age six, you would not expect the child to understand the psychological meanings. By nine or ten, children usually show awareness of connections between meanings. Another approach, used by Winner, Rosenstiel, and Gardner (1976), involves having the child explain sentences using these words metaphorically. You can create your own sentences that are adjusted in length and vocabulary to the child—

e.g., She is a warm person and I like to visit her.

PROVERBS   Asking older children to explain proverbs provides interesting insight into their ability to use language in a nonliteral way and to understand the implicatures of society's conventional sayings. Preadolescents may explain proverbs in a nonliteral fashion but typically cannot understand the implicatures. Some examples of proverbs that may be used in elicitation follow:

Don't count your chickens before they're hatched.
The squeaky wheel gets the grease.
The grass is always greener on the other side of the fence.

ASSESSING CONCEPTUAL DOMAINS

We now move from assessment of the meanings of individual words to investigation of the ways words relate to one another. These procedures are obviously not entirely separate, but our primary concern now is how words reflect concepts and which concepts are related. Since there is an infinite number of possible concepts, we do not attempt to assess them all. Instead, we are interested in the concepts or conceptual domains within which the child has shown confusion of single-word meanings or the domains operational for the child with a limited expression of concepts.

Working from Language Samples

In order to assess the child's ability to relate words from language samples, we will look for evidence of different conceptual domains. By seeing how various domains are referred to, we can begin to understand how the child views that domain and relates concepts within it. If syntactic analysis has previously been done, the summary sheets will be helpful in identifying some conceptual domains, since different word classes tend to express particular kinds of concepts. Rather than begin with our list of domains that each word class may code, it is better to look first at the sample and see what the child is trying to express. We are not looking to see which words the child uses but rather what kinds of meaning the child has command of. This analysis would be used only if the child's sample appears to be very restricted in the domains expressed. If, for example, the child uses only a few adjectives, we would want to determine if they all fall within a common class of meaning. You would not necessarily also investigate the conceptual domains expressed by other word classes, unless they were similarly restricted. We suggest the following way to proceed.

1. Locate adverbials and determine which conceptual domains they express. They may fall within the list that follows, or you may need to form additional or altered categories that better fit the child's intended meaning.

Time	(tonight, on Wednesday)
Location	(in the tree, over there)
Characteristic of action	(slowly)
Instrument	(with a brush)
Accompaniment	(with my mom)
State of person	(cheerfully)
Causation	(because it's old)
Motivation	(because I want it)
Recurrence	(twice, a lot)

2. Locate adjectivals and determine which conceptual domains they express. The following list is not complete; you will find adjectives that fall in subclasses or outside of the classes we have listed.

Sensory qualities

Vision	(blue)
Sound	(loud)
Touch	(soft)
Taste	(sour)
Smell	(smelly)

Logical qualities

Shape	(round)
Size	(big)
Number	(four)
Substance	(brick)
Condition	(new)

Affective qualities

Feelings	(happy)
Bodily states	(tired)
Judgments	(kind)

Relations

Possession	(my)
Exclusivity	(only)
Qualification	(enough)
Relative position	(last)
Comparison	(best)
Opposition	(long-short)
Disappearance	(all gone)

3. Locate lexical verbs and classify them according to the type of action or state change they express. Some possible classifications are

Pro-verbs	(do)
Change of state	(tear)
Action of body	(sit down)
Action with object	(throw X)
Sensory state	(hear)
Sensory process	(listen)
Deictic	(come)
Locomotion	(run)
Function	(sweeps)

4. Locate nouns and determine if they tend to fall within a few conceptual domains or if several are represented. A few of the categories you might find are

Names	(Sally)
People	(the lady)
Animals	(dog)
Toys	(dump truck)
Food	(french fries)
Clothing	(shoe)
Body parts	(finger)
Abstract	(imagination)

**Elicitation Procedures for Assessing
Conceptual Domains**

CATEGORIZATION When we have children sort objects into related groups, such as foods, or animals, or furniture, they are demonstrating the conceptual grouping that is the foundation for a semantic domain. One way to assess this ability is to use a variety of toys or pictures and have the child put together the ones that go together. To see if they can shift categories, young children can be given blocks or cut outs in a variety of shapes (e.g., circle, square, triangle), colors (red, blue), and sizes (big, small) and asked to sort them according to the different dimensions. A more complex categorization task involves having children fill in elements missing from a sequence or identify elements that do not belong in a category:

> Cow, horse, sheep, elephant. Which one doesn't belong?
> Morning, afternoon, evening. What's missing?

ANALOGIES   Solving analogies shows that children not only have established semantic relatedness but also can be selective in the type of relationship they express—that is, they can identify that a particular conceptual domain is relevant. The vocabulary and the complexity of the relationship can be adjusted for the child. Analysis of children's responses to analogies should involve investigation of the particular conceptual domains that they can respond within rather than simply indicating the number missed or correct. You may want to probe the child's analogic reasoning by giving only the incomplete part of the analogy rather than the whole thing to determine if the child is simply completing the statement, without regard for the relationship expressed in the stem of the analogy—

> Rabbits are fast; turtles are _____.
> Give only "Turtles are _____" on another occasion.

VERBAL ABSURDITIES   Children can be asked questions involving both true and false propositions, such as

> Can cups fly?
> Can birds fly?

It is usually best to ask children to explain answers that seem "wrong." If, for example, a child responds to the first question with "Yes" and then explains that you have to throw a cup in the air for it to fly, the yes answer is not absurd. Older children can be asked to tell what is funny about absurd statements, such as

> It was raining so the boy went outside to get dry.

SIMILARITIES AND DIFFERENCES   When we describe how two or more things are alike and how they are different from each other, we have to establish some category of relatedness between them. This is what we are investigating when we ask children to do this task. This task can be adjusted in difficulty to see if the child can shift from objects to actions, abstraction or nonliteral language—

> How are a bus and a car alike?
> How are they different?
>
> How can a person be like a turtle?

DEFINITIONS   As we mentioned earlier, children's definitions sometimes are informative in identifying the conceptual domains within which words fit.

We can look for a number of things in children's definitions, such as whether they see the word as a label for a specific referent rather than a category, and if they have the central features of the category. We also can note whether a child defines words by putting them in sentences, giving synonyms, making comparisons, or listing features.

EXERCISES

1. Give examples of semantic errors the child might make for "dog" if he or she were
   a) overextending meaning
   b) underextending meaning
   c) referring to wrong referent
   d) having word finding problems
2. The following examples were drawn from several children's language samples. Indicate for each italicized segment the kind of semantic error that seems to be present, choosing from the list presented here or deriving your own description.
   a) Word deficit resulting in use of term from same conceptual domain
   b) Word deficit resulting in overuse of pro-forms
   c) Overextension of lexical meaning of prefix
   d) Underextension of meaning
   e) Confused prepositions indicating movement away from place
   f) Confused prepositions indicating place
   g) Inconsistency between pronoun and anaphoric referent

   Adult: Here's a brother.
   _____ Tony: That's *not a brother;* he's too small.
   Adult: The other baby was crying? Why?
   Lisa: Because she wanted a big toy; *this much.* (spreading arms)
   Adult: Oh, she couldn't have the toy?
   _____ Lisa: I give her the big truck; *this much.* (spreading arms)
   Adult: Where's the ball?
   _____ Eden: *Under* my back.
   Sally makes the following statements in one language sample:
   I *got* Girl Scouts last night.
   I *got* born.
   I *want* we could drop all the pennies in here.
   I *went* in a hospital before.
   I *went* in a hospital a long time.
   I *went* at ballet I eight years old.
   Adult: Do you go every day?
   _____ Amy: No, I go *next days.* You see, today I didn't has no school. Tomorrow I got school. Then I don't got school.
   _____ Amy: (Comparing two rings, one with a stone and one which is a solid band) It's gold like this, sep' it doesn't have this. It's *all circle.*
   _____ Jake: I still got two cups and *it's* in my closet.
   _____ Michael: I will *unrase* it. (with eraser)
   Adult: What about the cows on your farm?
   _____ Brian: Cause when we was leaving *at the house*, Daddy said they was milking away.

Adult: What did this guy do?

_____ Brian: Sent him *out the tent.*

3. The following is a listing transcript of all utterances with prepositions drawn from a language sample. How many different meanings are expressed by each preposition? Describe them.

Felt *on* my tummy and my back.
Boy walk up *on* top.
No toes *on* boy.
First I put jelly *on* it.

I talk *in* there. (microphone)
In the cup.
I put it *in* my tummy.

Under the cup.
Under the light.
Under my back.

Stick it *to* the page.
Will you come *to* my house?

I eat *off* Roy dish.
Is the light *off?*

4. In the following sample, Jeannie is playing with an adult. Her sister Sherry is present. Underline all the words in the sample that depend on context for their meaning. Indicate whether each has exophoric or anaphoric reference provided.

Jeannie: I broke it. Here, fix it.
Adult: It's all right. It's old.
Jeannie: It's old.
Adult: Did mommy make these?
Jeannie: Yes her did. I'll break it. See, it's out.
Take it please. I can't get it out. That's out.
That's out. Trying this out. Trying this thing out.
Adult: You're trying to get it out? You're breaking it.
Jeannie: No I not. Trying this one out, Sherry.
Sherry touched me. She touched me.
Adult: Where's the sewing machine?
Jeannie: It's all gone.

5. Look through the following utterances for evidence of conceptual domains this child expresses in the short sample. Which word classes seem restricted or not present? What conceptual domains are expressed by the restricted word classes (for example, sensory qualities, logical qualities, functions, affective qualities, time, and specific relationships such as possessors).

I fell down
Me read Scott's book
Mommy fell down
Scott is sleeping
Come here, Poppy
Tell me a story
Going sleep
Read book, Poppy
Eat banana
Get up
Go out

Go up
Nana come
Mama is coming
Nana do
Scott's dog
More cookie
No more book
All gone
No play now
Two cookie
Two points
Rocking chair
Tape recorder on bed

6.   On an elicitation task to assess conceptual domains, a child is asked "Do chairs sit?" and replies "Yes." Is this a semantic problem? If not, what kind of a problem is it?

REFERENCES

ACHENBACH, T. M.   Standardization of a Research Instrument for Identifying Associative Responding in Children, *Developmental Psychology,* 2, 1970, 283–91

ASCH, S. E., AND H. NERLOVE.   The Development of Double Function Terms in Children, in *Perspectives in Psychological Theory,* eds. B. Kaplan and S. Wagner. New York: International Universities Press, 1960.

ATKINSON, M.   Prerequisites for Reference, in *Developmental Pragmatics,* eds. E. Ochs and B. Schieffelin. New York: Academic Press, 1979.

BANGS, T. E.   *Vocabulary Comprehension Scale.* Austin, Tex.: Learning Concepts, 1975.

BATES, E.   *Language and Context: The Acquisition of Pragmatics.* New York: Academic Press, 1976.

BELLUGI, U., AND R. BROWN, eds.   The Acquisition of Language, *Monographs of The Society for Research in Child Development,* 29, 1964 (serial no. 92).

BILLOW, R.   A Cognitive Developmental Study of Metaphor Comprehension, *Developmental Psychology,* 11, 1975, 415–23.

BILLOW, R.   Spontaneous Metaphor in Children. Unpublished paper, Adelphi University, 1977.

BLOOM, L.   *Language Development: Form and Function in Emerging Grammars.* Cambridge, Mass.: The M.I.T. Press, 1970.

BLOOM, L.   *One Word at a Time: The Use of Single Word Utterances Before Syntax.* The Hague: Mouton Publishers, 1973.

BLOOM, L., AND M. LAHEY.   *Language Development and Language Disorders.* New York: John Wiley, 1978.

BLOOM, L., M. LAHEY, L. HOOD, K. LIFTER, AND K. FIESS.   Complex Sentences: Acquisition of Syntactic Connectives and the Semantic Relations They Encode, *Journal of Child Language,* 7, 1980, 235–62.

BLOOM, L., P. LIGHTBOWN, AND L. HOOD.   Structure and Variation in Child Language, *Monographs of The Society for Research on Child Development,* 40, 1975 (serial no. 160).

BOWERMAN, M. *Early Syntactic Development: A Cross-Linguistic Study with Special Reference to Finnish.* Cambridge, Mass.: Cambridge University Press, 1973.

BOWERMAN, M. Semantic Factors in the Acquisition of Rules for Word Use and Sentence Construction, in *Normal and Deficient Child Language*, eds. D. M. Morehead and A. E. Morehead. Baltimore, Md.: University Park Press, 1976.

BRAINE, M. D. S. Children's First Word Combinations, *Monographs of The Society for Research in Child Development,* 1976 (serial no. 164).

BRODZINSKY, D. The Role of Conceptual Tempo and Stimulus Characteristics in Children's Humor Development, *Developmental Psychology,* 11, 1975, 843–50.

BROWN, R. *Psycholinguistics.* New York: Fress Press, 1970.

BROWN, R. *A First Language: The Early Stages.* Cambridge, Mass.: Harvard University Press, 1973.

BROWN, R., AND C. FRASER. The Acquisition of Syntax, in *Verbal Behavior and Verbal Learning: Problems and Processes,* eds. C. N. Cofer and B. Musgrave. New York: McGraw-Hill, 1963, pp. 158–97.

CARR, D. B. The Development of Young Children's Capacity to Judge Anomalous Sentences, *Journal of Child Language,* 6, 1979, 227–41.

CHOMSKY, N. *Language and Mind.* New York: Harcourt Brace Jovanovich, 1968.

CHUKOVSKY, K. *From Two to Five.* Berkeley, Calif.: University of California Press, 1968.

CLARK, E. V. Nonlinguistic Strategies and the Acquisition of Word Meanings, *Cognition,* 2, 1973a, 161–82.

CLARK, E. V. What's in a Word? On the Child's Acquisition of Semantics in His First Language, in *Cognitive Development and the Acquisition of Language,* ed. T. Moore. New York: Academic Press, 1973b.

CLARK, E. V. Some Aspects of the Conceptual Basis for First Language Acquisition, in *Language Perspectives-Acquisition, Retardation and Intervention*, eds. R. L. Schiefelbusch and L. L. Lloyd. Baltimore, Md.: University Park Press, 1974.

CLARK, E. V., AND O. GARNICA. Is He Coming or Going? On the Acquisition of Deictic Verbs, *Journal of Verbal Learning and Verbal Behavior,* 13, 1974, 559–72.

CLARK, E. V., AND C. J. SENGUL. Strategies in the Acquisition of Deixis, *Journal of Child Language,* 5, 1978, 457–75.

CLARK, H. H. Linguistic Processes in Deductive Reasoning, *Psychological Review,* 76, 1969, 387–404.

CLARK, H. H., AND E. V. CLARK. *Psychology and Language.* New York: Harcourt Brace Jovanovich, Inc., 1977.

COX, M. V. Young Children's Understanding of In Front Of and Behind in the Placement of Objects, *Journal of Child Language,* 6, 1979, 371–74.

deVILLIERS, P., AND J. deVILLIERS. On This, That, and the Other: Nonegocentrism in Very Young Children, *Journal of Experimental Child Psychology,* 18, 1974, 438–47.

DONALDSON, M., AND G. BALFOUR. Less Is More: A Study of Language Comprehension in Children. *British Journal of Psychology,* 59, 1968, 461–72.

DUCHAN, J. F., AND N. J. LUND. Why Not Semantic Relations? *Journal of Child Language,* 6, 1979, 243–52.

ELKIND, D. Piagetian and Psychometric Conceptions of Intelligence, *Harvard Educational Review,* 39, 1969, 319–37.

ENTWISTLE, D. R., AND N. E. FRASURE. A Contradiction Resolved: Children's Processing of Syntactic Cues, *Developmental Psychology,* 10, 1974, 852–57.

ERVIN, S. Changes with Age in the Verbal Determinants of Word Association, *American Journal of Psychology,* 74, 1961, 361–72.

FILLMORE, C. J. The Case for Case, in *Universals in Linguistic Theory,* eds. E. Bach and R. T. Harms. New York: Holt, Rinehart & Winston, 1968.

FILLMORE, C. Space. Unpublished ms., 1971.

FOWLES, B., AND M. E. GLANZ. Competence and Talent in Verbal Riddle Comprehension, *Journal of Child Language,* 4, 1977, 433–52.

GARDNER, H. Metaphors and Modalities: How Children Project Polar Adjectives into Diverse Domains, *Child Development,* 45, 1974, 84–91.

GARDNER, H., M. KIRCHER, E. WINNER, AND D. PERKINS. Children's Metaphoric Productions and Preferences, *Journal of Child Language,* 2, 1975, 125–41.

GARDNER, H., E. WINNER, R. BECHHOFER, AND D. WOLF. Figurative Language, in *Children's Language,* Vol. I., ed. K. Nelson. New York: Gardner Press, Inc., 1978.

GENTILE, J. R., AND L. H. BELCHER. Associative Relatedness as a Predictor of Differential Performance on Analogy Items, *APA Experimental Publication System,* 9, December 1970. Ms. no. 309–34.

GENTILE, J. R., AND R. SEIBEL. A Rating Scale Measure of Word Relatedness, *Journal of Verbal Learning and Verbal Behavior,* 8, 1969, 252–56.

GENTILE, J. R., L. TEDESCO-STRATTON, E. DAVIS, N. J. LUND, AND B. C. AGUNANNE. Associative Responding versus Analogical Reasoning by Children, *Intelligence,* 1, 1977, 369–80.

GENTNER, D. Validation of a Related-Component Model of Verb Meaning, *Papers and Reports on Child Development,* No. 10. Stanford University, September 1975.

HILL, C. Linguistic Representation of Spatial and Temporal Orientation. Proceedings of the Berkeley Linguistics Society, Vol. 4, 1978, 524–39.

HUXLEY, R. The Development of the Correct Use of Subject Personal Pronouns in Two Children, in *Advances in Psycholinguistics,* eds. G. D'Arcais and W. Levelt. New York: American Elsevier Publishing Co., 1970.

INHELDER, B., AND J. PIAGET. *The Growth of Logical Thinking from Childhood to Adolescence.* New York: Basic Books, 1958.

KIRK, S., J. McCARTHY, AND W. KIRK. *The Illinois Test of Psycholinguistic Abilities* (rev. ed.). Urbana, Ill.: University of Illinois Press, 1968.

KUCZAJ, S., AND M. MARATSOS. Front, Back, Side: Stages of Acquisition. *Papers and Reports on Child Language Development,* 8, 1974, 111–28.

LAKOFF, R. Remarks on This and That, in *Berkeley Studies in Syntax and Semantics,* Vol. 1, eds. C. Fillmore, G. Lakoff, and R. Lakoff. Berkeley, Calif.: Department of Linguistics, 1974.

LEOPOLD, W. *Speech Development of a Bilingual Child* (4 vols.). Evanston, Ill.: Northwestern University Press, 1939.

LORD, C.   Variations in the Patterns of Acquisition of Negation, *Papers and Reports on Child Language Development*, No. 8. Department of Linguistics, Stanford University, Palo Alto, California, 1974.

LYONS, J.   *Introduction to Theoretical Linguistics.* Cambridge, England: Cambridge University Press, 1968.

LYONS, J.   Deixis as the Source of Reference, in *Formal Semantics of Natural Language*, ed. E. L. Keenan. Cambridge, England: Cambridge University Press, 1975.

McGHEE, P. E.   Development of the Humor Response: A Review of the Literature, *Psychological Bulletin*, 76, 1971a, 328–48.

McGHEE, P. E.   The Role of Operational Thinking in Children's Comprehension and Appreciation of Humor, *Child Development*, 42, 1971b, 123–38.

McGHEE, P. E.   On the Cognitive Origins of Incongruity in Humor: Fantasy Assimilation versus Reality Assimilation, in *The Psychology of Humor: Theoretical Perspectives and Empirical Issues*, eds. J. H. Goldstein and P. E. McGhee. New York: Academic Press, 1972.

McGHEE, P. E.   Cognitive Mastery and Children's Humor, *Psychological Bulletin*, 81, 1974, 721–30.

McNEILL, D.   A Study of Word Association, *Journal of Verbal Learning and Verbal Behavior*, 5, 1966, 548–57.

McNEILL, D.   *The Acquisition of Language: The Study of Developmental Psycholinguistics.* New York: Harper & Row, Pub., 1970.

MERVIS, C. B., J. CATLIN, AND E. ROSCH.   Development of the Structure of Color Categories, *Developmental Psychology*, 11, 1975, 54–60.

MUMA, J. R., AND C. ZWYCEWICZ-EMORY.   Contextual Priority: Verbal Shift at Seven? *Journal of Child Language*, 6, 1979, 301–11.

NELSON, K.   Structure and Strategy in Learning to Talk, *Monographs of The Society for Research in Child Development*, 38, 1973 (serial no. 149).

PALERMO, D.   *Psychology of Language.* Glenview, Ill.: Scott, Foresman, 1978.

PIAGET, J.   *The Language and Thought of the Child.* New York: Harcourt, Brace, 1926.

POLLIO, M., AND H. POLLIO.   The Development of Figurative Language in Children, *Journal of Psycholinguistic Research*, 3, 1974, 185–201.

PRENTICE, N. M., AND R. E. FATHMAN.   Joking Riddles: A Developmental Index of Children's Humor, *Developmental Psychology*, 10, 1975, 210–16.

QUIRK, R. S., S. GREENBAUM, G. LEECH, AND J. SVARTVIK.   *A Grammar of Contemporary English.* London: Longman, 1972.

RICHARDSON, C., AND J. A. CHURCH.   A Developmental Analysis of Proverb Interpretations, *Journal of Genetic Psychology*, 94, 1959, 169–79.

ROSCH, E.   On the Internal Structure of Perceptual and Semantic Categories, in *Cognitive Development and the Acquisition of Language*, ed. T. E. Moore. New York: Academic Press, 1973.

ROSCH, E., AND C. B. MERVIS.   Family Resemblances: Studies in the Internal Structure of Categories, *Cognitive Psychology*, 7, 1975, 573–605.

SAPIR, E.   Grading: A Study in Semantics, *Philosophy of Science*, 11, 1944, 93–116.

SHULTZ, T. R.   Development of the Appreciation of Riddles, *Child Development*, 45, 1974, 100–105.

SHULTZ, T. R., AND F. HORIBE. Development of the Appreciation of Verbal Jokes, *Developmental Psychology*, 10, 1974, 13–20.

SLOBIN, D. I. Initiation and Grammatical Development in Children, in *Contemporary Issues in Developmental Psychology*, eds. N. S. Endler, L. R. Boulter, and H. Osser. New York: Holt, Rinehart & Winston, 1968, 437–43.

SNYDER, A. D. Notes on the Talk of a Two-and-a-half Year Old Boy, *Pedagogical Seminar*, 21, 1914, 412–24.

TANZ, C. Learning How "It" Works, *Journal of Child Language*, 4, 1977, 225–36.

TANZ, C. *Studies in the Acquisition of Deictic Terms.* Cambridge, England: Cambridge University Press, 1980.

VENDLER, Z. *Adjectives and Nominalizations.* The Hague: Mouton Publishers, 1968.

WARDEN, D. The Influence of Context on Children's Use of Identifying Expressions and References, *British Journal of Psychology*, 67, 1976, 101–12.

WERNER, H., AND B. KAPLAN. *Symbol Formation.* New York: John Wiley, 1963.

WINNER, E. New Names for Old Things: The Emergence of Metaphoric Language, *Journal of Child Language*, 6, 1979, 469–91.

WINNER, E., A. ROSENSTIEL, AND H. GARDNER. The Development of Metaphoric Understanding, *Developmental Psychology*, 12, 1976, 289–97.

WINNER, E., A. ROSENSTIEL, AND H. GARDNER. The Development of Metaphoric Understanding, *Developmental Psychology*, 12, 1976, 289–97.

WOODROW, H., AND F. LOWELL. Children's Association Frequency Tables, *Psychological Monographs*, 22, no. 97, 1916.

8

Language Comprehension

What do we mean when we say a child can comprehend words or sentences or narrative? Are we saying simply that when presented with a word or sentence or set of sentences that children can derive the corresponding meanings? Would we call it comprehension if they derived the wrong meanings? Would we call it language comprehension if the children used cues such as the intonation contour of the utterances they hear, the nonverbal accompaniments such as facial expression or gesture, or the situational context of the utterances to derive meaning? Are there degrees of comprehension such that we could talk about full vs. partial comprehension? Is there more than one way to understand something correctly? What can one take as evidence that a child understands the utterances?

These issues, and others related to them, have plagued those who are researching or assessing children's language comprehension. Their solution has been to try to study children's language comprehension in broad as well as systematic ways and to attempt to control for the many factors that are involved in children's so-called language comprehension.

We will begin our approach to comprehension assessment by discussing the pragmatics aspects of language comprehension, specifically in terms of situational context, intentional context, and listener context. Once we have emphasized the importance of these contextual factors, we will talk about approaches to purely linguistic understandings, for example, how syntax and semantic strategies and knowledge come into play. We finish the chapter with suggestions for arriving at a structural approach for assessing how particular children with language problems are understanding the language they hear.

THE PRAGMATICS
OF COMPREHENSION

The Situational Context

As with language production, the situational context has a strong effect on language comprehension. Young children are reputed to rely on the situation for their interpretation of language, but it is not only children who comprehend language in terms of their sense of the situational context. We all do. Bransford and his colleagues (Bransford and Johnson, 1972; Bransford and McCarrell, 1974; Bransford and Nitsch, 1978) have distinguished two senses of comprehension—that of interpreting language in terms of linguistic knowledge and that of interpreting language in light of the situation. The first they describe as linguistic interpretation, which requires *knowing about* language; the second they see as interpreting the entire situation, or *knowing with* language. They illustrate by offering sentences to their research subjects, such as "The notes were sour because the seam split." They present the sentences both with and without a physical referent. In the case of the sentence about notes, the referent was a picture of a man trying to play music with a set of torn bagpipes. The torn bagpipes, then, offer a situational context which gives sense to the otherwise opaque sentence.

The way situational context influences the interpretation of language can be examined through the same views we used in relation to language production (Chapter 3). These are physical context, context of the speech event, event frames, and topic.

THE PHYSICAL CONTEXT   Language about the concurrent physical context is understood before language about nonpresent objects, events, and relations (see Chapter 9). Children whose orientation in time and space is centered on the here-and-now will not understand requests which require that they obtain objects not within their view (Dihoff and Chapman, 1977; Huttenlocher, 1974), nor will they carry out an action stipulated by a command unless the object of the action is present to act on (Shipley, Smith, and Gleitman, 1969).

This description may seem to imply that children with here-and-now comprehension would respond to anything talked about as long as it is in the current situation. However, what becomes apparent upon further scrutiny is that children's sense of here-and-now is different from that of the attending adult. This can be witnessed when an adult holds up an object or points to a picture and asks "What's that?" The child responds with the label of the object of current attention, which may be the object in his or her own hand or the picture he or she is looking at and not what the adult question is about. Bruner (1975) emphasizes this when he points out the importance of mutual referencing in early language learning. He feels that for a young child to understand or learn a new word he or she must be looking at the referent being designated when the word is said.

Clark's (1973) research can also help us conceptualize this here-and-now set for children's comprehension. She has shown that children view the physical situation in terms of their perceptual or functional preferences—that is to say, certain attributes of their here-and-now focus are more salient to children than others. Clark's (1973) study of prepositions shows, for example, that the shape of the objects being referred to will affect young children's interpretation of commands for manipulating those objects. If one object is a container, a second smaller object will be placed *in* the container, whether the command specifies to put it *in, on,* or *under* the first object. Likewise, if the first object is not a container but has a flat surface, the second object will be put *on* the surface, even if the request is for placement *in* or *under.* Clark (1973) has attributed these responses to a *perceptual saliency strategy* used by children to interpret language in terms of what they perceive as the salient, or noticeable, perceptual aspect of the situation.

This reliance on nonlinguistic strategies to react to commands with the locatives *in, on,* and *under* has been identified as the first stage children go through in comprehending the meaning of these words (Clark, 1973). At this stage, children do not understand the words at all, except perhaps that they are locatives. Clark's data show children from approximately eighteen months to two years utilize this strategy predominantly. The response of children at this stage to *in* is always correct, since it would be dictated by a container being present; *on* is responded to correctly some of the time—that is, when a noncontainer is presented; while *under* is never correct. At a second stage noted between two and three years of age, the child shows partial comprehension of the locative words. These children respond correctly to *in* and also to *on* most of the time, with *under* responded to correctly up to half of the time. The third stage, when all these locatives are linguistically interpreted correctly, occurs after age three years.

We see then that the physical immediacy of objects and actions, the focus of the child as language is used, and the saliency of particular attributes of objects all draw children to relate the language they hear to the physical situation. This leads them to understanding language that fits the situation they are experiencing but not understanding language that is not bound to the situation. While this is particularly apparent with young children, we can also see the influence of physical context for older listeners, especially with certain words and circumstances, such as words with shifting referents as we discussed in Chapter 7, Semantics.

THE SPEECH EVENT   Along with the influence of immediacy, focus, and saliency of objects in the physical setting, it is also the case that children understand language in light of the ongoing speech event, i.e., the event in which the utterance occurs. Thus, the child is more likely to understand "Where is your belly button?" in a game involving naming body parts than if the utterance were to occur outside of that game context. Shatz (1975) studied this phenomenon and found that children interpreted "Can you talk on the telephone" as a request for action in one context (with utterances such as "Come get the telephone," "Push the button," etc.) and as a request for information in another context (with utterances such as "Who talks on the telephone in your house?").

Similarly, Mayrink-Sabinson (1980) found in her study of mothers' interpretations of children's utterances that the speech event influences adult interpretations. When the children's utterances were related to ongoing book-reading episodes, or any type of game, the utterances were more interpretable than when they had as their referent something unrelated to that event. For example, when one of her subjects said "doggie" upon hearing a dog bark in the distance, the mother took much longer to respond than when the child said "doggie" referring to a dog in the book they were both looking at.

EVENT FRAMES   The effect of the degree of framing on children's language comprehension has only recently begun to be appreciated and is still somewhat undefined. What is apparent is that there are many tightly framed *routine exchanges* in the language of adults to children (Duchan, 1980; Thomas, 1979) and that these routines may be one important way that children move from their prelanguage stage of situational comprehension to their beginning language comprehension. Thomas's (1979) description of the routines used by fathers to children suggests that the children understand the parent's routine "syntactic amalgams" and that these forms may, in the early stages of child language development, function as vocables do in their language production; that is, the utterances in a routine do not yet mean anything but rather are part and parcel of the complex cluster of happenings within which they occur. So the attention-getting routines such as "Look it" can be construed by the child as an event which is about to begin rather than as a command meaning "Look over here."

The notion of routines as something verbal to comprehend seems to violate their very nature, since they are by definition prefabricated units which involve some interaction, perhaps including productions by the child as well as nonverbal action exchanges. As we continue to study routines we may need to develop a deep structure construct, such as routine packages or unities, through which children conceive of and participate in repeating events. This, then, will prevent us from mistakenly assuming that just because children respond appropriately to a verbal initiation that they understand it as a linguistic entity. Rather, they may be working from a routine package conceptualization—a tight frame which, when triggered, moves automatically and unanalytically through a particular sequence. What we can say now is that there is evidence that routines undoubtedly play a role in early comprehension and must therefore be assessed and perhaps used in therapy by language clinicians.

Story frames are less tight but still involve framing. Attempts to describe the structures underlying comprehension of integrated passages have often focused on stories since this particular form of discourse has an internal structure or frame that is to some degree predictable and experimentally manipulable. Comprehension of these complex units cannot be understood merely as a composite of individual words and sentences within that discourse. When children listen to stories, it is assumed that they expect this internal structure and that the incoming information is assimilated to this story frame. Stories that follow the expected pattern should thus be recalled more accurately than those that violate it.

Several descriptions of story frames have been offered (e.g., Mandler and Johnson, 1977; Rumelhart, 1975; Stein and Glenn, 1976, 1979). For example, Stein and Glenn (1979), in describing folk tales, find that there are categories of information which recur in most stories and further that there is a network that exists between categories specifying the logical order of the categories. In addition to some provision of setting which introduces the main characters and describes the context for the rest of the story, each story consists of two or more episodes. The episodes consist of predictable elements, such as initiating events, responses, plan sequence, plan application, attempt, consequences, and reactions. Stein and Glenn (1979) investigated the relative saliency of categories by having first and fifth graders retell stories or answer probe questions and noting which categories of information were most frequently recalled. They consistently found that the major setting, the consequences, and the initiating events most frequently appeared in children's recalled versions of several stories. The primary goal of the protagonist was always well recalled, and inferences were generally made about feelings and motives of the characters, particularly by the older children. It appears that these categories of information are structurally more important in recall and may be the basic frame that children use when retelling stories, with other information being embedded within this frame.

The temporal organization of discourse was investigated by Brown (1975) through use of sequenced pictures with five and seven year olds. She found that when the original description of the story specified the causal relationship between the pictured events, seven year olds' recall of the correct temporal order was greatly improved over presentations that did not include the causal information. The five year olds did not appear to make use of this information to aid recall.

An interesting study by Omanson, Warren, and Trabasso (1978) with five and eight year olds illustrates that goals and motivation play a role in listener's development of inferences about stories over and above facilitating recall of the propositions of the story. Each story in this study had two parts—a setting and a core. The core, which was presented to all of the children, consisted of actions that were unclear as to referents and motives of people in the story. For example, the following core was used:

> Nancy saw what she wanted on the shelf. When the man came over, she pointed to it. She accidentally knocked over a lamp. The lamp fell with a crash. Nancy said she was sorry. The man said it was okay. He handed her the box. As she was walking out, Nancy saw Fred. Nancy hid behind the door. (Omanson, Warren, and Trabasso, 1978, pp. 340-41)

Along with this core, children were presented with one of three settings for the core—one provided the protagonist with negative motivations for the actions (Nancy stole money from Fred to buy a skateboard for herself); one provided positive motivation (Nancy wants to buy a skateboard for her brother Fred with her own money); and a third, neutral condition did not present any information relevant for resolving ambiguity in the core (Nancy wants a handkerchief and finds one in her pocket).

The children were asked both to recount the stories and to answer questions that required them to draw inferences that went beyond the given content (e.g., Why did Nancy hide behind the door?). It was found that while children's recall of the events of the stories was not significantly affected by the statement of goals, they were better able to answer the inference questions when the goal was presented, suggesting that their comprehension of the story was greater. This finding also suggests that retelling of stories is not as sensitive an indicator of comprehension as use of inferential questions is. This is consistent with the findings of Stein and Glenn (1979) that children who were asked probe questions about stories were likely to indicate the central importance of intentions and motives more so than in their retellings of stories.

Taken together, these studies indicate that children's comprehension of stories tends to be structured according to the information they expect to be presented. If the anticipated information is not provided, they may fill it in (Stein and Glenn, 1979) or alter the story to fit their psychological frame. When cause of events and motivation of characters is explicit, children's comprehension seems to be improved.

THE TOPIC   One element of all discourse that can be identified as having a strong influence on comprehension is provision of the topic. The role of topic is illustrated in the research of Bransford and his associates (Bransford and Nitsch, 1978). They have shown in their comprehension studies that listeners as well as speakers have an internal construction of what is happening in a speech event. So, for example, when a speaker is describing the process of washing clothes, listeners understand the particular linguistic units in terms of that clothes-washing topic, and an utterance such as "First you arrange things in different groups" can be understood. Thus, although listeners may understand something about the propositional content of the sentence, they sometimes do not understand it fully unless they can derive a general topic (either from the situation or from the discourse) for fitting sentences together into a coherent whole. As adults, we are likely to signal this lack of comprehension by saying something like "I don't know what you're talking about." Children are less likely to do this. The clearest evidence that children have missed the point is when they retell a story or joke and demonstrate their original failure by leaving out or changing crucial parts.

In sum, we have discussed children's dependency on situational context in their comprehension of language and found that they depend heavily on the physical here-and-now; they rely, for interpretation, on present objects, those objects which they are focused on, and the features which they find most salient in the situation. We also found that even the youngest children use the ongoing speech event to interpret language contained in these events, relying first on tightly framed routines and later developing frames for particular speech events. Recognition of topics also emerges at a later age.

The Intentional Context

We have been describing ways the listener's conceptualization of the situation affects his or her understanding of the language embedded in it. One very important aspect of the situation is, of course, the speaker. Listeners' interpretations of what speakers are saying will vary depending upon their assumptions about what speakers want, i.e., the presumed intention of the utterance and the relative power relationship and interactional history between particular speakers and listeners. Clinicians will be familiar with the experience in which they ask a child to repeat an utterance and the request is taken as a correction because the child sees the clinician as seeking "good speech" rather than simply requesting clarification. So the intentional context for comprehension has to do with the listener's perception of the speaker, or the intentions attributed to the speaker by the listener and their effect on listener comprehension.

As we discussed in the pragmatics chapter (Chapter 3), intentions can be expressed in various ways. There are indirect requests where intention differs from the propositional meaning of the utterance. Further, there are more direct requests which are stated but couched in a larger syntactic frame such as a question. Finally, there are clearly stated requests, usually indicated in an imperative sentence wherein the verb tells the listener what the speaker wants done. The verbs can be about the listener's action ("answer the phone") or can be a performative which describes the speaker's wish ("I want . . .").

If children produce all types of requests, we have evidence that they understand indirect as well as direct expression of intention (see Chapter 3). Evidence for their comprehension of requests produced by others is more difficult to determine (Ervin-Tripp, 1977; Reeder, 1980). It may be that they fail to carry out the request because it is an indirect expression of the speaker's intentions and they cannot interpret the request. It may also be that they don't want to do it, or that they succeed in carrying out the request not because they understand it as stated in its full form linguistically but because they know what the speaker wants them to do from the situational and social clues or gestures. They then combine their situational knowledge with bits and pieces of the linguistic request to understand what the speaker intended. Thus they are not understanding the illocutionary force of the utterance from the linguistic information but rather from its situational context. For example, Shatz (1975), in her study of children's responses to requests embedded in questions ("Can you find a truck?"), found that children as young as age two carry out the act rather than answer yes or no. Shatz (1975), Ervin-Tripp (1977), and Reeder (1980) doubt that children at this age are understanding the entire yes-no indirect request form, but rather they are probably extracting the request nucleus ("find-truck") and responding to it in accordance with their sense of the entire situational meaning. Some of Shatz's older children responded to yes-no questions with yes or no when the questions were in a context where the adult was asking the child for information, but these older children also had a preference for carrying out the action rather than answering the question. Ervin-Tripp (1970) found that if the children were asked to do an impossible or unfeasible act ("Can you fly in the sky?"), they would answer yes or no rather than attempt to carry out the unlikely act. She also found three year olds were likely to respond to "Why don't you" with an answer rather than treating it as a request for action. This was related to their preference for answering *why* questions with "because + statement" responses.

Perhaps the most difficult type of illocutionary force for children to decipher is that involving a logical implication not stated in the utterance or situation. Grice (1975) has called these conversational implicatures and Dore (1977) has studied them in contexts where three year olds answer their teacher's questions. Dore found highly sophisticated responses to yes–no questions. He called them "qualified responses" and subclassified them as (1) presuppositions,

(2) pragmatic conditions, (3) extra conditions, and (4) remote associations. Type 1, presuppositions, occurs when the answer contains a semantic contrast with some information in the question (Q: Did you do that? A: Tasha did it.). The pragmatic condition, type 2, assumes that the child and questioner share knowledge of some real-world condition which prompts the question, and the child's answer contains information about that condition (Q: Shall I give you the truck? A: No it's broken. Condition: I don't want to play with broken toys). The extra condition answer does not answer the question with a simple yes or no but adds unpredictable information (Q: Does this look like a bean? A: Those are green beans). Finally, there are remote answers which, in Dore's examples, were explanations related to a question taken as a reprimand (Q: Did you make a hole for the grapefruit seed? A: I want to take one of these. Implication: That's why I'm not making a hole).

In sum, the listener's comprehension of language is affected by the intention attributed to the speaker. Requests stated in question forms or in other indirect ways require the child to interpret what the speaker wants in order to respond correctly. Children also show that their comprehension of language takes the speaker's intentions into account when they respond to logical implicatures that are not stated. From these indirect acts we can see how subtle the process of language comprehension can be. The listener must know not only what the words and sentences mean linguistically, but why the speaker said them and what they mean in the context of the particular situation.

The Listener Context

BACKGROUND KNOWLEDGE   When we talked about how the situation influences language comprehension, we only briefly emphasized the idea that the situation is not something given to the child or adult, but rather that it is interpreted according to the background knowledge of the listener with regard to physical entities, speech events, and topics. We will now focus on what the listener brings to the situation in the way of pertinent background knowledge.

We know that children understand language about *familiar referents* before language about something less familiar or new or anomalous (Miller, 1980). The most obvious effect of familiarity on children's comprehension is vocabulary or lexical comprehension—that is, at first they only know words which refer to familiar objects, relations, and events. Huttenlocher (1974) says it this way:

> My impression of the learning of words is as follows: The child became familiar with certain objects and object classes; among these salient objects were his pets, his bottle, cookies, etc. He learned certain distinctive acts, such as standing up or sitting down, or carrying out particular routines like the games of peekaboo or patty cake. Some of these salient familiar objects, object classes, or acts became linked to the sound-patterns of particular words. These sound-patterns then came to serve as retrieval cues for these salient experiences. (Huttenlocher, 1974, p. 355)

Ervin-Tripp (1970, 1974, 1977), in her studies over the years of children's comprehension of adult directives, has summarized her observations, saying that young children's compliance or even acknowledgment of a directive depends upon their knowledge (1) that objects have characteristic acts associated with them (e.g., pictures are to name, puzzles are to assemble), (2) that objects belong in certain places (e.g., shoes are kept in the closet), and (3) that objects or behaviors are subject to constraining household or classroom rules (e.g., lamps shouldn't be touched). Such background knowledge offers the set within which the directives are understood, or misunderstood.

A concrete demonstration of this reliance on background knowledge is Lewis and Freedle's (1973) description of a thirteen-month-old child who, when given the two commands "Throw the apple" and "Eat the apple," responded to both by eating the apple when she was in her high chair and by throwing the apple when she was playing in the play pen.

Sachs and Truswell (1978) tried to control for such situational influences in their testing of one and one-half to two year olds' comprehension of usual and unusual two-word commands. The experimenters did not, for example, issue a command when the child was looking at or handling the object-referent named in the command. Nor did the researchers use gestures or routines in their presentations of the command. Under these more controlled circumstances, the young children could, on occasion, respond to unusual commands such as "Kiss the flower" or "Pat the bottle."

Despite Sachs and Truswell's (1978) findings, it is apparent that most comprehension under normal, less controlled conditions is heavily influenced by the child's knowledge of what usually happens. Strohner and Nelson (1974) have called this the *probable event strategy*. They found that two- and three-year-old normal children assigned meanings to the utterances they heard on the basis of what they experienced as probable relationships between the referents designated by the utterance. For example, when Strohner and Nelson (1974) asked their young subjects to interpret "The ball carries the wagon," the children responded by putting the ball in the wagon.

Others have studied the probable event strategy under different rubrics—e.g., cognitive bias (Duchan, 1980; Duchan and Siegel, 1979), response bias (Chapman, 1978), and semantic probability (Bever, 1970). The effect is common in young children's response to utterances regardless of the utterance type. Bever studied it in noun-verb-noun and embedded relative clauses; Duchan and Duchan and Siegel found it operating in noun-preposition-noun sequences. The outcome of all the studies is that children as well as adults interpret linguistically difficult sentences in terms of their most likely meanings, which they know from their background knowledge of how their world operates.

Before we leave the issue of probable occurrence as a basis for understanding language, we should emphasize that it is not the only strategy people use. We and others have observed certain idiosyncratic strategies which children use. For example, in our study of children's response to locative commands (Duchan, 1980), we found a child who had a favorite object strategy, wherein she interpreted the second noun of an utterance but ignored the first and instead combined the referent of the second noun with a favorite object (in her case it was a key). For example, in response to the request "Put the scissors under the paper," she put the key on the paper. We also have seen favorite position strategies, such as the child who had a next-to preference in which he placed the nearer object next to the further object, ignoring the preposition in the command.

The main point we have been making is that listeners—adults as well as children—develop an understanding of language not just from the information in sentences, but also from what they supply from their background knowledge. The most advanced sense of this is when speakers rely on listeners to do what Clark and Haviland (1977) have called bridging and what we have called making implicatures. Take Clark and Haviland's example "John is a democrat. Bill is honest, too." The unstated implication is that democrats are honest, and the speaker probably assumes that the listener shares that value judgment. Children listening to such sentences must build an implicature or bridge from one to another sentence in order to understand their relationship.

Besides building implicatures between sentences, adults and children must be able to go beyond the meanings given by the words in sentences by presupposing certain ideas. For example, if a sentence contains a factive verb such as *know, notice, is happy, is aware,* the adept listener presupposes that the proposition following that verb is true. Take the sentence "John knows that the book was lost." You, as a listener, can assume from this sentence that the speaker believes the book is in fact lost. This would not be the case for nonfactive verbs, such as *think, assume,* and *is sure.* "John thinks that the book is lost" leaves you not knowing whether or not the speaker thinks the book is lost. Other kinds of verbs, which have been called *implicatives* (e.g., *pretend*) assume that the following proposition is not true. Ability to understand presuppositions built into these verbs differs depending upon the verb. For example, Scoville and Gordon summarize their own and other findings as follows:

> First, the major conclusion is that the acquisition of factivity seems to proceed on a verb-by-verb basis. Verbs do not fall neatly into factive versus nonfactive categories. Secondly, the acquisition of factivity appears to progress gradually, but there are some conflicts among the studies concerning exact acquisition times. (Scoville and Gordon, 1980, p. 398)

In sum, children interpret language in light of background knowledge they have acquired from previous experiences. This includes the amount of previous exposure to referents and the characteristic or probable events involving referents in the child's experiences. It may also involve the child's predilection for relating to referents in idiosyncratic ways. Eventually, comprehension includes presuppositions based on previous experience with the particular words used.

LINGUISTIC KNOWLEDGE

In spite of the frequent success of the nonlinguistic sensitivities in aiding a child to interpret language, children eventually come to understand language itself as a system. We need, then, to assess children's ability to understand the semantics of lexical items, as well as of longer sequences, and we also need to evaluate their ability to understand syntactic constructions. Let us examine children's acquisition of linguistic knowledge, proceeding from the one-word stage of comprehension to the two-word stage and from simple sentences on to longer and more complicated linguistic entities.

The One-Word Period in Comprehension

Children's understandings of single words, one at a time, has been one way of characterizing their early acquisition of semantics. Evidence for this stage is that children either ignore the longer utterances (Shipley et al., 1969); pick out one familiar word from a group of words, ignoring the others (Benedict, 1979); or treat the whole group of words as if it were one word (Thomas, 1979). As we have said in the pragmatics section of this chapter, these one-word understandings are context bound in that they are only understood if they pertain to present, familiar, and perceptually salient objects. Nonetheless they do carry some of their own decontextualized meaning, since children will occasionally switch their attention from what they are doing to the referent designated (Sachs and Truswell, 1978).

The first words learned are familiar and favorite people and then familiar objects; only after that, at age two and one-half or so, do children seem to respond to less favorite things and to action words (Miller, 1980).

Research that has uncovered these early trends in comprehension has tested for the children's lexical knowledge as if the lexical items have fixed meanings with adultlike circumscribed boundaries. Typically, adult words are used and children are asked to designate the referent that an adult would judge to be an examplar of that category. However, as we learned from looking at the literature on language production (Chapters 3 and 7), children often do not work with fixed meanings—their meaning boundaries fluctuate and are context bound; and their meanings when they *are* fixed may not coincide with the adult senses. These boundary "problems," which have been called overextension and underextension, also occur in language comprehension. The difference is that there appears to be less overextension in comprehension than in production of lexical items (Huttenlocher, 1974; Rescorla, 1980; Thomson and Chapman, 1977).

The Two-Word Stage in Comprehension

Children have been described as passing through a telegraphic stage in their sentence production (Brown and Bellugi, 1964). What about their comprehension? Some reports suggest that they seem to single out two content words in the constructions they hear and form a relational meaning such as agent-action, action-object, possessor-possessed, or object-location (Miller, 1978, 1980). This would suggest that their comprehension is telegraphic and would benefit from telegraphic stimuli where the selection of the words to be understood is already done for the children. For example, it seems they should do better in understanding "Mommy sock" than "Mommy will sock you." This has not been found to be true, however (Duchan and Erickson, 1976; Petretic and Tweney, 1977). Indeed, children who are at the one- and two-word stage in their production do more poorly in responding to commands that are telegraphic than to commands that contain function words (for an exception, see Shipley et al., 1969).

Might it be that children benefit from the intonation contour offered by the full-formed utterance and that they disregard the sounds in the function words? This is apparently not the case. Duchan and Erickson (1976) found that when nonsense fillers were inserted to replace the function words, the children's comprehension was even worse than for the telegraphic forms. Thus, while children do seem to ignore the meaning of function words and some content words, they seem at the same time to notice that something is wrong when these words do not occur in an utterance. This suggests that they do not hear telegraphically, although they might be responding meaningfully to only two of the lexical items contained in the utterance.

Once we start examining descriptions of children's interpretations of two content words, we are met with the same difficulties that we find in the descriptions of two-word semantic relations in language production (see Chapter 6). That is, we are in danger of assuming too much knowledge, while instead the child may be working from a very limited or different sense of the relationship from adult language users. An example of this rich interpretation problem is revealed by a detailed longitudinal study of a child progressing from age one and one-half to two years by Miller and Weissenborn (1978). They found that early comprehension of locative commands (e.g., "Where is X?") was only in game contexts of pointing to pictures in books and body part identification and did not require that the child understand the idea of location as separate from the object being identified. While we may have assumed the child had the notion of location when she responded and pointed, saying "There" to "Where is your pacifier?" at age sixteen months, it was not until she was twenty-four months old that she answered "where" questions with place-naming answers. Extending the implications of this study to commands involving placing objects (N_1) in places

$$(N_1) \qquad (N_2)$$

(N_2), as in "Put the apple in the bathtub," we can see that the child could simply put both objects together without understanding that the command carried the idea of locative relation.

An investigation of the comprehension of possessive relations (Golinkoff and Markessini, 1980) likewise raises questions about the degree of knowledge that can be attributed to young children. Using children in five MLU groups from 1.00 to 4 (mean ages 1.8–5.5), they sampled comprehension of several possessive relations—alienable ("girl's shoe"), "intrinsic" or body part ("mommy's face"), and reciprocal or reversible kinship relations of either a child-parent type ("baby's mommy") or parent-child type ("mommy's baby"). They also included anomalous relations of both alienable and intrinsic types ("shoe's boy"; "face's mommy"). Most of the children, excepting the youngest group, correctly interpreted the alienable possession items, but only the oldest group predictably used word order to interpret the reciprocal relations correctly. It is interesting to note that all children interpreted the parent-child relations correctly more frequently than the child-parent relations, indicating that children probably view parents as possessors of children more so than the reverse. Their performance on anomalous relations, where children overwhelmingly chose the first noun ("Show me the face's mommy"; shows face), also shows their strong predilection to interpret utterances to be consistent with their knowledge of the world, at least until MLU 4 when the children began to interpret anomalous alienable phrases as adults do ("Show me the ball's mommy"; shows mommy).

A further problem with the conceptualization of the two-word semantic relations stage in language comprehension is that different relations require different kinds and levels of processing for deriving an answer that appears correct (Duchan and Erickson, 1976). That is, comprehension is not just deriving the meaning relationship between two words, but rather it involves recognizing that the words signal different grammatical relations. With the locative, for example, we require not only that the child understand that the first noun (N_1) is located in relation to the second (N_2), but we also require that the specific nature of the relation, expressed in English by a preposition occurring in a phrase with N_2 ("on the table," "in the attic," etc.) be understood. Prepositions are notably hard to learn (Slobin, 1973), thereby making locatives harder to comprehend than some other relations. In contrast, the possessive relation requires that the child respond by indicating only one of the nouns—the second one—and does not require the interpretation of a preposition. To get "mommy's hat" requires that the child hear and show a hat, not a mommy as well as a hat. Finally, other so-called semantic relations require understanding of action words, which are more difficult to understand and are acquired later than nouns (Miller, 1980). It is indeed the case, in keeping with predictions made from the preceding comments, that two-word locatives are relatively late to develop in language comprehension, following, in consecutive order, possessives, action-objects, and agent-action relations (Duchan and Erickson, 1976; Miller, 1980).

Finally, while we are describing here the child's linguistic knowledge, we can not ignore context, although this is typically done. It is certainly the case, for instance, that comprehension of the relation of two content words will depend upon whether they occur in familiar contexts, whether one of the content words is known information or not, or whether it is within the perceptual saliency or attention of the child at the time the command is given; or whether a linguistic or nonlinguistic strategy is applicable to the sentence. Like the points made earlier, these pragmatic circumstances will affect the various semantic relations differently. This leads us to be suspicious of a conceptualization of a unified semantic relations stage in children's language comprehension.

Simple Clauses

Noun-verb-noun sequences have frequently been studied in the language acquisition literature, probably because they have been thought to represent the most basic sentence type, the simple active declarative sentence. Also, one of the most documented strategies used by children in their language comprehension is that of noun-verb-noun = subject-verb-object (NVN = SVO). Or if the orientation is a semantic one rather than one of grammatical relations, the strategy is described as NVN = agent-action-patient (NVN = AAP). The prevalence of this strategy perhaps reveals that children regard this as a basic sentence form which they use to interpret or misinterpret all sentences.

While agent-action-patient is the most common semantic relation expressed in the NVN string, others are also possible, such as the first noun acting as instrument or the second acting as locative or dative. The agent and patient can even be in reverse order, as in "The apple is eaten by the cow" (NVN=PAA). The interpretation for an adult will depend upon the verb and what comes between the verb and the second noun. For children, these relations may be determined by the probabilities of events in the real world—that is, cows eat apples and apples do not eat cows. So, a sentence with these words in it would be interpreted by early language learners as cow=agent; eat=action; apple=patient, regardless of word order or other aspects of the sentence, thus overriding the NVN=AAP strategy. Sentences that have nouns that cannot be both agents and patients have been called irreversible or probable sentences. These sentences are the earliest to be understood because regardless of word order, the agent is always clear since the reverse is improbable, e.g., "The apple eats the cow."

Comprehension of Multiple Clauses

As we have seen in the chapter on syntax, sentences with multiple clauses include compound clauses, which use a coordinating conjunction (*and, but, or*), or embedding, in which one clause is inserted in another either as a subordinate clause, where it serves as a major constituent to the main clause (subject, or object), or as a relative clause, where it modifies the constituent of the main clause.

The NVN=AAP strategy, because it includes two nouns and a verb, does not work for more complex sentences which have more than two nouns and a verb. Children may try to make it work, as can be evidenced by four year olds who act out sentences such as "The boy who hit the girl, hit the man" by having the girl hit the man, since the girl can be seen as the beginning of a NVN sequence. Relative clause sentences such as the previous ones require more and different kinds of linguistic knowledge. Bowerman (1979) describes the inadequacy of NVN=AAP as follows:

> Problems may arise because one clause interrupts another, because major constituents such as subject or object are replaced by pronouns or missing entirely in embedded and conjoined clauses, because the normal word orders of free-standing sentences are rearranged, and for a variety of other reasons. (Bowerman, 1979, p. 288)

The types of linguistic knowledge involved in interpretation of multiple-clause sentences require that the interpreter determine what propositions are expressed by the embedded or coordinated clauses and how the clauses work with one another. As we saw from the above misinterpretation of the hitting example, one of the difficulties with complex sentences is the determination of the grammatical relations for the various nouns and verbs within clauses and across clauses. Even when these determinations are made for the general case, the exceptions to these generalizations remain to be learned. Furthermore, certain complex sentences are difficult to learn because of their semantic or cognitive complexities. We will first discuss children's comprehension of compound sentences, then those involving embedding, then the exceptions to the rules, and finally some multiple-clause sentences with difficult semantic components.

COMPOUND SENTENCES   Compound sentences, at first glance, should be the easiest of the multiple-clause sentences to understand, since the same word order strategies should apply to them as to the simple sentences—just more than once. However, one of the characteristics of these sentences is that if there are overlapping ideas in the constituents, such as both having the same subject, the language allows for dropping out the duplication. So, if John both went to the store and bought some sardines, the apt speaker would not say "John went to the store and John bought some sardines" but rather would probably omit the second *John* and say "John went to the store and bought some sardines." Thus, ellipsis becomes a complicating factor in children's comprehension of compound sentences. The deletion can be one in which an element is mentioned and then, upon second mention, is omitted ("Mary sang and [Mary] played"); this has been called forward deletion. Or the deletion can be backward—it is made before the first mention of the duplicated element ("Mary [ran] and Jane ran").

Although one might predict that forward deletions are easier to understand, the evidence for this pattern is not clear. DeVilliers, Tager-Flusberg, and Hakuta (1977) found that there was no difference between children's comprehension of backward and forward deleted sentences. Further, their three and four year olds were able to interpret full sentence coordination and deletion within subject and verb phrases equally well. Using elicited imitation and spontaneous production as a measure of mastery of coordination, Lust (1977) and Lust and Mervis (1980) found that two and three year olds frequently use *and* coordination in a forward direction, while backward reduction is rare to nonexistent. Also, unlike deVilliers, Tager-Flusberg, and Hakuta, they found that the children first acquired sentence coordination, often with redundancy (e.g., "That's a daddy and that's a daddy"), and then later acquired coordination within phrases (e.g., "The mommy and daddy"). This is consistent with other, previous findings (Limber, 1973; Menyuk, 1969, 1971; Slobin and Welsh, 1973).

Ardery (1980) also found a trend in her study of three to six year olds toward acquiring coordinations involving forward deletions prior to those requiring backward deletions. But, she argues, there are other factors involved making the picture more complicated. Some forward deletions are quite difficult, as for example, "The giraffe kissed the horse and the frog the cat," which was one of the most difficult and was not understood correctly until age 5.7. Ardery accounts for the difficulty of this type of "gapped verb" structure by postulating a verb primacy hypothesis which says that the verb serves as the primary unit of clausal structure in children's language. Ardery examined children's comprehension of a number of different types of coordinate sentences. The sentence types, an example of each, and their mean age of acquisition are listed in Table 8.1. It can be seen that sentences with redundancy were not used in this study; this, along with possible differences between processing for production and for comprehension of coordination structures, may account for different findings in various investigations. The age differences among children participating in this and other studies could also be a factor in interpreting results.

VERB COMPLEMENTS Some sentences have verb complements following the clause object:

I told you *to go.*
I want you *to jump.*

Table 8.1 Coordinate Sentence Types and Age of Acquisition

	MEAN AGE OF CHILDREN CORRECT
Intransitive verb: The frog ran and fell	3.11
Object noun phrase: The giraffe kissed the tiger and the cat	4.0
Sentential intransitive: The dog ran and the cat fell	4.3
Verb phrase: The dog kissed the horse and pushed the tiger	4.5
Subject noun phrase: The tiger and the turtle pushed the dog	4.9
Sentential transitive: The turtle pushed the dog and the cat kissed the horse	5.0
Gapped verb with particle: The horse bumped into the cat and the dog into the turtle	5.0
Transitive verb: The turtle kissed and pushed the frog	5.2
Gapped verb, no particle: The giraffe kissed the horse and the frog the cat	5.7
Gapped object: The cat kissed and the turtle pushed the dog	5.9

Source: From Ardery, G., On Coordination in Child Language, *Journal of Child Language*, 7, 1980, 305–20. Reprinted by permission of Cambridge University Press.

Typically, these complement verbs have as their subjects the noun immediately preceding them, which is the object of the main clause (*you* in both of these examples). This strategy of going to the immediately preceding NP for a subject has been called the *minimal distance principle* (Chomsky, 1969; Rosenbaum, 1967).

Tavakolian (1976, cited in Bowerman, 1979) found that three- and four-year-old children, instead of following the minimal distance principle, overgeneralized the subject-object deletion strategies used for interpreting coordinate clauses when assigning subjects to complement verbs—that is, they used *compounding strategies*. The children interpreted the main clause subject as the subject of the complementary clause in the same way they interpreted the coordinated subject of a compound clause. The result was the following:

1. *Stimulus with compound clause:* Donald told Bozo a story and lay down. Make him do it.
    Response: Child shows Donald laying down.
    Strategy: Main clause subject is Donald, lay down is compound clause with subject Donald deleted.
2. *Stimulus with complement:* Donald told Bozo to lie down. Make him do it.
    Response: Child has Donald laying down.
    Strategy: Donald treated as main clause subject, and lie down incorrectly treated as compound clause with subject Donald deleted.

RELATIVE CLAUSES   Tavakolian (1976) also found that her three- to five-year-old subjects used a compounding strategy in interpreting sentences with relative clauses; that is, they selected the first NP as the subject of both main verb and the verb in the relative clause. This led to their systematic misinterpretation of sentences such as

The cat bit the dog that the rat chased.

The compounding strategy led them to have the cat bite the dog and the cat chase the rat.

DeVilliers et al. (1977) found a different strategy was used by their three to five year olds in interpreting relative clauses. These children elaborated on the NVN=AAP strategy and used the second noun both as object of the first clause and subject of the second. In the preceding example, the child with this NV$\{^N_N\}$ = AA$\{^P_A\}$ strategy would show the cat biting the dog and the dog chasing the rat.

The order of acquisition of different types of relative clause constructions depends, of course, on whether the children's strategy leads to a correct or incorrect interpretation. Thus, children who have a coordinated strategy would appear to learn center-embedded sentences first, such as "The boy who hit the girl ran away," while those with the complex AP$\{^P_A\}$ strategy would acquire sentences such as "The boy hit the man who kissed the doll" before other forms. Studies have combined children who are working with all these strategies, and thus the results are difficult to interpret and are in disagreement (see Bowerman, 1979, for a review).

ADVERBIAL CLAUSES   Adverbial clauses begin with adverbials such as *before, after, when, if, because, so, until.* What is interesting and different about them is that they require different interpretations depending upon the adverb involved and its placement in the sentence. Take *before* and *after* as examples. There are four possible permutations:

1. Clause with *before* in first position
   e.g., Before Mary ran, Tom ran
2. Clause with *before* in second position
   e.g., Mary ran before Tom ran
3. Clause with *after* in first position
   e.g., After Mary ran, Tom ran
4. Clause with *after* in second position
   e.g., Mary ran after Tom ran

Clark (1971) found for *before* and *after* clauses that her three- to five-year-old subjects used a NVN=AAP interpretation for each clause and combined the two clauses with a semantic order-of-mention strategy—that is, they interpreted the first clause as happening first followed by the second. This would result in an apparent correct interpretation for examples 2 and 3 in the preceding list, but an incorrect interpretation for examples 1 and 4. Amidon and Carey (1972) found a different pattern. Their five- and six-year-old subjects responded only to the main clause, ignoring the adverbial clause. A possible resolution of the apparent contradiction in results is that the order-of-mention strategy occurs earlier in development than identification of the main clause.

Typically, in the study of any phenomenon, the exception to the rule offers the best test of that rule. So, if we postulate that children understand complicated sentences according to strategies such as compounding, NVN=AAP, minimal distance principle, or order-of-mention, then we would expect them to make mistakes interpreting sentences which violate these regularities. This is due to overgeneralization of the rule to instances where it does not apply.

The most often cited example of this is children's interpretation of passive sentences which violate the NVN=AAP rule. So, for example, "The boy is chased by the dog" in which the patient comes first is interpreted as "The boy chased the dog."

A second interesting exception is verbs such as *promise* and *ask* which fail to operate by the minimal distance principle (MDP) (Rosenbaum, 1967). For example, in the sentence "John promised the man to leave," it is John and not the man who will leave. Similarly, *ask*, when combined with a wh- question, deviates from this principle—e.g., "Ask Mary what to do next." In this case, it is "you" that will perform the action, and not Mary, as would be predicted from the MDP. Not surprisingly, these exceptions are late ones to be acquired and are misinterpreted by typical children as late as age ten years (Chomsky, 1969; Kessel, 1970).

Another sentence type which has been studied because of the violation of the MDP is that in which the main subject becomes the object of the complement verb. Compare, for example, "John is easy to see," where John is the object of *see*, with "John is eager to see," which follows the MDP in that John is the subject of *see*. Typical children come to understand these correctly between four and seven years of age (Cromer, 1970; Fabian, 1979).

SENTENCES IN NARRATIVE   We said earlier in this chapter that sentences are not understood out of context. An important beginning is being made in this regard—specifically, an investigation of how the semantic cohesiveness between clauses within a sentence as well as preceding clauses affect children's comprehension. Tyler and Marslen-Wilson (1978a, 1978b) have presented five to eleven year olds with stories which were controlled for semantic overlapping between clauses. An example of overlapping clauses with high cohesion is

Sarah went running up to Peter and gave him a big hug.

An example of low-cohesion clauses would be

When the children were at school, Sarah and Peter visited their friends.

The experimenters stopped the story at various places and asked the children to repeat the last sentence they heard. While the older children, like adults, used syntactic information to process and recall clause by clause, the five year olds relied primarily on semantic information and tended to give back an integrated sense of the sentence, particularly for sentences with high cohesion between clauses. It was also found that their verbatim recall suffered most when both clauses in a test sentence referred to the same event as the prior text rather than introducing a new event. They then tended to "lose" clauses by integrating them into preceding discourse. This effect was also noted with the seven year olds but to a lesser extent. The difficulty the younger children experienced separating and processing clauses rapidly needs further exploration, since it looks as if it may be a deficit of children who have academic problems but who seem to perform well on single-sentence evaluation measures.

We will now turn to the application of the literature we have reviewed to assessing children's comprehension abilities.

ASSESSMENT OF LANGUAGE COMPREHENSION

When assessing language production, we can directly observe the product we are interested in describing, that is, the spoken words and sentences. This is not the case when assessing language comprehension, thus forcing us to make inferences about what children understand from their behavior. This leads to the possibility of overly rich interpretation of what children understand about language, giving rise to the same problem we have when attributing meaning to children's productions. The researcher and clinician must guard against unfounded assumptions that children understand questions just because they answer them or understand the language of commands simply because they comply with them. It should be obvious simply from introspection that answering yes does not mean you understand the question, just as carrying out a request does not mean you would understand the same request in a different context. Thus, we need to be clever in our assessment procedures to guard against the tendency toward rich interpretation.

There are several aspects of comprehension that we may be interested in assessing. We may want to know if children can respond appropriately to particular lexical items or to particular grammatical structures. Or our interest may be in whether or not children can comprehend connected discourse. Our goal may be to determine which elements in the context lead to comprehension or to determine a child's understanding of decontextualized language. We may be interested in the linguistic strategies the child employs as well as the nonlinguistic strategies based on context. We will discuss some examples of each of these approaches to assessment of language comprehension, using elicitation procedures.

Comprehension of Particular Words or Relations

Techniques can be designed to include or control for the effects of the situational context and the listener's background knowledge when we are assessing a child's comprehension of particular words or grammatical relations. Children can be asked to do something that is expected in that situation, thereby examining their ability to interpret language in *compatible contexts*. These contexts place the least reliance on linguistic interpretation, since the situation typically calls for a particular response. Examples of such procedures for assessing a variety of structures follow.

RESPOND TO THE EXPECTED   In this assessment procedure, children are asked to follow expected directions in familiar naturalistic situations or appropriately answer questions relating to present objects.

> Sit down (when approaching table and chair)
> Throw the ball (when holding ball)
> Drink your milk (milk in glass)
> Make the baby go night-night (with doll and bed)
> Where's the kitty? (child looking at kitty)
> Do you want to go outside? (holding coat)

ACT OUT THE EXPECTED   Here, children are asked to perform a described action which is the most probable event in the given context. Items may be chosen to assess particular structures.

> Put the baby in the bed (preposition)
> Make the lady pat the dog (agent-object)
> Show me the apple is eaten by the horse (passive)
> Where's the lady's hat? (possessive)

We can also create a language measure of decontextualization, wherein there is a dissonance between what is said and what is expected. These would be *dissonant contexts*. These contexts are the most difficult, since the child must override the tendency to interpret the expected in the situation. Some examples follow.

UNEXPECTED DIRECTIONS IN FAMILIAR SITUATIONS

> Stand on the chair (when approaching table and chair)
> Kiss the ball (when holding ball)
> Stir your milk (milk in glass)
> Make the kitty go night-night (with doll and bed)
> Where's the puppy (child looking at kitty)
> Do you want to go to bed? (holding coat)

ACT OUT THE UNEXPECTED   Children are asked without forewarning to do something which is contrary to the most probable event, given the situation.

> Put the baby under the bed
> Make the dog pat the lady
> Show me the horse is eaten by the apple
> Where's the hat's lady?

IDENTIFY WHAT'S SILLY   Children are presented with improbable commands or statements, such as those above, and asked to tell what's silly about them.

Another possibility is to create a situation and a linguistic event which carry no expectation for one another, since the elements generally would not occur together in the child's experience. These are *neutral contexts* and offer little contextual support for interpreting language. Some examples are

USING FAMILIAR REFERENTS IN UNPREDICTABLE RELATIONS   Children are asked to carry out actions involving referents that are not typically related to each other or otherwise have no predictable relationship.

Put the spoon in the tree
Make the block hit the ball
Show me the pen is bumped by the shoe

NONSENSE WORDS   Some researchers have taught children new or nonsense words and then measured their comprehension in different linguistic or situational contexts. For example, Werner and Kaplan (1952) asked eight- to- thirteen-year-old children the meaning of a nonsense word after presenting the word in the context of six sentences. They expected that the children would be able to derive the meaning *stick* or *piece of wood* for the nonsense word *corplum* from the following six sentences.

1.   A corplum may be used for support.
2.   Corplums may be used to close off an open space.
3.   A corplum may be long or short, thick or thin, strong or weak.
4.   You can make a corplum smooth with sandpaper.
5.   A wet corplum does not burn.
6.   The painter used a corplum to mix his paints.

Comprehension of Discourse

We now turn to comprehension of connected clauses and sentences to see if children can understand them as cohesive units. The speech event context becomes important, since we all tend to understand language in terms of what we perceive to be the event that is going on. Also, we can determine whether children's comprehension is shaped by the expected frames or provision of topics within speech events. We must also consider the intentional context to see if children are sensitive to speaker's intentions in their interpretation of language. We will discuss some elicitation procedures to assess these aspects of comprehension of discourse.

RETELLING   Children are read or told stories and then asked to retell them. Determine if their version differs significantly from the original in ways such as nature or sequence of events, motivation of characters, or outcome. Note if they fill in parts by drawing reasonable implications from what is given or if they go beyond the presented elements. If parts are left out or altered, determine if these reflect lack of understanding of parts of the original story.

The following story from Stein and Glenn (1979) is first given in an abbreviated version that eliminates details of setting and motivation which have been found to be important parts of the story frame. This is followed by the original version. Children's comprehension of the two versions can be compared by their retelling and by asking inference questions.

THE TIGER'S WHISKER

A woman wanted a tiger's whisker because her husband was very sick. So she went to a tiger's cave and put down a bowl of food in front of the opening and sang some soft music. The tiger came out and ate the food. Then he walked over to the lady and thanked her for the delicious food and lovely music. The lady cut off one of his whiskers and ran down the hill very quickly. The tiger felt lonely and sad again.

THE TIGER'S WHISKER (Original form)

Once there was a woman who needed a tiger's whisker. She was afraid of tigers, but she needed a whisker to make a medicine for her husband who had gotten very sick. She thought and thought about how to get a tiger whisker. She decided to use a trick. She knew that tigers loved food and music. She thought that if she brought food to a lonely tiger and played soft music the tiger would be nice to her and she could get the whisker. So she did just that. She went to a tiger's cave where a lonely tiger lived. She put a bowl of food in front of the opening to the cave. Then she sang soft music. The tiger came out and ate the food. He then walked over to the lady and thanked her for the delicious food and lovely music. The lady then cut off one of his whiskers and ran down the hill very quickly. The tiger felt lonely and sad again. (Stein and Glenn, 1979, p. 79)

DRAWING IMPLICATIONS   Children can be asked probe questions to determine if they understand implications of statements from discourse they hear. For example:

Ask the puppet if the water is too hot.
Puppet answers: I can put my hand in it.
Is the water too hot?
Ask the puppet if he wants a glass of milk.
Puppet answers: I'm going to bed.
Does he want a glass of milk?
Ask the puppet if he had a good time at the party.
Puppet answers: The food was good.
Did he have a good time?

Ask the puppet if he knows where the toy is.
Puppet answers: I wasn't playing with it.
Does he know where it is?

Children can also be told stories and then asked inferential questions. You might compare their understanding of stories that have clear settings and explicit motives with those that leave elements ambiguous, such as those used by Omanson, Warren, and Trabasso (1978).

UNDERSTANDING THE UNEXPECTED   Jokes, riddles, and puns often are funny because the punch line is a switch from the usual or expected meaning of words. If children understand a joke, they are showing their ability to shift orientation to accommodate the unexpected portions into the discourse. Just because children find jokes funny does not mean they understand them, so it is best to have them explain the joke as a check on comprehension. See Chapter 7 for some examples of jokes to use with children; try to identify the types of jokes that children do and do not comprehend.

UNDERSTANDING INTENTION   Language often takes on different interpretations when we take the speaker's intention into account. When the same utterance is spoken to children in different intentional contexts, we can see if they use this information for comprehending language. Some examples of how we might do this follow:

In context of toy vehicles, ask "Can you drive the car?"
In context of who drives the car at your house, ask "Can you drive the car?"
In context of pointing to body parts, ask "Where's your sweater?"
In context of getting dressed to go out, ask "Where's your sweater?"
In context of reviewing items bought on a pretend shopping trip, ask "Do you have any cookies?"
In context of pretend tea party, ask "Do you have any cookies?"

UNDERSTANDING SENTENCES IN DISCOURSE   Using the techniques of Tyler and Marslen-Wilson (1978a, 1978b), we can investigate school-age children's ability to deal with multiple-clause sentences in discourse—we can determine if children are able to deal with successive clauses or if they display the primarily semantic memory typical of younger children and lose the syntactic information. Children can be read stories and asked to repeat the immediately preceding sentence exactly as heard at various points throughout the story. Observe if recall is significantly poorer for sentences with redundant information. Note if the child blends together clauses or sentences that refer to the same event together and if he or she gives back the basic meaning but not the structure of the sentence. The following story is an example of one that contains several multiple-clause sentences, some of which offer redundant information about events already referred to, others with new information about old events, and some with new information about new events:

Terry and Blackie were two dogs that lived with the Jones family. They woke up early each day just as the sun was coming up. They woke up very hungry and wanted to eat. They ran to the back door and barked to be let in. They wanted to get in and eat their breakfast. While they were eating their breakfast, the children came downstairs to the kitchen. After the children left for school, Terry and Blackie visited their friends. They visited all their friends because they wanted to find out all of the dog news. After a day of visiting their friends, they waited for the children to come home. That was their favorite part of the day.

Discovering Linguistic Strategies

In addition to examining the effects of various contexts on language comprehension, we can give special attention to children's use of particular linguistic strategies in interpreting sentences. A technique which has become popular in the language acquisition literature is finding sentences that violate expected linguistic strategies and observing whether children misinterpret them. If they have a strategy worked out, children are likely to employ it to interpret the exceptions incorrectly. We will present some examples of strategies and exceptions to them to show you how it works. It is important to use neutral contexts and reversible sentences so the correct interpretation of the sentence cannot be deduced nonlinguistically.

NOUN-VERB-NOUN = AGENT-ACTION-PATIENT   The following are examples of utterances that fit this strategy and will be interpreted correctly:

The cat chases the squirrel
The boy hugs the mother

Exceptions to the rule that will be interpreted incorrectly with this strategy are

The cat is chased by the squirrel
The boy is hugged by the mother
The boy who hit the girl chased the man
The dog who chased the cat bit the mouse
The boy, because he wanted to see his mother, went home

MINIMAL DISTANCE PRINCIPLE   The noun preceding the complement is the agent for that complement—utterances that fit this rule and will be interpreted correctly are

I want you to go to the store
John asked Mary to play
John is eager to please

Exceptions to the rule that will be interpreted incorrectly with this strategy are

	INTERPRETED AS
I promised you to go to the store	You go to the store
John asked Mary what to play	Mary will play
John is easy to please	John will please

$$NV \begin{Bmatrix} N \\ N \end{Bmatrix} VN = \begin{Bmatrix} A \\ A \end{Bmatrix} AP \qquad AA \begin{Bmatrix} P \\ A \end{Bmatrix}$$ The second noun in a NVNVN sequence is the patient of the first clause and the agent of the second clause. Utterances that fit this strategy and will be interpreted correctly are

The cat bit the rat that chased the dog
Jack told Mary to catch the ball

Exceptions to the rule that will be interpreted incorrectly with this strategy are

	INTERPRETED AS
The cat bit the rat that the dog chased	Rat chased the dog
Jack told Mary he caught the ball	Mary caught the ball
The boy patted the dog and chased the cat	Dog chased the cat

COORDINATE CLAUSE STRATEGY $N \overset{VN}{\underset{VN}{\diagdown}}$ The first noun in a NVNVN is the subject of both the clauses that follow the noun. Utterances that fit this strategy and will be interpreted correctly are

The boy hugged the girl and kissed the baby
The car raced the truck and hit the train

Exceptions to the rule that will be interpreted incorrectly with this strategy are

	INTERPRETED AS
The boy hugged the girl that kissed the baby	Boy kissed the baby
The car raced the truck that hit the train	Car hit the train

ORDER-OF-MENTION STRATEGY   The order of clauses corresponds to the order of events mentioned. Utterances which fit this strategy and will be correctly interpreted are

The bell rang before they ate
After the bell rang, they ate
First the bell rang and then they ate

Exceptions to the rule that will be interpreted incorrectly with this strategy are

	INTERPRETED AS
They ate after the bell rang	Eating before bell
Before they ate, the bell rang	Eating before bell
They ate when the bell finished ringing	Eating before bell

IDIOSYNCRATIC STRUCTURES Besides testing for the existence of strategies found in normally developing children, it is important to allow yourself to discover new strategies which may be peculiar to the particular child you are evaluating. Thus, you will need to be sensitive to how the child consistently interprets a set of utterances. An effective procedure is to place a number of objects in front of a group of children and ask them to carry out the directions you give. Videotaping the event will prevent you from having to keep track of all of the responses as children carry out the directions. What is relevant to your assessment will depend upon the child; the following areas of observation might be helpful in leading you to discover a strategy:

1. The delay time
2. The search pattern, i.e., what children look at
3. The order of selection of objects
4. The assignment of agent and patient
5. The order of carrying out the propositions in multiple-clause utterances
6. A puzzled look or request for more direction

Assessment of Comprehension from Language Samples

We have been describing elicitation procedures which can be used to sample particular forms of language comprehension. Additional insight into the child's understanding of language can be obtained by examining transcripts of naturally occurring interactions. In such interactions, language is generally supported by compatible context, so we must be aware that the child often has more than linguistic information on which to rely for interpretation.

Each transcript is likely to show quite a bit about the words and structures that the child comprehends. Some things that might be of particular interest to look for in spontaneous samples include

INAPPROPRIATE RESPONSES TO QUESTIONS OR REQUESTS

Adult: Bring me my shoes.
Child brings book he is holding.
Here the child understands a request is being made and interprets it in terms of the object on which he is focused.

Adult: Did Daddy go bye-bye?
Child waves.
Here the child seems to be responding to the initiation of a routine that pairs the word *bye-bye* with the action. The child does not interpret utterance as a request for information.

Adult: When did you get that?

Child: From my Grandma.

The child understands that information is being requested, and not understanding the question word, probably responds with the most salient bit of information.

Adult: Give me the paper that Billy brought home.

Child gives paper to Billy.

Child may be responding to a "give the X to Y" routine, or otherwise having difficulty assigning the patient role.

UNDERSTANDING INFERENCES

Adult: Where did the dog get that sandwich?

Child: I was done with it.

Adult: It's time to put these away.

Child: This one's not done.

Adult: Do you know what time it is?

Child: I don't wanna go to bed.

EXERCISES

1. Which of the following instructions would follow a probable event strategy (compatible context)? Which are counter to the probable event (dissonant context)? Which are neutral? Indicate C, D, or N for each of the following, and say why you classified it as you did. Some can have more than one answer.

   a) _____ Put the baby in the bed.

   b) _____ Put the pencil through the paper.

   c) _____ Put the marble in the cup.

   d) _____ Put your hat under your foot.

   e) _____ Put the spoon in the bowl.

   f) _____ Put the baby under the bed.

   g) _____ Put the bowl on the spoon.

   h) _____ Put the block beside the chair.

   i) _____ Put the key under the paper.

   j) _____ Put the key on the bed.

2. Match up the sentence in the left column with the appropriate description in the right column. More than one answer is permitted.

   _____ The boy pushed the girl.   a) Violates MDP

   _____ The boy pushed the swing.   b) NVN=AAP

   _____ The boy was pushed by the girl.   c) Redundant

   _____ The girl runs and the boy runs.   d) Backward deletion

   _____ Henry promised Mary to feed the dog.   e) Order of mention

   _____ After you eat, you can go outside.   f) Reversible sentence

   _____ The baby eats and sleeps.   g) Forward deletion

   _____ Before you go outside, we'll eat.   h) Nonreversible sentence

   _____ The boy saw the dog and fed him.   i) Overlapping clauses

   _____ The boy and the girl walked to school.   j) Violates order of mention

3. How would the following sentences be interpreted by children using (a) the compounding strategy and (b) NVNVN = AA $\left\{ {P \atop A} \right\}$ AP

The girl tickled the baby who cried. Who cried?
a)
b)
The girl, because she saw the dog, ran. Who ran?
a)
b)
The car was bumped by the truck and turned over. What turned over?
a)
b)
The dog chased the cat who ran away. Who ran away?
a)
b)
The girl who hit the boy kissed the baby. Who kissed the baby?
a)
b)
The baby who was kissed by the girl cried. Who cried?
a)
b)
The baby didn't like the boy who yelled. Who yelled?
a)
b)
The boy pushed the baby who fell down. Who fell down?
a)
b)
The boy patted the dog and sat down. Who sat down?
a)
b)

4. The following questions from Stein and Glenn (1979) could be asked about the long version of the story *The Tiger's Whisker* (see p. 244). Indicate for each question whether it asks for information given in the story (G), or inferred in the story (I). Tell the story to a child and then ask the probe questions. Which are easiest for the child to answer?
a) _____ Why did the lady need a tiger's whisker?
b) _____ Why was the lady afraid?
c) _____ Why did the lady need to make medicine?
d) _____ Why did the lady decide to use a trick?
e) _____ Why did the lady go to the tiger's cave?
f) _____ Why did the lady sing a song and give the tiger food?
g) _____ Why did the tiger come out of his cave?
h) _____ Why did the tiger eat the food?
i) _____ Why did the tiger walk over to the lady?
j) _____ Why did the tiger thank the lady?
k) _____ Why did the lady cut off the tiger's whisker?
l) _____ Why did the lady run down the hill quickly?
m) _____ Why did the tiger feel sad and lonely again?

REFERENCES

AMIDON, A., AND P. CAREY. Why Five Year Olds Cannot Understand Before and After, *Journal of Verbal Learning and Verbal Behavior*, 11, 1972, 417–23.

ARDERY, G. On Coordination in Child Language, *Journal of Child Language,* 7, 1980, 305–20.

BENEDICT, H. Early Lexical Development: Comprehension and Production, *Journal of Child Language,* 6, 1979, 183–200.

BEVER, T. The Cognitive Basis for Linguistics, in *Cognition and the Development of Language,* ed. J. R. Hayes. New York: John Wiley, 1970.

BLOOM, L. Why Not Pivot Grammar? *Journal of Speech and Hearing Disorders,* 36, 1971, 40–50.

BOWERMAN, M. The Acquisition of Complex Sentences, in *Language Acquisition,* eds. P. Fletcher and M. Garman. London: Cambridge University Press, 1979, 285–306.

BRANSFORD, J., AND M. JOHNSON. Contextual Prerequisites for Understanding: Some Investigations of Comprehension and Recall, *Journal of Verbal Learning and Verbal Behavior,* 11, 1972, 717–26.

BRANSFORD, J., AND N. MCCARRELL. A Sketch of a Cognitive Approach to Comprehension, in *Cognition and the Symbolic Processes,* eds. W. Weimer and D. Palermo. Hillsdale, N.J.: Lawrence Erlbaum Associates, 1974.

BRANSFORD, J., AND K. NITSCH. Coming to Understand Things We Could Not Previously Understand, in *Speech and Language in the Laboratory, School, and Clinic,* eds. J. Kavanagh and W. Strange. Cambridge, Mass.: M.I.T. Press, 1978.

BROWN, A. L. The Development of Memory: Knowing, Knowing about Knowing, and Knowing How to Know, in *Advances in Child Development and Behavior,* Vol. 10, ed. H. W. Reese. New York: Academic Press, 1975.

BROWN, R. *A First Language: The Early Stages.* Cambridge, Mass.: Harvard University Press, 1973.

BROWN, R., AND U. BELLUGI. Three Processes in the Child's Acquisition of Syntax, *Harvard Educational Review,* 34, 1964, 133–51.

BRUNER, J. The Ontogenesis of Speech Acts, *Journal of Child Language,* 2, 1975, 1–19.

CHAPMAN, R. Comprehension Strategies in Children, in *Speech and Language in the Laboratory, School and Clinic,* eds. J. Kavanagh and W. Strange. Cambridge, Mass.: M.I.T. Press, 1978.

CHOMSKY, C. *The Acquisition of Syntax in Children from 5 to 10.* Cambridge, Mass.: M.I.T. Press, 1969.

CLARK, E. V. On the Acquisition of the Meaning of Before and After, *Journal of Verbal Learning and Verbal Behavior,* 10, 1971, 266–75.

CLARK, E. V. Nonlinguistic Strategies and the Acquisition of Word Meaning, *Cognition,* 2, 1973, 161–82.

CLARK, E. H., AND S. HAVILAND. Comprehension and the Given-New Contract, in *Discourse Production and Comprehension,* ed. R. O. Freedle. Norwood, N.J.: Ablex Publishing, 1977, pp. 1–40.

CROMER, R. Children Are Nice to Understand: Surface Structure Cues for the Recovery of a Deep Structure, *British Journal of Psychology,* 61, 1970, 397–408.

DEVILLIERS, J., H. TAGER-FLUSBERG, AND K. HAKUTA. Deciding among Theories of the Development of Coordination in Child Speech, *Papers and Reports on Child Language Development,* 13, 1977, 118–25.

DIHOFF, R., AND R. CHAPMAN.   First Words: Their Origins and Actions, *Papers and Reports on Child Language Development,* Stanford University, 13, 1977, 107.

DORE, J.   Oh Them Sheriff: A Pragmatic Analysis of Children's Responses to Questions, in *Child Discourse,* eds. S. Ervin-Tripp and C. Mitchell-Kernan. New York: Academic Press, 1977.

DUCHAN, J., AND J. ERICKSON.   Normal and Retarded Children's Understanding of Semantic Relations in Different Verbal Contexts, *Journal of Speech and Hearing Research,* 19, 1976, 767–76.

DUCHAN, J., AND L. SIEGEL.   Incorrect Responses to Locative Commands: A Case Study, *Language Speech and Hearing Services in the Schools,* 10, 1979, 99–103.

DUCHAN, J.   Interactions with an Autistic Child, in *Language: Social Psychological Perspectives,* ed. H. Giles. New York: Pergamon Press, 1980a.

DUCHAN, J.   The Effect of Cognitive Bias on Children's Early Interpretations of Locative Commands, *Language Sciences,* 2, 1980b, 246–59.

ERVIN-TRIPP, S.   Discourse Agreement: How Children Answer Questions, in *Cognition and the Development of Language,* ed. J. Hayes. New York: John Wiley, 1970.

ERVIN-TRIPP, S.   The Comprehension and Production of Requests by Children. *Papers and Reports on Child Language Development,* Committee on Linguistics, Stanford University, No. 8, 1974, 188–96.

ERVIN-TRIPP, S.   Wait for Me Roller Skate, in *Child Discourse,* eds. S. Ervin-Tripp and C. Mitchell-Kernan. New York: Academic Press, 1977.

FABIAN, V.   When Are Children Hard to Understand? Paper presented at the Second Annual Boston University Conference on Language Development. Boston, Mass., 1977.

GOLINKOFF, R. M., AND J. MARKESSINI.   Mommy Sock: The Child's Understanding of Possession as Expressed in Two-Word Phrases, *Journal of Child Language,* 7, 1980, 119–35.

GRICE, H.   Logic and Conversation, in *Syntax and Semantics, Vol. 3: Speech Acts,* eds. P. Cole and J. L. Morgan. New York: Seminar Press, 1975, 41–58.

HUTTENLOCHER, J.   The Origins of Language Comprehension, in *Theories in Cognitive Psychology,* ed. R. L. Solso. Potomac, Md.: Erlbaum, 1974.

KARMILOFF-SMITH, A.   Language Development After Five, in *Language Acquisition,* eds. P. Fletcher and M. Garman. London: Cambridge University Press, 1979.

KESSEL, F.   The Role of Syntax in Children's Comprehension from Ages Six to Twelve, *Society for Research in Child Development Monograph,* 35, 1970.

LEONARD, L., J. BOLDERS, AND J. MILLER.   An Examination of the Semantic Relations Reflected in the Language Usage of Normal and Language Disordered Children, *Journal of Speech and Hearing Research,* 19, 1976, 371–92.

LEWIS, M., AND R. FREEDLE.   Mother-Infant Dyad: The Cradle of Meaning, in *Communication and Affect: Language and Thought,* eds. P. Pliner, L. Krames, and T. Alloway. New York: Academic Press, 1973.

LIMBER, J.   The Genesis of Complex Sentences, in *Cognitive Development and the Acquisition of Language,* ed. T. E. Moore. New York: Academic Press, 1973.

LUST, B.   Conjunction Reduction in Child Language, *Journal of Child Language,* 4, 1977, 257–88.

LUST, B., AND C. A. MERVIS.   Development of Coordination in the Natural Speech of Young Children, *Journal of Child Language,* 7, 1980, 279–304.

MANDLER, J., AND N. JOHNSON.   Remembrance of Things Parsed: Story Structure and Recall, *Cognitive Psychology,* 9, 1977, 111–51.

MAYRINK-SABINSON, L.   Study of Mother-Child Interaction with Language-Learning Children: Context and Maternal Interpretation. Unpublished Dissertation, State University of New York at Buffalo, 1980.

MENYUK, P.   *Sentences Children Use.* Cambridge, Mass.: M.I.T. Press, 1969.

MENYUK, P.   *The Acquisition and Development of Language.* Englewood Cliffs, N.J.: Prentice-Hall, 1971.

MILLER, J.   Assessing Children's Language Behavior: A Developmental Process Approach, in R. Schiefelbusch, *Bases of Language Intervention.* Baltimore, Md.: University Park Press, 1978, pp. 269–318.

MILLER, J.   *Assessing Language Production in Children.* Baltimore, Md.: University Park Press, 1980.

MILLER, M., AND J. WEISSENBORN.   Pragmatic Conditions on Learning How to Refer to Localities. *Papers and Reports on Child Language Development,* Stanford University, 15, 1978, 68–77.

OMANSON, R., W. WARREN, AND T. TRABASSO.   Goals, Inferential Comprehension and Recall of Stories by Children, *Discourse Processes,* 1, 1978, 337–54.

PETRETIC, P., AND R. TWENEY.   Does Comprehension Precede Production? *Journal of Child Language,* 4, 1977, 201–10.

REEDER, K.   The Emergence of Illocutionary Skills, *Journal of Child Language,* 7, 1980, 29–40.

RESCORLA, L.   Overextension in Early Language Development, *Journal of Child Language,* 7, 1980, 321–36.

ROSENBAUM, P.   *The Grammar of English Predicate Construction.* Cambridge, Mass.: M.I.T. Press, 1967.

RUMELHART, D. E.   Notes on a Schema for Stories, in *Representation and Understanding: Studies in Cognitive Science,* eds. D. G. Brown and A. Collins. New York: Academic Press, 1975.

SACHS, J., AND L. TRUSWELL.   Comprehension of Two-Word Instructions by Children in the One-Word Stage, *Journal of Child Language,* 5, 1978, 17–24.

SCHLESINGER, I. M.   Production of Utterances and Language Acquisition in *The Ontogenesis of Grammar,* ed. D. Slobin. New York: Academic Press, 1971.

SCOVILLE, R. P., AND A. M. GORDON.   Children's Understanding of Factive Presuppositions: An Experiment and a Review, *Journal of Child Language,* 7, 1980, 381–99.

SHATZ, M.   How Young Children Respond to Language: Procedures for Answering, *Papers and Reports in Child Language Development,* 10, 1975, 97–110.

SHIPLEY, E., C. SMITH, AND L. GLEITMAN.   A Study in the Acquisition of Language: Free Responses to Commands, *Language,* 2, 1969, 45.

SLOBIN, D. I.   Cognitive Prerequisites for the Acquisition of Grammar, in *Studies of Child Language Develpment,* eds. C. A. Ferguson and D. I. Slobin. New York: Holt, Rinehart & Winston, 1973.

SLOBIN, D. I., AND C. A. WELSH. Elicited Imitation as a Research Tool in Developmental Psycholinguistics, in *Studies of Child Language Development,* eds. C. A. Ferguson and D. I. Slobin. New York: Holt, Rinehart & Winston, 1973.

SNOW, C. Conversation with Children, in *Language Acquisition,* eds. P. Fletcher and M. Garman. Cambridge, England: Cambridge University Press, 1979, 363–76.

STEIN, N. L., AND C. G. GLENN. An Analysis of Story Comprehension in Elementary School Children: A Test of Schema, *Resources in Education,* 11, August 1976.

STEIN, N. L., AND C. G. GLENN. An Analysis of Story Comprehension in Elementary School Children, in *New Directions in Discourse Processing,* Vol. 2, ed. R. O. Freedle. Norwood, N.J.: Ablex Publishing Corporation, 1979.

STROHNER, H., AND K. NELSON. The Young Child's Development of Sentence Comprehension: Influence of Event Probability, Nonverbal Context, Syntactic Form, and Strategies, *Child Development,* 45, 1974, 567–76.

TAVAKOLIAN, S. Children's Understanding of Pronominal Subjects and Missing Subjects in Complicated Sentences. Paper presented at the Winter Meetings of the Linguistic Society of America, 1976.

THOMAS, E. It's All Routine: A Redefinition of Routines as a Central Factor in Language Acquisition. Paper presented at the Fourth Annual Boston University Conference on Language Development, Boston, Mass., 1979.

THOMSON, J., AND R. CHAPMAN. Who is "Daddy" Revisited: The Status of Two-Year-Old's Overextended Words in Use and Comprehension, *Journal of Child Language,* 4, 1977, 359–75.

TYLER, L., AND W. MARSLEN-WILSON. Some Developmental Aspects of Sentence Processing and Memory, *Journal of Child Language,* 5, 1978a, 113–30.

TYLER, L., AND W. MARSLEN-WILSON. Understanding Sentences in Contexts: Some Developmental Studies, *Papers and Reports on Child Language Development,* 15, 1978b, 102–13.

WERNER, H., AND E. KAPLAN. The Acquisition of Word Meanings: A Developmental Study. *Society for Research in Child Development Monograph,* 15, 1952, 190–200.

9

Cognitive Precursors
to Language Acquisition

Until now, our structural approach to assessment has assumed that the child being evaluated has some language comprehension or production. In recent years, there has been an increased emphasis by speech pathologists on working with the preverbal child, i.e., the child who has no knowledge of language. This new focus on the preverbal child has been the result of a composite of trends. One is that many psycholinguists have shifted their attention to studying how the nonlinguistic context affects people's understanding and production of language. This pragmatics emphasis has led to new techniques for analyzing communicative situations that can be used in assessing the preverbal child. Another trend is that child developmentalists have evolved new methodology for determining competencies in infants and preschoolers. A third trend is that legislation has mandated services for all handicapped populations, including the severely and profoundly retarded, autistic, and emotionally disturbed. These populations include many who have no language. Finally, and perhaps as a result of the preceding factors, practitioners have found success in using communication systems other than the auditory-verbal ones in their work with nonverbal children and adults.

The literature and techniques in this area of assessing the preverbal child are as yet highly exploratory, although the efforts have in common the goal of discovering a set of abilities which children need to develop in order to learn language—the so-called *cognitive precursors*. One approach to discovering these abilities has been the *correlational* approach, wherein skills in one area are examined for their developmental correlation with language. For example, Moore et al. (1977) studied eleven Down's syndrome infants and found a high correlation (.75) between their MLU and performance on object permanence tasks. Similarly, Bates (1979) studied gestural communication at the onset of verbal language and found communicative pointing to be a good predictor of first words. Bates (1979) and Harding and Golinkoff (1977) also found positive correlations between children's ability to make means-end distinctions and their language acquisition.

The correlational approach is theoretically motivated in that the areas of behavior examined are selected as those most logically related to language acquisition. A second approach, the *developmental checklist* approach, is not theoretical in that it assumes that if children with language delay have all the skills which are present in normally developing children at the onset of their language, the slowly developing children will be able to learn language. Those operating under this approach typically proceed to assess children by evaluating whether they can perform a predetermined set of tasks which are usually age graded and often, except for age equivalence, unrelated to one another. Examples of such checklists are contained in popular developmental tests, such as the Denver, Utah, Houston, or Bayley (see Chapter 10).

Our approach is, as you know, structural. We proceed by examining the individual child's behaviors, preferably in natural interactions, and then we analyze the data for patterns in order to develop a sense of how the behaviors are structurally related and how they may function for the child. The structural approach, like the correlational approach, is theoretical in that we do not examine all behaviors but select out those which seem from our inclinations most telling or salient for the child and/or those most logically related to the goals of the structural analysis. In the structural approach, our aim is to analyze the behavioral patterns which would seem to have a bearing on language acquisition, whether it be of a verbal or nonverbal language system.

We will begin by thinking about how to analyze structurally and understand various actions performed by preverbal children. Our goal for this structural analysis is to help the preverbal child progress to the use of a symbol system; so once we have discussed structural methodology, we will offer guidelines for how one might work from what the child knows, toward knowledge which would be functional in acquiring such a symbol system. We will be basing our analysis on four types of actions which the children may be displaying: *spontaneous actions, imitated actions, actions directed toward a goal,* and *make-believe actions.* We will be concerned with how to classify actions and then how to cast them into one or more of the four types. For example, "reaches" are a class of actions which are usually directed toward a goal and are unlikely to be pretend in nature.

The unit of action and type of action will be influenced by the presenting situation and its sequence in a series of actions. Thus, just as a language analysis entails looking at the context, an action analysis also involves pragmatics. The purpose here is to think about how bound to the context these preverbal children are, since language learning, by its very nature, involves decontextualized thinking.

Once we have classified the actions of interest and have assessed their degree of context boundedness, we can determine how these actions may be functioning for the child. Thus we not only do an action classification analysis and a context analysis, but also a functional analysis. Of course these analyses will influence one another. Indeed, Bates and MacWhinney (1979) would probably argue that we should start with a functional analysis, since they see the actions and the context boundedness as deriving from the child's intended functions. However, we have chosen to start with the more observable levels of analysis and move to the more mentalistic categories.

How does our analysis pertain to language? How do we go from our results to thinking about actions as precursors to language? We will offer here a theoretical and tentative approach to this issue. Borrowing heavily from cognitive theorists such as Piaget and Bates, we will try to devlop a way to draw a cognitive model that would represent the findings of the other analyses. The model will be one which will help us think about whether or not children are using symbolic thinking in their performance of actions and whether they have a sufficient degree of intentionality and interaction competance to be moved into using a symbol system.

In sum, we will proceed (1) by identifying the significant actions of preverbal children; (2) analyzing them for context embeddedness; (3) attributing functions to them; and (4) postulating a theoretical cognitive model which could account for such behaviors. We will begin with a discussion of the movement types.

TYPES OF ACTIONS

Spontaneous Actions

We find when we start analyzing actions that children are in constant motion and that a movement analysis of all their actions is formidable. A few must be selected from the many. The easiest movements to identify and there-fore the ones most studied are those that involve spontaneous *actions on objects* (Piaget, 1952; Uzgiris and Hunt, 1975).

Soon after normal babies are born, they begin to differentiate what they do with different objects (Piaget, 1952). Piaget calls this *recognitory assimilation* and views it as a differentiation of different sensorimotor action schemes. Uzgiris and Hunt (1975) describe the evolution of this differentiation in one of their developmental scales. The earliest actions are holding, mouthing, and visually inspecting the object. The developmental progression is to simple motor schemes such as hitting or banging with the object—an action which only by happenstance conforms to the cultural meaning of the particular object (e.g., hammering with a hammer). The children then develop to a stage where they examine the object by turning it and feeling its surface in various places. A stage of complex motor schemes follows where the actions are more diversified and relate to the sensory-perceptual nature of the objects, such as sliding slidable objects, tearing tearable objects, crumpling flexible objects. From there, accord-ing to Uzgiris and Hunt, the children pass through a "letting go" stage where they seem to be actively investigating an object's properties by repeatedly drop-ping or throwing it. Finally, at around two years of age for normal children, they perform culturally conventional actions on the object, such as drinking from a cup, putting on a necklace, smelling a flower.

Another yet later stage, that of combinational play, is reported by Bates

(1979) and Nicholich (1977). This involves several actions related to the same objects, as might be seen when children put in and take out a series of objects, or when they put rings on and off a peg.

An integral part of some of these sensorimotor spontaneous actions are children's vocalizations. These *action-vocalization packages* have been described as vocables by Ferguson (1978) and Carter (1975); as sensorimotor morphemes by Carter (1975); and as primitive consistent forms by Dore et al. (1976). They are characterized by a stable short vocalization unit which is temporally connected with a particular action, such as a point, push away, or reach and give. Most of them relate to objects. These noises emerge into stable symbolic entities which become less tied to the action (Carter, 1979) and indeed may become a request for it (Menn, 1976).

A second grouping of spontaneous movements which are readily identifiable are *social gestures*. These are different from the actions on objects in that the child's focus is on a social interaction. Bates et al. (1975) forwarded this distinction of social- and object-focused actions. They found, for example, that children under age ten months perform different actions on animate vs. inanimate objects. Children smile at, rub, and hug animate objects, while they bang, hit, and mouth the inanimate ones. Further, Bates and her colleagues found that social- and object-related actions may occur under different circumstances. They describe a child who typically stops playing with her toys and goes to her parent when a stranger approaches. The distinction of object-focused and socially focused activity is maintained, according to Bates's research, beyond this ten-month age when children perform either in their object-focus mode, using people to get objects, or in their social mode, using objects to get people's attention.

Unlike actions on objects, social actions may involve objects or they may not. Examples of object-related social gestures are giving and showing (or pointing to indicate); examples of non–object-related actions are engaging in showing off, raising arms to be picked up, and initiating interactive routines.

Bruner's research (1975, 1977) on how children engage in joint activity has emphasized the importance of social interaction in early language learning. Bruner sees as crucial to language acquisition those interactive sequences in which children and their caretakers both look at the same object and the adult names the object. He also sees interactive routines, such as patty-cake and peekaboo, as cognitive origins for turn taking in later verbal conversations. Bruner (1977) calls the labeling activities *joint referencing* and the games *joint activities*. Stages in both move from adult-initiated to child-initiated, from short sequences to longer events, and from sequences which involve close face to face proximity to those interactions which involve participants or objects which are further away.

Bates and her colleagues (1979) have dimensionalized aspects of children's development in areas of social actions and looked at how they are correlated. One dimension is conventional social actions, such as waving bye-bye, vs. unconventional ones, such as whining for a request; another is externally related actions (e.g., showing, giving) vs. self-focused ones (showing off). The researchers found that there was a correlation in acquisition of those actions which were social, conventional, and externally related and that the actions tended to be highly correlated to the emergence of language. Bates called the actions communicative, and her examples were giving, showing, communicative pointing, and ritual requests such as reaches.

Siebert (1979) has built on the research of Bruner and others and has distinguished several types of social actions:

1. Actions which initiate social interactions (joint activity)
2. Actions which initiate joint reference
3. Actions which are responsive to others' initiations of joint action
4. Actions which are responsive to others' initiations of joint reference.

Siebert and his colleagues are developing psychological scales for these social actions as Uzgiris and Hunt did for the object-related actions. Among the observation categories which they are using in their pilot work are the following, in order of acquisition:

1. Action comprehension
2. Initiation of social action
3. Use of agents to obtain objects
4. Use of agents to act on objects
5. Initiating joint reference
6. Responding to joint reference

Just as with actions which are object focused, social actions involving joint activity and joint referencing also can involve vocalization. Some of the early action-vocalization units noted by researchers are those which are woven tightly into these social activity sequences.

A third set of identifiable spontaneous movements are *repetitive movements,* or what have been called *self-stimulatory behaviors.* These are neither object nor socially focused but are self or internally focused in that they involve repeated actions that appear to have as their interest their sensorimotor effect. For example, one witnesses actions performed by babies such as thumb sucking, rocking, moving their hands or fingers in front of their eyes, or babbling. Typically, at these times, the children's eyes are not focused on a particular object, and an interactant will often call them as if they were somewhere else (Duchan, 1979). These movements are sometimes regarded as characteristic of abnormal populations, such as the retarded or autistic, but they occur in all populations (Duchan, 1979).

So far we have classified three types of spontaneous actions commonly reported in the literature: actions directed toward objects, actions directed toward people, and actions directed toward oneself. We have begun with these generalized categories of movement based on their directed focus. As we said earlier, we can also subclassify movement types within these generalized categories on the basis of the general contour of the movement. Carter (1979), for example, classified what she calls "ridding" actions displayed by her subject David on the basis of general similarity in movement (waving his hand or performing a rubbing or slapping gesture) and similarity in goal directedness (to get someone's help to remove an object).

In sum, we have reviewed the literature on spontaneous actions that focus on objects, social events, and self and have suggested that within each there are subtypes which can be identified by their movement contours and goal directedness. We will now move on to our discussion of imitated actions.

Imitated Actions

Imitation in language acquisition is considered to be of primary importance by behaviorists. Their notion is that children learn language by imitating it; language knowledge is seen as the storehouse or memory repertoire of responses learned through imitation. With the coming of transformational theory in linguistics came the effort to purge the notion that imitation contributed to language learning. The attempt by early transformationalists was to replace behaviorism with a strict nativism which claimed that language is learned because speakers are genetically endowed to learn it. Cognitive psychologists have since de-escalated this unequivocal nativist stance. They are again looking at nonlinguistic precursors to language acquisition and are again examining the role which imitation may play.

The first issue we must confront when thinking about imitation is a definitional one: How do we know an imitation when we see it? We will skirt the details of this problem temporarily and at this point define imitation as behavior exhibited spontaneously by the child which is modeled after and resembles behavior immediately preceding it. This, then, eliminates from our definition deferred imitations, which are events that follow the model minutes or more later, and it eliminates elicited imitation, wherein the child is trained or stimulated to produce particular behaviors upon request. What the definition includes are spontaneous imitations of movement and vocalization which could be imitations of one's self, someone else, and of objects. These spontaneous imitations will be our focus.

If we were to classify the imitations reported in the literature, we could come up with a list of what types of events or objects are imitated. The most typical distinction made among imitated behaviors in preverbal children is their division into modalities of movements and vocalizations (e.g., Piaget, 1952; Uzgiris and Hunt, 1975). Under movements, one finds descriptions of head and arm gestures, as well as facial expressions and postural shifts. These movements may be imitations of one's self or another person. Also under movements, we find occasional references to imitations of repeated or cyclical movements, such as rocking, waving, etc., where what is being imitated is the rhythm, beat, or tempo of the model; these rhythmic imitations may be of objects as well as of people (Werner and Kaplan, 1963). In these descriptions of imitation and movements, one can find references both to children imitating movements of objects (e.g., spinning like a top) and imitating movements which act on objects (e.g., pushing a toy car back and forth). Thus, we see in Piaget (1952) the well-cited reference of Lucienne opening and closing her mouth as an imitation of a matchbox opening and closing, and in Lezine's research (cited in Inhelder, 1976) we find children are reported to imitate conventional functions of objects such as moving trucks back and forth.

For imitated vocalizations, one finds citations of children's self-imitations and imitations of others. Piaget (1952) referred to the former as primary circular reactions and the latter as secondary circular reactions. Children's imitation of the noises made by objects, and their imitations of familiar and unfamilar sounds, are also distinguished in the literature.

From our example, it can be seen that children often imitate an aspect of an action rather than the entire action. For example, Werner and Kaplan (1963) describe a thirteen month old who rocked his head as a presumed imitation of his father's arm and hand movements. What the experimenters say is imitated in this case is the dynamic vectoral nature of the patterns. Another example was our observation of a one and one-half year old child standing above Niagara Falls and making a loud roaring noise, which we believe was possibly an imitation of the noise of the falls. These types of imitations are difficult to identify unless one knows the child. This raises the issue of methodology in determining which behaviors are imitative. It is likely that we are only studying imitations which we see to be topologically similar to the target and are missing the others that are similar but not full renditions of the model.

Finally, imitations have been looked at for their temporal contiguity with the target. Prizant and Ferraro (1979) found in their study of echolalia in autistic children that the time lag between target and imitation coincided with the function of the imitation. The longer lags represented the more cognitively advanced imitations—that is, the imitations that involved more psycholinguistic processing.

Now that we have described some different aspects of imitations as reported in the literature, we are ready to return to the definitional issue and develop a framework for defining imitations. In so doing, we raise only a few of the many problems which will ultimately need to be resolved when doing analyses on imitations; problems which are inherent in analysis of how particular children use imitations and which ones they use. First consider the following examples and accompanying questions:

1. Mother smiles, child smiles. Is the child's smile an imitation of the mother's?

2. Child draws a picture of a tree while looking at a real tree. Is the drawing an imitation of the tree?

3. Mother opens her own mouth as she feeds the baby. Is the mother imitating what she expects to happen?

4. Child moves hands in time with the beat of the music. Is the movement an imitation of the music?

5. Child responds by clapping hands when mother initiates patty-cake by clapping hands, but does not so respond when he observes the mother applauding. Is contextually bound duplication considered imitation?

6. Child says "bababa" in response to adult's "rarara."

Is this an imperfect copy or a new response? Is the last "ba" of the child an imitation of the first or second "ba"?

7. Child bangs on table.

Could a particular bang be considered an imitation of the one(s) before?

8. Child moves one car back and forth, then does the same with a truck.

Is the truck event an imitation of the car event, and is the car event an imitation of what the child saw real cars do?

9. Mother looks at an object; child turns head to look at the same object.

Is the child imitating the mother's positioning of her gaze?

10. The child poorly imitates a target, such as raising hand when imitating another's pointing.

How do we recognize imperfect imitations?

11. Child has a mental image of a familiar toy, i.e., a representation.

Is the image an imitation of the original?

12. Child draws a composite picture, abstracting the essential qualities from different situations.

Can an imitation be an abstraction or generalized version over several original events?

13. The child wipes her own face upon seeing the dog's wet face.

Is the child imitating the feeling of wetness?

14. The family is just served soup and they begin eating it; the child does the same.

Is the child imitating the others eating, or would he have done it without the immediate model?

15. Adult says "Hi"; child answers "Hi."

Is the answer an imitation?

16. Child tries to put an object upright, fails, then tries again.

Is the second attempt an imitation of the first?

17. Children tease one another by exaggerating the traits of the one being teased.

Is making fun by doing a caricature of someone the same as doing an imitation of them?

18. Child babbles.

Does this involve imitation?

19. Adult corrects child's productions by repeating the child's utterance— e.g., "Not wug, rug."

Is correction the same as imitation?

If our stand on what imitations entail is workable, it should help us decide which of the above events we are going to classify as imitations. Our definition should also be motivated by a consideration of what is psychologically real for the children rather than simply arbitrarily assigned for purposes of our own methodological convenience. Let us assume, then, that imitations are for the children separable psychological events in that they involve a particular mental state in the child which differs from others. Let us characterize this state as one in which the child is focused on a model and in which he or she deliberately duplicates that model, for whatever reason. Thus the mental state, if the child could verbalize it, is "I'm doing that again" or "I'll do that again with this variation." This implies, then, that the child would not be carrying out the act unless an original event occurred. It is in this sense we appropriate Piaget's notion of accommodation—that is to say, the child is oriented to an external model.

Let us also assume that the main focus of the imitation is on the form, content, or effect produced by the model rather than on the effect achieved by the imitation itself. This is another way of establishing the externally directed nature of the imitation. In other words, the child may be wondering "How did that work?" or "Isn't that interesting, let's run it through again" rather than "What would be the effect on the interaction or object or event if I do it?" or "I wonder how well or if I can do that."

While our formulation is theoretical, and the attitude of the imitator inaccessible, it does allow us to distinguish what we are calling imitations from events such as immediate perceptions, interactive routines, teasing by imitative exaggeration, or mutual looking in joint activities. Similarly, it allows us to postulate that imitations can serve different functions, and it allows for there to be different kinds of imitations, such as simple re-presentations and elaborate symbolic ones, with and without understanding. It also allows for the same behavior to be imitative in one instance and something else in another instance, offering us a way to separate similar surface structures from one another. Thus, babbling may in one instance be a function of the child's involvement in a particular constellation of sounds, rhythms, or intonation patterns of an outside model, which is then imitated to reproduce it for further examination. In a second instance, the babbling might be a game or a means for keeping the interaction going. It is the first instance that we would call imitation. The second is not focused on the model but on the interaction, since the child could just as well be saying or doing something less similar to the model and produce the same effect.

We would like to incorporate one further stipulation in our definition—that imitation occurs immediately after the model behavior. This excludes deferred imitations, which occur minutes or days after the original. Like Bates (1979), we feel deferred imitation is something qualitatively different from immediate imitation and suggest that deferred imitation be classified as self-initiated action with context boundedness. We will discuss this more in a later section on context boundedness.

Our definition, then, involves three components.

1. An attitude on the part of the child of deliberateness, as if saying "I'm doing that again."
2. A focus on the model—that is, a feeling the child has that "I'm interested in that" rather than in the effects of reproducing it.
3. A sense of "nowness," wherein what is being imitated has just occurred.

What about the development of imitated actions in normal children? Piaget (1962) studied this in detail and traced the development of his children through a reflexive stage, in which they imitated crying, to one of primary circular reactions, in which they imitated their own visible and familiar behaviors or sounds, to secondary circular reactions, in which they imitated visible and familiar actions on objects. From there the children progressed to a point where they were able to imitate invisible but still familiar actions, such as facial expressions, and finally to where they imitated unfamiliar and invisible actions.

Uzgiris and Hunt (1975) designed two scales to measure levels of imitations, one for vocal imitation and another for gestural imitation. Their scales are based on Piaget's sense that the children progress from imitating what they can already do to imitating novel actions and from imitating things they can see themselves do (visible imitation) to imitations involving actions invisible to them.

Moore and Meltzoff (1978) found a stage, much earlier than that reported in Piaget's work, in which twelve- to twenty-one day old infants were able to imitate tongue protrusions, mouth openings, and lip protrusions. They postulate a supramodal representation wherein the modality is irrelevant to the child, unlike the later and more advanced imitator who knowingly matches his face to the model. What they seem to be implying is that the infant's imitations are not specific to body parts and thus might not be recognized as imitations.

Actions Directed to a Goal

So far we have been discussing single actions, either self-initiated or imitated, and have only alluded to their sequential arrangement. Now we can begin to think about how to interpret sequences of actions and their relationship to one another. This is a different problem than if we were to study sequences of words because children's actions are occurring continually rather than in sequences that can be isolated, as one or more morphemes can. In the case of action sequences it becomes a problem as to what we will be calling units and sequences of units and further what the relationships are between these units in the various sequences.

We are likely, for example, to find children who display a sequence of actions such as a reach for an object, followed by a grasp once they get it, and then a lift to the mouth, where they proceed to suck on it and then fall asleep. Do we interpret this as a unit made up of actions and call it a plan to acquire an object for sucking? Do we see each action as a means to the next one and do we see each one as the achievement or end of the preceding one (i.e., reaching to grasp, grasping to lift, etc.)?

Let us begin our solution to this identification and segmentation problem by recalling that three kinds of actions were described when we talked about self-initiated movements and vocalizations: (1) actions directed to objects, (2) actions directed to people, and (3) actions directed to one's self. As we have said, any of these actions may be made intentionally or not. If they are, they can be thought of as a means the children use to achieve a goal or end. Further, we would suggest that the focus of the means is on the act, while the desired end may be an action on the part of the child (sucking), or an object (acquisition of a particular toy), or a situational event (getting the adult's attention).

Means can, of course, involve objects as instruments, as when Kohler's (1927) famous chimps used a stick to get an out-of-reach banana; but we see the cognitive focus of the act as being the means, not the stick. These early intentional actions have been seen as the beginnings of means-end knowledge.

What about our longer strings of actions and their means-end function? We suggest that these can be viewed on two levels—one of simple action pairs, the other as a string of actions to achieve an ultimate goal. Thus reaching would be a means to grasp an object, grasping a means to lifting it. These adjacency pairs of the child's actions relate to one another hierarchically in that they all function to get toward the ultimate goal, sucking the object. Note we are allowing ourselves to make the assumption that the ultimate goal of the sequence described earlier is not to fall asleep but rather to suck on the object.

Action sequences may or may not be serving one another in the means-end relations. Some action sequences may be unrelated or equally coordinated elements in a string. So, for example, the banging actions in a circular reaction do not pair up in means-end action pairs, nor do they lead hierarchically to an ultimate goal. Our contention, then, is that we can identify means-end sequences as those in which the first actions operate toward an end, as if the child were thinking "Do this or these in order to achieve this." We distinguish these sequences from other actions sequences. For example, they are different from

1. Unrelated activities, as in the sequence "Do this and then do this" (bang the headboard, throw a toy)
2. A cyclical action sequence, as in "Do this again and again" (several games of patty-cake), or
3. A single repetitive series, as in "I'm doing this" (banging).

Now let us look at various acts and try to identify means and ends distinctions within them. From there we will proceed to a set of criteria which we can use to designate behavioral evidences of means-end distinctions and then to some developmental literature.

MEANS-END IDENTIFICATION   Which of the following activities contain a means-end relationship, and what would it be?

1. Child pushes truck.
2. Child bumps one truck into another.
3. Child puts rubber band around a pencil.
4. Child throws a ball to the wall and catches it.
5. Child uses a stick to get a cookie.
6. Child crawls toward the mother.
7. Child spits out food when doesn't want any more.
8. Infant cries when uncomfortable.
9. Child follows moving object with eyes, then reaches for it.
10. Child nests objects.
11. Child throws a cup and breaks it, then looks at adult guiltily.
12. Piaget's match box example: L. opens her mouth when she can't open the box.
13. Child pulls a string on a toy whose main part is out of reach.

14. Child plays with object by making it perform different functions.
15. Child finishes book by turning the last page.

If we were to assign every action sequence a means-end relationship, we would find ourselves, for example, saying a push of a toy car is a means to have it move. This seems contrived and not what we want to include in a means-end distinction.

We are now ready to put forth some ways to distinguish actions which serve as means to goals or ends and to develop strategies for answering the questions posed in the preceding list.

EVIDENCE FOR MEANS-END DISTINCTION

1. There should be some evidence for a plan or some indication that the means action was preplanned (e.g., child looks to a goal). Evidence for goal behavior would be a sign of surprise or frustration if attempt is thwarted.
2. Means action should be different and separable from goal action. The resolution of the series of actions is not inherent in the means; but rather a new event, the end, is required before the steps in the activity are ended.
3. It would also be helpful in identifying means to end to observe the creation of new means toward the same end if earlier attempts do not succeed. This is repair work or detour behavior.
4. For imitations, or self-initiations to be defined as means, we need evidence that there is a productivity in the relationship and not just an imitated sequence of events experienced previously; that is, the child should show evidence of thinking "this achieves that."
5. Peaks and pauses in movement sequences can also give hints about separable action sequences, with the means action and end action receiving peak action focus.
6. It is helpful when the means and end occur close together in time.

What are some developmental trends for normal children's acquisition of means-end knowledge? As for imitations, children's performance on means-end tasks progresses from the ability to use their own familiar actions as a means (reaching, grasping) to a later ability to develop novel means using external objects to get things (using a stick to get an out-of-reach object) (Miller et al., 1980; Siebert, 1979; Uzgiris and Hunt, 1975). Further, children progress from being able to design means for obtaining or manipulating easily accessible and visible objects to a point where they can plan ahead and obtain invisible or inaccessible objects. Finally, Bates (1979) has found that the similarity and contiguity of the means object to the goal object makes a difference in a nine month old's ability to perform means-end tasks. It helped these infants when the means object was touching the goal (e.g., an attached string), and it hurt their performance if the tool used to get the goal was similar in texture or shape to the goal object (Bates, 1979).

Make-Believe Actions

The actions we have been discussing so far are either spontaneous or imitated or actions which serve as a means for directly achieving an intended goal. There is another type of action which has been seen as an important aspect of the behavior of nonverbal children—the type of action which children use in their "play." As with directly expressed actions, identification of play actions is no trivial or easy task. The most common attempt at a definition is separating play from work actions. This is obviously not a tenable distinction when applied to children, since one is hard put to describe anything children do as work. Some definitions circumvent this by separating pleasurable from serious activities, with the pleasurable activities being defined as "play." This allows us to identify a single action, say, banging a block, as play when it is accompanied by a pleasure mood, and as serious when done in a serious mood. Fein and Apfel (1979) argue against a definition using this criterion, since they feel play activities, such as games, can create frustration for a loser and thus have nonpleasurable aspects but still deserve the classification as play.

A second distinguishing feature commonly used to define play is its occurrence in speech events which do not have adult goals. That is to say, play time is not like meal time or bath time wherein adult agendas of having the child eat or be washed are the focus of the activity (Mayrink-Sabinson, 1980). Again, this definition is adult centered and not likely a psychologically real one for the child.

A third common sense of "play" is that it is what children do with toys. Thus we have studies which trace the development of children's play by watching what children of different ages do with blocks, miniature furniture, dolls, etc. (Lowe, 1975; Nicholich, 1977). This toy definition assumes that playing with toys requires different cognitive abilities from actions on nontoys. Further, the developmental studies assume that the progression from banging blocks to stacking them to building an imaginary bridge with them are qualitatively similar and evolve from one another. Even if this evolution were the case, we would find ourselves hard put to distinguish what we have described as simple or combination-of-action schemes from those which could be defined as play.

Our solution to these definitional problems is perhaps a cheating one—we try to avoid the general category of play. Instead, we confine our attention to the idea of symbolic play, specifically make-believe. We feel justified in that we are particularly concerned with the symbolic nature of play, which is inherent in the definition of make-believe but not necessarily involved in all kinds of play.

Let us concretize now our definition of make-believe by calling forth some examples which we would like you to classify as either involving or not involving make-believe pretense:

Blowing bubbles
Sticking out tongue, as if licking
Sucking in anticipation of eating
Making faces

Contagion laughter
Saying "zoom" while pushing a toy truck around
Feigning crying
Role playing
Pretending not to hear when called
Thinking about pretending
Pretending to be sisters when really sisters
Playing games
Pouring from an empty pitcher
Sucking on a pacifier

If you experienced what we did as you selected symbolic play episodes from the examples, your response in many cases was "It depends." For us it seemed to depend on (1) what we regarded as the child's learning history with the action; (2) whether it felt as if the child expressed the action directly toward a goal or used it in a nondirect way; or (3) whether the child seemed to be amused by the action or actions. We will elaborate on each of these in order to better lay out the criteria and nature of what we will be calling "make-believe."

One reason that you cannot tell whether an action is make-believe or not is that it seems to depend upon the child's history with the action. For example, a cognitively naive child who tries to drink from an empty glass may be doing so in order to quench his or her thirst, while a more advanced child performing the act may know full well that the result of the act will not be to get water. Only in the second case can we call the act one of make-believe. Similarly, when we watch these two children play with a car and see them make engine noises as they move it back and forth, we are unfortunately likely to assume they are both playing. However, in the case of the naive child, he or she may be imitating what someone else was seen to do earlier, while the advanced child may be thinking of how this act compares to what real cars do. Thus, one must know something about the child's history in order to define an act as pretend.

Another example of this problem of distinguishing delayed imitation from play is evaluating children's reenactments. We know from our own intuitions and from the literature on child development that reenactments of familiar scenes are cognitively easier than novel fantasies. A child creating a new version of the story of the three bears uses competencies beyond those she would use to enact the rehearsed rendition. Once again the learning history, that is, the child's previous familiarity with the original version, is needed to define the degree of departure from the original learning.

A second reason there are problems in defining "play" is that the term implies that actions or objects function differently in the play sequence than they ordinarily do. This displacement of the action or object from its ordinary goal or use allows us to call it play when animals pretend to fight, when children pretend to cry, or when adults tease one another. While the actions or objects ordinarily have as their focus a goal or direct experience, in play the focus is on the subjective experience. This contrast is further verified when we observe that the one doing the playing marks it with an exaggeration or abbreviation of some of

the movements. So the pretend sequence has sometimes a quality of a caricature or a feel of lack of consummation when compared with the real event (e.g.,
pretend crying that is much louder and more dramatic than a real expression of
unhappiness).

The problem of using displacement as a criterion for identifying play is
that the subjectivity is attributed to the pretender by the observer, and unless the
child indicates it in some way, one is left with the dilemma of making a rich
interpretation and ascribing a play mode when indeed the intent may be a direct
or nondisplaced one.

Finally, there often is a sense of amusement accompanying the play
which identifies it as a nonserious activity. While it is helpful to use laughter as an
identifier, it is not a sufficient criterion in itself, since play can occur without
laughter and laughter can occur in nonplay situations.

Let us summarize now by restating three features which can, but need
not, act as identifier of pretend play sequences.

1. A background history which distinguishes the sequence as nonimitative
    and creative
2. A quality of distortion which indicates that the child is not viewing the
    sequence as directed toward its usual goal or experience
3. A sense of amusement which marks the pretend sequence as nonserious
    fooling around

What are the various types of pretend play that would fit these general
criteria, and what kinds of play are excluded by our definition? The excluded
activities would be simple reenacts or imitations of earlier experiences.
These are simple recollections without distortion and would thus be better
classified as delayed imitation. Also excluded would be (1) simple exploration of
miniature toys unless there is evidence of contrast with real events, (2) play-
ground play that is not pretend, and (3) ritualized games which do not involve
pretend play. Included are (1) symbolic reenactments, (2) actions in which one
object is substituted for another ordinarily used object, (3) feigned actions which
are removed from customary goals, and (4) role playing.

STAGES OF MAKE-BELIEVE   The complexity of make-believe activity is
matched by the complexity of the studies of stages in normal children's development of this ability to pretend. The literature suggests that children do not
just progress from a point where they cannot pretend to one where they can;
rather, children display various stages in their development which depend upon
the objects they are pretending with, the agents or recipients of their pretense, the
complexity of the actions involved, the length of the pretend episodes, and the
particular kind of tasks they are pretending in.

Pretend objects are those which are substituted for real objects. They are
important to development in that children progress from pretending with objects similar in form and function to real objects (a toy phone for a real phone,
for example), to pretending with dissimilar objects (a block for a phone), and
finally to a stage of pretending with imaginary substitutes (Jakowitz and Watson,

1980). It is also the case that children's familiarity with and attitude toward real and substituted objects are important. Pretending with toy cups (Lowe, 1975) and pretending to feed with spoons occur at a different age than pretending to feed with bottles (Fein and Apfel, 1979). Furthermore, the number of substituted objects involved in the pretense makes a difference, with more substituted objects being used in later pretense (Lowe, 1975).

In early pretense, children themselves are the agents carrying out the episode, and only later can they imagine dolls or others as the agents in the pretend sequence (Fein and Apfel, 1979; Lowe, 1975; Piaget, 1962). Young children are also better able to place themselves in the position of recipient in a pretend sequence, such as one of feeding the baby, than projecting others into that role.

Early pretend sequences are made up of brief single-action units which progress to multiple-action and longer episodes (Fein and Apfel, 1979). The advanced sequences involve more planning and are self-initiated, unlike the more spontaneous and context-bound beginning pretenses of younger children (Fein and Apfel, 1979; Fenson and Ramsey, 1980; Golomb, 1979; Nicholich, 1977; Piaget, 1962).

Finally, and following logically from the research listed so far, the particular kind of pretend task which the child can engage in varies with age and developmental stage. The easier tasks are with object substitution under conditions of imitation; the more difficult are fantasy interactions, such as puppet shows, involving long decontextualized and interaction sequences (see Golomb [1979] and Duchan and Meyer [1977] for studies of task influences).

ACTIONS AND THEIR CONTEXTS

Decontextualization has been used to describe and explain children's progression from a primitive, infantlike state where they interpret things only in terms of the currently perceived context to an adultlike state where they think about things outside of the presenting contexts. Stages in their progression toward decontextualization have been discovered by Piaget and his followers for each of the action types we have been discussing. For example, according to Piaget, knowledge of spontaneous actions progresses from actions on objects which are present to actions on objects which are imagined; imitations progress from immediate imitations to those which are deferred in time; goal directed actions progress from using familiar means to obtain obvious and immediately occurring ends to using novel means to achieve temporally distant ends; and pretending progresses from substituting present and perceptually similar objects for one another to imagining objects or making perceptually dissimilar object substitutions (Piaget, 1952, 1954, 1962).

We would like to explore these progressions toward decontextualization in terms of some of the contexts which we delineated in the pragmatics chapter— i.e., in terms of the immediate situation, the children's intent, their sense of their interactant, and their background knowledge.

As we proceed through our discussion, we ask that you be wary of the rich interpretation problem which has perhaps been even more influential in interpreting cognitive precursors than in the other areas we have been discussing; that is, adult observers have generally assumed that their sense of context is the true reality and have evaluated children's behaviors in terms of that, neglecting to ask the necessary question, What is the child's sense of context? With this in mind, we will turn to an outline and review the four different types of contexts that are relevant here.

Immediate Situational Context

When we say children are context bound to the immediate situation, we mean they have regard only for the current spatial and temporal situation. Decontextualized actions would involve regard for nonpresent objects, people, or actions or a view toward the ongoing situation which considers the communicative event or theme, and not each perceptual experience as it occurs.

Intentional Context

The intentional context highlights the relationship between the action and its goal. This distinguishes actions which are goal oriented from those which are not—that is, it focuses on actions which point toward a hoped-for result, as in a means-end relationship, rather than those that are automatic, non–goal-directed reactions. Actions are bound to intentional context if they lead directly to a goal and if their relationship to the goal is temporally short and cognitively obvious. Actions with decontextualized intents are also goal oriented but might involve much more planning, or more steps to obtaining that goal, or more time between the intent and its consummation.

Other Person Context

The dichotomy of context bound vs. decontextualized thinking in relation to another person is described as egocentric on the one end and decentered on the other. Egocentric children fail to appreciate the physical perspective of the other person in interpreting the context and others' actions. Decentered children, on the other hand, are empathic and considerate of the other person's perspective.

Background Knowledge

Finally, we can find evidence for a fourth domain contained in the theoretical notion of context bound—that of the child's background knowledge. Context-bound actions are children's reenactments of typical actions performed on familiar objects. In other words, they are action schemes that are part of children's background knowledge about particular objects. The progression is from this literal recollection to a stage where objects and functions can be disassociated or creatively determined. Children can then progress from typical culturally defined activities, such as sweeping with a broom, to those which are innovative, such as using the broom handle for a flag pole. This type of progression has been explained by Piaget as one where action schemes become more mobile.

We have briefly described four domains of context boundedness: (1) being bound to the immediate situation, (2) being bound to obvious goals, (3) being bound to one's own perspective, and (4) being bound by background knowledge of typical conditions. These have all been seen to stem from a child's conceptual limitations. Children can free themselves from contextually bound thinking only when they can do such things as re-present past experiences to themselves, or translate particular experiences or images into abstract concepts, or conceptually operate with given knowledge to produce new ways of thinking about things.

We can summarize our view of context boundedness by imagining how the most cognitively naive children experience context. These children make no distinction between action and object, between self and others, between now and then, between present and absent. Their sense of context is highly limited and they are bound by these limitations. When we say these children are maximally contextually bound, we are not saying that they see the context as we do and are more bound by it than we are; rather, we are saying they are limited by their conceptual naiveté from multiple-context perspectives or decontextualization. They would conceive only of presently occurring events, and they act only with their limited set of action schemes and without intention. As children mature, their sense of contexts changes. Our job is to explore this by explaining how they operate in terms of various contexts. Through our contextual analysis, we try to determine what their context is and how bound they are to it.

ACTIONS AND THEIR FUNCTIONS

If we were committed to confining our structural analysis to a level of structural categories whose existence we could demonstrate by looking at behaviors, we would not be including such intangible categories as functions. However, as we argued in the pragmatics chapter (Chapter 3), a treatment of intentionality is critical in the conceptualization of a child's language and so too for his or her prelinguistic movement and vocalization.

Our approach to a functional analysis of actions entails answering two questions: Why did the child perform the action? and What was the effect of the action? The first question gets at the child's intention, the second at the function of the action.

Explanations for why children perform actions can be answered in as many ways as one's imagination allows. Some possibilities for why children grasp a toy, for example, are (1) to get it. (2) to put it in their mouth, (3) to show off, (4) to practice grasping, (5) to avoid doing what they do not want to do, (6) to utilize their opposing fingers and thumbs, and (7) to perform the reflexive grasping scheme they are born with. Certainly all may be true; so how do we decide which ones are applicable?

We would like to eliminate from this analysis the biological and developmental explanations—that is, those explanations which appeal to stages in learning, or genetically determined origins, which are not seen as answering the question in a useful way. Examples of this kind would be numbers 4, 6, and 7 in the preceding list.

Further, we would like to eliminate from our sense of intentionality causal factors which are abstract psychological mechanisms, such as attention, interest, and motivation. Some examples appealing to such mechanisms are to practice, to have fun, to learn, and to explore.

Before we specifically lay out our sense of what an analysis of intentionality would include, let us take another direction and talk about actions which would not be analyzed for intentionality. These are individual actions which are parts of larger units of intentionality, such as the sequences involved in means toward an end (e.g., reach then grasp then lift then suck). Each step would not be analyzed outside of the broader context. Then there are actions which are not what the child is focused on, such as moving one hand while kicking a ball. These do not emerge from an intent except in an incidental way. There are also those actions which are directly tied to emotional states, such as cries, which are not performed to get the caretaker's attention but rather as expressions of say, discomfort. And there are those acts which are responses to others' imitations, such as smiles in response to being talked to, which we do not assume emerge from intentional states.

The acts we want to call intentional are those which are (1) purposeful, (2) initiated by the child for an apparent reason, (3) discrete from others, and (4) those which involve the single-directed cognitive emphasis that can be witnessed in coordinated actions such as body orientation, gaze, hand movement, and vocalization. These intentional acts include means-end relations—but include more than that in that they need not be tied to a plan or indicate evidence of being a step toward a goal.

The second part of our functional analysis involves an examination of how the actions affect the situational context. Actions which serve to take a turn or to shift a topic, for example, are considered as having interactive functions not necessarily intended by the child.

COGNITIVE MODELS OF ACTIONS

In order to make comparisons across the different actions we are observing, we, like Piaget and Bates, feel a need for developing an abstract model or sense of underlying structure which could be producing such behaviors. We will develop our thinking by using Piaget and Bates as touchstones. We will first explore their theoretical frameworks in order to understand what kinds of cognition we might be assessing, and then we will look to their research as well as other's research to see what we might take as behavioral evidence for these knowledges. This, then, will lead us to our focus for structurally analyzing the behaviors of preverbal children.

Piaget sees the child in the first two years of life as constructing a variety of knowledges from interactions with the world. The knowledges are different in kind in that they are operating on different cognitive domains, but they are similar in that they all lead in the direction of representational thinking. In his studies of the sensorimotor stage of development, Piaget examined in detail the way babies from birth to two years come to understand objects, to play, to imitate, and to understand causality (Piaget, 1952, 1954, 1962). He studied these domains, among others, by watching children in naturalistic contexts and sometimes by structuring the contexts to elicit more examples of the behaviors he was interested in studying. Piaget then performed a structural analysis using his observational notes as data and in so doing discovered patterns in the acquisition of each area of sensorimotor performance. From these patterns, as well as from his theoretical notions of how the mind works, Piaget built his constructivist theory of representational thought.

One form of re-presentational thinking is what Piaget describes as children's ability to re-present something to themselves by thinking about it. This term is hyphenated, since it means "present again." Piaget reports that children learn during the sensorimotor period (0 to 2 years) to re-present an event or object to themselves by performing a mental operation. According to Piaget, this re-presentation operation derives from children's ability to internalize a particular referent—that is, an object is seen at time 1 and the thinker internalizes or stores a mental image of it which can then be mentally re-presented at time 2. We have drawn a model of this in Figure 9.1. The figure shows a differentiation between what is presented in external reality (above the horizontal straight line) and the children's perception of that reality (below the line). Of course the children's perception will be influenced by their past experiences with the elements in the presented reality. These background knowledges which are influential in immediate perception are depicted below the horizontal wavy line. The new elements in the situation are "stored" or added to background knowledge to be re-presented at time 2 in the form of a mental image.

Re-presentational thinking revolves around the relationship between the internalized experience and the experience of the original external or real-world event. In re-presentational thinking the internal event has as its base those sensorimotor schemes involved in the original event. Later that mental construct can become more abstract, that is, generalized and dissociated from the particular instances, forming more abstract concepts or operations. Furth (1969) elaborates:

> Piaget refers to interiorization aptly as an increasing dissociation of general form from particular content. The sensory-motor scheme of weight

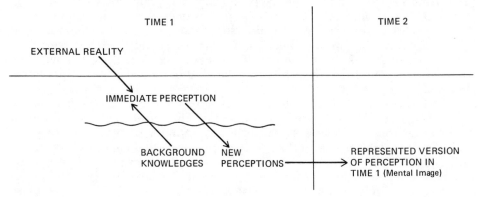

Figure 9.1

in the very young child requires the feeling and sensing of heaviness of objects.... Later interiorization dissociates the concept from the experiential content. (Furth, 1969, p. 60)

The particular and earlier developing version of imagery we will call *re-presentation,* and the second, the conceptual and abstracted sense of the object, will be a necessary component to what we will be calling *symbolization.*

Bates (1979) characterizes symbolization as an act that involves two mental constructs—the internal referent and the internal symbol, say, a word or abbreviated image. The internal symbol stands for the internal referent. Others have described this symbol-meaning relationship in different terms. For example, Piaget describes it as a distinction or separation between what he refers to as signifier (the symbol) and the signified (the concept). In some depictions, such as Piaget's and Bates's, it involves two mental constructs, with the symbol standing for or representing the other, its concept, meaning, or internal referent. In other depictions the symbol is described in relation to an external referent in the same way as re-presentation has been depicted in Piaget, thus making re-presentation and symbolization indistinguishable.

In Figure 9.2 we have drawn this relation between internal symbol and internal concept. We see this kind of symbolization differing from re-presentation thinking in Figure 9.1 in several ways. First, there may no longer be clear ties to a particular original learning experience, or even to the presenting reality—that is to say, the mental constructs need not have sensorimotor ties to particular experiences but can be abstractions from these experiences.

Secondly in the case of symbolic thinking there is a relationship between the two mental constructs. The relationship can take various forms—it can be *indexical,* wherein the symbol is physically associated with the concept, as in smoke symbolizing fire; *iconic,* wherein the symbol has some sensorimotor features in common with the concept, as in a picture which symbolizes a three dimensional

EXTERNAL REALITY

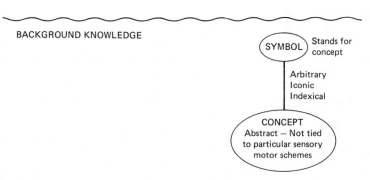

Figure 9.2

object; or *arbitrary,* wherein the symbol is simply assigned to the concept, as when words are assigned meanings by the speakers of a language. We will elaborate on these when we get to particulars of assessment.

We need to address one final issue in our model of symbolization and that is the issue of cognitive complexity. So far we have treated the symbol-concept relationship as one between a symbol and a single concept. However, this is inadequate when we try to model the concepts involved in pretending or in thinking about complex events, such as strings of actions, whole situations, or stories. Thus we must extend our idea of a concept to include categories such as themes or situations or interaction events. We have called this process of constructing complex units *thematization* (Duchan and Palermo, 1979) and will model symbolization of such themes in the form of Figure 9.3.

So far, then, we have learned from Piaget and Bates that there are two kinds of representational thinking—one is re-presentation of an absent external event and the second is symbolic in that the symbol is associated with a more abstract concept. The symbol (an index, icon, or arbitrarily constructed item) acts to recognize, identify, recall, label, or stand for the concept. Both kinds of thinking emerge only at the later stages of the sensorimotor period. We have added to Bates and Piaget a third kind of thinking, that of thematizing, or symbolizing themes.

Let us back up now and ask what Bates and Piaget see as the precursors or building blocks to those two achievements, re-presentation and symbolization. Bates adopts a "specific abilities" model which says that certain precursors are important for certain subparts of the development of thinking, while Piaget sees the same precursors affecting all domains of knowledge. For example, Bates found from her correlational studies that children's development of means-end, or what she calls social, instrumentality is highly related to their acquisition of early communicative acts, and she believes the acquisition of object concepts are related only to object naming.

How, then, have we decided what to emphasize in our assessment of the preverbal child? First, we have taken those areas of behavior which both Bates and Piaget say are strongly related to language acquisition—initiated actions, imitated actions, actions directed to a goal, and pretend play. We have presented them as separable but also see them as different facets of one another—that is,

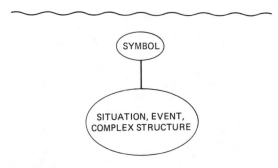

Figure 9.3

actions may be self-initiated or imitated and may also be used for achieving goals (means-end relations) or creative exploration (play).

We will now summarize by looking at some specific behaviors and trying to formulate a cognitive modeling procedure for them in Piaget's tradition.

As we have said, re-presentational actions are those wherein children present to themselves in the absence of contextual hints—that is, the reaching, giving, and pointing to objects would not be evidence for re-presentational thinking, since the actions would be triggered by the objects present in the immediate social situation. Evidence for re-presentational activity would be found in anticipatory situations where the child performs an action without the support of the event which the action was previously associated with (e.g., going into another room to get something from a drawer).

Symbolic actions would be indicated in those situations where the action has some symbolic meaning outside its performative or intentional force. This would be the case if the child were mimicking, signing, or pretending, since such acts must be accompanied by a subjective meaning or concept in order to be sensible. As we have said, the relationship between the manifest symbol and its concept can vary. It can be iconic, where the action resembles its concept, as when a child's stirring activity has as its significance the stirring act involved in baking a cake; it may be indexical when the action resembles part of its concept, as when the child raises his or her arms to be picked up; and it can be arbitrary when the action fails to resemble what it means, as in the conventional actions involved in sign language. Assigning an action to one of the three kinds of symbols is particularly difficult, since the assignment will necessarily depend upon the child's history with the action. That is to say, actions which appear to us to be arbitrarily related to their meaning may have an iconic or indexical history for the child.

Another kind of symbolic thinking, that involving thematization, would be indicated when children clap their hands to request a patty-cake sequence or a whole temporally sequenced set of events. Indications are that the entire routine has been conceptualized by the child, and the hand clap initiates it and serves as an indexical sign for the routine.

ASSESSMENT FOR COGNITIVE PRECURSORS

Where have we been in our discussion of cognitive precursors to language, and how can we apply what we have said to developing an assessment procedure? We have discussed four categories of action: spontaneous, imitated, goal oriented, and make-believe. We have implied that we can classify actions into one of the four types and, once classified, can evaluate their characteristics in terms of context boundedness, intentionality, and cognitive trend. Further, we imply that if we can determine that the actions reflect re-presentational or symbolic thought, we can conclude that the child can then be taught a symbol system.

Our approach is a departure from the developmental framework, wherein children are presented with tasks and their responses are evaluated for their place in a set of stages gathered from normal children's performance on the same tasks. Rather, we want to be able to develop a sense of how the child is performing and to use those behaviors to build a model from which we can work to teach that child to communicate symbolically and effectively. Thus we would engage a child in some naturalistic situations, videotape his or her performance, and then study the video for recurring patterns, extracting from them what we take to be the child's cognitive and communicative competencies.

Step 1 in our assessment procedure, then, is to do a videotape of the child engaged in a familiar activity or interaction.

Secondly, we would peruse the video to determine what would be worthwhile to study in detail. If the child is limited in the use of action schemes, we might look at what variety there is, listing types and what they are directed to. If the child seems inattentive to the activity defined by the adult, we might examine what the substituted object of attention is and the quality of the inattention. If the child is perseverative in action, we could do an analysis of the nature or quality of the perseverations. We could also select those behaviors that might indicate symbolization, such as pretending or consistent use of vocables, and study them in more detail. The general approach at this level of perusal is to pick a set of behaviors that occur frequently and which can be used to build upon or to modify, thereby helping the child progress.

Step 2, then, is to select a set of behaviors to study by examining the video and making notes about what might be pertinent to analyze.

Thirdly, a transcription or depiction of the videotape data needs to be done so that an analysis can be performed. This transcript will vary with what is being studied and will change as you begin to narrow what is relevant and omit what seems extraneous to your analysis. If you begin with a general depiction of what is going on, you might figure out a way to classify spontaneous actions, imitations, actions used as means, and those in the service of make-believe. Just classifying them into one of the four types may not be as crucial as determining how context bound they are or how they function for the child. Any actions, whether spontaneous, imitative, goal oriented, or pretend, are important insofar as they reflect the child's ability to think in a decontextualized or symbolic mode or to communicate an intention. The transcript, while it should include evidence for the type of action, should do so in such a way that the contextual base of the action is clear. This could require a description of (1) an action sequence carried out by the child or the interactant, (2) the involvement of objects in the execution of the sequence, (3) the match of the action to its model if the action is imitated, (4) the sense of how the action fits the event, (5) any breakdown or repair in accomplishing the act or its intent, and so on.

Step 3, then, is to design a transcript of the actions of initial interest and in so doing to decide what to include that is relevant to the interactants and to the analysis.

We now have delimited a data base, a transcript which we can analyze; and indeed, we designed it with a sense of what we want to analyze. The analysis would involve examining the transcripts, along with viewing the tapes. If the goal is to determine a child's readiness for a symbol system, we would look for evidence of the child's ability to decontextualize and to construct intentions. Each issue would be treated somewhat differently, so we will discuss each separately.

The analysis for the degree of context boundedness would involve looking at the tapes and transcripts for actions or action sequences which are decontextualized. A list of these actions could comprise the analysis, along with a description of how the action appears decontextualized—that is, references should be made to which context is involved, what the suspected background knowledge is, and the reason for your sense of decontextualization.

Step 4 is to do an analysis of the actions which could lead to a determination of the degree to which the child is context bound.

Analysis of means-end intentionality might have been part of the context boundedness study. Such an analysis can also serve the study of a child's intentionality, since construction of means to achieve an end is evidence of intentional behavior. Studying intentionality involves examining the tapes for actions initiated by the child which are directed to objects or people that involve the child's cognitive energies. Clues to such sequences would be reaches, shows, points, and the like.

A multilevel transcript of suspected intentional acts allows you to determine their quality and variability and to understand what gives them their intentional character. The transcript would logically include the effect of the act, therefore encompassing not only the intent of the act but its function. This could lead to a sense of appropriateness and effectiveness of the child's acts, giving you an idea of how to improve your responsiveness, or others' responsiveness, to the child's intentions.

Step 5 is an analysis of the child's intentionality by designing multilevel transcripts to illustrate the single directedness, the structure, and the success or failure of the intentional acts.

A final area has to do with building a cognitive model to account for the structural or functional categories which you found in the analysis. This endeavor is theoretical and requires a spirit of adventure, as we have been saying all along. The basic question is how the categories found in the preceding analyses articulate with the world—that is, in order to think in those ways, does the child need to engage in re-presentational thinking, or better yet in symbolic thinking or thematization.

This is an extension of the decontextualization analysis as well as the functional analysis in that it asks whether the degree of decontextualization discovered requires symbolic thinking. The analysis can begin with the results of step 4. Assume that when the action is decontextualized, it involves symbolization. Also when the intent is constructed different from the goal and not present in the context or emerging from well-rehearsed experience, it *too* is symbolic.

A more detailed aspect would be to match the assumed symbol to its referent and decide whether the relationship is iconic, indexical, or arbitrary. Arbitrary symbols are of course clearly symbolic; the others may or may not be depending upon whether they are conjured up in contexts where their referents are not there to give contextual support.

Step 6, then, is to create a model for the decontextualization and intentional acts found in steps 4 and 5, with the goal of determining whether or not they involve symbolic thought.

EXERCISES

1. The following are criteria for judging whether or not an action is an imitation. Using the examples listed on pp. 161-62, determine whether or not they qualify as an imitation in light of the three criteria. Add or change the criteria to better fit your sense of imitation.

      a) "I'm doing that again" attitude
      b) Focus on the model
      c) Sense of "nowness"

2.   Below is a list of tasks which have been used to evaluate children's stages in the development of means-ends comprehension. Organize the tasks moving from easy (early developing) to difficult (late developing). Proceed in your organization from the context bound, simple actions, to decontextualized, complex actions. Write a paragraph justifying your choices.
      a) Pulls a support to get the object on it
      b) Uses a stool to get to the sink to get a drink
      c) Pushes away your hand which interferes with an attempt to get a toy behind it
      d) Lets go of one object when handed another

3.   Intents are different from functions. Describe two events in which the intent is different from the function, and two in which the intent and the function are the same.

4.   Postulate a cognitive model to represent the following sequences:
      a) Child moves a block back and forth in the same way she does her toy car
      b) Child claps his hands to request patty-cake
      c) Child puts on her coat when she sees the bus pull up in front of the school

5.   Are the relationships between the following indexical, iconic, or arbitrary?
      a) A clap to request music
      b) A meow to indicate cat
      c) Saying buh for bubbles

REFERENCES

BATES, E. *The Emergence of Symbols.* New York: Academic Press, 1979.

BATES, E., L. CAMAIONI, AND V. VOLTERRA. The Acquisition of Performatives Prior to Speech, *Merrill Palmer Quarterly,* 21, 1975, 205–26.

BATES, E., AND B. MACWHINNEY. A Functionalist Approach to the Acquisition of Grammar, in *Developmental Pragmatics,* eds. E. Ochs and B. Schieffelin. New York: Academic Press, 1979.

BRUNER, J. The Ontogenesis of Speech Acts, *Journal of Child Language,* 2, 1975, 1–19.

BRUNER, J. Early Social Interaction and Language Acquisition, in *Studies in Mother-Infant Social Interactions,* ed. H. R. Schaffer. New York: Academic Press, 1977.

CARTER, A. The Transformation of Sensorimotor Morphemes into Words: A Case of "More" and "Mine," *Journal of Child Language,* 2, 1975, 233–50.

CARTER, A. Prespeech Meaning Relations: An Outline of One Infant's Sensorimotor Morpheme Development, in *Language Acquisition,* eds. P. Fletcher and M. Garman. London: Cambridge University Press, 1979.

DORE, J., M. FRANKLIN, R. MILLER, AND A. RAMER. Transitional Phenomena in Early Language Acquisition, *Journal of Child Language,* 3, 1976, 13–28.

DUCHAN, J. Temporal Aspects of "Self-Stimulating" Behaviors in Abnormal Speakers, Paper presented at Interactions Rhythms Conference, Columbia University, 1979.

DUCHAN, J., AND L. MEYER. An Analysis of Pretend Play in Four Children. Paper presented at New York State Speech and Hearing Association, Monticello, New York, 1977.

DUCHAN, J., AND J. PALERMO. Thematization: A New Look at Autism. Unpublished ms, 1979.

FEIN, G., AND N. APFEL. Some Preliminary Observations on Knowing and Pretending, in *Symbolic Functioning in Childhood,* eds. N. Smith and M. Franklin. Hillsdale, N.J.: Lawrence Erlbaum Associates, 1979, pp. 87–100.

FENSON, L., AND D. RAMSEY. Decentration and Integration at the Child's Play in the Second Year, *Child Development,* 51, 1980, 171–78.

FERGUSON, C. Learning to Pronounce: The Earliest Stages of Phonological Development in the Child, in *Communicative and Cognitive Abilities—Early Behavioral Assessment,* eds. F. Minifie and L. Lloyd. Baltimore, Md.: University Park Press, 1978.

FURTH, H. *Piaget and Knowledge.* Englewood Cliffs, N.J.: Prentice-Hall, 1969.

GOLOMB, C. Pretense Play: A Cognitive Perspective, in *Symbolic Functioning in Childhood,* eds. N. Smith and M. Franklin. Hillsdale, N.J.: Lawrence Erlbaum Associates, 1979, pp. 101–16.

HARDING, C., AND R. GOLINKOFF. The Origins of Intentional Vocalizations in Prelinguistic Infants. Paper presented at the Biennial Meeting of the Society for Research in Child Development, New Orleans, April 1977.

INHELDER, B. The Sensorimotor Origins of Knowledge, in *Piaget and His School,* eds. B. Inhelder and H. Chipman. New York: Springer-Verlag, 1976, pp. 150–65.

JAKOWITZ, E., AND M. WATSON. Development of Object Transformations in Early Pretend Play, *Developmental Psychology,* 16, 1980, 543–49.

KÖHLER, W. *The Mentality of Apes.* New York: Harcourt Brace, 1927.

LOWE, M. Trends in the Development of Representational Play in Infants from One to Three Years—An Observational Study, *Journal of Child Psychology and Psychiatry,* 16, 1975, 33–47.

MAYRINK-SABINSON, L. Study of Mother-Child Interaction with Language Learning Children: Context and Maternal Interpretation. Unpublished dissertation, State University of New York at Buffalo, 1980.

MENN, L. Pattern, Control and Contrast in Beginning Speech: A Case Study in the Development of Word Form and Word Function. Ph.D. thesis, University of Illinois at Urbana-Champaign, 1976.

MILLER, J., R. CHAPMAN, M. BRANSTON, AND J. RICHELE. Language Comprehension in Sensorimotor Stages V and VI, *Journal of Speech and Hearing Research,* 23, 1980, 284–311.

MOORE, K., D. CLARK, M. MAEL, G. DAWSON-MEYERS, P. RAJOTLE AND C. STOEL-GAMMON. The Relationship between Language and Object Permanence Development: A Study of Down's Syndrome Infants and Children. Paper presented to the Society for Research in Child Development, New Orleans, April 1977.

MOORE, K., AND A. MELTZOFF. Object Permanence, Imitation and Language Development in Infants: Toward a Neo-Piagetian Perspective on Communicative and Cognitive Development, in *Communicative and Cognitive Abilities–Early Behavioral Assessment,* eds. F. Minifie and L. Lloyd. Baltimore, Md.: University Park Press, 1978, 151–84.

NICHOLICH, L. Beyond Sensorimotor Intelligence: Assessment of Symbolic Maturity through Analysis of Pretend Play, *Merrill Palmer Quarterly,* 23, 1977, 89–99.

PIAGET, J.   *The Origins of Intelligence in Children.* New York: International Universities Press, 1952.

PIAGET, J.   *The Construction of Reality in Childhood.* New York: Ballantine, 1954.

PIAGET, J.   *Play, Dreams and Imitations in Childhood.* New York: W. W. Norton, 1962.

PRIZANT, B., AND B. FERRARO.   Automaticity in Echolalic Behavior as Measured by Response Latencies. Paper presented at Conference on Communicative Behavior, State University of New York at Buffalo, 1979.

SIEBERT, J.   A Model for Analyzing the Development of Early Communication Skills, Based on Levels of Cognitive Organization. Paper presented at Boston University Conference on Child Language Development, Boston, November 1979.

UZGIRIS, I., AND J. HUNT.   *Assessment in Infancy.* Urbana, Ill.: University of Illinois Press, 1975.

WERNER, H., AND B. KAPLAN.   *Symbol Formation.* New York: John Wiley, 1963.

10

Tools of Assessment

The structural model we have presented emphasizes assessment in naturalistic contexts in order to find the patterns that emerge when the child is part of a communicative interaction. Formal tests have not been included in our assessment procedures because tests by their very nature and purpose present language removed from ordinary intentionality. When taking tests, children do not respond to a test item to share information or make requests. Rather, these items entail specialized demands that do not typically occur in real situations. Part of the unnaturalness of tests comes from the removal of contextual clues in order to assure the child "knows" the answer only from the language forms given. As we have attempted to demonstrate, this is an artificial separation, since language typically depends on context for interpretation. Not only is the intention and the context artificial in test situations, the language itself is often characteristically different from language in everyday communicative exchanges. We ask children to label objects, fill in missing words, or imitate words or sentences that elicit different structures from those they would ordinarily use. We have previously discussed some of the problems in assessing phonology with one-word responses or syntax with imitation. These caveats should be applied to most tests.

Arguments against the use of formal tests to assess language have been repeatedly and persuasively made (e.g., Siegel and Broen, 1976; Duchan, 1982). We obviously agree with the others that tests cannot be substitutes for structural analysis in finding regularities in children's performance. Tests can be helpful, however, if we understand their limitations. We include this chapter to discuss how tests and other formalized procedures relate to the questions asked in language assessment. We will introduce various concepts that we consider to be relevant to the use and interpretation of tests and relate these to some commonly used language tests. Our intent is not to provide the clinician with a comprehensive list of tests, since such a list is rapidly outdated and other authors have compiled extensive and useful descriptions of commercial language tests (e.g., Darley, 1979; Wiig and Semel, 1980). Rather, our intent is to provide a framework for evaluating these and other tests to determine their role in addressing the assessment questions we posed in Chapter 1.

PURPOSE OF A TEST

The general purpose of any test is to provide a sample of behavior for analysis, and the type of sample desired depends upon the specific purpose of the test. Tests are generally designed to accomplish one or both of the following goals.

1. RANK INDIVIDUALS   Tests that are designed to determine relative ranking of individuals who take the test are described as *norm referenced*. In using these tests, we compare the score of a given child with the scores of other children who have taken the test and determine where our child's score falls within the distribution of scores. The population of children our child is compared to is taken to be representative of the general population and thus the "norm." Norm-referenced tests are typically used to make decisions, including whether or not the child should be considered as having a language disorder.

Tests that are designed to determine a child's ranking in an area (language or otherwise) will be constructed from selected items that should be representative of that area, without attempting to be comprehensive in its coverage. For example, school achievement tests and intelligence tests do not attempt to include every skill that would indicate achievement or intelligence but rather are constructed to be a sample of such skills. Some norm-referenced language tests sample several kinds of language behavior, with the intent being to give a ranking of general language skill. Other tests are restricted to one or a few specific areas of language and thus are used to assess ranking within those areas only.

The ranking obtained with norm-referenced tests can help us to answer the first assessment question: Does the child have a language problem? If the child's rank is comparable to other children of the same age, we judge that there is no problem within the area tested; if the rank is very low, we have found evidence that a problem exists—if we have confidence that the child's performance on the test is representative of nontest abilities. These tests may also help us identify areas of deficit and thus address the third assessment question—the child's areas of deficit. If a test primarily covers one area of language and a child ranks low on that test, we have evidence of one area of deficit; it may not be the only or the most handicapping area of deficit. If a test covers several areas in some depth, we may find that the child shows deficits in one or more areas and not in others.

2. DESCRIBE REGULARITIES OF PERFORMANCE   Tests designed to meet this second purpose of testing sample many instances of a specified type of behavior, with the goal of identifying the specific behaviors the child does or does not possess. If, for example, a teacher wants to determine if a child knows the multiplication tables, a test would be chosen or constructed that includes all

numbers from one to nine as the multiplicand to assess this. The teacher's interest in this case is not in how the child ranks relative to a group of children, so this test does not have to be norm referenced. Rather, the question is whether or not the child knows the specific objectives that the teacher has chosen to be important to know. This type of test has been called *criterion referenced*. Some commercial tests of this type have been norm referenced so it is possible to use them to rank children, but ranking is not the primary purpose. Since the intent of these tests is identification of specific kinds of knowledge that the child has or lacks, it is appropriate to teach the objectives of the items that are missed; on the other hand, this is inappropriate with tests designed to rank individuals, in which items should be representative but not inclusive of knowledge being sampled.

Language tests of this type are designed to answer the fourth assessment question: What are the regularities in this child's language skill? When they are used to supplement structural analysis of spontaneous language, they are helpful in identifying goals for intervention.

MEASUREMENT ISSUES

When choosing a test for either purpose, that is, to rank an individual or to describe regularities of performance, there are two relevant issues the clinician needs to consider. First, how comprehensively does the test cover the area it purports to test? If, for example, it is designed to test prepositions, how inclusive or representative is the set of prepositions presented? This is particularly critical when we are testing for regularities of performance, since we want to make sure we have sampled enough to make generalizations about the child's patterns. A second question concerns the appropriateness of this test for a given child. A clinician would generally not give a test unless there were some indications in the child's behavior that there might be a problem in the area of language covered by the test. A clinician's wholesale use of tests simply because they are available is the mark of one who is insecure in making any clinical judgments; this clinician has the mistaken assumption that finding the right test or battery of tests is the answer to all assessment questions.

Use of tests designed to determine ranking raises some other measurement issues that come from the need for confidence in the scores when we are making decisions based on an individual's rank relative to others. We will briefly discuss types of scores, reliability, validity, and standardization population. More detailed explanations can be found in texts on testing, such as Cronbach (1970) or Salvia and Ysseldyke (1978).

Types of Scores

An individual's rank on a test can be derived from comparison to the original sample of people taking the test in two ways, resulting in age-equivalent scores or scores of relative standing.

AGE EQUIVALENT SCORES   The individual's score can be compared to all age groups in the original sample to determine which group he or she scores most like. If, for example, a child's score is the same as the average (mean) score for six year olds, her age-equivalent score would be 6 years. Scores falling between means for adjacent age groups are interpolated or estimated to yield an intermediate age-equivalent, such as 6.2 (six years, two months). These scores might be identified in various ways, such as language age, mental age, or receptive vocabulary age. Age-equivalent scores can be converted to *developmental quotients* by comparison to the child's chronological age.

$$\text{Developmental quotient} = \frac{\text{age-equivalent}}{\text{chronological age}} \times 100$$

There are several problems with age-equivalent scores and developmental quotients. First, they provide no way of knowing the amount of significance to attach to a discrepancy between the child's chronological age and the derived age-equivalent score. Some behaviors may be most typical of one age group but may still be exhibited by a significant proportion of normal children at an older age. It becomes impossible to interpret age-equivalent scores on a single test or to compare them between two different tests unless the amount of variability shown by normal children is known. Some clinicians follow the guideline that if the child earns an age-equivalent score that is eighteen months or two years below chronological age, he or she can be considered to have a language problem. One problem with this approach is that it assumes a two-year gap is equally significant across the age-range of childhood, while it is obvious that the proportional discrepancy would be greater the younger the child. Using the developmental quotient has similar problems, since the variance of age scores within the chronological age groups is different, and thus the same quotient means different things at different ages.

Another problem with these scores is that they assume that equal scores indicate equal performance. The six year old who achieves a score equal to the mean score for four year olds may not in fact have performed at all like a four year old. The approach to items as well as the specific items missed may be different. Further, this age-equivalent score tends to foster the false assumption that there are "average" four year olds to whom our child is being compared, when this is merely the mean of four year olds' scores.

As we have already mentioned, scores that fall between the means of each age group in the original sample are interpolated on the assumption that increase in knowledge is linear and even. Thus, if the mean score for four year olds is 20, and the mean score for five year olds is 30, a score of 25 will be assigned the age-equivalence of 4-6, even though it has not been demonstrated that this is the average score for children of this age (4-6). Likewise, scores are sometimes extrapolated or estimated for ages younger and older than the children in the original sample. This presents another obvious weakness of these scores. In general, we do not recommend using age-equivalent scores due to the problems of interpretation.

SCORES OF RELATIVE STANDING   The second way a child's score can be interpreted is by comparing it to others of the same age group in order to determine the child's standing relative to his or her peers. One type of comparison is based on the statistical concept of the normal curve, or "normal" distribution of test scores. The mean score for each group, which is the average obtained by adding up all the scores of each member of the group and dividing by the number in the group, is in the middle of the distribution. To get an idea of how far away an individual's score is from the mean, we must know the standard deviation for the group. This is a measure of the range of scores that were obtained by a certain proportion of the group. One standard deviation above the mean and one standard deviation below the mean (± 1 S.D.) give us the score range of 68 percent of the group; ± 2 S.D. account for 95 percent, and ± 3 S.D. give us the score range for 99 percent, or almost the entire group. To give an example, on the Peabody Picture Vocabulary Test, the mean score ($\overline{X}$) for the 11.6 to 12.5 age group is 86.23, with S.D. $= 10.79$. So we know

68% of this group scored between 75.4 and 97.0 ($\overline{X} \pm 1$ S.D.)
95% scored between 64.6 and 97.0 ($\overline{X} \pm 2$ S.D.)
99% scored between 53.9 and 118.6 ($\overline{X} \pm 3$ S.D.)

The decision as to what constitutes the "normal range" is an arbitrary one. Most people would certainly accept that at least 68 percent of the population must be considered "normal," so would not see any score falling between ± 1 S.D. as deviant. It is common for makers of test classification schemes to take ± 2 S.D. as the division between normal and deviant, on the assumption that 95 percent of the sampled population should be considered normal. With this guideline, a twelve year old taking the PPVT would have to score below 65 before we would consider his or her performance to be outside of normal limits.

Some tests use *standard scores*, which are derived by assigning the mean an arbitrary number, such as 100 in intelligence tests, and a constant value to indicate 1 standard deviation. This makes it possible to compare groups with different means and degrees of variability with each other. A child's score can be converted to a standard score to indicate in standard deviation units how much the given score deviates from the mean of the group. This can be computed as a *z-score* in the following manner:

$$z = \frac{\text{child's score (X)} - \text{mean } (\overline{X})}{\text{standard deviation (S.D.)}}$$

For example, your child scores 45 on a test; you find in the test manual that the mean for the child's age group is 55 and standard deviation is 7.00. To find the child's z-score, we follow the formula

$$z = \frac{45 - 55}{7} = \frac{-10}{7} = -1.42$$

We can now see that this child's score is within -2 S.D. of the mean and not in the deviant range. This is a simple and useful means of comparing ranking on different tests as well.

Another way a child's score can be compared to his or her age peers is by using *percentile ranks.* These norms are established by arranging the scores of everyone within the sample age group from high to low and computing the percentage of individuals at and below each score. If 10 percent of the group score at and below 28 on a given test, then a child who receives a score of 28 is in the 10th percentile. It should be emphasized that this is not a measure of the percent correct for a given child, but rather an indication of relative standing in comparison to peers.

Percentile ranks are not based on a normal distribution, as are standard deviations and standard scores. When used with a normally distributed population, we can note a relationship between these two types of measures. The 16th percentile corresponds to approximately -1 S.D. The 2nd percentile is closest to -2 S.D., which might lead us to interpret performance below the 3rd percentile as deviance from normal, to be consistent with the -2 S.D. cut off. We can also note that the range of scores in the middle of a normal distribution is going to be much smaller for each percentile point than at the extremes. Thus, each item scored correct or incorrect will influence an individual's rank more in the middle of the distribution than at the extremes. Using the Peabody again as an example, we find that the difference in scores between the 61st and the 69th percentile for 12 year olds is 3, while between the 1st and 9th percentile the range is 13.

SUMMARY   Tests designed for ranking individuals can have the following types of scores:

1. *Age-equivalent scores,* which compare a child to children at all ages sampled, and assign an age-equivalent score corresponding to the age group the child scores like. These can be converted to developmental quotients, but either method of reporting has intrinsic problems of interpretation.
2. *Relative ranking scores,* which compare a child to children of the same age, with the score indicating how the child ranks relative to peers. There are two basic ways of doing this:
   a. *Standard scores,* which can be used to compare a child's score to a presumed normal distribution of scores to determine the degree of deviation from the mean of the age group. Scores within -2 S.D. of the mean are generally considered to be in the normal range.
   b. *Percentile ranks,* which indicate the percentage of peers who score below a given child's score.

Reliability

The reliability of a test is a measure of the stability or consistency of test results and indicates the amount of confidence one can have in the score. If children's performance on a test is dependent primarily on their knowledge of the material being tested rather than extraneous factors, reliability should be high. Several kinds of reliability are generally reported.

Interexaminer reliability refers to the consistency of scores when the test is administered by more than one examiner. *Test-retest reliability* is derived by administering the test to the same children twice within a short period of time to determine the stability of scores. Tests that have *alternate forms* (two or more versions of the same test) will report reliability coefficients between the forms to show how comparable they are. To measure the internal consistency of the test, *split-half* or *odd-even* reliability is derived by comparing the score on one half of the items to the score on the other half. If all items are testing the same general ability, this should be high.

Reliability can be adversely affected by factors other than the test items. If test directions are unclear or complicated, individual testers or children being tested may then interpret them differently, thus changing the nature of the test. Test makers generally indicate the kind of training examiners should have prior to administering the test, in order to achieve reliable results.

Reliability is a minimal requirement for any test, and most tests on the market report reasonable reliability when directions for administration are followed.

Validity

The validity of a test is an indication of how well it measures what it purports to measure. A test can be highly reliable but have little validity, as would be the case, for example, if we took shoe size as an indicator of language ability. It would be easy to demonstrate that shoe size is stable, but that does not make it a reasonable way to measure language skill. Demonstrating validity is more difficult than showing reliability, particularly in the area of language, since the ability or disability being measured is usually ambiguously defined.

There are various ways of reporting validity, and type as well as degree of validity should be a major concern of a clinician choosing a test. One common measure of validity is showing a correlation with other standardized tests that are presumed to measure the same skill. The questions that are then relevant are whether or not that skill is what you intend to measure and how well the validity of the comparison test has been demonstrated. Being highly correlated with an intelligence test does not necessarily indicate a language test is valid, unless we make the assumption that language ability is a direct reflection of intelligence or that the intelligence test measures primarily language ability, which violates the assumptions of most such tests. Another common way to describe validity is to report the correlation between test scores and age—that is, to show that older children get more items correct than younger children. This correlation should be high, since this would be the trend on almost any measure, including shoe size. It is at best a weak argument for the validity of the test. A more meaningful measure of validity is whether the test identifies those children who have language problems and whether the test scores are correlated with severity of the problem. The best reference criterion is probably the clinical judgment of experienced clinicians as to whether the test predicts nontest language behavior, since ultimately the diagnosis of language disorder must be based on the child's nontest performance. Most language tests do not report impressive validity data, if any at all, so usually the clinician must make judgments about the appropriateness of individual items. This is known as content validity and is the responsibility of the test user. The model of language on which the test is developed becomes an important question in this judgment, since that will determine the type of items that are seen as relevant to measuring language. If clinicians do not understand or accept the model of the test maker, it is not a valid test for their purposes, i.e., to identify the children who have language problems.

Standardization Population

The norms on a test are derived from administering the test to a number of individuals and then using their scores as representative of the population at large. Since those tested are not usually selected at random from the general population, it is relevant to determine the particular characteristics of this standardization population. If they differ in some significant way from the individual child we are testing, it may be inappropriate to compare our child's score to this group. Just as we would not compare the performance of a child speaking French to the norms for English speakers, we cannot use the performance of a dissimilar geographic or social group to judge the normalcy of a child. The standardization populations generally do not include individuals who deviate from the "typical" in any way. Thus, in order to compare an atypical child to this group, we must assume that his or her pattern of language development is the same as the normally developing child but perhaps at a slower rate. It is not clear that this is an acceptable assumption to make. If the clinician is seeking a test to determine ranking for a particular child, it is important to choose one which was standardized with a population similar in cultural background to that child.

Another question that needs to be raised about the standardization population is its size. Since the performance of this group is assumed to represent the general population, it should be large enough to make this a reasonable assumption. The total size of the sample is not as informative as the number of individuals in each age group sampled, since the norms to which a child is compared are derived within these subgroups. If there are 100 individuals in a subgroup, each person represents 1 percent, so that the lowest scoring person's score would identify the 1st percentile, etc. Since by definition 2.27 percent fall below -2 S.D. there would be less than 3 people in the standardization group in that range. Most normalizing populations have considerably fewer than 100 persons in each age group, so norms are often extrapolated or inferred from data on a few individuals, particularly at the extremes of the distribution.

SUMMARY   When evaluating the usefulness of tests to rank individual children, the clinician should determine that the test is

1. *Reliable*—that is, results can be assumed to be stable and repeatable. We can have most confidence in the reliability of tests with high reliability coefficients, which should be reported in the test manual.
2. *Valid*—validity measures, when reported by test makers, may or may not be of significance to the clinician, depending on the type of validity that is reported. Predictive or content validity are probably the most meaningful for making clinical decisions; these are rarely demonstrated.
3. *Standardized* on a population to which the individual child can reasonably be considered similar in background.

TYPES OF TESTS

While recognizing that any classification system can lead to artificial distinctions, we have chosen to discuss some of the existing language tests according to our perception of the purpose and scope of the instruments. Our impression of these attributes does not always correspond with that of the test maker but reflects our own examination of test items. We begin again with our two broad categories of tests—those to determine an individual's rank and those for finding regularities in performance.

The norm-referenced tests for ranking can all be used to address the question of normalcy, as the individual's score is compared to a larger population. It must be kept in mind, however, that the determination of which ranks are "normal" and which are "deviant" is arbitrary and based on clinical judgment. If the clinician has already judged a child's language to be deviant, data from these tests are useful only to document this judgment when required for administrative purposes; they are not useful for planning remediation.

Some ranking tests or combinations of tests are helpful in determining relative areas of strength and deficit, thus addressing another assessment question. It must be cautioned, however, that these are not tests covering all potential deficit areas, so they cannot be relied on to get a complete profile of language ability. Further, these tests can be used only to suggest general areas of deficit— they do not sample any specific area in enough detail to find regularities.

Tests of regularities, on the other hand, are always confined to specific areas, since the intent is to determine patterns of performance within an area. Analysis of items that are right and wrong is the essence of scoring these tests, rather than quantifying results. Our goal here is to analyze the child's response structurally so we can understand what led to it.

Some available tests are clearly of the ranking type and others are for revealing regularities. Several tests attempt to do some of both. We will discuss examples of each type. Table 10.1 shows how some of these tests can be categorized according to their purpose and the areas of deficit they assess.

TESTS FOR RANKING

Developmental Scales

All developmental scales are based on a normative model of assessment and are designed to rank children. They are characterized by having ages attached to specific behaviors and scores which are reported as age-equivalent curves. Typically, there are several behaviors reported to be normal at each age level, so an individual child is observed or directed to perform these behaviors and then scored according to which age group his or her score is closest to. There are some variations on this scoring system with the individual scales, as well as differences in the number and scope of behaviors sampled.

Following are some examples of popular developmental scales. Some are broad and cover other areas as well as language skills. Others are addressed primarily to a level of general language functioning. None offer a coherent picture of the child's language competency or identify areas of deficit.

Table 10.1 Representative Language Tests by Type and Purpose

TEST	PURPOSE		AREAS OF DEFICIT				RECEP	EXPRESS.
	Ranking	*Regularity*	*Phon.*	*Morph.*	*Syn.*	*Sem./Vocab.*		
Developmental Scales (Age Equivalence)	X							
Preschool Language Scale	X							
Sequenced Inventory of Communication Development	X							
REEL	X							
Communicative Evaluation Chart	X							
Denver Developmental Screening Test	X							
Survey Tests (Pass/Fail)								
DIAL	X							
Fluharty Preschool Speech and Language Screening Test	X							
Area of Deficit Tests								
Bankson Language Screening Test	X		X	X	X	X	X	X
Test for Auditory Comprehension of Language	X		X	X	X	X	X	
The Test of Language Development	X		X	X	X	X	X	X
Northwestern Syntax Screening Test	X			X	X		X	X
Peabody Picture Vocabulary Test	X					X	X	
The Illinois Test of Psycholinguistic Abilities	X			X		X	X	X
Articulation Tests								
Goldman-Fristoe		X	X					X
Fisher-Logemann		X	X					X
A Deep Test of Articulation		X	X					X
Berry-Talbott Test of Grammar	(X)[a]	X		X			X	X
Michigan Picture Language Inventory	(X)	X		X			X	X
Carrow Elicited Language Inventory		X		X	X			X
Oral Language Sentence Imitation Screening/Diagnostic Tests	(X)	X			X			X
Boehm Test of Basic Concepts		X				X	X	
Vocabulary Comprehension Scale	(X)	X				X	X	
McCarthy Scales of Children's Ability (subtests)	(X)	X				X	X	X
Wechsler Intelligence Scales (subtests)	(X)	X				X	X	X
Environmental Language Inventory		X			(X)	X	X	X
Assessment of Children's Language Comprehension		X				X	X	X

[a] (X) indicates information is available to use the test for this purpose, but we consider it secondary.

The *Preschool Language Scale* (Zimmerman, Steiner, and Evatt, 1969) has separate sections for evaluating comprehension and expression of language. Each section has four behaviors at each 6-month interval from age 18 months to 7 years. Receptive vocabulary, concept acquisition, and understanding of commands are sampled on the comprehension scale. The expressive section (verbal ability) samples some labeling, expression of concepts, memory span for digits, limited syntax and morphology, and articulation. Age equivalence is derived for each of the two sections by adding together the number of behaviors displayed and counting each as 1½ months of development (a method of calculation which actually violates the assumptions of a norm-referenced measure).

The directions for administering and evaluating each of the items on the Preschool Language Scale are very clear and explicit. A picture book is included for use with some of the items. No information on reliability or validity is available. The authors do not view this as a test but rather as an instrument to isolate areas of strength and deficiency in language. It is scored, however, as a standardized test.

The *Sequenced Inventory of Communication Development* (Hedrick Prather, and Tobin, 1975) is also divided into receptive and expressive language behaviors, with an age range of from 4 months to 4 years. Rather than assigning each behavior to a given age, the authors indicate the ages at which 25, 50, 75, and 90+ percent of their standardization population accomplish each behavior, which is useful information on normal development. It should be noted, however, that this population consisted of only 252 children. Receptive and expressive communication age-equivalent scores can be computed. Items on each scale are arranged developmentally, with receptive items ranging from awareness of sound to speech sound discrimination. Expressive items include motor and vocal imitation as well as answers to questions and a spontaneous sample. Play behaviors and prelinguistic responses sampled, along with viewing language as part of a social system, are interesting features of this scale.

The *Houston Test of Language Development* (Crabtree, 1963) and the *Utah Test of Language Development* (Mecham, Jex, and Jones, 1963) are similar in their orientation and types of items. Both include items chosen from older scales of language and intellectual development, utilizing many nonlinguistic items as well as items intended to sample concepts, and a variety of expressive and receptive language skills. Little attention is given to language structure. The Houston Test is divided into two parts: part I for ages 6 months to 3 years; part II for ages 3 years to 6 years. The Utah Test has an age range of 1.6 to 14.5 years. Both scales yield an age-equivalent score.

The *Verbal Language Development Scale* (Mecham, 1971) and the *REEL* (Bzoch and League, 1971) are two assessment scales that are administered primarily through interviewing parents rather than direct observation. Both can therefore be administered quickly but provide very limited information and would be of little use to a clinician. These scales might be of value to nonprofessionals for use in identifying those children needing referal to a speech-language pathologist.

There are several scales that provide for a cursory assessment of language along with other aspects of development.

The *Communicative Evaluation Chart* (Anderson, Miles, and Matheny, 1963), for infants from 3 months to 5 years old, presents receptive and expressive language behaviors along with items to assess motor coordination and visual-motor perceptual skills at each age level. No normative data are available, and there are no directions or suggestions for how to elicit each behavior.

The *Denver Developmental Screening Test* (Frankenburg et al., 1975) is divided into four areas: personal-social, fine motor, language, and gross motor. An age range for each item is shown by giving the age at which 25, 50, 75, and 90 percent of children pass that item. Language behaviors sampled are very limited but include some items that assess structure as well as vocabulary. Detailed directions are given for each test item. This scale was standardized in Denver using 1,036 normal children aged 2 weeks to 6.4 years.

Survey Tests

Survey tests are designed to provide a sampling of relatively broad-based behavior in a brief period of time for the purpose of selecting children who need further language evaluation and/or identifying areas of deficit in which further assessment is indicated. They are often identified as "screening" tests, but since this label is applied to such a wide variety of standardized and informal assessment procedures, we choose not to use it here. Survey tests are norm referenced, but unlike the developmental scales, they do not yield age-equivalent scores. Instead, they have established criteria for what is considered adequate performance at a given age. If a child fails to meet this criteria, he or she is considered a candidate for more extensive testing or observation to determine the nature and severity of the language disorder. The survey tests are ranking tests because they match the child's performance to a normal sample in several language areas, as well as in some nonlanguage areas.

The *DIAL* (Mardell and Goldenberg, 1975) was developed to assess the needs of large numbers of prekindergarten children for follow-up services due to deficits in motor or language abilities. It is designed to have each child observed individually by a team of four examiners in the areas of gross motor skills, fine motor skills, concepts, and communication. Points are given for each task, and scores are computed for each of the four areas tested. The need for follow-up intervention or further assessment is determined by comparing the child's score in each area with the cutoff score specified by chronological age, with the 10th percentile of the standardization population being used as the criterion for arriving at cutoff scores. Items were selected from a battery of norm-referenced tests and developmental scales. The concepts and communication subtests cover a variety of receptive and expressive language skills, including articulation, vocabulary use and recognition, following directions, and formulating original sentences in response to questions and story pictures (parts of speech and length of longest sentence are scored). There is no breakdown of performance into areas of language, and individual items should not be interpreted as identifying areas of deficit.

The authors of the DIAL indicate that the examiners need only limited training to administer the test. We suspect that the reliability of scoring, particularly of the communications portion, would be heavily dependent upon the examiner's training or experience. The DIAL kit includes most of the materials needed for the survey, except for a Polaroid camera and film for photographing each child. The justification of the expense of this procedure is questionable if the picture is used only in the limited way outlined in the instruction manual. The DIAL is intended for use with children from 2.6 to 5.5 years of age. It takes approximately 25–30 minutes for a typical child to complete the four subtests. It could be administered to an individual child by one examiner, but its uniqueness is primarily in a format which facilitates surveying a large number of children at a time. It would not be useful as a language test for a child who is already suspected to have a language impairment, as it could provide little additional information.

The *Fluharty Preschool Speech and Language Screening Test* (Fluharty, 1978) is an example of a survey test that is designed to be given quickly to a large population to indicate which children need further evaluation, and in which areas of deficit. Expressive vocabulary and articulation are assessed by having the child label objects. Comprehension is assessed by having the child respond to a set of sentences with varying syntactic structures, and several grammatical forms are sampled through sentence imitation. Cutoff scores are presented for each of the four areas tested for 2, 3, 4, and 5 year olds, thus giving a general indication of deficit areas. Typical testing time is 6 minutes. Tests of this type are obviously not designed to determine presence of a language problem but only to identify potential problems. Effective referrals can serve the same function.

Area-of-Deficit Tests

These tests differ from the survey tests in that they are designed to determine the child's ranking in a specific area or to compare more than one area, rather than to determine a general age equivalent or adequacy.

The *Bankson Language Screening Test (BLST)* (Bankson, 1977) consists of a battery of seventeen subtests covering semantics, morphology, syntax, and auditory and visual perception, thus reflecting an attempt to identify areas of deficit for further assessment. It focuses on expression rather than comprehension. The semantics subtests range from concrete vocabulary items to more abstract generalizations, such as functions and opposites. Most of the early grammatical morphemes are covered in various subtests, with syntax getting less emphasis. The auditory perception subtests include memory for words and sentences, following commands, story sequencing, and phonemic discrimination. The visual perception subtests are included on the rationale that children with oral language deficits often will also have difficulty with reading and that this test can serve as a tool for early detection of such problems.

Items on the BLST are scored as right or wrong. Total raw score can then be converted to percentile rank, with the author recommending further language evaluation for children with scores at or below the 30th percentile, with a strong therapy recommendation for those below the 16th percentile. The validity of these criteria points has not been demonstrated, and clinicians may find other cutoff points more useful when using this test to identify children for further evaluation. It is also possible to score each subtest separately, for comparison with means and standard deviations presented by age group. This would be more helpful than overall percentile rank in identifying areas of deficit. The BLST was norm referenced on 637 children between the ages of 4.1 and 8.0 years. It takes approximately 25 minutes to administer. A shorter version is possible by administering 38 items identified as being the most discriminating. There are no norms available for this version, however. A preferable means of shortening the test would seem to us to be eliminating the subtests on visual and auditory perception that are less directly relevant to identifying language areas of deficit. Norms for the remaining subtests could still be used, but of course the total score would not be converted to an overall percentile rank.

While the *Test for Auditory Comprehension of Language (TACL)* (Carrow, 1973) is designed to "measure in depth the auditory comprehension of linguistic structure" as well as to determine the level of functioning on comprehension, we see the TACL as most appropriately used for the latter function. It includes 101 items to sample receptive vocabulary, syntax, and morphology, making it roughly comparable in length and coverage to the first three sections of the BLST. It differs in that it samples only receptive abilities, and the vocabulary items are identified by word class rather than by concept as in the semantics portion of the BLST. Total raw score can be converted to age equivalence, or errors can be summarized by type to arrive at vocabulary, morphology, and syntax subscores. No norms are available for these subscores, so while they may be helpful in identifying areas of deficit, ranking within these areas cannot be determined.

Mean and standard deviation are reported for each 5-month age group, along with partial percentile ranks. Each item indicates the ages at which 75 percent and 90 percent of children pass it. It should be noted that the standardization population was only 200 children, ranging in age from 2.10 to 7.0 years, and distribution of scores was uneven. A briefer version of the TACL is available that consists of 25 items from the larger test. It was standardized on 400 middle-class children from 3 to 6 years of age. It is intended for group administration, and norms are not applicable when it is used to test children on an individual basis. Both versions of the TACL are available in Spanish.

The *Test of Language Development (TOLD)* (Newcomer and Hammill, 1977) was developed on a linguistic model, including subtests that assess facets of semantics, syntax, and phonology both expressively and receptively. The semantic subtests are limited to identifying named pictures and giving definitions. Comprehension of morphology and syntax is tested through identification of pictures described with sentences. Along with comprehension of a variety of grammatical forms (e.g., negatives, plurals, subordinate clauses), several specific vocabulary items are assessed by the subtest (e.g., *different, middle*), thus making it difficult to isolate comprehension of morphology and/or syntax. Expressive syntax and morphology are assessed through imitation of 30 sentences, and morphology is also sampled through sentence completion, with plurals, possessives, various verb tenses, and comparatives being elicited. Phonology is assessed through single-word responses to pictures. A word discrimination subtest is also included. Items for all subtests were chosen as representative of the area being tested, rather than as comprehensive.

Scores for each subtest are computed separately and can be converted to age-equivalent scores or scaled scores. A "linguistic quotient" is derived by adding together the scaled scores of each subtest. Scores are analyzed by comparing scaled scores on each test to criteria established to determine if a child's performance is "average," "below average," "above average," "poor," or "superior." Means of establishing these criteria are not presented. The scores thus do not provide a measure of deviance from average performance but are more similar to the survey tests in that a pass-fail criterion is given. Scaled scores on subtests can also be compared to each other to get an indication of deficit areas.

The TOLD was standardized on 1,014 English-speaking children between ages 4.0 and 8.11 from varied geographical, socioeconomic, and ethnic backgrounds.

The *Northwestern Syntax Screening Test* (NSST) (Lee, 1971) was also developed on a linguistic model and consists of items to sample receptive and expressive morphology and syntax. It was designed to identify children significantly impaired in these skills (defined as those scoring more than 2 standard deviations below the mean), as well as those who need further testing to establish the existence of a clinically significant language delay (as evidenced by scores below the 10th percentile). Separate scores are derived for expressive and receptive portions, and each can be compared to percentile ranks by age group.

The inappropriateness of using this test as a diagnostic tool for children who have already been identified as language-impaired has been emphasized by Lee (1977) as well as by others who have found a lack of consistency on particular structures between test performance on the NSST and spontaneous language (Prutting, Gallagher, and Mulac, 1975). The standardization sample consisted of children from middle to upper middle suburban communities in the Midwest, with less than 50 children in some of the age groups. Subsequent studies have shown that the norms are not appropriate for children from other populations (Larson and Summers, 1976). Lee emphasizes that the NSST is applicable only to children learning the standard English dialect. The age range of the test is given as 3 to 8 years, but it is apparent from looking at the norms that the test is not sensitive to differences beyond the 6.11 age level. Even below this age, the statistical support of reliability and validity is meager.

The *Peabody Picture Vocabulary Test–Revised (PPVT)* (Dunn and Dunn, 1981) of receptive vocabulary evolved out of a normative orientation to language, with the words chosen for their frequency of occurrence rather than semantic content. Raw scores can be converted to age equivalents, stanines, standard scores, or percentiles with an age range of 2.3 to 18.5.

The PPVT is one of the best standardized language tests available, but it should also be emphasized that it can only identify a deficit in the area of receptive vocabulary and should not be used as a measure of general language functioning.

The *Illinois Test of Psycholinguistic Abilities (ITPA)* (Kirk, McCarthy, and Kirk, 1968), as we mentioned previously, has evolved into a self-defining view of language. Designed for children from 2 to 10 years of age, it consists of 12 subtests, each intended to identify a potential area of deficit. It could be argued that some of the subtests, such as auditory sequential memory, are also used to identify a possible cause of a language problem, depending on the clinician's view of the nature of language disorders—that is, poor auditory memory may be seen as either a symptom or a cause of a language problem. The raw score for each subtest is converted to a scaled score to allow for comparison across subtests. An age-equivalent score ("psycholinguistic age") is calculated for the entire test.

The ITPA was standardized on predominately middle-class Illinois and Wisconsin children, all of whom demonstrated average intellectual functioning, academic achievement, adjustment, and sensorimotor integrity, which severely limits the population of which the norms are representative. Test-retest reliabilities are relatively low, ranging from .12 to .86. Validity as a test of language function has not been demonstrated, but it correlates highly with chronological age (Salvia and Ysseldyke, 1978) and intelligence tests (Huizinga, 1973).

The subtests of the ITPA follow:

COMPREHENSION SUBTESTS

Auditory reception. This subtest includes 50 questions of the type "Do dogs eat?" "Do dials yawn?" with vocabulary becoming increasingly more difficult.

Visual reception. This subtest includes 50 items, each consisting of a stimulus picture and 4 response pictures from which the child is to choose the one conceptually similar to the stimulus picture.

EXPRESSIVE SUBTESTS

Verbal expression. An object is presented and the child is asked "Tell me all about this." The score is the number of discrete, relevant, factual concepts expressed. The manner or structure of expression is not regarded, thus making this a vocabulary test or test of conceptual attribution.

Manual expression. The child is shown 15 pictures of common objects and asked to pantomime the appropriate action of each.

ASSOCIATION SUBTESTS

Auditory association. The child is presented with 62 verbal analogies of the form "I cut with a saw; I pound with a _____?" with items of increasing difficulty.

Visual association. This subtest has two parts. On the first, the child is to choose one of four pictures that "goes with" the stimulus picture. On the second part, visual analogies are presented (e.g., tennis ball, tennis racket; baseball, _____).

Grammatic closure. The child is given 33 orally presented items accompanied by pictures and is to complete the second statement through use of automatic habits acquired through redundancies of the language. Items are of the form "Here is a bed; here are two _____?"

Visual closure. This subtest consists of 4 scenes, each containing 14 or 15 common objects concealed in varying degrees. The child is to identify them from incomplete visual representation.

Auditory sequential memory. This tests ability to recall sequences of digits increasing in length from 2 to 8 digits.

Visual sequential memory. The child is asked to reproduce a sequence of nonmeaningful figures from memory.

Auditory closure (optional). Thirty words with sounds omitted are said to the child, who is to identify and repeat the word, filling in the missing sounds.

Sound blending (optional). The sounds of a word are spoken singly at half-second intervals, and the child is asked to synthesize the word and say it correctly.

TESTS FOR REGULARITIES

Unlike the ranking tests, the assessment tools discussed here are designed to identify specific problems a child has with language rather than simply determining whether or not, or to what degree, a problem exists. It thus is appropriate to look at each item individually and to compare it with other items to determine what regularities are present in the child's performance. These measures are all restricted to specific areas of deficit rather than representative of general language function. As we have mentioned, some of them have been norm referenced and so can be used to arrive at a level of functioning on a specific task, but this is not their primary purpose. These norms do make it possible, however, to quantify children's performance and thus report scores when they are desired. Many of these tools have not been adequately standardized to use as measures of relative rank. This is not a serious criticism of them as long as they are not used for that purpose. In any event, scores are of little value for the purposes of describing language and planning therapy, so clinicians must analyze performance on each item. Again, we have not attempted to be comprehensive in our coverage, but rather we give examples of various types of descriptive tools. We have organized this discussion according to the area of deficit being investigated. An important criterion for the usefulness of these measures is the adequacy of the sample obtained for indicating regularities in performance.

Phonology Assessment

There are numerous articulation tests available that sample expressive phonology, usually by having the child say the name of pictured objects or read test sentences. The *Goldman-Fristoe* (1972) and the *Templin-Darley* (1969) tests are popular examples of this type; both provide normative data for comparison. With these tests, each phoneme is sampled in one to three words. If a child consistently produces one or more of the phonemes in an atypical manner, these tests will provide an adequate sample for describing that difference. If, however, the child's phonological rules are atypical, samples obtained will not be comprehensive enough to identify the regularities that exist. Limitations of the traditional articulation tests for assessing phonology are discussed in our chapter on phonology. We will only comment here on a few tests that offer some unique features.

There are no tests of receptive phonology that we take to be descriptive of that area of deficit. Despite the fact that the authors of some discrimination or perception tests have described their instruments as useful in describing or identifying the cause of language (or learning) problems, the relationship of the skills tested to understanding language has not been demonstrated.

A Deep Test of Articulation (McDonald, 1964) assesses error phonemes in multiple-phonetic contexts, thus making it possible to observe the degree of variability in the child's production. Words are produced in combinations, which more closely approximates phonological sequences involved in formal discourse than does production in single words, even though the combinations are semantically unlikely.

The *Fisher-Logemann Test of Articulation Competence* (Fisher and Logemann, 1971) not only aids in the identification of misarticulated phonemes, but also facilitates analysis of the nature of misarticulations. Consonants are analyzed on the basis of a three-feature system (place of articulation, manner of articulation, and voicing), with errors of phoneme substitution or distortion described in terms of feature differences.

Phonological Process Analysis (Weiner, 1979) is a departure from traditional articulation tests in that it focuses on underlying rule-ordered articulatory patterns rather than listing specific sound errors. Stimuli were selected to detect particular phonological rules rather than to sample all standard sounds. Tests words are elicited both in isolation and in phrases through delayed imitation. The phonological processes identified by Weiner are

1. Syllable structure processes
    a) deletion of final consonants (/wɛ/ for *wet*)
    b) cluster reduction (/tap/ for *stop*)
    c) weak-syllable deletion (/tɛfon/ for *telephone*)
    d) glottal replacement (/bæʔ/ for *back*)

2. Harmony processes
    a) labial assimilation (/wʌm/ for *thumb*)
    b) alveolar assimilation (/lɛ lo/ for *yellow*)
    c) velar assimilation (/gɔg/ for *dog*)
    d) prevocalic voicing and final consonant devoicing (/bIg/ for *pig;* /pIk/ for *pig*)
    e) manner harmony (/nImI/ for *swimming*)
    f) syllable harmony (/wɑwɑ/ for *water*)

3. Feature contrast processes
    a) stopping (/tʌn/ for *sun*)
    b) affrication (/tʃu/ for *shoe*)

c) fronting (/tar/ for *car*)
d) gliding of fricatives (/wɪʃ/ for *fish*)
e) gliding of liquids (/wʌn/ for *run*)
f) vocalization (/lɪto/ for *little*)
g) denasalization (/doz/ for *nose*)
h) neutralization (a number of different sounds are replaced by one sound, such as /d/ for all stops)

Administration time for the complete list is approximately 45 minutes with a cooperative child, with little additional time needed for analysis, since stimulus words are grouped according to the author's phonological processes.

Natural Process Analysis (NPA) (Shriberg and Kwiatkowski, 1980) also focuses on rule-ordered deviations. It is a further departure from traditional articulation testing in that it utilizes a sample of continuous speech for phonological analysis rather than a test-generated sample. Eight phenomena are identified as natural processes that frequently occur in the samples of speech-impaired preschoolers and school-age children. Five processes are identical to those identified by Weiner. These are final consonant deletion, stopping, cluster reduction, unstressed syllable deletion, and liquid simplification (gliding). Weiner's "fronting" category is divided into velar fronting (/tæt/ for *cat*) and palatal fronting (/si/ for *she*) in NPA. Also distinguished in NPA (but counted as one process) are regressive assimilation (/gɔg/ for *dog*) and progressive assimilation (/dɔd/ for *dog*).

Other deviations are noted but not included in the analysis. Detailed guidelines are provided for sampling and transcribing connected speech and for interpreting observed process deviations from standard productions. Analysis includes attention to syllable configuration and contextual influence. Measures of reliability are provided, and a discussion of construct and predictive validity is included. The authors find that experienced clinicians can transcribe a 200-word sample in approximately 50 minutes, with another 50 minutes spent completing analysis. This seems to be fairly efficient for the amount of information that is obtained from the sample.

Ingram (1981) has recently extended his original list of phonological processes identified in normal phonological development (Ingram, 1976; see our Chapter 4) to include procedures for analysis of deviant phonology. Sampling is either through use of an articulation test or language sample. The entire elicited lexicon is then listed in alphabetical order and transcribed phonetically to show variations in production of the same word. From this list, the child's repertoire of sounds and syllable configurations is summarized. The analysis also includes identifying the phonological processes accounting for deviations from adult forms. Ingram lists twenty-seven types of phonological processes. In general, these are the same procedures described by Weiner and by Shriberg and Kwiatkowski, but with more detailed distinctions. For example, Ingram divides "deletion of final consonants" into consonant type, including separate processes for deletion of nasals, voiced stops, voiceless stops, voiced fricatives, and voiceless fricatives. Table 10.2 is a comparison of the processes analyzed by Ingram with

Table 10.2 Patterns Identified for Phonological Analysis with Four Different Systems[a]

LUND & DUCHAN	PPA	NPA	INGRAM
Substitutions	Feature Contrasts		
Place features			
fronting	fronting	velar fronting	velar fronting
		palatal fronting	palatal fronting
backing			
alveolarizing			
etc.	glottal replacement		apicalization
Manner features			
stopping	stopping	stopping	stopping
			initial fricatives
			initial affricates
frication			
nasalization	denasalization		denasalization
affrication	affrication		deaffrication
gliding	gliding	liquid simplification	liquid gliding
vocalization	vocalization		vocalization
Voicing features			
voicing			
devoicing			
Position + feature			
Context Sensitive	Harmony		
Assimilation	Assimilation	Assimilation	Assimilation
perseverative	velar	progressive	velar
anticipatory	labial	regressive	labial
bidirectional	alveolar		prevocalic
	prevocalic voice		devoicing final C.
	final C. devoice		
	manner harmony		
Coalescence			
Syllable Structure			
Coalescence			
Weak syl. delet.	Weak syl. delet.	Unstressed syl. delet.	Unstressed syl. delet.
Reduplication	Syllable harmony		Reduplication
Restricted syllable			
CV structure			reduction of disyllab.
final C. deletion	final C. deletion	final C. deletion	final C. deletion
Cluster reduction	Cluster reduction	Cluster reduction	Cluster reduction
Syllable addition			
Transposition			

[a] See text for description of systems.

Phonological Process Analysis (Weiner, 1979), Natural Process Analysis (Shriberg and Kwiatkowski, 1980), and the processes described in Chapter 4 of this book. A unique feature of Ingram's system is analysis of homonymy. He defines a homonymous form as a phonetic form of the child's that represents two or more lexical types (Ingram, 1981, p. 45). For example, a child's homonymous form /dɔ/ may mean *dog, call,* and *talk.* This analysis leads the clinician to determine the extent of homonomy in a child's language.

Assessment of Morphology

Most tests that assess morphology also sample syntax. The morphology tests are directed specifically at describing a child's use of particular grammatical morphemes.

The *Berry-Talbott Test of Grammar* (Berry and Talbott, 1966) was derived from Berko's (1958) classic investigation of children's morphological rules through use of nonsense words on her "wug" test which was never commercially available. Each nonsense word is associated with a unique picture representation, and the appropriate grammatical morpheme is solicited with items such as "This is a kubash. Now there are two of them. There are two _____?" In this manner, plural and possessive nouns, third person singular, progressive and past tense verbs, and comparative and superlative adjectives are tested. Although this is identified as a comprehension test, all items require verbal production. This is not a norm-referenced test, so its usefulness comes from analyzing specific items. While Berko's original use of nonsense words for her research had important theoretical implication, it is questionable whether this unique format is advantageous for describing individual children's morphology (e.g., Dever, 1972).

The *Michigan Picture Language Inventory,* as developed by Lerea (1958) and revised by Wolski (1962), was intended to serve as a ranking test for vocabulary and grammatical structures, but we feel its usefulness lies in some of the subtests for sampling morphology. The manual directs the clinician to use the pictures to test comprehension only if the child fails an item expressively, but this restriction need not be followed if this is not used as a normative measure. The morphemes tested are not extensive but include plural and possessive nouns, articles, adjectives, adverbs, personal pronouns, demonstratives, prepositions, and progressive, present, and past tense verbs, and *will* modal. Each morpheme is tested several times, which makes it useful in identifying patterns. The format of the test may help clinicians develop some original items for deep testing particular forms.

Syntax-Morphology Assessment

Children's ability to use syntactic rules to produce word combinations can be meaningfully described only through analyzing their connected speech. The two most common approaches to getting such a sample are through *elicited imitation* and *spontaneous discourse.* There are advantages and limitations to both sampling techniques, as we will discuss.

ELICITED IMITATION FOR ASSESSMENT OF SYNTAX   Elicited imitation refers to a sampling procedure in which the child is instructed to imitate a model, as distinct from analysis of child-initiated imitation. The assumption behind using elicited imitation to assess expressive language is that it is an efficient and valid means for sampling the child's grammatical performance. It is efficient because sentences can be formulated to contain all grammatical structures of interest to the examiner, including those that may occur only infrequently in spontaneous discourse. The assumption of validity is based on research findings of Menyuk (1963) and Ervin (1964) among others that a child's imitations of sentences will closely resemble the manner in which the child would spontaneously produce those sentences—that is, in general, children cannot imitate structures in sentences that they would not ordinarily use, but instead reformulate the sentences to fit their grammatical capabilities. The primary limitation of elicited imitation tasks for syntax assessment lies in the exceptions to this generalization. Some children can imitate accurately certain grammatical structures that they cannot use spontaneously, particularly if the model sentence is short or if the child is inclined to echo adult utterances. There are also children who are unable to imitate utterances which they are capable of producing spontaneously. This could be described as due to difficulty with "auditory processing" (Weiner, 1972), but it also demonstrates that the speech act of imitation is different from speaking spontaneously. Slobin and Welsh (1973) describe a child's inability to imitate her own spontaneously produced utterance at a later point in time when the situation is no longer appropriate for the utterance. Thus, while imitation tasks can provide an efficient way to sample many structures, they may overestimate or underestimate some children's grammatical capabilities.

When results are interpreted with some caution, sentence imitation tasks can be useful for describing many children's syntactic production. They can also provide some indication of comprehension deficit, since children cannot maintain the meaning of a sentence in their reformulation if they do not understand it. For example, if in response to the model "The girl is pushed by the boy" the child responds "Girl push boy," it appears that the passive form of the verb is not understood. Of course, we cannot be sure how the child is conceptualizing the actual event related to "Girl push boy" (i.e., who is pushing whom), but it gives a clue to possible misunderstanding of the syntactic construction presented.

While there are some sets of sentences available that are widely used for elicited imitation, such as those presented by Menyuk (1963) and Carrow (1974, see the following), it is possible to construct original lists to test all structures of interest to individual clinicians, as we have suggested in Chapter 6. Since the primary purpose of such assessment is to describe a child's regularities, it is best to sample each structure more than once. Several structures can be sampled in each sentence to keep the number of sentences to a minimum. Vocabulary, of course, should be well within the range of the child being assessed to eliminate confusion on those grounds. These criteria of completeness, multiple occurrence of structures, and simplicity of vocabulary can also be used to evaluate published sentence imitation tests.

The *Carrow Elicited Language Inventory* (CELI) (Carrow, 1974) consists of 1 phrase and 51 sentences, ranging in length from 2 to 10 words. It samples primarily simple clause structures; a few subordinate clauses are included, but there are no coordinate or relative clauses. Negatives, wh- questions, imperatives, pronouns, prepositions, and various types of noun phrases are sampled. Plural (but not possessive) noun inflection is included, and verb inflections are extensively covered. Uninflected adjectives and adverbs are included.

An elaborate scoring procedure is presented in the CELI manual, along with a training guide and tape to facilitate accuracy of scoring. If the test is to be scored for normative purposes, it is necessary to undergo this training because of the unique categorization and scoring conventions used, some of which seem of questionable accuracy. When it is used to describe regularities of production, clinicians can derive their own categories for reporting results.

The *Oral Language Sentence Imitation Screening Test* (OLSIST) and the *Oral Language Sentence Imitation Diagnostic Inventory* (OLSIDI), both developed by Zachman, Huisingh, Jorgensen, and Barrett (1977) are two complementary tests that use imitation for assessment of syntax. Although the goal of the screening version as described is to ascertain normalcy of function, it is not norm referenced and should not be used for this purpose. It is useful, however, in identifying particular structures that are difficult for the child, through use of 20 sentences that include multiple occurrences of 18 to 23 different morphological and syntactic forms, depending upon the language level of the child. The diagnostic test is designed as a deep test for those structures missed on the screening version. It is composed of 27 individual sentence imitation tests, each with 10 sentences containing a particular structure.

SPONTANEOUS DISCOURSE FOR SYNTAX ASSESSMENT   Spontaneous discourse refers to utterances that occur when interacting with another person in a conversational manner. It excludes performance on tests or elicited imitation. This method of assessing children's language has come into favor in recent years because it is seen as providing the most relevant kind of information about children's language production. The disadvantage of relying on discourse for assessment of syntax lies in the amount of time required for all structures to emerge spontaneously. Also, the skill and experience of the adult interacting with the child have a great influence on the richness of the sample obtained. We have discussed some approaches to eliciting discourse in Chapter 2, Structural Analysis. Here we will comment briefly on some systems for describing syntax based on spontaneous discourse. The specific structures assessed by each system, including the structural categories outlined in this book, are compared in Table 10.3.

The *Developmental Sentence Types* (DST), described by Lee (1966, 1974) and followed by *Developmental Sentence Scoring* (DSS) (Lee and Canter, 1971; Lee, 1974), was the first widely used approach to analysis of spontaneous discourse. DST is based on 100 utterances and is used primarily to classify "presentence" utterances according to the grammatical relationship between the words produced. It distinguishes between noun phrases, clauses with lexical verbs, clauses with copulas implied, and "fragments" that have no subject or verb, such as prepositional phrases. Morphological inflections and some syntactic features are noted as elaborations and modifications of basic sentence types. Since this is intended to be a descriptive measure rather than normative, Lee encourages clinicians "to modify, enlarge or simplify the DST procedure in any way that is appropriate to their needs" (Lee, 1974, p. 131).

The DSS analysis is based on 50 consecutive utterances that contain a subject and verb, thus qualifying as sentences. Scores are assigned for each

Table 10.3 Comparison of Grammatical Structures Analyzed Using Different Language Sample Analysis Procedures

STRUCTURE	LARSP	LSAT	DSS	L&D
Noun Phrase Structure				
Articles	+	+	−	+
Demonstratives	+	+	+	+
Possessives	−	+	−	+
Adjectives	+	+	−	+
Qualifiers	G	G	+	+
Quantifiers	G	+	+	+
Ordinals	G	G	+	+
Initiators		G	−	+
Pronouns		+	+	+
Subject	G	G	+	+
Object	G	G	+	+
Possessive	G	G	+	+
Reflexive	G	G	+	+
Indefinite	G	G	+	+
Verb Phrase Structure				
Verb	+	+	+	+
Copula	+	+	+	+
Auxiliaries	+	+	+	+
Modals	+	+	+	+
Particles	+	+	−	+
Irregular past tense	+	+	+	+
Regular past tense	+	+	+	+
Present participle	+	+	+	+
Past participle	+	+	+	+
Third person singular indicative	+	+	+	+
Passive	+	−	+	+
Questions	+	+	+	+
Rising intonation	−	G	−	+
Auxiliary inversion	+	G	+	+
Do insertion	−	G	+	+
Tags	+	G	+	+
Wh- questions	+	G	+	+
Negatives	+	+	+	+
Simple Clause Structure	+	+	−	+
Complex Clauses				
Compound	+	+	+	+
Subordinate	+	+	+	+
Relative	+	+	−	+
Other	+	+	G	G
Other Parts of Speech				
Prepositions	−	+	−	+
Adverbs	+	+	−	+
Gerunds, Infinitives	−	+	+	G

Note: + means system analyzes this feature.
     − means system does not analyze this feature.
     G means system does not specify this feature but covers general area.

pronoun, verb, negative, question, and conjunction used, with the size of the score depending on the identified developmental sequence within each category. Many morphological and syntactic forms are thus not scored. Total score can be compared to norms presented or compared on subsequent analysis to assess progress over time. In view of the considerable time and training involved in using this procedure, analysis beyond derived scores would be warranted. DSS uses standard dialect for the criterion for correctness of production, and Lee cautions against using this analysis with children who come from other language backgrounds.

The *Language Sampling, Analysis, and Training* procedure described by Tyack and Gottsleben (1974) relies on a 100-sentence sample of spontaneous speech. The child is assigned a "linguistic level" based on a ratio of mean number of words to mean number of morphemes per sentence. For each level, there is an inventory of grammatical features that according to the authors should be expected for children at or above that level. The data for this assignment of grammatical features to various levels come from a study of 15 normal and 15 language-deviant children (Morehead and Ingram, 1973) and should not be interpreted as a standardized measure. Various types of clause structures are included in analysis, as well as negatives, questions, pronouns, prepositions, and conjunctions. Noun and verb inflections are thoroughly covered. As the title implies, the analysis portion of this procedure is designed to lead directly to identification of therapy goals and training, which is touched upon in the manual.

The *Language Assessment, Remediation, and Screening Procedure* (LARSP) described by Crystal, Fletcher, and Garman (1976) takes a more comprehensive view of syntax than the other systems discussed. It is based on a structural linguistic model of syntax which is thoroughly described and is in many ways similar to our description of syntactic structures. They identify seven stages of syntactic development corresponding to chronological age (9 months to 4.6+ years) and describe the syntactic characteristics of each stage. Analysis of structures present and absent at the child's age level leads to remediation goals. Assignment of particular features to the various levels is based on the literature in developmental psycholinguistics and apparently the authors' experience with this assessment procedure. Several "patterns" of language disabilities are discussed that correspond to profiles obtained from the LARSP, but no normative data are presented, since the emphasis is on describing individual children's regularities.

Assessment of Semantics

SPECIFIC VOCABULARY ASSESSMENT   These tests may be identified as "conceptual domain" tests, since the vocabulary assessed is associated with specific conceptual categories. The tests are not intended to provide a measure of general vocabulary functioning, and although they present some normative data for comparison, they are more useful for identifying specific problems than for answering the question of establishing normalcy. Thus their general deficiency in meeting standardization criteria is not a problem.

The *Boehm Test of Basic Concepts* (Boehm, 1971) includes 50 vocabulary items in the categories of space, quantity, and time, along with a miscellaneous category, that are typically used in work materials for kindergarten children. Comprehension of individual words is tested by having the child choose from a set of pictures with items arranged developmentally. Each item is tested only once, so clinicians will want to follow up this test with deep testing of items missed. Although the manual identifies the items as useful for a population of kindergarten to second grade children, many of the items would be appropriate for use with preschoolers. There are two equivalent forms of the Boehm and also Spanish directions for each form available.

The *Vocabulary Comprehension Scale* (Bangs, 1975) has the unique feature of assessing vocabulary comprehension through use of toy objects (which are included) rather than pictures. The vocabulary items test for the concepts of spatial relations, size quantity, and quality, and also for personal pronouns. As with the Boehm, there is only one item for testing each word, so follow-up assessment would be necessary for items.

The *McCarthy Scales of Children's Ability* (MSCA) (McCarthy, 1970) has several subtests in its verbal scale that can be useful in assessing children's semantic knowledge. In particular, there are the following:

> Word knowledge: In part 1 of this subtest, children point to 5 common objects and name 4 pictured objects. In part 2, they define words.
>
> Verbal memory: Part 2 of this subtest has children relate the highlights of a paragraph read to them and thus demonstrate awareness of theme as well as semantics.
>
> Verbal fluency: Children must name words that fall into each of 4 different categories within a time limit.
>
> Opposite analogies: Children provide opposites in an analogy form.

The MSCA is designed for children from 2½ to 8½ years of age. It is norm referenced if the entire scale is used, but no norms are available for individual subtests, which is not a problem when used to assess regularities.

The *Wechsler Intelligence Scale for Children–Revised* (WISC-R) (Wechsler, 1974) and the *Wechsler Preschool and Primary Scale of Intelligence* (WPPSI) (Wechsler, 1967)—these scales sample similar behaviors but are intended for different age groups. The WPPSI is used with children from 4 to 6½ years of age, and the WISC-R with 6 to 16 year olds. The verbal subtests include

> Comprehension: This subtest assesses ability to understand specific customs and mores as well as verbal directions.
>
> Similarities: Items require identification of similarities in verbal stimuli.
>
> Vocabulary: The child is required to define words.

The *Detroit Tests of Learning Aptitude* (DTLA) (Baker and Leland, 1967) were developed from a behavioral model of language that analyzes language in terms of stimuli and responses and equates meaning with association. While there has been a general move away from this model, some of the subtests of the DTLA can still be used profitably to sample aspects of children's semantic knowledge by structurally analyzing their responses rather than scoring them.

Subtests included in the DTLA have norms for children from ages 3 to 19 years and thus have a wide range of difficulty in the items. Not all subtests are appropriate for all ages. Some of the subtests that may be helpful in assessing semantics are

Verbal absurdities: There are 20 statements in this subtest, each consisting of 1 or 2 sentences. Each statement contains a contradiction which the child is to identify.

Verbal opposites: The examiner says each stimulus word and the child supplies its opposite. Words range from simple to difficult vocabulary.

Social adjustment: The child is asked a series of questions about social dilemmas in the first part of this subtest, which can demonstrate understanding how word meanings relate to each other. In the second portion, the child defines vocabulary related to the social environment.

Orientation: The child is asked questions that require space, time, age, and size concepts to answer correctly.

Free association: The child is to produce a run-on series of words within a given time period, with the time alloted depending on the age of the child.

Likeness and Differences: This subtest consists of 32 word pairs which are related in meaning, and the child is to describe how the members of the pair are similar and how they are different.

Semantic-Syntactic Relations

Bloom and Lahey (1978) present an extensive discussion of semantic-syntactic relations along with an assessment approach that coordinates semantic relations with syntactic structure. This approach, which is designed for analysis of spontaneous discourse, identifies 21 relations that have frequently been reported in the speech of children up to 3 years of age. The emergence of syntactic structures to express the various relations is tied to 8 developmental phases, which are based on MLU (phases 1–5) and successive samples of three children (phases 6–8). Assessment involves comparing the syntactic forms used by a child to express various relations with the description of the forms expected at the various phases. For example, attribution is described as occurring at successive phases with the following forms:

phase 1	single word	hot
phase 2	adjective + noun	dirty pants
phase 3	combined with existence relation	that's a yellow one
phase 4	combined with action relation	make a big tree

| phase 5 | combined with state relation | I got a new pair |
| phase 6 | combined with locative action relation | here goes a green wheel |

The child's failure to express particular relations can also be noted. The intent of assessment is not to determine normalcy, but rather to lead to an appropriate sequence of therapy goals.

The *Environmental Language Inventory* (ELI) (MacDonald, 1978) was the first test to emerge designed to assess regularities in children's use of semantic relations. It is designed to evaluate multiword utterances according to the presumed semantic roles. Eight semantic-grammatical rules, based on Schlesinger's (1971) position rules and Brown's (1973) early sentence types, are assessed.

1. agent + action
2. action + object
3. agent + object
4. agent or object + location
5. action + location
6. negation + X
7. modifier + head (attribution)
                          (possession)
                          (recurrence)
8. introducer + X

Description of these rules is included in the manual. The child's expression of each semantic relation is sampled three times for a total of 24 items. Each item consists of a nonlinguistic cue (object or event), a conversational cue (e.g., "What did I do?"), and an imitation cue (e.g., "Say, 'Kick big ball'"). The child is presented the conversation cue twice for each item, before and after the imitation cue. This manner of presentation is to provide the clinician with information regarding the child's stimulability through imitation. For diagnostic purposes, the imitation and second conversational cue are included only if the child does not respond to the first conversational cue with an expression of the intended rule. A sample of speech in free play is also recorded and scored for semantic relations expressed as well as several measures of utterance length and intelligibility. Analysis of assessment results determines goals for intervention, with suggested training procedures following a behavioral model of stimulus-response-consequence and the stimuli being the same nonlinguistic, conversational, and imitative cues used in assessment.

The ELI model of assessment and training focuses entirely on production. It is most appropriate for use with individuals with good receptive skills and expression limited to two- and three-word utterances. Before using this test, the examiner should be thoroughly familiar with semantic relations theory in order to understand the categories.

The *Assessment of Children's Language Comprehension* (ACLC) (Foster, Giddan, and Stark, 1973) was not formulated on a semantic relations model, but it can be interpreted within this framework. It was designed to assess children's comprehension of different word classes in various combinations of length and complexity. Although these word classes are identified as "critical elements," they could be analyzed according to their semantic roles of agents, actions, objects, locations, and attributes. The test is organized into four sections. Part A is a 50-item vocabulary test that serves as a pretest to assure that the child is familiar with the vocabulary used in the remaining sections. The remainder of the test presents combinations of two (part B), three (part C), and four (part D) critical elements for the child to interpret by choosing the right picture from several foils. Parts B, C, and D each have 10 items representing several semantic relations in each. Combinations appear to be selected somewhat arbitrarily and are sometimes agrammatical ("Show me 'on table'"). Performance can be evaluated either according to the length of the stimulus by comparing scores on each part or by analyzing patterns of error on each part.

Assessment of Cognitive Precursors to Language

In some situations, clinicians frequently see individuals who are not talking or are using only minimal speech. It is then useful to investigate some areas that may give indications of cognitive precursors to language and may be helpful in understanding the nature of the individual's interaction with the environment.

The *Environment Pre-Language Battery* (EPB) (Horstmeier and MacDonald, 1978) has a verbal and a nonverbal section and is intended for individuals with language skills at or below the one-word level. Prior to administration of this battery, the authors recommend completion of the *Oliver: Parent-Administered Communication Inventory* (MacDonald, 1978). With this, the parent provides comprehensive information about communication behaviors and typical activities at home. Based on this information and initial observation, a beginning level of assessment is selected. The nonverbal section of the EPB includes a brief history of sound production and observation of "preliminary skills" (attention, sitting, object permanence, gestures), along with tests of functional play with objects, motor imitation, identifying objects, understanding action verbs, identifying pictures, and following directions. Each of these tests has four items. If response to any item is not correct, the adult first models and then physically assists the child to perform it correctly, and then the child repeats the item without assistance. This is to assess response to this training procedure. Points are assigned for each item and totaled to give a pass, not pass, or "emerging" designation for each test. Tests are supposedly arranged developmentally so that if two consecutive tests are not passed, testing is discontinued on the assumption that subsequent tests would also not be passed. Tests in the verbal section are likewise constructed and scored and include sound, single-word, and two-word phrase imitation and spontaneous production. Scores on the EPB are designed to indicate the level at which to begin intervention or to evaluate change over time. They are not normative scores.

In *Assessment in Infancy* (1975), Uzgiris and Hunt present six assessment scales based on Piaget's descriptions of the sensorimotor period of development. Each scale tests for a certain area of sensorimotor performance by eliciting specific behaviors that demonstrate cognitive functioning in that area. For example, in the scale entitled "Visual Pursuit and the Permanence of Objects," a beginning task is to observe the child's reaction to a moving object. Low-ranking performance on this task is for the child not to follow the object; high-ranking performance is to follow it visually through its 180 degree arc. This particular scale progresses from this primitive task to the advanced level of finding an object which has been seen hidden several times. Good performance on the hidden-object task is to search for it in the reverse order of the hiding sequence (i.e., looking in the last place the object was hidden, then the next to last, and so on).

The six scales are:

Scale 1: Visual Pursuit and the Permanence of Objects
Scale 2: Means for Obtaining Desired Environmental Events
Scale 3a: Vocal Imitation
Scale 3b: Gestural Imitation
Scale 4: Operational Causality
Scale 5: Construction of Object Relations in Space
Scale 6: The Development of Schemes Relating to Objects

The scales are not scored, but behaviors are arranged developmentally within each. Use of these scales can help the clinician to structure observation of the nonverbal child; and, while it has not been demonstrated that a given level of cognitive development is necessary for the acquisition of language, some of the scales have been found to be particularly useful in predicting readiness for language (e.g., Bates, 1976; Chapman and Miller, 1980).

REPORTING ASSESSMENT FINDINGS

The diagnostician's view of language determines the assessment procedure chosen and the type of observations made and thus is reflected in the information that goes into the diagnostic report. We began this book by posing five assessment questions.

1. Does this child have a language problem?
2. What is causing the problem?
3. What are the areas of deficit?
4. What are the regularities in the child's language performance?
5. What is recommended for this child?

While a report may address each of the five assessment questions, there generally is an emphasis that corresponds to the kind of information that is viewed as most central to assessment. A report that consists primarily of test scores and normative measures reflects the clinician's view that language assessment is documenting deviation from norms. Some reports are primarily extensive and detailed case history reviews, revealing the diagnostician's bias for an etiological model of language disorders—that is, finding the cause of the problem is central to their assessment. Reports that are organized in sections that correspond to areas of deficit identify the areas that are salient for the clinician.

The clinician that is trained in doing structural analysis emphasizes the child's regularities when reporting assessment findings. The goal is to make observations from which the child's behavior can be predicted and intervention can be planned. Areas of deficit may be identified, but only as a summary of the pattern of errors noted, not as an unsupported generalization. The deficit area or areas that are described will depend on the patterns presented by the individual child. The report will include specific recommendations for further analysis and for intervention goals. Interviews with the child's caregivers are likely to focus more on the child's present status than on past events. History and other kinds of information are not excluded from the reports, but information is emphasized which is relevant to the question of the child's language regularities and relates to planning intervention.

When tests are used in assessment, their purpose is clearly specified in the report. Tests are chosen carefully for the kind of information they can provide, and their limitations are recognized.

As you have progressed through the chapters of this book, you have become prepared to write assessment reports that reflect your structural analysis of various aspects of language. You have acquired the terminology and concepts basic to each area, and you are equipped to go beyond the specific structures presented to find your own patterns and transmit the valuable information you have gathered for planning and evaluating the effectiveness of intervention. Appendix A contains excerpts from reports we or our students have written that reflect our structuralist orientation. Your reports will not sound the same because your observations will be different, but seeing how various kinds of language problems have been described may be helpful as you develop your own style.

EXERCISES

1. It is often difficult for clinicians to know what information should be included in a diagnostic report. We find it helpful to think in terms of our five assessment questions when reading and writing reports. It then becomes clear when there is information missing or when something has been unnecessarily included. The following report was written by a student clinician. As you read it, try to decide the purpose for including the information it contains. Rewrite the report, putting all the information under one of the following headings depending upon the question it is directed toward answering.
    a) Is there a language problem?
    b) What condition(s) causes the language problem?
    c) What are the areas of deficit?
    d) What are the regularities in the child's language performance?
    e) What are the recommendations?

Also look for

    a) Identifying information
    b) Other information that should be included
    c) Other information that it is not necessary to include

Name: Nathan Smith
Age: 3.6

HISTORY

Nathan was a full-term baby with no complications during or after birth.

Nathan sat up and crawled during his ninth month. He is not yet toilet trained, but "nearly so." There are no bed-wetting problems. He has a tendency to cry in his sleep, but this behavior is diminishing. He is unable to suck out of a straw.

At 10 months of age, Nathan was hospitalized with whooping cough. He has also had croup and bronchitis. No other physical problems were noted.

DESCRIPTION OF PRESENT STATUS

Nathan was described by his mother as shy and insecure with strangers and tending to be possessive of people. She feels his fear of being left alone is a result of his earlier stay at the hospital.

Punishment is handled by both parents and consists of spanking or having him sit in a chair. Nathan is very close to his grandfather, and has been "spoiled" by his grandmother in his mother's opinion. Mrs. Smith reports that she works on speech with Nathan, but that her husband lacks the patience to do so. She reported that there is tension in the home at times.

Mrs. Smith feels Nathan's language is moderately delayed. Family and friends are able to understand him, but strangers have problems. She estimated his expressive vocabulary to be approximately ten words. He is able to count to three or four. He cannot say his name, nursery rhymes, or the alphabet. He responds to his name, *no,* and simple directions. He is able to identify simple pictures and animals.

LANGUAGE ASSESSMENT

    a) Utah Language Development Scale:
       Results indicate a language age of 3 years.
    b) Language Sample:
       Nathan used one-word utterances and echoic responses.
       He also used question intonation.
    c) Peabody Picture Vocabulary Test:
       Nathan's raw score was 26, placing him in the 20th percentile for his chronological age.

HEARING

Nathan would not wear the earphones. He was able to respond to a whispered voice.

IMPRESSIONS

At age 3.6, Nathan exhibits a mild delay in language.

RECOMMENDATIONS

It is recommended that Nathan be enrolled in language therapy. Preparation for further audiometric testing should be pursued.

---

2. The following sample contains portions of a report which was written by a clinician trained in doing structural analysis. Indicate the question or questions from exercise 1 that each italicized segment addresses.

Name: Nathan Smith
Age: 3.6

REASON FOR EVALUATION

This speech and language evaluation was requested by Nathan's mother who [1]*feels that Nathan's language is moderately delayed.*

DESCRIPTION OF PRESENT STATUS

Information was provided by Mrs. Smith prior to this evaluation through responses to a questionnaire sent to her home and also through an interview at the time of evaluation. [2]*She describes Nathan as having approximately a ten-word expressive vocabulary, including family names* (mama, dad, /titi/ sister, no, /m/ more, /wu/ all done). [3]*She reports he will count to three or four when started on the sequence, but otherwise has no connected words.* He frequently repeats a single word from an utterance directed to him (e.g., A: That's a tomato. N: mato). Mrs. Smith indicated that Nathan responds to his name and to *no* as a reprimand. [4]*He will carry out simple, frequently used directions, such as "Go get your shoes."* He will point to pictures in books when asked "Where's the X?" Mrs. Smith reports that Nathan plays with toy vehicles in appropriate ways and while making car noises. He also likes to watch "Sesame Street" for up to an hour. He has shown little interest in books or puzzles on his own, but likes it when his older sister reads to him or plays with puzzles or takes apart toys with him.

[5]*Nathan lives with his mother and father and sister Cara, age 6 years.* His maternal grandparents live in the neighborhood. Mrs. Smith described him as very close to his grandfather. Both grandparents and the immediate family generally understand Nathan's speech, but most other people have difficulty. Nathan was described as shy and insecure with strangers.

LANGUAGE ASSESSMENT

[6]*Nathan was observed initially with his mother prior to meeting the examiner. Mrs. Smith was asked to interact normally with Nathan for a few minutes while they were observed through a one-way mirror.* She had brought some of Nathan's toys from home, as requested. Other toys were also available. During this observation, which was approximately ten minutes, [7]*Nathan was observed to frequently point to toys, or hold them up to show his mother, with the gestures accompanied by similar vocalizations, generally /di/ or /si/.* When used with question intonation, this seemed to be a request for a name, and Mrs. Smith usually responded by naming the object. The same syllable with downward inflection appeared to be an attempt to direct attention to an object, but this was not usually successful.

[8]*A few identifiable words were heard: /ka/ for car;* moo *for cow; /fa daU/ for* fall down; mama *was used frequently to get attention;* yup *and* nope *in response to yes-no questions.*

(Description of language continues)

EVIDENCE FOR CAUSE OF PROBLEM

There is nothing in Nathan's history that points to a cause of language disorder. His mother feels he is shy, possibly due to a hospitalization at age 10 months, but he interacted readily with the examiner. [9]*Although there was an early history of upper respiratory problems, his health in the last two years has been good.* Hearing was checked informally, as Nathan resisted wearing earphones. Further testing will be done, but hearing appears to be adequate to acquire language.

IMPRESSIONS

[10]*Nathan has a limited repertoire of expressive vocabulary, syntactic structure, and phonology.* His utterances are primarily single or reduplicated syllables with a variety of consonants used initially. His comprehension of single words appears to be adequate, but understanding of connected speech may be somewhat delayed.

RECOMMENDATIONS

1. Further evaluation of Nathan's comprehension of connected speech is indicated. This should include structured observation of naturalistic situations to analyze his reliance on contextual cues. Administration of a broad-based language comprehension test is also recommended.

2. Nathan should be provided with models for questions and requests, such as ''What's that?'' ''Look,'' ''Give me X.'' These models should be used in context.

(Recommendations continue)

3. Compare the reports in exercises 1 and 2 in terms of their helpfulness to the clinician planning therapy. Indicate for each the information that is not included that you want before beginning therapy.

4. Take a report from your clinical files and try to reorganize it in terms of the five diagnostic questions.

REFERENCES

ANDERSON, R., M. MILES, AND P. MATHENY. *Communicative Evaluation Chart.* Golden, Colo.: Business Forms, Inc., 1963.

BAKER, H., AND B. LELAND. *Detroit Tests of Learning Aptitudes.* Indianapolis, Ind.: Bobbs-Merrill, 1967.

BANGS, T. *Vocabulary Comprehension Scale.* Boston, Mass.: Teaching Resources Corporation, 1975.

BANKSON, N. *Bankson Language Screening Test.* Baltimore, Md.: University Park Press, 1977.

BATES, E. *Language and Context: The Acquisition of Pragmatics.* New York: Academic Press, 1976.

BERKO, J.   The Child's Learning of English Morphology, *Word,* 14, 1958, 150–77.

BERRY, M., AND R. TALBOTT. *Exploratory Test of Grammar.* Rockford, Ill., 1966.

BLOOM, L., AND M. LAHEY. *Language Development and Language Disorders.* New York: John Wiley, 1978.

BOEHM, A.   *Boehm Test of Basic Concepts.* New York: The Psychological Corporation, 1971.

BROWN, R.   *A First Language: The Early Stages.* Cambridge, Mass.: Harvard University Press, 1973.

BZOCH, K., AND R. LEAGUE. *Receptive-Expressive Language Scale.* Gainesville, Fla.: The Tree of Life Press, 1971.

CARROW, E.   *Test for Auditory Comprehension of Language.* Boston, Mass.: Teaching Resources Corporation, 1973.

CARROW, E.   *Carrow Elicited Language Inventory.* Austin, Tex.: Learning Concepts, 1974.

CHAPMAN R., AND J. MILLER.   Analyzing Language and Communication in the Child, in *Nonspeech Language Intervention,* ed. R. Schiefelbusch. Baltimore, Md.: University Park Press, 1980.

CRABTREE, M.   *The Houston Test for Language Development.* Houston, Tex.: The Houston Test Co., 1963.

CRONBACH, L.   *Essentials of Psychological Testing.* New York: Harper & Row, Pub., 1970.

CRYSTAL, D., P. FLETCHER, AND M. GARMAN.   *The Grammatical Analysis of Language Disability: A Procedure for Assessment and Remediation.* London: Edward Arnold, 1976.

DARLEY, F.   *Evaluation of Appraisal Techniques in Speech and Language Pathology.* Reading, Mass.: Addison-Wesley, 1979.

DEVER, R. A.   A Comparison of the Results of a Revised Version of Berko's Test of Morphology with the Free Speech of Mentally Retarded Children, *Journal of Speech and Hearing Research,* 15, 1972, 169–78.

DUCHAN, J.   The Elephant Is Soft and Mushy: Problems in Assessing Children's Language, in *Speech, Language and Hearing,* eds. N. Lass, L. McReynolds, J. Northern, and D. Yoder. Philadelphia: W. B. Saunders, 1982.

DUNN, L.   *Peabody Picture Vocabulary Test.* Circle Pines, Minn.: American Guidance Service, 1965.

DUNN, L. AND L. DUNN. *Peabody Picture Vocabulary Test–Revised (PPVT).* Circle Pines, Minn.: American Guidance Service, 1981.

ERVIN, S.   Imitation and Structural Change in Children's Language, in *New Directions in the Study of Language,* ed. E. Lenneberg. Cambridge, Mass.: The M.I.T. Press, 1964.

FISHER, H., AND J. LOGEMANN. *The Fisher-Logemann Test of Articulation Competence.* Boston, Mass.: Houghton Mifflin, 1971.

FLUHARTY, N.   *Fluharty Preschool Speech and Language Screening Test.* Hingham, Mass.: Teaching Resources, 1978.

FOSTER, R., J. GIDDAN, AND J. STARK. *Assessment of Children's Language Comprehension.* Austin, Tex.: Learning Concepts, 1973.

FRANKENBURG, W., AND OTHERS. *Denver Developmental Screening Test.* Denver, Colo.: LADOCA Project and Publishers Foundation, Inc., 1975.

GOLDMAN, R., AND M. FRISTOE. *Goldman-Fristoe Test of Articulation.* Circle Pines, Minn.: American Guidance Service, Inc., 1972.

HEDRICK, D., E. PRATHER, AND A. TOBIN. *Sequenced Inventory of Communication Development.* Seattle, Wash.: University of Washington Press, 1975.

HORSTMEIER, D., AND J. MACDONALD. *Environmental Pre-Language Battery.* Columbus, Ohio: Chas. E. Merrill, 1978.

HUIZINGA, R., The Relationship of the ITPA to the Stanford-Binet Form L-M and the WISC, *Journal of Learning Disabilities,* 6, 1973, 53–58.

INGRAM, D. *Phonological Disabilities in Children.* New York: Elsevier, 1976.

INGRAM, D. *Procedures for the Phonological Analysis of Children's Language.* Baltimore, Md.: University Park Press, 1981.

KIRK, S., J. MCCARTHY, AND W. KIRK. *The Illinois Test of Psycholinguistic Abilities* (rev. ed.). Urbana, Ill.: University of Illinois Press, 1968.

LARSON, G. W., AND P. A. SUMMERS. Response Patterns of Pre-School-Age Children to the Northwestern Syntax Screening Test, *Journal of Speech and Hearing Disorders,* 41, 1976, 486–97.

LEE, L. Developmental Sentence Types: A Method for Comparing Normal and Deviant Syntactic Development, *Journal of Speech and Hearing Disorders,* 31, 1966, 311–30.

LEE, L. *Northwestern Syntax Screening Test.* Evanston, Ill.: Northwestern University Press, 1971.

LEE, L. *Developmental Sentence Analysis.* Evanston, Ill.: Northwestern University Press, 1974.

LEE, L. Reply to Arndt and Byrne, *Journal of Speech and Hearing Disorders,* 42, 1977, 323–27.

LEE, L., AND S. CANTER. Developmental Sentence Scoring: A Clinical Procedure for Estimating Syntactic Development in Children's Spontaneous Speech, *Journal of Speech and Hearing Disorders,* 36, 1971, 315–41.

LEREA, L. Assessing Language Development, *Journal of Speech and Hearing Research,* 1, 1958, 75–85.

MCCARTHY, D. *McCarthy Scales of Children's Abilities.* New York: Psychological Corporation, 1970.

MCDONALD, E. *A Deep Test of Articulation.* Pittsburgh, Pa.: Stanwix House, Inc., 1964.

MACDONALD, J. D. *The Environmental Language Inventory.* Columbus, Ohio: Chas. E. Merrill, 1978.

MARDELL, D., AND D. GOLDENBERG. *DIAL: Developmental Indicators for Assessment of Learning.* Highland Park, Ill.: DIAL, Inc., 1975.

MECHAM, M. *Verbal Language Development Scale.* Circle Pines, Minn.: American Guidance Service, 1971.

MECHAM, M., J. JEX, AND J. JONES. *Utah Test of Language Development.* Salt Lake City, Utah.: Communication Research Associates, 1963.

MENYUK, P. A Preliminary Evaluation of Grammatical Capacity in Children, *Journal of Verbal Learning and Verbal Behavior,* 2, 1963, 429–39.

MOREHEAD, D., AND D. INGRAM. The Development of Base Syntax in Normal and Linguistically Deviant Children, *Journal of Speech and Hearing Research,* 16, 1973, 330–52.

NEWCOMER, P., AND D. HAMMILL. *The Test of Language Development.* Austin, Tex.: Empire Press, 1977.

PRUTTING, C., T. GALLAGHER, AND A. MULAC.   The Expressive Portion of the N.S.S.T. Compared to a Spontaneous Language Sample, *Journal of Speech and Hearing Disorders,* 40, 1975, 40–48.

SALVIA, J., AND J. YSSELDYKE.   *Assessment in Special and Remedial Education.* Boston: Houghton Mifflin, 1978.

SCHLESINGER, I.   Production of Utterances and Language Acquisition, in *The Ontogenesis of Grammar,* ed. D. Slobin. New York: Academic Press, 1971.

SEMEL, E., AND E. WIIG.   *Clinical Evaluation of Language Functions.* Columbus, Ohio: Chas. E. Merrill, Pub. Co., 1980.

SIEGEL, G., AND P. BROEN.   Language Assessment, in *Communication Assessment and Intervention Strategies,* ed. L. Lloyd. Baltimore, Md.: University Park Press, 1976.

SHRIBERG, L., AND J. KWIATKOWSKI.   *Natural Process Analysis: A Procedure for Phonological Analysis of Continuous Speech Samples.* New York: John Wiley, 1980.

SLOBIN, D., AND C. WELSH.   Elicited Imitation as a Research Tool in Developmental Psycholinguistics, in *Studies in Child Language Development,* eds. C. Ferguson and D. Slobin. New York: Holt, Rinehart & Winston, 1973.

TEMPLIN, M., AND F. DARLEY.   *The Templin-Darley Tests of Articulation,* 2nd ed. Iowa City, Iowa: University of Iowa Bureau of Educational Research and Service, 1969.

TYACK, D., AND R. GOTTSLEBEN.   *Language Sampling, Analysis and Training: A Handbook for Teachers and Clinicians.* Palo Alto, Calif.: Consulting Psychologists Press, 1974.

UZGIRIS, I., AND J. McV. HUNT.   *Assessment in Infancy.* Urbana, Ill.: University of Illinois Press, 1975.

WECHSLER, D.   *Intelligence Scale for Children (WISC).* New York: Psychological Corporation, 1949.

WECHSLER, D.   *Preschool and Primary Scale of Intelligence (WIPSI).* New York: Psychological Corporation, 1967.

WECHSLER, D.   *Wechsler Intelligence Scale for Children—Revised.* New York: Psychological Corporation, 1974.

WEINER, F.   *Phonological Process Analysis.* Baltimore, Md.: University Park Press, 1979.

WEINER, P.   The Perceptual Level Functioning of Dysphasic Children: A Follow Up Study, *Journal of Speech and Hearing Research,* 15, 1972, 423–38.

WIIG E., AND E. SEMEL.   *Language Assessment and Intervention for the Learning Disabled.* Columbus, Ohio: Chas. E. Merrill Co., 1980.

WOLSKI, W.   *Michigan Picture Language Inventory.* Ann Arbor, Mich.: University of Michigan, 1962.

ZACHMAN, L., R. HUISINGH, C. JORGENSEN, AND M. BARRETT.   *The Oral Language Sentence Diagnostic Inventory.* Moline, Ill.: Linguisystems, Inc., 1977a.

ZACHMAN, L., R. HUISINGH, C. JORGENSEN, AND M. BARRETT.   *The Oral Language Sentence Imitation Screening Test.* Moline, Ill.: Linguisystems, Inc., 1977b.

ZIMMERMAN, I., V. STEINER, AND R. EVATT.   *Preschool Language Scale.* Columbus, Ohio: Chas. E. Merrill, 1969.

Appendix A

Sample Clinical Reports Based on Structural Analysis

The following are excerpts taken from assessment reports we have done that are based on structural analysis. We include them to show how the results of this analysis can be reported and how to report recommendations based on the analysis. You may find that the excerpts are different from the reports you are used to reading because they reflect a different methodology and report different kinds of information. Some of these descriptions are of structures which have not been discussed (dysfluency, intonation). They are mentioned to show how the methodology can be expanded to any domain.

DAVID

Dear Karen:

In response to your request that I see David, I have just spent three hours observing him in his classroom with his teacher and have watched him on videotape. I would like to report to you about how his language now appears to me and on some possible directions for future work with him.

I agree with you that he has made wonderful progress. The degree of progress is especially apparent when he is doing a familiar, but open-ended, activity which lacks a teaching-learning-performing tone. For example, he likes to dress and play with the Peabody plastic mannequin. In these free-flowing contexts, he used language naturally to achieve his ends, and he responds appropriately and with savvy.

In contrast, we all have observed David in his most autistic-like moods, where he is highly ritualized; his language sounds as if it proceeds through an imaginary script which may or may not relate to what is going on; it has an ethereal tone as if being spoken or sung in an echo chamber. These lack in productive quality and give one the feeling that he is singing a song he has heard before. This less normal use of language seems to occur in structured situations, in those with a pedogogical flavor, or when he is bored or upset.

David seems to use language in different ways: One to get himself things, another to reflect to himself what he is thinking, a third as an object to play with, a fourth as a vehicle for expressing emotions such as fear, frustration or anger, and a fifth as a way to interact with others. How wonderful to have such versatility; yet his and our problem with it is that he doesn't always use conventional ways to carry out these functions, so he fails to achieve what he sets out to do. For example, his requests are often phrases which he has heard used in relation to the activity he is requesting ("They're cutting the saw" meaning *"Can I saw?"; "The baby crying"* meaning *"Can I play with the pictures of the baby crying?").* People tend not to respond to these as if David were asking for something, so they fail to work for him as requests.

David's emotional expressions are often an issuance of a series of directives or reprimands which are probably delayed echoes (e.g., "Don't put your boogers in your mouth" or "Don't eat the playdough"). He uses them differently, sometimes as if threatening or teasing someone, other times as if a self-warning.

David's sound play has gotten wonderfully elaborate since I last saw him. He likes /r/ sounds, he plays with intonation, sings phrases, and breaks up words into syllable or sound units by placing a glottal stop between the sounds (e.g., "Where the bab.y cr.y.ing").

His language of thinking to himself is characterized by verbal free association of single words and phrases and is accompanied by a faraway look in his eyes. I think it is important that he use language in this way and, although it appears abnormal, I think he should be allowed to continue with it.

Finally, David's language used to interact with other people is usually a singsong response containing a sentence structure which sometimes does not seem productive or appropriate to the context David is working from.

LINDA

Linda functions best in the communicative context which she understands to have as its meaning something other than her ability to perform correctly or incorrectly. This is very important to consider in interacting with Linda because it appears that she has learned her negative experience about answering questions and labeling or matching items very well. Expressive language has proven dangerous for her. How sensitive she is to negative experiences can be seen in her severe regression with toilet training of three years' duration after a negative incident this summer. Linda will need to be convinced of the benefits of expressive language before she will use it extensively.

When Linda interprets the significance of the speech event to not be directed at her performance, and to be immediately relevant to both participants, Linda responds with appropriate gestures and signs, relatively smooth hand or body movements, and relaxed facial expression. If she interprets the significance of the speech event to be directed at her performance, she exhibits perseverative responses, immobile posturing, inappropriate staring and tears.

What qualities does a speech event need to have for Linda to perceive it as nonthreatening? The topic must obviously be of interest to the initiator and not just a question asked of Linda. It is interesting to note that what Linda has brought to me for inspection has been rocks, scraps of plastic, nuts and bolts from a cabinet. Toys do not hold as much interest for Linda as "real" objects. She also is genuinely interested in door handles, tape containers, water fountains, sinks and swivel chairs. The voice tone and pitch are important cues to Linda as to the intentionality of the person speaking. A normal pitch with clear, slow, simple statements made once, rather than repeated several times, seems to focus her attention on the topic rather than on the person.

Linda frequently has long latency of response time, especially if the question is factual ("Is this my coat?") rather than one of desire ("Do you want to go outside?"). It is important to allow lots of time and silence for Linda to process auditory information and to plan her response. It may seem initially that lots of verbal support and cheerful chatter are helping Linda feel acceptable, but it does not seem to facilitate her making appropriate responses. It also undercuts the importance of her participation in the interaction. Linda seems able to sense if the quiet is peaceful or awkward. She is very content with silent spaces if she feels they are acceptable to the other person.

These conclusions point to a mode of therapy that would be very short on quantity of expressive language initially, but the quality would come from being produced in meaningful interactions rather than trained responses. The major aim of therapy that I see for Linda is to develop a stronger need to communicate and a meaningful structure of interaction in which to communicate.

BILL

Bill's use of adjectives and adverbs in this sample indicates restriction of semantic domains expressed. His adjectives consisted of colors, which he knows well; numbers, which are his favorite topic; and the judgmental terms—"bad," "nasty" and "big." His only adverbs indicated destinations (*down* and *back*), although he seems to understand temporal adverbs well.

Bill exhibits a pattern of overextension based on shape. He refers to any rectangular or square object as a fire alarm. These associations seem to be so strong because of Bill's predilection for pulling fire alarms in his group home. The overextension applies to both objects and drawings.

Some confusion was noted on Bill's concepts of "boy" and "man." When shown a picture of a male baby, child, or man, Bill consistently refers to the picture as "man." However, when referring to himself, Bill inappropriately uses "boy." Both terms appear to be overly restricted, but it may be that attempts to teach Bill that he is a man and not a boy have resulted in this confusion.

MITCH

Mitch speaks in one-, two-, and three-syllable utterances. In this sample, only 14% of the utterances began with lax vowels that were unstressed. There were few exceptions to this vowel selection.

There is a clear difference between utterances that were spoken in a conversational tone and those that were said when Mitch was angry. The angry utterances, which were intelligible, began with a primary stressed vowel, whereas the conversational utterances began with a weak or tertiary stressed vowel.

The following regularities in vowel and consonant selection were noted. The angry utterances and his frequently used "I don't know" were exceptions to these rules in that phoneme selection is less constrained.

Syllable harmony was noted when multiple-syllable utterances began with /au/, with the same vowel then occurring in a later syllable. For example

17. au dau #

20. aŭ dʌz aû #

The only exception to this rule was when he was emphasizing the new information "red" in #31 in response to a question.

Two-syllable utterances beginning with /ə/ have an alveolar consonant in the second syllable, perhaps due to the central position of the shwa. For example

8. ɚʌn

16. ɚdudû #

In only one case, a glottal fricative was the consonant in the syllable following /ə/, possibly due to the back vowel of the second syllable.

When three-syllable utterances begin with /ə/, the following syllable contains an /ʌ/ with or without a consonant, as though it marks a beat. If the second syllable has a consonant, the third syllable will have either a consonant with the same place of articulation and voicing or a reduplication of the same consonant. If the second syllable does not have a consonant, the third syllable likewise consists of only a vowel. The only exception to this pattern had question intonation.

MARK

Analysis of Dysfluency

Mark's speech has an unusual amount of dysfluency which can be classified into at least four different types—unfilled pauses, filled pauses, repeats, and rephrasings. The pauses, both filled and unfilled, seem to fall primarily at the beginnings of sentences and major syntactic units, sometimes before rarer words such as "barrel." This would suggest that they are formulation pauses where he is trying to decide what to say or how to phrase it. This, in itself is not unusual except that they are more frequent for Mark. The filled pauses are noises which are also used by all of us to keep our turn in the conversation (otherwise the other person would start talking). However, most of us use "um's" or "uh's" and Mark's, I think, are fast unintelligible and unrecognizable insertions which make the listeners feel they have not understood him. I say "I think" because they may, indeed, be part of the sentence rather than fillers, but judging from the rest of the sentence, I feel they are better categorized as condensed filler phrases. Their frequency, like the unfilled pauses, suggest he is having trouble with formulating an idea or its expression.

Mark's repeats are usually a sound or syllable, such as *re re re,* said several times followed by a word which does, indeed, start with the sound being repeated. These seem to occur more with multisyllabic words, especially for those which have similar syllables (*recre*ation) and seem to reflect a problem he has with how to sequence the syllables in the words. To restart then allows him stalling time while he thinks about the way the word goes. In this case, Mark's error patterns suggest that he is not having trouble choosing the word or formulating the idea as with formulation pauses, but rather deciding how to order the syllables.

The rephrasings are yet another kind of nonfluency and are often of a backtracking type where he substitutes a like word (*restaurant* for *building*) or fills in a phrase (*my sister,* changed to *my parents, my brother and my sister*). Sometimes he doesn't complete the rephrased word, as when he said /kI kI/ and then changed what was possibly going to be "kicked' to "fighting with him." These seem different from the multisyllabic restarts, since the word is changed and the rephrased units often seem to have already been formulated in terms of word selection in sound sequencing, and in syntactic organization.

Perhaps the most disconcerting rephrasings are those where Mark corrects his pronunciation. These backtracks disrupt the timing of his utterance more and are the hardest for his listeners to follow since they can't recognize what he is saying, as when he pronounced *train* as *chain* when saying *train jumped.*

I believe most of these errors are anticipations of future sounds or sound features. For example, he said *ch* for *tr* in the last example because he was anticipating saying the next word *jump* where the *ch* is said like the *j.* There are many examples of these anticipatory assimilations.

Analysis of Speech Intelligibility

Mark has spurts in his talking which are totally unintelligible even though they are fluent. These occurred with me when we first started talking and when we finished and got up to go into another room, suggesting they may be related to emotional state or "cognitive overload." I believe these are actual phrases and not just jargon or fillers, and that what makes them unintelligible is that they are said very rapidly, that sounds (especially stops and weak syllables) are omitted, and that many sounds are underarticulated. An easy example is *rof* for *reel off.* This "telescoped" or "coalesced" speech has been considered as a symptom of "cluttering," and that label would therefore be an accurate description of this aspect of Mark's speech, but it's not the whole story.

GARY

Concerning the content of Gary's speech, four patterns appear:

1. *Conditionals.* These are statements which bracket limits of the idea Gary is expressing. For example, Gary was describing what his mother has done

for him: "She has done alot. Not a little bit or not a small amount. She did alot." When the clinician asked Gary when and if he would come to therapy he said "It would depend on what day and what time. I couldn't come on Monday or Friday. You could not do anything on the weekends could you? So you are off. So you are off Sunday, Monday, Friday, and Saturday. That leaves Tuesday, Wednesday, and Thursday. Monday I have to go to Boy Scout meeting."

2. *Tangential or Wandering Speech.* This pattern appears frequently in Gary's speech. When asked a question, he responds with information not related to the topic. Additionally, during these responses Gary elaborates, which tends to take him further away from the original topic. One example of this was when Gary noticed he and the clinician were being observed through a one-way mirror. The clinician asked him if he were bothered by this, and he responded by saying it didn't bother him at all, it wouldn't bother him if someone were sitting there with a machine gun. Gary then went on to talk about laws concerning machine guns and how they are sold illegally.

3. *Comprehension.* Gary does display comprehension problems when he is unfamiliar with the topic or when, as in the subtests, the material is lengthy. When the clinician asked Gary if he would come to this clinic to work on his language, Gary asked if he would be able to work on a neon beer sign he owns that is not working. As previously reported, Mabel feels she has to use, "plain" words when talking to Gary.

4. *Literal Interpretations.* This is related to Gary's overall comprehension. When the clinician used sarcasm in a joking manner, Gary responded seriously to the statement. This pattern applies pragmatically as well as semantically.

JAMES

Recommendations

It is recommended that James receive five days a week language therapy from a speech and language pathologist, and that he be placed in an educational program with an emphasis on one-to-one interactions and an emphasis on developing and building on James' communication attempts and interests. The new program should be one which builds on his current interests using as a base his fascination for rough surfaces, shiny objects, physical play, affectionate interaction, and most of all, food.

A beginning and primary emphasis should be to get James involved in direct and nonfrustrating interactions, and to initiate those interactions. This would build intentionality upon which a communication system could be designed and without which it will undoubtedly fail. The gestures need not at first be symbolic, but simply points, tugs, grunts, reaches, which involve having people get things for him and having him do things he likes for himself.

Continued emphasis on comprehension training would be important, with the language being tied to what he enjoys (e.g., "Get the milk from the refrigerator") rather than disciplinary.

In sum, James shows sufficient communicative competence and interests to benefit from an educational program which is highly individualized and which is designed to get him to communicate about his likes and dislikes.

RICK

Rick displays a variety of self-stimulatory behaviors. There are vocal noises, chin and head hits, and head and body rocks. His vocal noises have an identifiable form which allows one to classify them into two kinds. The first is a "henshui"—a stereotypic form which is two or three syllables in length. The first syllable is usually a very high-pitched consonant and vowel—the consonant is an /h/, the vowel is nasalized. The second syllable is said on a much lower pitch and shorter, and begins with a fricative or affricate followed by a vowel, usually a /u/. The last syllable, if present, is either a vowel or bilabial consonant and vowel. It is also short in duration and low in pitch. Rick's other noises are an "oioioi," said with a glottal fry, and a buccal fry. The noises all involve extremes in articulatory positioning, i.e., front to back vowels, glottal to alveolar movement. The "fry" aspect suggests his focus on kinesthetic as well as, or instead of, auditory features for those sounds.

Rick's hits are most often chin and head hits with the palm or heel of either hand. Sometimes there are quick sequences made with alternating hands on alternate sides of his head. His repetitive sequences were often combinations of several types of behaviors rapidly following one another, such as hits, noises, then rocks. They were sometimes irregular in temporal organization—that is, they were not equally timed, had an unequal number of identical segments per sequence, and were unequal in the amount of time given to each identical sequence. Those sequences which were more regular were where Rick or the adult was talking. In these cases, he hit himself or jerked on the strongly stressed syllable of the utterances. Sometimes every syllable was stressed, as when he said "this is a 'puh'" and hit his leg with his left hand on each word.

In Rick's interaction with his mother, his repetitive behaviors were infrequent, consuming about ten seconds of a two minute sequence. They occurred between activities or when his mother was looking away from him. Contrastively, his repetitive behaviors were more frequent with his teacher, with the longest sequences following the teacher's nonacceptance of his attempts to perform for her. In both interactions, the adults sometimes continued to talk to Rick during his repetitive sequences. At other times, they waited until the behaviors subsided or told him to put his hands down.

Appendix B

Answers to Some of the Exercises

Our exercises at the end of each chapter were intended to help you think about the ideas presented in the chapters. We have found that many of them engender useful disagreements about the issues in the text and that they have no "right" answers. Rather, the answers will depend upon your perspective and the assumptions you make. They do have wrong answers, however. These are answers that either show a lack of understanding or an incorrect conclusion from the material. You will know as you work through the exercises whether you understand the chapters or not, since a debate about right answers will require the knowledge we are presenting. That is what we want the exercises to do for you.

We are including in this appendix the answers which require less debate to show you how we would answer them. This section does not include answers to all exercises, and it is not intended to hand-feed you. Feel free to argue with our answers. It is this kind of interaction that goes on when we work with real children in real clinical contexts, after all.

CHAPTER 1

1.	1	8.	1	15.	3,4	22.	2
2.	1	9.	3	16.	4	23.	4
3.	2	10.	3,4	17.	2	24.	3,2
4.	2	11.	4	18.	4	25.	3
5.	2,3	12.	1	19.	3	26.	4
6.	2	13.	2	20.	3		
7.	1	14.	3	21.	4		

CHAPTER 3   PRAGMATICS

1.

a) c

b) c

c) a

d) b or c

e) a

f) b

g) c

h) b or c

3.

a) a

b) e

c) c

d) cs

e) a

f) e

g) c

h) c

i) cs,a

j) a

k) a

l) a

m) e

n) e

o) e

4.

a) I,A

b) A,I

c) I,A

d) I,A

e) A,I

f) I,A

g) I,A

h) I,A

7.

Orienting terms
  do you remember
  the the one
  well
  you know
  the one
  do you know
Relative clauses
  which involved the sale
  the assistant D.A.
  who prosecutes real estate
  who sold the house
Identifying adjectives
  old white
  new
Identifying prepositional phrases
  over on Fulton Street
  for Judge Stone
  at the Statler Hilton
  across from the bank

CHAPTER 4   PHONOLOGY

1.

c,k

b
d
k (c)
d
g,j,e
h,i
j
e,f,j
f
a,g

2.

a)	place	l)	none
b)	manner	m)	voicing
c)	manner	n)	none
d)	manner	o)	none
e)	manner	p)	manner
f)	none	q)	none
g)	voicing	r)	place
h)	place	s)	none
i)	manner	t)	place, voicing
j)	place, voicing	u)	place
k)	place, manner, voicing	v)	none

3.
a)   Bidirectional assimilation of fricatives to /f/
b)   Anticipatory assimilation of /l/ and /r/ to /t/ and /d/
c)   Reduction of /s/ + stop clusters to stop

CHAPTER 5   MORPHOLOGY

1.

g	j
d	i
h	a
b	e
f	c

2.
a)   present and correct: modal (gonna, adj.)
     missing: aux., art.
b)   present and correct: cop. (was)
     error: cop. (was/were)
c)   error: overregularized past (eated)
d)   present and correct: progressive (picking)
     missing: aux., art., poss.
e)   present and correct: reg. past (walked)
     error: adv. (really/real)
f)   error: third pers. sing. for irreg. past (gots/got)
     missing: compar., art.

g) error: overreg. past (runned)
   missing: art
h) present and correct: modal (hafta), adj., reg. plural (marbles)
i) present and correct: third pers. sing. (drives), adj.
   missing: art.
j) present and correct: modal (could)
   error: perfective (had do)

CHAPTER 6   SYNTAX

1.

a) SVC	e) SVA	i) SVO
b) SVC	f) SVC	j) SVCA
c) SVO	g) SVA	k) SVDO
d) SVOD	h) SV	l) SVAA

2.

a) SVA	g) SVC	m) $VA
b) SV	h) VO	n) SVOC
c) SVOD	i) SVO	o) SVO
d) SVO	j) SVC	p) SVØD
e) $VA	k) SVD	q) SV
f) VOA	l) SVC	r) SVA

3.

a) SV+VA

b) SVO$\frac{+SV}{A}$

c) SVC$\frac{+SVO}{A}$

d) SV$\frac{SVC}{O}$

e) SV$\frac{+SV}{C}$

f) $\frac{SVC}{S}$VC(RVO)

g) $\frac{\$VO}{O}$SV

h) SVC(SVA)

i) SVO(SV)

j) SV$\frac{+SV}{C}$

k) SV+SV

l) SV$\frac{+SVOA}{O}$

m) ASVA$\frac{+SVO}{A}$

n) SV$\frac{+SVO}{A}$

o) SVC(RV)

4a and b

SVO	S	V	O	C	D	A
Eric mix them up	name	mix up	PN			
Eric make a boy	name	make	NP			
Lady put glue on	name	put on	N			

SVOC						
Eric make it red	name	make	PN	adj		

SVOD

*Eric give (you) a man	name	give	NP	—
Eric show mommy	name	show	name	—
*Eric give (it to) mommy	name	give	—	name

SV(A)

I talk in there	PN	talk		prep
I don't know	PN	d.n.		
Eric push	name	push		
Boy walk up on top	N	walk		prep
(They) Talk on telephone	—	talk		prep
(Doctor) Felt on my tummy and my back	—	felt		prep

VO(A)

	S	V	O	A
Stick it to the page	—	stick	PN	prep
Make a boy	—	make	NP	

SVC

I (am) Eric	PN	—	name
He (is) sick	PN	—	adj
You (are) a piggy	PN	—	NP

4d

Summary: In this limited sample we can see that Eric uses a variety of simple clause types. All subject-verb-object sentences, including one with an object complement are structurally correct. Some subject-verb sentences are also correct, but two in this sample lack subjects, making them structurally similar to imperatives, which Eric uses correctly. Sentences with dative elements give Eric problems; he omits either the object or the dative in all instances. Eric uses no copulas in the sample, instead producing subject-complement clauses. The subjects of all the SC clauses are pronouns, with the complement being a name, adjective and noun. Clauses with lexical verbs in contrast typically have names as subjects, infrequently beginning with pronouns or nouns.

4c

COMPOUND CLAUSES

	conj.
*He ran and go down like that	and
*I didn't want to but I can't	but

RELATIVE CLAUSES

	Rel. PN
What is inside are wires *that control this*	that
This is powder *we put on after baths*	—
I know something *you don't know*	—
*That not mine *you gave me*	—
*It's the one *that go broke*	—

SUBORDINATE CLAUSES	act as	conj
I hate owls *cause I can't read*	adverbial	cause
It's time to go home *when we finish our spelling*	adverbial	when
I think *she's upset*	object	—
A palace is *where a king lives*	complement	where
What is inside are wires...	subject	What
Try to eat them, you know	object (invert)	—
*It's like *the sky is*	complement	like
I don't know *if I can get it back*	adverbial	if
*In summer I no have go school *cause it gonna be very hot*	adverbial	cause
I will *if you want me to*	adverbial	if
I will if you want *me to*	object	—

4d

Summary: This child shows a good command of multiple clauses, using a variety of types. Most common are subordinate clauses, which generally serve as adverbials and objects, but also include complements and a subject subordinate clause. A number of relative clauses were used, all modifying objects or complements. Both compound clauses, as well as a few of the relative and subordinate clauses, had morphological and semantic errors that are not characteristic of this child's simple clauses, perhaps indicating that combining clauses adds psychological complexity and causes breakdowns in other systems.

5.
c) a little car (art. + adj. + N)
d) My big wheel (gen. art. + adj. + N); her big wheel (gen. art. + adj. + N)
e) my piece of paper (gen. art. + quant. + N); in (prep)
f) a red nose (art. + adj. + N)
g) all the fur (initiat. + art. + N)
h) my own seat (gen. art. + adj. + N)
i) my nose (gen. art. + N); (missing preposition)
j) my cold (gen. art. + N); for (prep)
k) my van (gen. art. + N); my daddy (gen. art. + N); in (prep)
l) that part (dem. + N)
m) the wall (art. + N); through (prep)
n) a funny one (art. + adj. + N)
o) this little one (dem. + adj. + N); at (prep)
p) very much games (quant. + quant. + N)
Longest noun phrase: noun + 2 modifiers (variety of forms)
Correct: Initiators, articles, demonstratives, adjectives, quantifier
Error: Quantifier (much/many)
Not sampled: Qualifiers, ordinals
Prepositions used correctly: in, for through, at; Errors: missing in
6.
missing auxiliary in c,d,e,o
double negation in g
wrong negative form in m

nonsyntactic negative in h
all others are syntactic and correct

7.

Personal pronouns present and consistently correct: me, mine, myself, you
(subj. and obj. sing.), she, he, we, them, they

Errors/Inconsistencies: I sometimes correct, with occasional substitution of
child's name or me.

Not sampled: Remaining forms

Indefinite pronouns present and consistently correct: it (subj. and obj.), this
(subj. and obj.), that (obj.)

Not sampled: Remaining forms

CHAPTER 7   SEMANTICS

1.

a)   calling a cat "dog"

b)   calling only stuffed animal "dog"

c)   Child thinks that tall men are dogs because she heard her mother say "look
at that big dog" when tall man was walking Great Dane.

d)   Child says "you know, it says 'bow-wow'"

2.

d

a

f

b

a

b

a

g

c

e

3.

ON	IN
surface	destination
upper horizontal surface	static location; contained
attached to	destination; contained
destination	

UNDER	TO
static location; in contact with lower surface	attachment
in direct vertical relationship	direction of movement
lower than	

OFF

negative location
state

4.

Summary: The class of adverbials is restricted. Those few that are used by this child are mainly in the conceptual domain of location. While the class of adjectives is also small, the conceptual domains they express are more varied. The number of nouns is consistent with sample size. They are restricted to tangible objects that would exist in the child's environment. Verbs are numerous and express a variety of conceptual domains.

CHAPTER 8   COMPREHENSION

1.
a) C
b) D
c) N, D, or C
d) D
e) C

f) D
g) D
h) N or D
i) N or D
j) D, N or C

2.
b,f
b,h
a,f
c,e
a
e
g
j
i
d

3.
girl, baby
girl, dog
car, truck
dog, cat
girl, boy
baby, girl
baby, boy
boy, baby
boy, dog

4.
a) G
b) I
c) G,I
d) I
e) I
f) G
g) I

h) I
i) G
j) G,I
k) G,I
l) I
m) I

CHAPTER 9   COGNITIVE PRECURSORS TO LANGUAGE ACQUISITION

2.
d
c
a
b

5.
a)   indexical
b)   indexical or iconic
c)   arbitrary

CHAPTER 10   TOOLS OF ASSESSMENT

1.   Comments directed at question of whether or not there is a language problem:

Mrs. Smith feels Nathan's language is moderately delayed
Strangers have problems understanding him
Utah results
Peabody results

Comments directed toward possible cause:

Most of history and description of present status and hearing test attempt

Comments directed toward identifying areas of deficit

Peabody results
Expressive vocabulary of ten words
Responds to simple directions
Can identify simple pictures and animals

Identification of regularities

able to count to 3 or 4
Cannot say name, nursery rhymes or alphabet
Responds to name and *no*
Uses one word utterances and echoic responses
Uses question intonation

Recommendations

Enroll in therapy
Prepare him for hearing testing

Identifying information

Name and age

Other information

*Means of punishment
close to grandfather and spoiled by grandmother
mother works on speech
*father lacks patience
*tension in the home at times

*These sections add no useful information and should not be included unless they are expanded to show how they are relevant.

2.
a) language problem?
b) regularities
c) regularities
d) regularities
e) other—include
f) other—include
g) regularities
h) regularities
i) cause
j) areas of deficit

Name Index

Subject Index